The Art of 3-D
Computer Animation
and Imaging

The Art of 3-D
Computer Animation and Imaging

Isaac Victor Kerlow

VAN NOSTRAND REINHOLD

ITP™ A Division of International Thomson Publishing Inc.

New York • Albany • Bonn • Boston • Detroit • London • Madrid • Melbourne •
Mexico City • Paris • San Francisco • Singapore • Tokyo • Toronto

Cover and Book Design: Isaac Victor Kerlow

Van Nostrand Reinhold Staff
Editor: Jane Degenhardt
Production Editor: Carla M. Nessler
Production Manager: Mary McCartney

Van Nostrand Reinhold
I(T)P ™ A division of International Thompson Publishing Inc.
        The ITP logo is a trademark under license

Printed in the United States of America

For more information, contact:

Van Nostrand Reinhold   Chapman & Hall GmbH
115 Fifth Avenue   Pappelallee
New York, NY 10003   64469 Weinheim
                                   Germany

Chapman & Hall   International Thomson Publishing Asia
2-6 Boundary Row   221 Henderson Road #05-10
London   Henderson Building
SE1 8HN   Singapore 0315
United Kingdom

Thomas Nelson Australia   International Thomson Publishing Japan
102 Dodds Street   Hirakawacho Kyowa Building, 3F
South Melbourne, 3205   2-2-1 Hirakawacho
Victoria, Australia   Chiyoda-ku, 102 Tokyo
                                   Japan

Nelson Canada   International Thomson Editores
1120 Birchmount Road   Campos Eliseos 385, Piso 7
Scarborough, Ontario   Col. Polanco
                                   11560 Mexico D.F. Mexico

1 2 3 4 5 6 7 8 9 10 QEB-HK 01 00 99 98 97 96

Library of Congress Cataloging-in-Publication Data
Kerlow,
     The Art of Three-Dimensional Computer Animation and Imaging
     /Isaac Victor Kerlow
        p.   cd.
     Includes bibliographical references and index
     ISBN 0-442-01896-7
     1. Computer graphics. 2. Computer animation.
     3. Three-dimensional display systems. I. Title.
T385.K45 1996   96-37902
006.6-dc20   CIP

Table of Contents

THIS BOOK IS DEDICATED TO ESTHER AND SERGIO KERLOW

Acknowledgements

MANY OF THE IDEAS contained in this book were developed throughout the years while teaching three-dimensional computer animation and imaging at several institutions, mainly Pratt Institute in New York, and the former Kodak Center for Creative Imaging in Camden, Maine.

I am indebted to all my students for their enthusiasm and interest. I am also grateful to my son Victor, friends, and colleagues who contributed to the process of completing this book.

I am especially indebted to the following individuals and companies: Lincoln Hu, Director of Advanced Technology at Industrial Light and Magic, for allowing me to reproduce in Appendix I his text about the creation of the feature film *Terminator 2*; Don Shay at Cinefex Magazine for allowing me to reproduce the chronological listing of all the *Cinefex* issues in Appendix III; Steve Cunningham, SIGGRAPH's Chairperson and former Director of Publications, for allowing me to reproduce a partial listing of the SIGGRAPH Video Review in Appendix IV; and Alias Research, autodessys, Softimage, and Specular International for allowing me to reproduce dialog boxes from some of their software products.

I also want to thank William Fasolino and Robert Anders, former Acting Deans of the School of Art and Design at Pratt Institute, for their support during my tenure there; and Jules van de Vijver, Simon Biggs, Johan Faber, and Hans Rijpkema for their hospitality during my residence as Guest Artist at SCAN in Groningen, The Netherlands. Steve Rittler applied his superb cartooning talents to turn my funny-looking sketches into hilarious black and white illustrations that will hopefully make people laugh while they learn. Iris Benado, currently at Rafael Viñoly Associates, and Tim Cheung, currently at Pacific Data Images, executed several three-dimensional models and images, and checked facts in a variety of software manuals. Dena Slothower provided consistent research and typing support, and managed most of the e-mail communication with contributors. Ben Luce reviewed portions of the manuscript and provided valuable suggestions. I also want to thank the many graduate students who helped with additional typing, scanning, and correspondance with contributors.

A special thanks to Dr. Irwin Sobel, currently at Hewlett-Packard Research Labs, who sparked my curiosity about three-dimensional computer animation by allowing me to learn and create in his computer graphics lab during his days at Columbia University. To him and his wife Ceevah goes my deepest gratitude.

Last but not least I am grateful to all the individuals and companies that gave me permission to reproduce their work in this book, each is credited next to their creations throughout the book.

Isaac Victor Kerlow
Manhattan, 1995

Preface

TODAY WE CAN use computer technology to create real or imagined worlds. This capability allows us to explore ideas in new ways.

Many of today's computer programs enable artists to simulate three-dimensional environments and to build detailed models that exist only in the computer's memory. With software we can change the shape and dimension of objects interactively, and rearrange them in a three-dimensional scene until we are satisfied. These models can be represented, or rendered, in an infinite variety of styles. In addition to being rendered as snapshots of real or fantastic worlds, these three-dimensional models can also be animated as if they were alive. Their motions can be recorded on film or videotape. Three-dimensional computer animation can be incorporated in a multimedia presentation or an interactive game, combined with traditional drawing and photography, or brought back to our real three-dimensional world in the form of sculptures built by computer-controlled machinery or as large-scale videogames that can simulate real-life experiences.

The speed, power, and graphics resolution of today's microcomputers make it possible to embark on sophisticated production quality three-dimensional computer graphics projects. Throughout this book we will limit our references to a variety of microcomputer and super-microcomputer systems. Although the techniques reviewed here can also be performed by larger computer systems (including minicomputers, mainframe computers, and supercomputers), we assume that most of the readers are not utilizing such systems.

This book extends over a wide range of topics in such a way that it can be read by professionals in a reasonable amount of time. It also addresses the time limitations of instructors and students who must present and digest, respectively, all this information in the context of one academic year (or less). Usually this learning process takes place in the midst of trying to complete related studio projects and while trying to master a specific software program.

It would require an encyclopedic work to fully document and present all the topics and techniques included in this work. This book does not pretend to be such work. A significant effort has been made to create a work that is not bound by the particularities of any specific computer program while, at the same time, offers detailed, practical information that goes beyond the mere theory. The knowledge contained in this book has been distilled from years of teaching three-dimensional animation and imaging with a vartiety of software programs, as well as from reading innumerable software manuals, and from practicing and making mistakes. Hopefully reading this book will help minimize the amount of mistakes you make!

This book conveys the excitement of three-dimensional computer animation and imaging, and provides technical and creative information that is both useful and inspiring. It will help you understand and perfect the techniques that make the creation of three-dimensional virtual worlds possible with computer technology. Enjoy!

How to Read this Book

The material in this book is structured to accommodate the fact that mastering the art and craft of creating three-dimensional computer models and animation can be achieved differently. Therefore, this book can be read in a variety of ways.

For those of you who like the systematic approach I recommend that you read the book from front to back and in sequential order, and refer to the illustrations and appendices to complement the knowledge presented in the main body of the text. It will also be beneficial to complete some of the exercises presented at the end of the chapter with your favorite three-dimensional software.

For those of you who prefer to learn by doing, or are too impatient to read the whole book from start to end, it might be best to look at the pictures first. But do not forget the read the captions as you look at the images. There is a lot of useful information contained in them. Next, try to do some of the exercises listed at the end of each chapter. Finally, you might want to read some of the sections in the book that complement the section you have already read in your software manual. In any case, Section One contains information rarely found in manuals presented by instructors on a "need-to-know" basis. The information contained in Section One is many times more important than it seems at first.

Using this Book with Software

Read this book as you learn and experiment with a specific three-dimensional program, or by itself without any hands-on. To those of you who prefer to learn by reading *before* you initiate the hands-on part of learning, this book offers a comprehensive theoretical introduction with plenty of practical references. Those of you who prefer diving straight into the particularities of a specific computer program—and reading *after* the fact—will find this book complements your experimental approach by offering clear explanations in a succinct form. Last but not least, to

those of you who learn best by combining the experimental approach with the conceptual comprehension, this book offers a logical progression of topics with clarity that goes beyond the particularities of software manuals.

Book Format

This book consists of five sections, each with several chapters. Each chapter starts with a summary, and concludes with sections about practical tips (Getting Ready), and quizzes and exercises (Review and Practice).

Section I includes general information about both historical background, and general design and production issues. This section deals with a summary of the major creative and technical trends, a short summary of milestones, and lots of advice regarding the planning of a three-dimensional project. Section I makes you think like an art critic, and a producer.

Section II goes right into the details of modeling three-dimensional objects and environments. This section has many examples in the form of black-and-white line drawings and halftones. Section II makes you think like a sculptor.

Section III covers many of the most useful rendering techniques, both simple and complex. This section contains many color figures. Section III makes you think like a photographer and a painter.

Section IV deals first with many of the issues associated with telling a story through moving pictures: basic screenplay writing, storyboarding, and cinematic techniques. Section IV makes you think like a cinematographer and a scriptwriter.

Section V presents many of the issues involved in recording and presenting your work, including compositing and special effects. Section V makes you think like a printmaker and a special effects technician.

What to Expect from this Book

This book presents the concepts required to understand the steps and procedures that lead to the completion of a fully rendered three-dimensional computer still image or animation. Many of the figures have been developed to present complex concepts in a way that is clear and easy to understand. A large effort in the writing process has also been made so that the structure and details of the book would be as inclusive as possible: many software programs and hardware platforms were tested and reviewed so that readers find a consistent treatment and point of view. The main goal of this book is to provide the reader with a solid conceptual and critical foundation by presenting an unusual combination of technique and creativity. This book seeks to inspire and to inform.

What Not to Expect from this Book

This book is not a general introduction to the use of computers. Instead it assumes that the reader is already familiar with the basic use of a computer system (such as saving files or knowing how to operate a mouse or a graphics tablet), or that the reader is in the process of gaining that knowledge elsewhere (several reference books that can be consulted for this purpose are listed in the Bibliography). Readers who have used computers and who have a basic understanding of the operation of computer systems might benefit from this book faster than readers who have never used a computer.

This book is not a computer software manual either. It is not based on a particular computer program for three-dimensional imaging. Readers who seek information regarding the detailed operation of a specific software or details about how specific techniques are implemented in particular programs are advised to consult specific software manuals. However, in the interest of linking the concepts presented here with today's available tools, various menus and dialog boxes from a variety of programs are reproduced throughout the book. These figures are for illustration purposes only and in no way is this book claiming to be a complete reference manual for any specific product. This book presents all concepts in a way that goes beyond the jargon or technical terminology of any specific program.

About Computer Manuals

Quite often I hear my colleagues or students complain that computer manuals are difficult to understand and that they never tell the whole story. I myself have been challenged when reading manuals that are incomplete or that require a significant effort from the reader's part before their contents can be put to any use. Virtually all software manuals contain some partial information and even some inaccuracies. This is not surprising if we take into account the complexity of some of the software, the constant upgrades of features and versions, and the extremely short production cycles that individuals and companies have for developing these complex programs and turning them into products within a highly competitive market.

Having been both a user and a writer of user manuals I am familiar with the frustrations experienced by both sides. My advice regarding the use of software manuals can be summarized as follows: take the useful information contained in the software manuals and build on it. Today's three-dimensional software is so complex and so changing that we cannot expect any manual to have every single piece of information perfectly digested. Some of the information required to be a proficient three-dimensional artist and technician can be found in manuals, some in magazines, some in books, some in individuals. Learning requires effort.

General Principles vs. Specific Techniques

Most of the techniques described throughout this book are available in many of the three-dimensional software programs available on the market. But instead of presenting these modeling, rendering, animation, and output techniques in exactly the same ways they are implemented in a specific computer system, we present them by focussing on their essential features and capabilities. Specific implementations of techniques—implementations that differ from system to system—are left untouched. Readers who wish to obtain highly specific information regarding a particular computer program mentioned in this book are advised to consult the program's reference manuals.

Differences and Similarities with Specific Software

The tools and techniques described in this book are quite generic but also closely resemble the types of tools and techniques available in today's three-dimensional computer graphics software. In fact a large variety of three dimensional software available in different computer platforms—such as Silicon Graphics, Apple Quadras and PowerPCs, IBM PC-compatibles, and Amigas—was used to formulate and test the concepts presented in this book.

Some of the tools and techniques described throughout the book might not be available in the particular software you are using. Today's programs are constantly upgraded and are in constant evolution. Even when the same feature is offered by two different programs, it might be implemented in different ways: some features might look the same but behave and perform very differently.

Introduction

CHAPTER 1

Art and Technology in Context

Summary

This chapter provides a brief summary of events and projects that contributed to the creative and technical development of three-dimensional computer animation and imaging techniques. The brief historical information presented here provides readers with a simple context in which to frame technical and stylistic discussions related to three-dimensional computer animation and imaging.

1.1 A Digital Creative Environment

Computers have become part of our life, and especially part of our creative life. They can be found everywhere: they coordinate the flow of information in our banking transactions, they digitize our voice and eliminate some of the noise in telephone conversations, they control the fuel injection systems in our cars, and they adjust the settings in photographic and video cameras so that image quality is always optimal. Most of the newspaper job listings in the visual professions and trades today require some degree of computer competency. Much of the broadcasting, manufacturing, graphic arts, and entertainment industries have computerized their production. Likewise, many independent artists and design studios develop their work with computers and often deliver it in digital formats.

The transition to increased reliance on computer systems affects many creators and technicians. Large numbers of established visual professionals have retrained to acquire new skills, and young students are eager to learn all the secrets and shortcuts. Expectations range from the sensible to the ridiculous. Those who resist the change altogether, for example, are left behind because the visual world is changing. Those who are overly enthusiastic often have unrealistic expectations. It is now time to find a new balance. It is time to accept the advantages that computer technology has to offer, to continue developing the promising possibilities, and to let rest the options that have not yet matured.

Much of today's creation and production of images is indeed performed with the aid of computers. Increasingly, professionals from a wide variety of visual disciplines are working with **digital information**. Some of the traditional visual techniques based on paint, photographic, and video methods are merging with **digital imaging techniques**. A creative environment that used to exist as a collection of totally separate and unrelated disciplines—each with its own tools, techniques, and media—is turning into an environment where visual people use more tools, techniques, and media are compatible with others. As a result some of the traditional barriers between visual disciplines no longer have to exist. There are now, for example, great overlaps between the traditional fields of graphic arts, broadcasting, and film. The creative **digital environment** has fostered this overlap because computer technology often provides more creative power to visual people. Decades ago, for example, visual professionals used to purchase tools specialized for their own profession. These tools were useful for doing the work just in their profession, but not in others. By using a computer for their own specialized work, many of today's professionals already own the tools used in other professions.

1.2 The Development of the Technology

Computers, and in particular their visual capabilities, are profoundly altering the way in which we create and distribute images. But the powerful computer systems that are so common today—and that everybody takes for granted—have existed for a relatively short period of time.

The ancestors of today's electronic digital computers were mechanical adding machines used to perform repetitive arithmetic calculations. Those early mechanical devices eventually evolved into machines that could be programmed each time to perform different sets of instructions. In the 1940s, electric versions of these computing machines were in operation.

The early computer models were called **mainframes** because all their bulky components were housed in large steel frames. During the 1960s two types of computers were developed to satisfy different needs. The **minicomputers**, smaller and less expensive than the mainframes but almost as powerful, were developed in an attempt to bring computers to a wider audience, and range of applications. **Supercomputers**, usually bigger and more expensive than mainframe computers, were developed to tackle the most taxing computing projects regardless of the cost, and with an emphasis on speed and performance.

Microcomputers were developed in the mid-1970s. Before then the large majority of artists found computers very uninteresting: they were too expensive and cumbersome to operate, and even the simplest tasks required extensive programming. Most models lacked monitors, printers, mice, or graphics tablets. Microcomputers contain millions of microscopic electronic switches on a single **silicon chip**. Some models of microcomputers, such as the Apple Macintosh and a variety of IBM PC-compatibles, were widely embraced by visual professionals during the 1980s. Many of today's powerful microcomputers are small enough to be carried in a briefcase.

The super-microcomputer and the parallel computer were developed during the 1980s and have had a great effect on the way visual people use computers. **Super-microcomputers**—also called **workstations**—are microcomputers built around a powerful CPU that is customized to excel in the performance of a specific task, for example, three-dimensional computer animation. **Massively parallel computers** deal with very complex processing challenges by dividing up the tasks among a large number of small microprocessors. Some of these computers may have between a dozen and thousands of processors.

Computer graphics technology was developed in the early 1950s to make visible what was invisible to the human eye. But virtually none of the early computer graphics systems was developed for artistic work. Most of these early applications were related to the military, manufacturing, or the applied sciences and included, for example, flight simulators to train fighter pilots without having to fly a real plane; computer-aided design and manufacturing (CADAM) systems to allow electrical engineers to design and test electronic circuits with millions of components; and computer-aided tomography (CAT) scanners to allow physicians to peek into the human body without having to physically open it.

During the 1950s and 1960s, the early years of computer graphics technology, the computer systems and techniques for creating images were rudimentary and very limited—especially by today's standards. During that period very few artists and designers even knew that computers could be used to create images.

During the 1970s and 1980s computer technology became more practical and useful. Therefore a significant number of visual creators changed their attitude and started to get interested in using computers. During the early 1990s a significant drop in the prices of computer systems encouraged many visual professionals to purchase the technology and to integrate it into their daily professional practices. Professionals from all visual disciplines accepted computer technology as it became more powerful, practical, and less expensive.

The computer technology necessary for creating three-dimensional imagery and animation has evolved tremendously since the first systems were developed in the 1950s. Within just a few decades the capabilities of hardware and software for creating three-dimensional environments went from simple to highly complex representations that often fool our visual perception.

A complete history of three-dimensional computer graphics technology and creative works remain to be written. However, the information presented in the rest of this chapter summarizes some of the highlights and landmarks. This summary is certainly not exhaustive, and it does not attempt to present a complete and detailed portrait of all the significant events. Instead it provides a personal account of individual examples and a summary of the major trends.

1950s and 1960s

The decades of the 1950s and 1960s saw the development of the first interactive computer systems, which were further improved during the following decade. The field of computer graphics was so new then that most of the technological innovations from this period are not very spectacular in terms of the results they produced. They were, however, fundamental in facilitating the impressive developments that would flourish 20 years later.

The first computer to use CRT displays as output channels was the *Whirlwind* computer at the Massachusetts Institute of Technology (MIT) in the early 1950s. This system was used to display the solutions to differential equations on oscilloscope monitors. During the mid- to late-1950s) the SAGE Air Defense System of the United States Air Force used command-and-control CRT displays on which operators could detect aircraft flying over the continental U.S. The SAGE operators were also able to obtain information about the aircraft by pointing at their icons on the screen with light pens.

During the 1960s various technology-intensive organizations developed the first Computer-Aided Design and Manufacturing (CADAM) systems. The goal of these early CADAM system was to make the design process more effective by offering users sophisticated design functions, and also to improve the organization of the manufacturing process by linking the numerical data that represents an image with other types of information, such as inventory and engineering analysis. One of the first CADAM systems was developed by General Motors, and it included various time-sharing graphic stations for designing cars. Other companies developed similar systems, among them were Boeing Aerospace, IBM, McDonnell Douglas, General Electric and Lockheed.

Early attempts to create computer-generated movies took place in several research institutions. Short pieces of animation were produced at Boeing by William Fetter and Walter Bernhart in the early 1960s. Three-dimensional drawings were plotted on paper and filmed one at a time to produce animations of an aircraft carrier landing. Fetter also modeled the human figure for ergonomic studies related to the design of cockpits. Michael Noll and Bela Julesz, at Bell Laboratories, produced various stereo computer animations on film to aid in the study of stereo perception. During this period some of the first animation programming languages were developed, but most of them resulted in programs that ran only in a non-interactive mode.

Only a few commercial companies were involved in computer graphics research during these two decades. Most of the technological developments during this period came out of government-funded academic research laboratories such as MIT's Lincoln Labs.

In the early 1960s, computer graphics were developed to visualize objects and situations that were too costly or just impossible to represent otherwise. Flight simulators, CADAM systems, and CAT scanners were among the pioneering computer graphics systems.

The first interactive system, called

Sketchpad, was developed in the early 1960s by Ivan Sutherland at MIT. This system allowed users to interact with simple wireframe objects via a light pen. This system made use of several new interaction techniques and new data structures for dealing with visual information. It was an interactive design system with capabilities for the manipulation and display of two and three-dimensional wireframe objects.

By the mid-1960s the first algorithms for removal of hidden surfaces were developed, and the systems for producing full color surface shaded animation in real time were improved. General Electric developed a flight simulator that animated and displayed simultaneously as many as 40 solid objects with hidden surfaces removed and in full color. The Mathematical Applications Group, Inc. (MAGI) in Elmsford, NY, was one of the first companies that offered computer-generated animation of fully rendered polygonal objects in the commercial environment. Its first contracts included simulations for the military and advertising-related projects.

The early three-dimensional computer animation and imaging systems depended on costly mainframe computers that were very slow by today's standards. Most of the programs would run only on a specific type of computer and display device, and were not portable to other systems. The use of computer graphic systems during the 1960s was clearly restricted by the high cost and limitations of the hardware involved.

Virtually all of the graphics software from this period was developed in-house. It was not marketed, and it was minimally documented. Most programs were executed in the batch mode, and very few had any interactive features at all. Users had to input their data almost exclusively through the keyboard; other types of input peripherals that encouraged more artistic freedom were just not available. Just a few computer systems had graphics screens, but most had monochrome alphanumeric CRT screens or even just teletype or dot matrix printers.

1970s

The 1970s was a significant decade for the development of three-dimensional computer animation and imaging technology. A large number of the basic rendering techniques still in use today were formulated during the 1970s. Microcomputer technology was also introduced to the consumer markets in the late part of the decade.

Compared to the mainframe computers, the minicomputers that became quite popular during the decade of the 1960s were easier to maintain. During the 1970s these systems also provided significantly more power at a reduced cost.

From the point of view of computer hardware, most of the research and production work done during this decade was predominantly based on minicomputers. The new microcomputer systems greatly contributed to the popularization of computer–generated graphics, mainly in the form of videogames. But the microcomputer's 8-bit computing power, memory capabilities, and output solution was insignificant when compared to their high-end counterparts. A standard configuration of an early 1970s microcomputer included an 8-bit CPU without any graphics co-processors, less than 100 kb of main (or RAM) memory, a clock speed of 10 Mhz, a low-resolution screen with a maximum palette of 8 colors (or slightly higher if dithering was used), and a limited amount of peripheral storage.

During this decade the University of Utah became a primordial force and a center of innovation in three-dimensional computer graphics research. Under the guidance of David Evans, co-founder of Evans & Sutherland, the Department of Computer Science at the University of Utah produced a distinguished roster of Ph.D. students. Many of them developed a large number of the major technical contributions of the decade, such as the original versions of polygonal, Gouraud, and Phong shading, image and bump texture mapping, and facial animation.

1980s

It was during the decade of the 1980s when computer graphics technology leaped from being a curiosity into becoming an area of proven artistic and commercial potential. Technologically speaking, this decade started with the uneven coexistence of powerful minicomputer systems with 8-bit microcomputers. But it ended with the combination of powerful 32-bit microcomputers and 64-bit RISC (Reduced Instruction Set Computer) graphics workstations at the forefront, and with minicomputers in the back seat. Commercially speaking, this decade started with a handful of companies that pioneered the production of three-dimensional computer animation and imaging. These companies included Digital Effects and MAGI on the East Coast; and Information International, Inc. (III) and Robert Abel Associates on the West Coast. These companies operated exclusively with software developed in-house and with much custom-built graphics hardware. The 1980s concluded with the closing of all of the pioneer production houses—or at least their production divisions—and with the creation of a new group of smaller, leaner, and less research-oriented firms that operated mostly with off-the-shelf hardware, and with a mixture of custom and off-the-shelf software.

The bulk of the software research and development during this decade was spent in refining the modeling and shading techniques inherited from the 1970s. Ground was broken with new rendering approaches such as radiosity and procedural textures, and with the development of the first generation of solid user-friendly computer-human interfaces for three-dimensional computer animation and imaging software.

Some of the leading academic centers in North America involved in three-dimensional graphics research during this period included Cornell University (radiosity rendering techniques), the Jet Propulsion Laboratory at the California Institute of Technology (motion dynamics), the University of California at Berkeley (spline modeling), the Ohio State University (hierarchical character animation, and inverse kinematics), the University of Toronto (procedural techniques), and the University of Montreal (character animation and lip syncing).

Significant original research efforts also took place at the University of Tokyo (blobby surfaces modeling techniques), and the University of Hiroshima (radiosity and lighting).

Some of the hardware research during the 1980s focused on the development of more powerful general-purpose microprocessors and special-purpose graphics processors, and techniques for the high speed transfer of visual data.

Most of the three-dimensional software products that were commercially available during the first half of this decade lagged behind the exciting work done in research institutions. This was due to the lack of capital investors who fully believed in the commercial potential of the technology. It was also due to the difficulty of implementing computing-intensive techniques with off-the-shelf hardware systems that were not quite as fast as needed and perhaps a bit overpriced.

In terms of output standards, few of the production companies at the beginning of the decade were capable of first-generation output to videotape. Most of the high-end work was output to film first and then transferred to videotape. By the end of the decade, however, video output established itself as the most common output method for computer-generated animation.

A standard mid-range computer system for three-dimensional production during the 1980s consisted of a 32-bit or 64-bit microcomputer or supermicrocomputer with one or several graphics processors, clock speeds higher than 50 Mhz, several dozens of megabytes for RAM memory, and extensive peripheral storage.

Early 1990s

The first half of the 1990s witnessed a major switch towards smaller and/or considerable more powerful computer systems than the average systems used in the 1980s. Virtually all of the low-end microcomputers currently in production are based on 32-bit microprocessors, while the powerful microcomputer models are centered around 64-bit CISC and RISC processors. A considerable number of models with different features were targeted at different segments of the market, and computer systems were sold in a modular form. Supermicrocomputers, or workstations, kept increasing in power while decreasing in price, or remained at the same price level but with additional features.

Research and development was mostly centered around issues of efficiency, cost, and ease of use. With the midrange hardware systems being powerful enough for most creative needs, a lot of energy and time was spent in optimizing the most successful existing software techniques. Taking small solid steps took precedence over making large groundbreaking advances. Computer-human interface issues also took precedence since the market was a buyer's market. Users of three-dimensional software became more sophisticated and more demanding than ever before, and they enjoyed the level of creativity and computing power provided by the standard systems of the early 1990s.

Two additional trends of this period include the rebirth of the electronic game industry (and the growth in jobs, volume, and quality associated with it), as well as the fact that, overall, the computer industry became friendlier and less technical as it tried to mass-market its products to the consumer market.

1.3 Visual Milestones

It is both refreshing and illuminating to view, enjoy, and analyze the visual works that became creative milestones in the development of three-dimensional computer animation and imaging. Two useful sources for viewing and reading about the three-dimensional computer animations developed since the late 1970s until today are the SIGGRAPH Video Review videotapes (listed in Appendix II), and the issues of the *Cinefex* journal (listed in Appendix V).

1960s

During most of the 1960s the computer was— in the opinion of most visual artists, critics, and spectators—too cold and technical to be involved in the creation of artistic projects. Similar prejudices about technology arose in the 19th century when machines were introduced on a massive scale to the industrial world, eventually becoming commonplace in everyday life. Many turn-of-the-century painters feared the new technology until they learned how to use it and became creative with it. During the 1960s the impact and influence of computers on the animation and imaging can be compared to the impact that photography had on the visual arts of the late 19th century. Miniature painters and engravers feared that the new invention would replace them, and some of them even called it the "invention of the devil."

As mentioned earlier, computers were used for the creation of images since the 1950s, but the first artistic experiments with computer-based systems did not take place until the early 1960s. Most of the early animations and images produced with computers were not created in art studios but in research laboratories. Furthermore, many of the first individuals who created these works came mostly from backgrounds in science and engineering, and they lacked formal training in the fine arts. Nevertheless, many of them displayed a strong artistic intention and a significant degree of aesthetic consciousness.

The computer systems that were used by these pioneers were not designed for the artistic creation. Such systems were not very interactive or not interactive at all. The machine-user interface of the 1960s was typically opaque, cryptic, and never self-explanatory.

Due to the fact that using the early computer systems to create animations and images was not easy, many of these early creators had to put more effort into the process of creating the works than into the form and contents of the works themselves. Many early computer artists were more concerned with the development of the computer-based imaging tools than with the style of their works. But in spite of all the limitations, the pioneers made effective use of the available technology.

The early computer-generated animations and images represent the early products of a technology still in the stage of development. The style of these early works was defined in a major way by the limitations of the computer equipment itself, and by the lack of computer programs that were capable of rendering complex images in a variety of ways. Very often complex methods and data structures did not yield correspondingly complex images. Among the American pioneers of computer art we can mention John Whitney, Sr. and Charles Csuri.

One of the earliest experiments with computer-generated character animation was "Mr. Computer Image ABC" created in 1962 by Lee Harrison III with the Scanimate system at Computer Image Corporation (the system won an Emmy Award in 1972).

1970s

The panorama in computer art changed greatly during the 1970s because of the development of techniques for representing three-dimensional environments, and because of the increased involvement of professional artists with computers. Computer-based animation and imaging systems became more interactive than what they were during the 1960s but were still not easy to use. Just a few of the artists who got interested in computer technology used it as their primary medium for artistic creation. In addition to their visual work, many of these early artists of three-dimensional computer animation and imaging also contributed to the technical development of their tools by collaborating in the development of software.

During the late 1970s one of the most widely viewed works of three-dimensional computer animation was *Voyager 2*, created by a team at the Jet Propulsion Laboratory (JPL) led by James Blinn. This work visualized the explorations of the Voyager 2 spaceship, and it is an excellent example of one of the earliest successful and extensive uses of image mapping techniques. Artist David Em, a visiting artist at the JPL, used the same software utilized to render the planets of the Solar System to create stills of his own fantastic planets.

Other notable examples of this period include *Vol Libre*, an animation by Loren Carpenter that shows renderings of fractal mountains with great lyrical force; the virtual character Cindy created at III for the science fiction film *Looker*, which is one of the earliest—if not the earliest—realistic models of the full human figure; and the Joggler, also created at III, an early example of an animated human character attempting complex motion. The commercial work done for advertising agencies at Digital Effects, III, MAGI, and Robert Abel and Associates is very illustrative of computer animation in the late 1970s.

1980s

In the area of three-dimensional computer animation, the 1980s started with a few exceptional works and ended with a flurry of outstanding projects. This was due to many factors, such as the enhanced technology, the larger market, the maturing of the artists working in the field, and the entry into the workforce of the first art students who attended computer animation and imaging educational programs.

The film *TRON* was produced in 1982 by Disney Productions, and included computer animations by Robert Abel and Associates, III, MAGI, and Digital Effects. *TRON* was the first feature film with over 20 minutes of computer animation, some of it composited with live action. The computer animation segments in *The Last Starfighter* were animated at Digital Productions in 1985. This was the first feature film to include a large amount of hyper-realistic computer animation of highly detailed models rendered with a Cray supercomputer. The Genesis Effect created by Industrial Light and Magic (ILM) for the film *Star Trek II* is also of historical interest because it includes one of the earliest examples of procedural modeling and animation.

Other notable works of the early and mid-1980s include some of the first ray traced imaging tests done by Turner Whitted; *Bio-Sensor* created in 1984 at Osaka University and Toyo Links, an impressive example of early figure locomotion and modeling with blobby surfaces; and the *Brilliance* commercial featuring a sexy female robot with convincing realistic motion created by Abel and Associates, and also the first entirely computer-generated TV ad to be aired during a Super Bowl football game.

The mid-1980s in three-dimensional computer animation were punctuated by the sublime simulations of light, fog, rain, and skies created at Hiroshima University (Fig. 7.5.2), and the intriguing simulations of clouds and smoke created by Geoffrey Gardner at Grumman Data Systems. The mid-1980s also saw the rise of leading commercial production houses such as Pacific Data Images (PDI), and Digital Productions in California; Cranston-Csuri in Columbus, OH; Sogitec in Paris; Toyo Links in Japan; and Omnibus in Canada.

Throughout the 1980s two constants exemplify the excellence reached by three-dimensional computer animation during the decade. On one hand there was *Growth*, a series of semi-abstract animations by Japanese artist-programmer Yoichiro Kawaguchi. The series portrays imaginary underwater creatures generated with procedural techniques. On the other hand there was the engaging and amusing character animations by the animation team at Pixar led by John Lassiter, including *Luxo Jr.* (1985), *Red's Dream* (1987), *Tin Toy* (1988), and *Knickknack* (1989). The Pixar projects not only pushed the Renderman shading language to its limits, but also proved that the traditional principles of character animation could be applied to computer-generated works.

The late 1980s witnessed experimentation with a wide variety of techniques ranging from the simulation of natural-looking hair growth to rigid body dynamics and modeling fabric with visible threads. *Stanley and Stella: Breaking the Ice*, produced by Symbolics Graphics and Whitney Demo Productions in 1987, is a solid and amusing early example of flock animation. The demo reels of design and production studios such as Rhythm & Hues and Metrolight in California, Ex-Machina in Paris, and Digital Pictures in London, are representative of the commercial work of the period. The 1989 *Study of a Numerically Modeled Severe Storm* is a good example of a simulation of natural forces and phenomena (Figs. 11.3.4–5). *Don't Touch Me*,

created in 1989 by the Kleiser and Walczak Construction Company, represents one of the earliest tour de force in character animation with motion capture techniques. The female singer in this piece displayed more body animation and faster motion than any previous attempt; the animation was achieved by applying the motion of a live singer to the virtual character. Cine d'auteur during the late 1980s has inspired examples in *Burning Love* (Pacific Data Images, 1988), *The Little Death* (Matt Elson at Symbolics Graphics, 1989), *Locomotion* (Pacific Data Images, 1988), and *Grinning Evil Death* (McKenna and Sabiston at MIT's Media Lab). *The Abyss* is a 1989 feature film that crowns the decade with convincing examples of three-dimensional animation, seamless compositing with 70 mm live action footage, and also of a complex production created to a great extent with off-the-shelf systems.

Early 1990s

The nature of three-dimensional computer animation and imaging is complex and full of varied styles and attitudes. Today's projects encompass an exciting body of work and a variety of styles and techniques. The creation of three-dimensional computer animation and imaging has become a mature and specialized field that requires a great amount of energy and interdisciplinary skills.

The 1990s have been defined so far by refined examples of computer animation as well as a succesful revival of special effects for feature films.

Several feature films created during the early 1990s used computer-generated visual effects extensively. *Terminator II*, for example, is a 1991 film by James Cameron with computer animation by ILM. This film was the first mainstream blockbuster movie to include outstanding morphing effects and also the first convincing simulation of natural human motion. *The Lawnmower Man*, a 1992 film with computer animation by Angel Studios, was the first feature film of the decade that explored the topic of virtual reality with computer animation. *Batman*

Returns is a 1992 stylized production with effective examples of flock animation (Fig. 11.4.2). *Jurassic Park*, a 1993 film by Steven Speilberg, is a great example of inverse kinematics, perfect compositing of live action with computer-generated images, hyperrealistic rendering, and a gigantic amount of processing performed in a relatively short period of time.

The early 1990s also saw great examples of broadcast-quality computer animation created entirely with off-the-shelf microcomputer systems. *Babylon 5*, for example, is a 1993 TV series and the first mainstream example of high-end three-dimensional computer animation produced entirely on 32-bit Amiga and Macintosh microcomputers.

Other notable examples of computer animation during the early 1990s include *Primordial Dance* (1991) and *Liquid Selves* (1992), both beautiful examples of computer animations created by Karl Simms with particle systems techniques; the irreverent and amusing *Le Xons Crac-Crac* and *Baston* created in 1991 by Ex-Nihilo and McGuff Ligne; Latham's hipnotic *Mutations* (1991); *Don Quichotte,* an ambitious keyframe animation created in 1991 by Video System; and *Leaf Magic* (1991), a good example of animation with motion dynamics by Alan Norton.

Some of the outstanding work for television commercials includes the 1993 *Coca-Cola Polar Bears* by Rhythm and Hues Studios, the 1994 *Listerine Arrows* by Pixar, and works by Topix in Toronto, Canada, such as *Lifesavers*. Many ambitious and exquisite architectural visualizations were also created in the early 1990s including *The Seven Wonders of the World* (1992) by Electric Images in England, *The Ancient World Revisited I-III* (1990-94) by Taisei Corp., and *De Karnak a Louqsor* (1992) by Ex-Machina.

Motion capture systems for character animation experienced an intense development during this period. Some of these efforts included the Facetracker system developed by the company SimmGraphics to animate the Super Mario character; *Moxy,* a virtual TV host animated by Colossal Pictures for the Cartoon Network (Fig. 11.2.6); Acclaim Entertainment's optical system with up to 70 sensors for simul-taneous two-person capture (Fig. 11.2.5); and a variety of commercially-available motion capture hardware and software.

1.4 A Bag of New Magic Tricks

Today's three-dimensional computer imaging and animation techniques provide us with a whole bag of new magic tricks.

Many of these visual tricks are described in this book. Some of them are simple, and others complex. Some can be learned in minutes while others take years, literally, to master. Modeling a sphere, a cube, and a pyramid, for example, can be simple and fast. But animating these shapes to behave like a wild trio of jungle animals is not a simple or quick task.

Some three-dimensional computer imaging and animation techniques duplicate effects that can easily be created with other media, while others produce results that are unique to the medium of three-dimensional computer imaging and animation. The effect of motion blur, for example, can easily be created by anybody with a point-and-shoot photographic camera. But simulating motion blur with three-dimensional computer techniques requires a significant effort and understanding of the tools. Three-dimensional morphing, on the other hand, illustrates a technique that is unique to the medium of three-dimensional computer imaging and animation. Computer-generated three-dimensional morphing can be produced efficiently, while creating similar effects with any other media would require an immensely laborious process. (Motion blur is covered in Chapter 8, and three-dimensional morphing is covered in Chapter 10).

Like all other performances of magic, the visual tricks of three-dimensional computer imaging and animation can be performed with exquisite subtlety or with disenchanting obviousness—audiences can be equally fascinated or disappointed. An obvious use of the technology, for example, is often a ray traced rendering of a group of reflective spheres without any further exploration on meaning: a cliché that no longer elicits surprise. The techniques that are often more promising are those that create results impossible to create with other media. These techniques may include, for example, transformations of color, matter, or shape.

As all other magic tricks do, the computer imaging and animation magic tricks require **practice**: a lot of study and practice. The more practice, the better. Reading this book will hopefully provide you with meaningful knowledge to guide your practice. This knowledge may include an understanding of both the technical and the creative issues. But practice is irreplaceable in the visual arts. Practice makes perfect.

Three-dimensional computer imaging and animation is a rich and complex medium. It requires constant learning because many of the techniques on which it is based are constantly changing. Incorporating computers in your creative work requires time and energy to learn many technical and creative issues. Do not be misled by promotional advertisements or by salespeople who characterize three-dimensional computer imaging and animation as "instant art" and "easy to learn." These techniques are just like any other: you get out what you put in, and the quality of the results equals the seriousness of purpose and the intensity of the effort.

However, the tools and techniques of three-dimensional computer imaging and animation are more than just a bag of new magic tricks. They have the power create visuals that communicate, inspire, and move the minds of people. How to use these tools is a challenge that artists can only solve through their practice. But there are so many styles to embrace, so many topics to explore! Using the creative power of computers to recreate and portray our reality, or simulating new dimensions and inventing virtual worlds is a common creative dilemma. The more fashionable option changes by the year or by the country. Another creative choice has to do with whether to use the new tools as specified in the manuals—following a logical sequence of steps—or whether to find new ways to use them—the equivalent of Jackson Pollock's paint dripping.

The discussion about how and what to create with our bag of new tricks continues.

Should we focus on creating images and animations about space travel and battles with aliens? Or should we be creating still lifes in the style of 18th century painters to decorate our dinning rooms? Or create expressionistic portraits of our friends? The strengths and weaknesses of new visual technologies throughout history have always influenced the creative directions of the time, but have rarely limited them.

It is unquestionable, for example, that the eventual development of non-representational and abstract painting was related to the fact that photographic technology liberated painters from just portraying the world in a realistic representational way. It is also clear that opposite creative styles can develop in parallel and enrich each other. Compare the work, for example, of the experimental animators that worked outside of the commercial and entertainment circles against the work of the animators who work within the Hollywood systems and who abide by the limitations imposed in a market economy. The former pioneered the use of experimental methods such as collage, cutouts, wax, pinhead shadow, object and abstract painting animation. Among them are found the French Leopold Survage, the Germans Hans Richter, Oskar Fischinger, and Lotte Reininger, the Canadian Norman McLaren, the French Alexander Alexeieff, and the Americans Claire Parker, and John Whitney, Sr. The later blossomed delivering gag after gag and amusing audiences with the likes of Popeye, Woody Woodpecker, Bugs Bunny, Tom and Jerry, and Mickey Mouse. Among them we find Max Fleischer, Walter Lantz, Tex Avery, and Walt Disney.

The 20th century has seen a string of innovations in visual technologies and also in visual languages, discourses, and styles. Whatever creative path you chose, keep the doors open so that others can have the opportunity to explore, and perhaps, to innovate.

The Future of Three-Dimensional Interactive Entertainment

The current trends, outstanding work, and original points of view in interactive entertainment that is based on three-dimensional computer animation and imagery demonstrate new levels of both creative and technical sophistication in a variety of ways. Some of the imagery, for example, is exquisite in its rendering. Several graphical interfaces go well beyond pointing and clicking. Some of the technology used is simpler than one would have imagined, yet the results are impressive.

During the 1890s the ultimate desire of Thomas Alva Edison and his assistant William K. Dickinson was to improve the devices for creating images in motion and, above all, the simultaneous recording of sound and motion. Edison and his assistant went on to develop the kinetoscope—which means "viewing in motion" in Greek—a closed box where 50 feet of looped film could be viewed through an opening. (The few kinetoscopes that were equipped with earphones to hear simultaneous music were called kinetophones.) The first kinetoscope parlor was opened in New York City in 1894. On the other side of the ocean, during the 1900 Paris Exhibition, a mechanical platform gently rocked by a steam machine presented riders with panoramic views of real and imaginary scenes of the world.

We certainly have come a long way since the kinetoscopes and the steam motion ride. But the interactive entertainment of today, however, does not present a unified creative vision. Some projects are slick products that are meant to be successful in the mainstream market. Other projects are explorations into new forms of entertainment that are not yet ready for commercialization. This apparent contradiction between creative directions is the engine of the three-dimensional interactive creations of today.

One of the reasons why there are so many variations of the idea of three-dimensional interactive entertainment is because it means different things to different people. For some, conversing interactively over tea and cookies is entertaining. For others, this kind of activity can be boring and perhaps too personal and interactive. Competing with imaginary opponents and defeating them through violent virtual destruction or scoring more goals is a satisfying inter-

action for many, and also their ticket to first-class entertainment. Others may find this kind of competition horrifying. And there is always good old movie watching, which is exciting for some and sleep-inducing for others.

The fact that there are so many ways of interacting and entertaining is an important issue for professionals and entrepreneurs of interactive entertainment. As we rush to produce the perfect three-dimensional game or the most stimulating entertainment, we can learn a lot by analyzing traditional forms of interaction and entertainment.

There are clearly many different concepts of what is truly entertaining and what is true interaction. This is an obvious point. What is less obvious is which of these concepts has the right combination of technology, imagery, plot, and pricing to be successful with the various potential audiences for interactive entertainment.

So far we seem to have focused most of our energies on the variety of interactivity that is based on quick reflexes and limited dialog. This has led to the creation of very sophisticated action games for distribution in both public areas (arcades) and private environments (homes). In these games, searching for and destroying the enemy is invariably the main priority, and impeccable hand-eye coordination is a condition for survival. But increasingly, as technology improves and as game plots get more ambitious, many action games are trying to incorporate more realistic imagery and motion. These improvements are based on technological developments such as faster and more powerful hardware, more efficient software, enhanced character development, and improved plots that allow a multitude of story lines.

There is also an increasing selection of successful games that require more analytical skills. Many recent examples in this genre also include stunning imagery. More ambitious plots are emerging, and the creative potential is limitless. How about more games based on history or real murder cases? How about crashing the stock market for fun, and then trying to recover it? Or rescuing the an entire state in the country from a extremist group that has taken it over? How about playing with our cultural myths? What if, for example, we have been charged by Zeus to stop Hera's jealous attacks on his mortal girlfriends? Or what if we have been called by the desperate members of a neighborhood watch to assist in eradicating drug dealers from their neighborhood, but someone from our team is corrupt and sabotages our plans? How about the trials and tribulations of the slaves escaping through the underground railroad? What if the American Indians had defeated their attackers? What if male players in a game could only play female roles?

In any case, it is essential to keep in mind that the goal of three-dimensional interactive entertainment, especially from the point of view of the audience, is not about technology at all. It is about being entertained, about being captivated by a story, or challenged by a mystery, or about fooling our senses and being transported to worlds of fantasy.

What's Next?

So, what's next? I hear that question all the time, whether it comes from impatient students, anxious clients, or frustrated colleagues. Some of us seem to need just a little more computing power, or additional branching options in an interactive three-dimensional game, or higher image resolution, or a larger screen size, or more models in a three-dimensional scene, or finer control over curve tools, or improved storage capacity. Others seem to want just a little less expense, or less complexity in the network, or less pages in the technical manuals, or less data volatility, or less pull-down menus to navigate through, or less waiting time for renderings to be completed.

The question of "what's next?" seems to always address issues related to the performance of the computer systems. But if past events can be an indication of the future, then we can expect many additional hardware and software innovations and breakthroughs that will continue to challenge our ingenuity and creativity.

But what about "what's next?" in terms of using the computer systems to create new art forms or to express the emotions of our times? Now that these systems have reached an impressive level of technical sophistication, it is a good time to invest some of our time and energy to reflect on the technology's effect on our creative lives. Integrating technology with people's creative lives and practices is as important as developing the technology in the first place.

Imagine how many artists could develop repetitive strain injury syndrome because they were never taught the correct way of holding the mouse or typing on the keyboard. Imagine how many clients could continue to have unreasonable expectations because we never made it clear to them what the strengths and weaknesses of this technology are. Imagine the nightmare of having interactive television with a poorly designed computer-human interface. Imagine how many individuals could go on believing that they create fine works of art just because they use the latest computer techniques. Imagine having millions of new CD-ROMs containing useless information. Imagine…

Key Terms

Computer graphics technology
Digital environment
Digital imaging techniques
Digital information
Mainframes
Massively parallel computers
Microcomputers
Minicomputers
Silicon chip
Super-microcomputers
Supercomputers
Workstations

Modeling

CHAPTER 2

Basic Modeling Concepts

Summary

The spatial description and placement of imaginary three-dimensional objects, environments, and scenes with a computer system is called **modeling**. This chapter explores the basic concepts of the modeling process, including the numerical description of objects, moving and resizing objects in three-dimensional space, common file formats, and advice on getting ready for a modeling session.

2.1 Space, Objects, and Structures

We live in a three-dimensional world. We move among other people, we climb mountains, run on the beach, and admire the landscape around us. We go in and out of buildings, we walk up and down the stairs, drive through bridges, and grab utensils for writing, cooking, and combing ourselves. Our daily life happens in three-dimensional environments and is full of three-dimensional objects. We see and feel three-dimensionality all the time. But unless we are involved in an activity or profession that is related to building things, like silverware or furniture, buildings or bridges, we rarely concern ourselves with how our three-dimensional reality was put together and what techniques were used for building it.

When it comes to the modeling of our reality we usually take a lot of things for granted. But if we want to model three-dimensional scenes with a computer program then we have to familiarize ourselves with the large selections of computer software tools that can be used for modeling objects and environments. In three-dimensional computer modeling it is quite common to use a combination of tools for building just one object. For example, think of the difference between a chair that was built by using just two tools—a manual saw and a hammer—and a chair that was built with six tools—a thick saw, a thin saw,

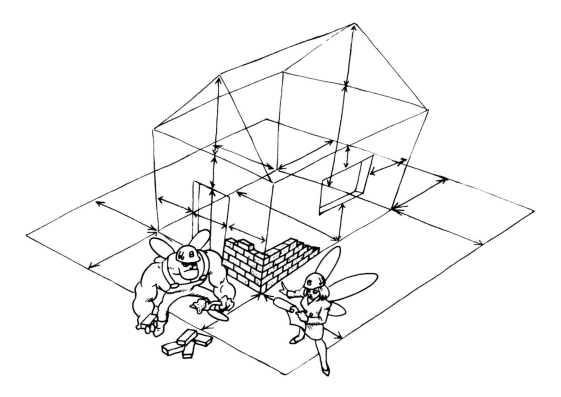

2.1.1 Building a simple rectangular room requires taking measurements that include the orientation of the walls, the location of the doorway, the windows, and the distance between the walls.

a lathe, a curved chisel, a hammer, and a sanding tool. It is obvious that while the first chair could have an interesting design the variety of shapes would be limited. The second chair would have richer and more refined modeling. The simple computer-based modeling tools are described in Chapter 3, most of the advanced modeling tools are covered in Chapter 4. Now let's step back and talk about some general issues involved in modeling in three dimensions.

Many of the basic conventions used in three-dimensional modeling software describing three-dimensional scenes are based on traditional conventions used in various disciplines. For example, in order to convey their space designed in a clear and concise way architects use all kinds of conventions related to measuring, composition, and sequence. Even the design of a simple rectangular room requires measuring many times so that all the components of the room end up where they were planned to be (Fig. 2.1.1). Furthermore, in order to interpret accurately an architect's drawing and build it, masons need to take measurements. Over the ages masons and architects have developed conventions so that they can be precise and clear about measuring **spaces**, building **objects**, and arranging them in **structures**.

We use similar conventions to describe the dimension, placement, and sequence of objects and environments in a three-dimensional space simulated with a computer program. A beginner builder will soon find out that there are many different methods available for measuring space, and at first this variety can be confusing. But experienced builders usually find this richness of methods very empowering, and have the option of using one or another depending on the requirements of the project.

Let's start our definition of three-dimensional space with the boundaries that define our **workspace** or **scene**. The simplest way to do this is to imagine that we are working inside a large cube. We can think of this cube as our world or environment. Objects that exist within the cube are visible, those that fall outside are invisible (Fig. 6.2.1).

The main point of reference in this world is called the world **origin**. This origin is usually located in the center of the space, but it can also be placed or repositioned elsewhere depending on the modeling needs and strategies (Fig. 2.1.2). For example, if we were building a model of the solar system it would make sense to have the world origin where the sun is, in the center, because all the other objects in the system are placed around the sun, and can be easily described in terms of the sun. If we were building an underwater scene that included both fish underwater and boats above water, we might want to position the origin at the point where air and water meet. In the case of a three-dimensional model of an airport the world origin could be placed at ground level, matching the position of the control tower.

All three-dimensional spaces have three basic **dimensions**: width, height, and depth. A common method for representing these dimensions in a three dimensional space is by using arrows or **axes** (Fig. 2.1.2). It is common to label the **axis** representing the width of a **three-dimensional space** with the letter X, the height axis with the letter Y, and the depth axis with the letter Z. The point in space where these three axes intersect or cross each other is the world origin.

The **rectangular coordinate system** can be used to define specific locations and accurately position the points of objects in three-dimensional space. René Descartes, an 18th-century French philosopher and mathematician, formalized the idea of using three axes labelled X, Y, and Z to represent the dimensions in three-dimensional space. The coordinate system he devised is commonly referred to as the **Cartesian** (or rectangular) **coordinate system**. Each axis in the system can be divided into many units of measurement. In principle these units are abstract values that can represent different units of measurement and scales of dimension. On each axis the values to one side of the origin are positive and the values on the other side are negative. As shown in Fig. 2.1.2, the positive direction of each axis in a right-hand-

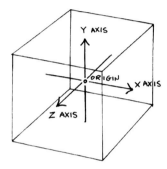

2.1.2 The origin is a point of reference usually located in the center of the three-dimensional space. It can also be located elsewhere in three-dimensional space. A three-dimensional space has width, height, and depth dimensions each represented by the three axes in the Cartesian coordinate system. The numerical values in the figure correspond to those in a right-handed coordinate system.

ed coordinate system is represented with an arrowhead.

There are many ways of representing the direction of an axis and, consequently, the directions in which values on that axis are positive or negative. Usually though, in what is called a **right-handed coordinate system**, the values on the X axis become larger to the right of the origin, the values on the Y axis increase as they move above the origin, and the values on the Z axis grow as they get close to us. In a **left-handed coordinate system** the values on the Z axis decrease as they get closer to us. There are several variations of the directionality of the rectangular coordinate system, but most three-dimensional modeling programs use the right-handed coordinate system to describe the virtual world.

The three axes in the rectangular coordinate system can be paired with each other in three different ways so that each pair of axes defines a plane or a view. The XY axes define the **front plane**, the XZ axes define the **top plane**, and the YZ axes define the **side plane** (Fig. 2.1.3).

There are other coordinate systems in addition to the popular rectangular coordinate system. The **spherical** or **azimuthal coordinate system** is also widely used because it provides a simple way for placing objects in a three-dimensional world in terms of their distance to the object, their angle around the point of interest, and their altitude angle above the point of interest. The spherical system is especially useful for placing and moving cameras and light sources in a three-dimensional scene (Fig. 2.4.6).

Any **world** or **global coordinate system** is useful for placing or moving objects in the world or in relation to each other. World coordinates are absolute values that are relative to the origin of the world. These coordinates do not depend on any specific object in the world, and are applied to all objects in the world indistinctly. (Global transformations, as we shall read later in this chapter, are easily expressed in terms of the world coordinate system.) In addition to the world coordinate system, however, each object in the world can have its own **object** or **local coordinate system** (Fig. 2.1.3). Object coordinate systems are values relative to the origin of the object, which is sometimes placed in the center of the object. For all practical purposes object coordinate systems are only used to specify positions, orientations, or transformations of the object in question. (Local transformations are almost always expressed in the coordinate system of the object.)

2.2 Building with Numbers

Throughout time we have developed a sophisticated vocabulary for describing with the spoken or written word the shape of three-dimensional objects and their relative positions to one

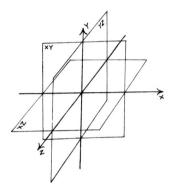

2.1.3 The three planes or views that can be defined with the XY, XZ, and YZ pairs of axes are useful for building models from different points of view. The world coordinate system is used to place and move objects in relation to the world origin. The objects' coordinate systems are useful to perform transformations only on specific objects.

another. We can use that vocabulary for communicating with others about three-dimensional objects and their positions in space. But, even though verbal descriptions of objects can be very concise, they lack precision. Verbal descriptions of objects can be interpreted in a variety of different ways, not only when it comes to obvious issues of dimension, but also subtle issues of proportion and shape. As you read the following verbal description of a flower vase try visualizing it in your head or by drawing it with pencil and paper.

> The vase has a very long neck and a short, round base. The neck is about five times the height of the base, the width of the base is about twice its own height. The cylindrical neck grows out of the base slowly. At the point where the neck touches the base it has a width that equals the height of the base. As it moves upward the neck gets narrow, and as it passes the first fifth of its height the neck reaches a thin, delicate width that remains constant until the end of the neck. A small section of the oval shape that constitutes the base of the vase is sliced off so that the bottom of the base is flat. The resulting sharp edge at the bottom of the base is rounded off just a little bit. Halfway between the edge of the base and its center, a thin slice of a short cylinder is attached to the base.

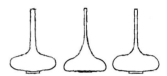

2.2.1 Different interpretations of the verbal description of a flower vase.

If you have some experience with modelmaking or pottery you were probably able to follow the description of the shapes in the vase and the relation between them, and your flower vase might look similar to the results shown in Fig. 2.2.1. But if you have little experience with three-dimensional models it is also possible that your sketch is quite different or even that you were unable to finish reading all of the description. Maybe you lost interest because you found it difficult to visualize all the shapes and the ways in which they were attached to one another.

Most individuals and today's computer systems are incapable of recreating in detail verbal descriptions of complex three-dimensional shapes. Computer modeling in three dimensions requires very precise and unequivocal descriptions of shape. The method of choice for precise and unequivocal descriptions of shape and their location in space consists of using numbers. With numerical description we can specify the position of an object in space and the details of its shape: height, width, depth, diameter, curvature, and number of sides. Figure 2.3.1 illustrates most of the numbers required for describing a fairly simple three-dimensional shape.

Much of the success in modeling three-dimensional objects and environments with a computer system lies in understanding how a particular computer system describes a shape with num-

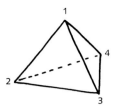

2.2.2 The difference between two geometry formats for the same object is quite evident here. These two listings were generated with two different types of modeling software.

2.2.3 This simple information dialog box provides quick numerical information about the position, orientation, size, and ranges of motion of an object. (Dialog box from Infini-D 3.0. © 1991-1995 Specular International, Ltd.)

bers. The exact same numbers sometimes mean different things to different software programs. For example, some systems give great attention to the decimal—or floating point—numbers (i.e. 5.379) that describe the subtle shape of a small curve, while other computer systems may ignore those numbers completely and recreate the curve based on a whole numerical value (i.e. 5). We must also keep in mind that some of the numbers that describe a shape may be of little value to us if we were building the object with traditional materials, such as wood. But those same numbers often provide the computer system with crucial information for building the object with computer modeling techniques. For example, the order in which we number points in a shape can yield very different results.

The essence of all software-based three-dimensional modeling techniques consists of creating a **data file**, or a list of numbers, that defines models in a way that can be understood by the computer program. Whether we create a simple cube or a collection of computer shapes representing a human hand, the numbers describing the object are kept in a file so that the program can load them into memory, display them, modify them, display them again, save them, and so on. The files that contain the data describing the object are called **geometry files**. Examples of all geometry file formats are discussed later in this chapter.

In most modeling systems, three-dimensional objects can be modeled by typing the numbers that describe the object directly into the system. This method of **direct numerical description** can be, however, quite tedious and time-consuming. We rarely use it except for those times when we are looking for an extremely specific shape or detail that can be hard to model with the regular modeling tools. Even when we use the interactive modeling tools provided by the software it is still possible to peek at the numerical information that the software uses to describe and manipulate three-dimensional shapes. Most systems allow us to get this numerical information in varying degrees of detail (Fig. 2.2.2).

Both the shape of an object and its position in three-dimensional space are expressed in terms of numerical values. From the computer's point of view, numerical values are easy to manipulate and easy to repeat. This facilitates the building of three-dimensional objects with modeling software, as well as the duplication of objects using the **cut-copy-paste** techniques used by most of today's programs (Fig. 2.2.3).

BASIC MODELING CONCEPTS

a   b

c

2.3 Points, Lines, and Surfaces

Now that you have learned how to locate points in three-dimensional space and how to create and edit lists of numbers that represent XYZ spaces you are ready to start thinking about building a simple model. The three-dimensional object illustrated in Fig. 2.3.1 is defined by four points, six lines, six edges, and four planes.

Points, lines, and surfaces are among the basic elements that can be used to build three-dimensional objects. A **point** can be easily defined by its XYZ location. A **line** can be defined by the XYZ location of its two endpoints. An **edge** is defined by two adjacent surfaces. A planar **surface** can be defined by the position of its bounding lines. An object is usually composed of several points, lines, and surfaces.

A three-dimensional object can be described to software as a list of numbers. This list is usually generated automatically by the computer program, but it can also be generated directly by the user. As stated earlier, it is not necessary in most cases to input all of these numbers by hand. In fact, we do not need to be aware that all this number-shuffling is taking place. But once in a while you will encounter modeling situations when it will be paramount that you understand the meaning and proper structure of these numbers. It is for those occasions when the information in this section will come in handy.

Simple objects like the one pictured in Fig. 2.3.1, and even much more complex objects, can easily be described or edited in most modeling software providing their point XYZ positions and the connectivity lists to the three-dimensional program. Whether this is done by typing their numerical values directly on the keyboard or by transferring the XYZ data collected by a three-dimensional scanner, a simple methodology can be followed. First label all the points and all planes in your sketch or print-out—if one is available (Fig. 2.3.1a). Then write down the XYZ position of each of the points in list form (Fig. 2.3.1b). Finally,

2.3.1 Three-dimensional objects are defined by points, lines, and planes. This simple object has a total of four vertices and four sides.

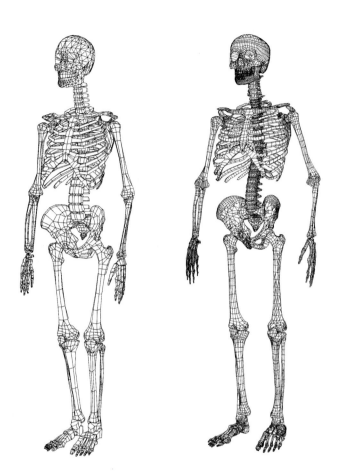

make another list that includes each of the planes and all the points that must be connected to define them. It is important that all the points in each plane are connected in the same direction—either clockwise or counterclockwise (Fig. 2.3.1c). Some computer programs require that you connect the points clockwise while others require counterclockwise, but usually all programs require that the order be consistent throughout the entire object.

The planar surfaces that define most three-dimensional objects are also called **facets**—as those in a cut diamond—or polygons. The word polygon has its roots in the Greek word *polygónon*, which means "with many angles." Polygons are closed planes bounded by straight lines. Polygons can be regular or irregular. Many of the three-dimensional shapes created with three-dimensional computer software are made of polygons. Simple geometric shapes may be defined with dozens of polygons. Objects like a teacup that require a fair amount of detail may also require hundreds of polygons to model that detail. Complex objects, such as the detailed model of a human, may require thousands of polygons (Fig. 2.3.2). The modeling of natural phenomena, such as a forest or simulation of the explosion of a supernova star, may require millions of polygons.

Sometimes we can define objects with curves instead of straight lines, and curved surfaces instead of flat polygonal surfaces. At first building objects with curved surfaces can be more demanding than using polygonal surfaces because curved surfaces are more complex. Read Chapters 3 and 4 for additional information on curves and curved surfaces.

2.4 Moving Things Around

Once we have built some objects we can move them around in

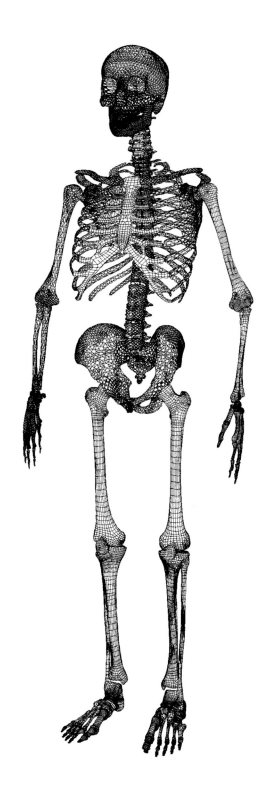

2.3.2 The first skeleton model is built with 141,788 polygons, the second one is built with 35,305, and the third one with 8,979 polygons. (Copyright Viewpoint Datalabs, used with permission.)

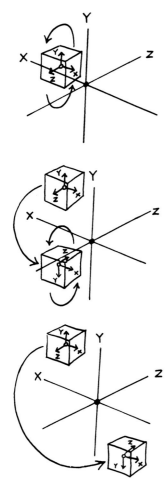

three-dimensional space and create a composition or a scene. Sometimes while we build objects it becomes necessary to move some of its components—a group of points for example—before the modeling is completed.

The functions used for modifying the shape of objects, their size and proportions as well as their position in space, are called **geometric transformations**. The name of these simple but powerful tools obviously comes from the fact that they can be used to transform—to change, to move, to modify—the geometry of objects. In effect, these **mathematical operations** can modify the numerical information that describes the objects that we build in the environment and even the environment itself. The most widely used geometric transformations are: translation, rotation, scaling, and perspective projection.

Geometric transformations can also be applied to the camera that "looks" at the scenes we model and arrange, and also to the lights that reveal our creations to the camera. See Chapter 6 for more information on camera motion, and Chapter 7 for more on moving lights around.

In general, when specifying transformations to be applied to a single object or a group of objects it is important to specify the type of transformation, the axis or axes in which the transformation is to take place, the point around which the rotation or series of rotations will occur (whether the transformation is local or global), and the order in which transformations are to take place in a sequence of several of them. Geometric transformations are usually calculated by most programs with the aid of a **transformation matrix**. This 4 x 4 matrix is used to calculate the new XYZ values after a transformation is applied to all the points of a three-dimensional element. A few programs allow users to manipulate XYZ values directly in the matrix in addition to—or instead of—using more user-friendly tools.

Global or Local Transformations

Geometric transformations can be performed on single objects or on entire environments. Transformations that are applied to the objects using the environment's axes and/or origin are called **global transformations**. When transformations are applied to a single object—or a limited selection of objects—using the object's own axes and origin, they are called **local transformations**.

In general, software programs offer two basic techniques for specifying whether a transformation—or a series of transformations—is global or local. It can be done by selecting the objects directly with the mouse or by typing the names of the objects on the keyboard.

We can start to define a local transformation by selecting or

2.4.1 The position of an object's center has very important implications in the results of the transformations applied to it. The first cube has been rotated locally around its own X axis and its own origin. The second cube has been rotated around the world's X axis and its own local origin. The third cube has been rotated globally around the world's X axis and origin.

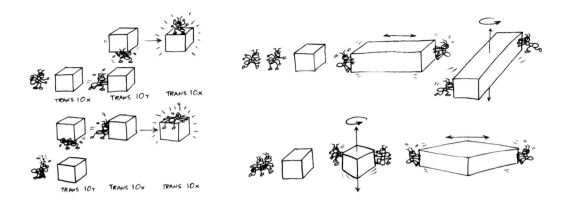

activating just one or several objects—but not all of them. In such instances, the transformation will be applied to the active objects only. In general, when one object is selected as the recipient of a local transformation, the object's center and axis are usually used as the centers of rotation and scaling, and the axis of translation, rotation, and scaling. (The centers of rotation or scaling are usually located in the center of the object unless specified otherwise.) Some programs, however, offer the option to apply local transformations to an object based on the environment's center and/or axis instead of the object's center and/or axis. The results can be quite different. For example, an object scaled along its axis after being rotated retains its shape, while an object scaled along the world's axes will not retain its shape (Fig. 2.4.1). Check the manuals of the software you use to find out how local and global transformations are implemented. Having a clear understanding of this is crucial to the correct operation of your software.

When performing global transformations, or local transformations that occur along or around the global axis, the order in which transformations are applied to an object or a series of objects can affect the final result. For this reason rotation and scaling sequences should be planned carefully, translation sequences can be applied in any order. **Concatenated transformations** is the name sometimes given to a series of global transformations applied in sequence. Figure 2.4.2 illustrates the different results obtained by applying the same global transformations to a trio of objects but in a different sequence each time.

In general, if all objects in a scene are active then the transformation is global and applied to all objects. Most software apply transformations to all the active objects. When performing a global rotation or global scaling, the center of the environment usually doubles as center of rotation and scaling for all the objects unless specified otherwise.

2.4.2 The examples on the left show the same translations applied to the same object in two different sequences. The results are identical, in both cases the object ends up in the same place. The examples on the right show two different results after applying the same rotation and scaling to an object, but in a different sequence.

Absolute or Relative Values

When working with most interactive modeling programs applying transformations to one or several objects is as easy as selecting them and dragging them to a new location in three-dimensional space. It is quite common to use the mouse and the mouse button for controlling the position, orientation, and size of the models in the environment. However, it is sometimes necessary to type specific values on the keyboard for controlling the exact position, orientation, and size of models. In those cases when typing values becomes a necessity one must keep in mind that all transformations can be specified as **absolute values** or as **relative values**. Absolute values, or numbers, always refer to an exact position in space where the object must be relocated regardless of where the object was located in space before the transformation. Relative values, as their name indicates, are numerical values that express the amount of units that must be added or subtracted to the current position of the object. Relative values are relative to an existing absolute position.

For example, if we have a sphere with a center located at XYZ coordinates 30 30 30, the command *trans sphere 0 20 0* (if the numbers were relative) would reposition the sphere's center at XYZ coordinates 30 50 30 because 20 units would have been *added* to the sphere's position. However, if the numbers being used were absolute numbers then the sphere's center would be relocated to the 0 20 0 XYZ position, regardless of the fact that the sphere's center was previously located at 30 30 30.

Translation

Translation is the simplest of all geometric transformations. This operation is used to move an object or group of objects in a linear way to a new location in three-dimensional space (Fig. 2.4.3).

Translation is the simplest, and easiest to control, of all geometric transformations. Translation can occur along one axis or

2.4.4 A bird's-eye view of an object being rotated.

along several axes at the same time. The order in which several global and local translations are applied to one object does not affect the final position of the object. For example, an object that is translated 5 units along the X axis, then 10 units on the Y axis, and finally -7 units on the Z axis would end up in the same positions as an object that is translated first 10 units along the Y axis, then -7 units on the Z axis, and finally 5 units on the X axis.

Rotation

Rotation is the geometric transformation used to move an element or group of elements around a specific center and axis. The amount of rotation is usually specified in terms of an angle of rotation (measured in degrees) and a direction of rotation (Fig. 2.4.4).

Depending on whether the rotation is global or local, objects can be rotated around their own center, the center of the environment, or even the center of their "parent" in a **hierarchy** of objects (for more on transformation of model hierarchies see Chapters 4 and 10). When rotating an object around its own center it is possible with many programs to reposition that center. Consequently, the center of rotation of an object may not always be placed in the geometric center of the object.

Rotations can be used to present different sides of an object to the camera. Rotations are very effective for arranging subtle details in a scene, such as to expose sides of a model with the most interesting shapes or detail, to simulate motion, or to emphasize the perspective of the objects in the scene.

Because rotations always happen around an axis, it is important to know which way rotations are supposed to occur. Depending on the value (positive or negative) that defines a rotation, the rotation can be clockwise or counterclockwise. In a right-handed coordinate system, positive rotations are always counterclockwise and negative rotations are clockwise. A simple method for remembering the direction of rotations consists of representing the axes on which the rotation is taking place with our extended right hand thumb as shown in Fig. 2.4.5. If the thumb points to the positive direction of the axes, the direction of a positive rotation is defined by the direction in which we close the hand and make a fist.

2.4.5 In a right-handed coordinate system the direction in which your hand closes to make a fist is the direction of a positive rotation around any axis represented by the extended right-hand thumb.

Scaling

Scaling is a geometric transformation used to change the size and/or the proportion of an element or a group of elements. Scaling can be applied to an object in a proportional or a non-proportional mode. **Proportional scaling** consists of resizing an object along each axis in equal amounts. The result of pro-

2.4.6 An object being scaled.

portional scaling is always a larger or smaller object with the same proportions as the original object. With **nonproportional scaling** the object may be resized by different factors along each axis. Nonproportional scaling can be used to change the proportions of a three-dimensional object so that it becomes taller or shorter, wider or narrower, or deeper or shallower (Fig. 2.4.6). Because of its ability to easily modify the shape of objects, nonproportional scaling is also widely used in computer animation to simulate the "squish-and-stretch" distortions typical of three-dimensional objects in motion.

When a scaling operation is performed, not on a single object but on all the objects in the environment, we get an effect that is similar to a camera zoom.

Perspective Projection

Perspective projection is a transformation of critical importance because it makes possible the representation of three-dimensional environments on the flat surface of the computer's monitor or a sheet of paper. A perspective view of a three-dimensional scene is created by projecting each point of an object from the viewpoint onto the picture plane. The points in the three-dimensional object coordinate system are then transformed to the two-dimensional image coordinate system.

Perspective projection is a transformation that happens automatically in virtually all three-dimensional software. It is not necessary that we ask for perspective projection each time we do something to our scene. The three-dimensional environment is con-

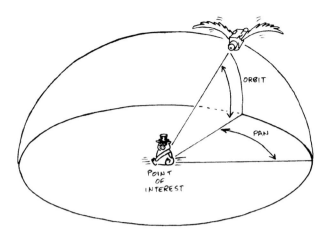

2.4.7 The spherical or azimuthal coordinate system.

stantly being transformed into a two-dimensional view using perspective projection techniques. The final two-dimensional images obtained on the screen can be modified by moving the objects in the three-dimensional environment or by altering the camera. See Chapter 6 for more information on perspective projection.

Navigation

Navigation usually refers to the motions that place the camera in different parts of the scene. Navigation can be used during the modeling process for looking at the models from points of view that show the model in more detail. Navigation can also take place before the rendering process to focus on areas of interest, or before the animation process to place the camera where it helps tell a story more effectively.

The spherical or azimuthal coordinate system is often used to navigate through the world by specifying camera positions in terms of the camera's angle around the horizon, its angle above the horizon, and its distance from the object (Fig. 2.4.7). Navigating through three-dimensional space by moving the camera can take place on any of the four view windows provided by almost all three-dimensional software. These windows include the perspective view and the three orthographic views: top/bottom, front/back, and right/left. All the camera motions described here can take place in the perspective window, but in some programs some camera motions—such as yaw/pitch or azimuth/elevation—cannot be viewed in the orthographic views because these motions can only be calculated in three-dimensional space, and not on a flat surface.

The basic characteristics of a virtual camera in three-dimensional space (what the camera sees) are defined by the camera position, its point of interest, and the camera lens. These characteristics can be quickly set by typing numerical values on the keyboard. These characteristics can also be set interactively by clicking on the control buttons provided by some programs, or by directly manipulating the camera with a variety of input peripherals that include the mouse, graphics tablet, trackball, joystick, or dial box.

Even though all camera positions and moves can be input from the keyboard, it is a lot more practical and fun to position and move the camera interactively. In any case, each possible camera move will result in the modification of at least one of the camera's three basic values: position, orientation, and focal length.

The motions of computer animation virtual cameras are based on the camera moves defined in traditional cinematography. Most programs use the same camera names used in traditional cinematography, but some use a different nomenclature. All of the camera moves, even the most complex ones, can be expressed in terms of translations or rotations around one or several camera axes (Fig. 2.4.8). A **dolly** is a translation of the camera along its X axis, a **boom** is a translation along its Y axis, and a **truck** is a translation along its Z axis. A **tilt** is a rotation of the camera around its X axis, a **roll** is a rotation around its Z axis, a **pan** is a rotation around its Y axis. Sometimes a tilt is called a **pitch** (as in airplanes pitching), and a pan is called a **yaw**. A **zoom** is a special type of camera move where only the camera's simulated focal length is modified but its position and orientation remain untouched. (Read Chapter 6 for additional information on cameras and camera moves.)

2.5 File Formats for Modeling

There are many formats for saving the information contained in three-dimensional geometry files. Many of the existing **file formats** containing descriptions of object geometry are exclusive of specific computer programs and are not portable. This means that the information contained in these files is formatted according to conventions that are particular to the software in question and are not compatible with other programs. But a few geometry file formats are **portable**, which means that they can be exchanged between several programs.

All three-dimensional models created within a modeling program can be save and retrieved in the application's own **native file format**. A specific three-dimensional software, for example, can save all of the three-dimensional models created with it in a file format that has been optimized for its own requirements.

The obvious advantage of using native—or custom—file formats is that it is easy and fast for any particular program to

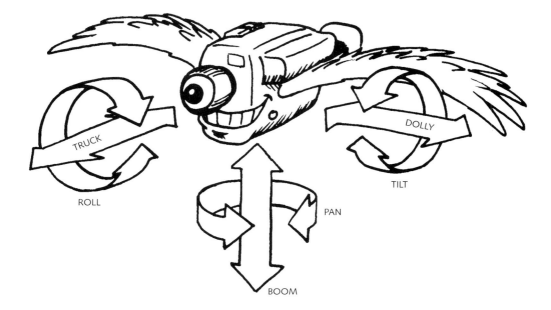

TRUCK

ROLL

BOOM

PAN

DOLLY

TILT

read files in its own native format. Files saved in native formats usually load faster and require less space for storage.

However, the disadvantage of saving files in native formats is that they may not be compatible with any program except with the program that was used to create them. The solutions to the format incompatibility problem include using "universal" file formats for saving information about three-dimensional models, or converting one native file format directly to the native file format of another program.

Some file formats are widely used for transporting three-dimensional modeling information between programs that use such data. These file formats are often called **universal file formats**, and one of the most popular ones is called **DXF**, short for Drawing Interchange Format. The DXF file format was developed by Autodesk, Inc. for handling both two- and three-dimensional geometry information. The DXF format is widely used in CAD (computer-aided design) applications along with the IGES and DES formats. However, even when using universal file formats to save three-dimensional information, there can be minor differences in the ways different programs interpret the information contained in these universal data formats. This latitude in interpretation is due to the fact that many of the universal file formats describe three-dimensional information in a very general way. The DXF file format, for example, may contain a lot of two-dimensional information that is usually discarded when

2.4.8 Navigating through three-dimensional space can be done by using the traditional cinematography camera moves: dolly, boom, truck, tilt, pan, and roll.

imported into the three-dimensional program. It is also common for many three-dimensional programs to have to clarify or interpret the precision and/or the curvature of a line that defines a three-dimensional surface.

Virtually all three-dimensional modeling programs offer some degree of **file conversion.** That capability is found either inside the standard file management options (under a command or menu option name such as Import or Retrieve) or as a standalone utility conversion program that can be executed outside of the modeling program. Most programs can also **export** its three-dimensional modeling data into other native or universal file formats.

Many of today's three-dimensional modeling programs offer some degree of **foreign-to-native** file format conversions. The number of data formats that a particular three-dimensional program may be able to convert may range from just a couple to several dozen formats. All file format conversions are controlled by **import filters,** which are tables that instruct the conversion utility program how to translate each and all of the elements encountered in the original—or foreign—file. Figure 2.5.1 illustrates a table that shows how a particular file conversion program deals with a foreign data file. Even when the most reliable file formats and conversion filters are used there are always small variations between the results obtained with different programs. Figure 2.5.2 illustrates the wide range of options available in software when importing or exporting data in the DXF format. One of the reasons for offering so many options in a format conversion to a "standard" format is because not all the aspects—or options—of the DXF format are supported by all programs that are capable of reading DXF files. Figure 2.5.3 illustrates how a specific program deals with one aspect of the native-to-DXF file format conversion.

The results obtained with different file conversion utilities vary widely. Some file conversions are almost flawless (with only minor details requiring adjustment) while others rarely produce desirable results. There is no easy way to know if a file conversion program will work perfectly or not: each has to be tried and evaluated.

The **Virtual Reality Modeling Language**, widely known as **VRML**, is quickly gaining popularity as a convenient way to describe three-dimensional environments in a portable format. VRML allows for the creation of virtual reality environments where multiple participants can interact with each other in three-

IGES Entity	ALIAS Entity
Boundary entity	Trim curve
Bounded surface	Trimmed surface
Circular arc	Arc or b-spline curve
Composite curve	B-spline curves (group)
Conic arc	B-spline curve
Copious data	B-spline curve
Copious data	B-spline curve
Copious data	Polyline
Copious data	Polyline
Curved on surface	Trim curve
Line	Polylines
Offset curve	B-spline curve
Offset surface	B-spline surface
Parametric curve	B-spline curve
Parametric surface	B-spline surface
Plane	B-spline surface
Plane	Face
Point	Control vertex
Rational b-spline	B-spline curve
Ruled surface	B-spline surface
Surface of revolution	B-spline surface
Tabulated cylinder	B-spline surface
Trimmed surface	Trimmed surface

2.5.1 This table illustrates how Alias software converts some of the modeling elements from the IGES file format into its own native file format.

dimensional spaces. VRML is in essence a **scene description language** that addresses object geometry, as well as rendering, navigation, interaction, and networking of virtual environments. The files created with VRML are saved in the **Open Inventor** ASCII file format developed by Silicon Graphics, Inc.

2.6 Getting Ready

Modeling can be a time-consuming activity because of the great attention to detail that is required. This can only be accentuated if one encounters a lot of unexpected hurdles along the process. In spite of the flexibility offered by many computer modeling systems, sometimes trying to fix complications due to poor planning can be more time-consuming and headache-inducing than to just start the process all over again. For this and other reasons—also related to practical issues such as time and budgets— it is very important to consider some of the preproduction guidelines listed below. All of these strategies are to take place before one actually starts building the three-dimensional models.

Sketch Your Ideas First

Sketching your modeling ideas on paper or modeling clay is usually faster and more economical than starting to model directly on the computer. While there is nothing intrinsically negative about creating three-dimensional models without having a sketch at hand, in most cases starting that way increases the chances of running into small problems that might have been easy to avoid. Small details such as the ways in which two complex shapes will blend into one another, for example, can be visualized faster and cheaper on paper or modeling clay. In most cases, it is not an issue of whether something cannot be "sketched" and visualized directly on the computer, but just an issue of having the budget clock tick much more expensively when one is sketching with the computer system than when one is sketching with a number two pencil, plain white paper, and an eraser.

Another advantage of sketching three-dimensional ideas on paper or modeling clay is that both media are absolutely portable and do not present any type of compatibility problem. This is especially important when you are required to present your work to others before actual production starts. It is very easy to show someone a sketch on paper, that can be done at anytime of the day and in any location. There is no need, for example, for your client to travel to your location because they do not have computers or for you to have to reserve one of the workstations in your company so that your client can see your ideas. There are few techniques for sharing your visual ideas with others as direct, portable, participatory, and friendly as a sketch on a piece of paper

2.5.2a Dialog boxes to control the import and export of files in the DXF format. (Dialog boxes from form•Z. © 1991-1995 auto•des•sys, Inc.)

DXF Entity	Alias Entity
ARC no thickness	B-spline curve
ARC with thickness	B-spline curve
CIRCLE no thickness	Face
CIRCLE with thickness	One b-spline surface and two faces (cylinder with end-caps)
3DFACE/SOLID/TRACE	SURFACE option: bilinear b-spline surface, POLYSET option; polygon of a polyset. Options in these entities determine how DXF 3DFACE, SOLID, and TRACE entities are translated to Alias entities. If set to SURFACE, then each instance of these DXF entity types is translated into an Alias bi-linear NURBS surface. If set to POLYSET, the default, then these entities form the polygons of ALIAS POLYSETS.
LINE/3DLINE no thickness	Linear b-spline curve
POLYLINE/3D open	B-spline curve
POLYLINE/3D closed	One polygon of a polyset. Options in this entityies determine how DXF POLYLINE and LINE entities, that describe surfaces, are translated into Alias entities. If set to SURFACE, then these DXF entities are translated into bi-linear, bi-quadratic, or bi-cubic NURBS surfaces. If set to POLYSET the default, then these DXF entities are translated into ALIAS POLYSETS.
POLYLINE/3D with thickness	Polygons of a polyset
POLYLINE/3D Mesh	SURFACE option: bi-linear, bi-quadratic, bi-cubic surface
POLYLINE/Polyface Mesh	Polygons of a polyset
LAYER	Multi set

2.5.2b A list of some of the DXF geometric entities supported by the Alias software.

or a clay scale model.

For those of you who are still unconvinced, keep in mind that a sketch is just a quick study, a rough drawing, a draft, a preliminary outline. A sketch is not a polished rendering or detailed sculpture. A sketch for a three-dimensional model should take just a few minutes to complete; it should be tentative but also offer more detail in those areas of the object that are more complex and therefore require more thinking than the bulk of the model. Sketches are meant to be aides in the production process and not works of art to be framed and admired by museum-goers. In some instances, it can be useful to complement the drawn sketches with short, written explanatory notes regarding details such as the proposed modeling technique or the number of polygons to define the curvature of a part, or the advantages and disadvantages of going with the solution proposed in the sketch.

Write Your Numbers Down

Writing your numbers down can often help not only before you start modeling but also throughout the modeling process. Initially it is important to write down (on a simple piece of paper, in the project spec sheet, or in your production journal) the numbers that describe general but important things such as: the general dimensions of your object, its position in three-dimensional space, and the boundaries of the active area or workspace. Writing down this type of information can be especially useful when you return to a project that was put on hold for a long time or when somebody else who is not familiar with the project has to take over because you have decided (or somebody has decided for you) to work on something else.

Do Not Lose the Blueprints

The creation of the blueprints becomes a necessity in cases where the objects to be modeled are too complex and detailed for improvisation and memory. In those instances, it becomes paramount to hold on to the original blueprints. Keep in mind that even after you think the models are finished, you or someone else on your team (or on the opposite team) may decide that the models are not finished after all. In such event, you or someone else may need the blueprints again.

Polygons or Curves?

Most of today's three-dimensional modeling programs are exclusively polygon-based, many are curved-based, and some offer both capabilities. Choosing between polygons or curves for modeling a three-dimensional object has obvious implications as far as the model's shape is concerned (for more on these implications see "Geometric Primitives" in Chapter 3). However, the rendering implications of modeling with polygons or curves are less obvious but critical in some cases.

As we will learn later in Section III: Rendering, a large number of rendering programs require polygonal structures from the modeling programs. This means that whenever curves are used at some point—but before the three-dimensional model can be processed by most rendering programs—the curves have to be converted to polygonal structures. In most cases, this conversion is not a problem: many programs perform this conversion automatically. However, in some cases, whether to start modeling with polygons or curves can become an issue that requires planning. For example, some modeling programs that are curve-based do not accept polygonal models, and likewise, some polygon-based modeling programs will have a difficult time reading files of models that have been specified with curves.

Furthermore, in many three-dimensional modeling programs—even those that offer both polygonal and spline-based modeling techniques—some advanced functions such as bevelling or clipping will work only on polygonal meshes. Most of the sophisticated programs that offer two-way conversions between polygon meshes and spline surfaces do so at the expense of the shapes involved. When these conversions are performed there is always a significant amount of distortion that sometimes requires time-consuming, point-by-point rearranging.

Will the Model Be Used for CADAM?

Objects that are modeled just to be rendered or animated are built very differently from objects that will serve as models for

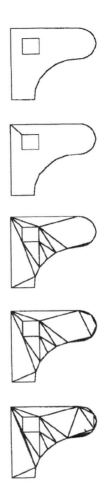

2.5.3 The decomposition process of a concave shape with a hole (a) when exported to the DXF file format. First all holes are connected to the edges of the shape (b), then the concave shape is decomposed into several convex parts (c), next all parts are further decomposed into four-sided parts (d), and finally, the shape is triangulated so that all the component parts become elements in a triangular polygonal mesh (e). (Courtesy of auto•des•sys, Inc.)

computer-aided design and manufacturing (CADAM). It is extremely important to know whether one's models will be used for CADAM purposes or not. If so, a specific modeling methodology has to be chosen and followed consistently throughout the project.

The two significant differences between modeling for CADAM projects or modeling for animation projects lie in the modeling technology used, and in the fabrication and structural implications of the objects modeled. Very few computer systems offer both modeling techniques. The majority of software is either just boundary-based or solid-based. In those situations this issue is automatically solved by the limitations of the software. It is in cases when the software has both capabilities that we have to choose between object shells or solid objects. When we build three-dimensional objects for rendering or animation purposes, in almost all instances we are interested just in the surfaces of the objects and very rarely in their inside volume. For that reason, when we model objects for rendering and animation we use, in most cases, **boundary** and **geometry modeling techniques**. Boundary geometry focuses on the surface or **shell** of objects, and ignores the **volume** and inner structure.

This is similar, for example, to making a photographic portrait of a person. In such case, we are mostly interested in capturing expression, gesture, skin texture, posture, eye color, and other details. In general, we are quite uninterested—as far as completing a successful portrait—by whatever is under the skin of this person: muscles, bones, and organs.

On the other hand, when we build three-dimensional computer models for the ultimate goal of fabricating them—with a computer-controlled milling machine or stereo lithography system—we are fundamentally interested in the inside of the object, its structural soundness, and whether the shapes we have included in our model can actually be fabricated efficiently. For all these reasons when we model objects for CADAM projects we use **constructive solid geometry** (or CGS) techniques. These techniques are not concerned at all with how fast a three-dimensional model would render or how realistic it would look or how efficiently it would animate. Instead, CGS techniques focus among other things on whether our three-dimensional model meets structural criteria, whether it has the exact required dimensions, and whether it contains the specified amount of material.

Modeling Is Related to Rendering and Animation

The life of a three-dimensional computer-generated model rarely ends with the modeling process itself. Most three-dimensional models go on to be rendered and many continue up the production process to be animated.

As you will read later in this book many creative and technical decisions made during the modeling process can simplify, complicate, and even paralyze either the rendering or animation processes or both. It would be premature to explain in detail which modeling solutions are more likely to complicate a certain rendering technique or an animation sequence. (It is certainly hoped that you will gain this information by reading the entire book.) For now, keep in mind that before you embark on future modeling projects you should get as much information as possible in terms of the plans regarding the rendering and animation of the objects, if any. For example, a certain rendering technique or production deadline or camera position may require that you cut in half the number of polygons used to define a section of the object, or perhaps the animation script might require that you group the objects a certain way. If either of these conditions is known in advance, you will avoid the difficulty of taking apart a model that is finished in order for you to try and reduce the number of polygons or having to undo a complex five-level hierarchical structure with hundreds of objects in order to re-establish some basic links in a different way.

Keep in mind the rendering and animation requirements of your project during the modeling process. This will help to keep wasted time to a minimum.

Check the Preferences File

Remember that both the three-dimensional modeling program that you may be using as well as your computer's operating system keep their preferred or default settings in a **Preferences File**.

The contents of the Preferences File are important because they control directly and indirectly the result of many operations, functions, and tools. Some of the settings contained in a preferences file may include, for example, the units used to specify the dimension of objects being modeled, or whether a tool for creating cubes will define by dragging from the center of the cube outwards or from one corner of the cube to the opposite corner. As you can see some of these settings may affect the result of your three-dimensional modeling, rendering, and animation.

In general, the last person who opened a file, or who used the program or the computer system is capable of altering the files with preferences. In some systems, the Preferences Files are attached to the three-dimensional computer program and in some cases to the model files themselves. Check your system for details.

Check Your Memory Requirements

Most of today's three-dimensional modeling software will allocate enough of the system's memory (RAM and/or virtual). This means that in most cases you do not have to be concerned about whether there will be enough space in the computer's memory for you to build your model. But sometimes, especially when complex three-dimensional models are being created in small computer systems, the issue of not having enough memory to work can become a problem. Sometimes when the system does not automatically make sure that there is enough memory for you to keep building, the system will unexpectedly run out of memory and freeze. Also keep in mind that many modeling programs can recover from errors very gracefully (and will allow you to restore all your data) while others cannot.

Save Your Work Often

Save your work often, every 15 minutes or so, and make constant backups of your important data files.

Use Multiple Camera Views While Modeling

2.7.1 A key outline.

It is often quite advantageous to model a three-dimensional object while using multiple camera views. A sculptor, for example, walks around the sculpture as he works on it in order to have a clear mental picture of how all the parts and shapes relate to one another. As soon as some of the shapes change others require reshaping and fine-tuning. In much the same way, it is convenient for an individual using a computer three-dimensional modeling system to look at the object from multiple points of view as it evolves. This can be easily accomplished by constantly rotating the object around its own center. However, it can be more convenient to have several views—often called windows—active while modeling. That way one can get immediate feedback from different points of view while concentrating solely on the modeling process itself.

Most three-dimensional modeling systems offer the capability of having four active views at once. It is common to use each of these views for a front view, a side view, a top view, and a camera view. The camera view usually allows for total control of the point of view: the simulated camera can be placed close to the object being modeled—for examining details—or far away—for evaluating the overall shape. Some viewing positions—such as 60-0-30, 45-0-45, 20-0-120, 45-0-220, and 30-0-60—are popular for positioning cameras during the modeling process because these positions resemble the angles of some of the standard three-dimensional projections commonly used in drafting.

Small computer systems usually recommend working with as few active views as possible in order to cut down on the processing time. In small systems, the more views required from the

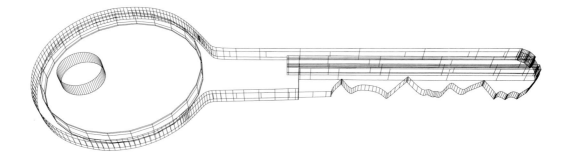

computer program, the longer it will take to process the information and to update the screen. Situations like this may force one to work with just the camera view and one more view that can be switched between front, top, and side views as needed. (Read Chapter 6 for more information on setting the camera.)

2.7 Sample Session

The process of modeling a simple object usually requires many steps and a variety of modeling techniques. In this section we present a sample overview of the modeling process. Detailed explanations of the techniques can be found in Chapters 3 and 4.

The key illustrated in Fig. 2.7.1 is a simple object that was built with several different modeling techniques. The first step consisted of creating a sketch of the object. This sketch was useful not only to visualize the shape of the key and some of its details, but also to annotate the different modeling techniques that may be used to illustrate each detail.

The outline was first drawn in the computer using b-spline curves on the XY (top) plane. The mouse was used to click on all the point locations and also to adjust the curvature of the lines. The resulting outline was extruded along the Z axis using simple extrusion techniques. Once the outline was extruded, the front and back faces were created. The result was a closed three-dimensional shape.

The round hole and the stripes around the head of the key were created by subtracting volumes with a technique usually called trimming or Boolean operations (Fig. 2.7.2). Finally, the key can be quickly rendered with a simple rendering technique to make sure that the model can be later rendered with more complex techniques and without any problems.

2.7.2 Using simple extrusion techniques the two-dimensional outline is extruded along the Z axis. The hole and the ridges along the head of the key were created with trimming functions.

Review and Practice

Matching

_____ Polygon

_____ Rendering

_____ Sketching on paper

_____ Vector
_____ File conversion

_____ Thumb rule

_____ DXF

_____ Constructive solid geometry
_____ Origin
_____ Preferences file
_____ Perspective

a. A popular file format supported by a large number of modeling applications.

b. Modeling techniques used when three-dimensional models are to be manufactured under computer control.

c. Many modeling decisions have a direct impact on this stage of the creative process.

d. The point at which the XYZ axes intersect.

e. A highly recommended technique that helps to foresee potential modeling problems and to choose a modeling strategy.

f. Its contents may affect the behavior and performance of the modeling program.

g. A transformation that projects three-dimensional environments onto a flat surface.

h. A straight line with a direction.

i. Can be used to easily determine the direction of rotations.

j. Closed plane bounded by straight lines.

k. Allows computer graphics software to import models that were not saved in the program's native file format.

Answers Matching: a. Polygon, b. Rendering, c. Sketching on paper, d. Vector, e. File conversion, f. Thumb rule, g. DXF, h. Constructive solid geometry, i. Origin, j. Preferences file, k. Perspective.

True/False

_____ a. A positive rotation in a right-handed coordinate system is clockwise.

_____ b. Scaling can change the size and proportion of a three-dimensional object.

_____ c. All three-dimensional modeling programs can retrieve models saved in the program's native file format.

_____ d. In the context of three-dimensional computer graphics, the environment or scene encompasses the three-dimensional space in which we place objects and the light sources.

_____ e. In order to describe one cube in XYZ space we need at least eight points and six connectivity lists.

_____ f. Import filters usually instruct the conversion utility how to translate the contents of a foreign file into the native format of the program.

_____ g. Three-dimensional space can be defined in terms of three axes.

_____ h. Geometric transformations are used to modify the shape, proportions, size, position, and orientation of three-dimensional objects.

_____ i. The DXF file format is generally used to export compressed geometry files.

_____ j. One hundred units is the absolute maximum width for the X axis.

_____ k. XYZ coordinate information is sometimes stored in the form of text files.

_____ l. One of the main uses for the spherical coordinate system is to position light sources in three-dimensional space.

_____ m. A "top view" of the Cartesian coordinate system generally describes a view of the XZ plane looking down the Y axis.

Answers True/False: a. False, b. True, c. True, d. True, e. True, f. True, g. True, h. True, i. False, j. False, k. True, l. True, m. True.

Key Terms

Absolute values
Axes
Azimuthal coordinate system
Boom
Boundary modeling techniques
Cartesian coordinate system
Computer-aided design and manufacturing
Concatenated transformations
Constructive solid geometry
Cut-copy-paste
Data file
Dimensions
Direct numerical description
Dolly
Drawing Interchange Format
DXF
Edge
Export
Facets
File conversion
File formats
Foreign-to-native
Front plane
Geometric transformations
Geometry files
Geometry modeling techniques
Global coordinate system
Global transformations
Hierarchy
Import filters
Left-handed coordinate system
Line
Local coordinate system
Local transformations
Mathematical operations
Modeling
Native file format
Navigation

Nonproportional scaling
Object coordinate system
Objects
Open Inventor
Origin
Pan
Perspective projection
Pitch
Point
Portable
Preferences file
Proportional scaling
Rectangular coordinate system
Relative values
Right-handed coordinate system
Roll
Rotation
Scaling
Scene
Scene description language
Shell
Side plane
Spaces
Spherical coordinate system
Structures
Surface
Three-dimensional space
Tilt
Top plane
Transformation matrix
Translation
Truck
Universal file formats
Volume
Virtual Reality Modeling Language
VRML
Workspace
World coordinate system
Yaw
Zoom

CHAPTER 3

Basic Modeling Techniques

Summary

This chapter covers the basic techniques for modeling three-dimensional objects with a computer system. The chapter starts with a short but important note about lines, their use in the creation of surfaces, and the general differences between polygonal meshes and curved surfaces. Following that is a discussion of the simplest geometric modeling tools available in most of today's systems. After that comes a survey of several derivative techniques including revolving, extrusion, and sweeping. Techniques for creating terrains and simple freeform objects are followed by a survey of utilities that are useful to modelers of all levels. An overview of hierarchical structures and file formats for modeling are presented just before the sample modeling session that concludes this chapter.

3.1 Introduction

Just like traditional modeling techniques, the computer-based three-dimensional modeling process begins with an idea. Before the modeling process can start we try to visualize this idea of what we want to create, perhaps by creating some sketches or even detailed blueprints.

The conceptualization and design of the three-dimensional model usually constitutes the first stage in the simulation of a three-dimensional scene with a computer. From an artistic point of view this step is probably the most decisive one in the process because it is here where the basic characteristics of the scene are laid out: the shape, position and size of the objects, the colors and textures, the lights, and the position of the camera. It is also at this stage where the basic ideas have to be analyzed and the best modeling methods chosen for each task.

I usually prepare the initial sketches that describe the three-dimensional objects and environments with traditional media, such as colored pencils or markers on paper. These sketches indicate the general characteristics of the objects such as size, relative position, color, and lighting effects. Once the sketches are finished I then analyze them and prepare a set of blueprints containing one or several detailed views of the object with dimensions.

There are many ways of translating the visual information contained in the sketches into numerical information suited for computer manipulation. Most three-dimensional modeling software allows users to build the model interactively. This means that the models that are being worked on can be displayed on the screen. Any and all model changes made by the user are displayed on the screen almost instantly. This interactive quality provides the visual feedback that is so important in developing the shapes of objects and the layout of three-dimensional spaces. Because of the lack of immediate tactile feedback when creating three-dimensional models with software, the real time visual feedback on the screen becomes almost indispensable.

When the modeling process is complete we usually end up with a file that contains a detailed description of the objects in our environment including information regarding their geometry, position, and hierarchy. Realistic images of the files can be obtained by rendering the file with some of the techniques presented in Chapters 5-8. There are many techniques for describing three-dimensional structures, and each one of them produces different results and requires a different type of approach.

Unless otherwise specified, all modeling techniques described in this chapter are based on boundary geometry and not on constructive solid geometry. As explained in Chapter 2, this means that the three-dimensional objects are built as hollow shells only and not simulated as true solid objects.

3.2 A Note About Lines

Lines are used to define the shape of the object and many of its surface characteristics. Lines are a fundamental component of all three-dimensional objects. Because of that reason it is important that we understand differences between types of lines, as well as their attributes and limitations. This section offers a short characterization of some of the standard lines most commonly used in three-dimensional modeling. Keep in mind that the names used here are as general as possible, but your computer system may have a different name for a specific type of line or a line tool. The classification presented here is based on the practical characteristics of different types of lines, on their advantages and disadvantages, and also on their mathematical nomenclature. The following paragraphs explain some of the differences between types of lines. Please read them carefully. These concepts are crucial for understanding much of the material presented in the other chapters about modeling and rendering.

One obvious difference between lines is that some are straight and some are curved. While straight lines are concerned with defining the shortest distance between two points, curves are concerned with subtlety of change and elegance of design. There are many great differences between straight lines and curved lines. They differ from each other in terms of: their mathematical description, their behavior as they are being used to model, the type of three dimensional structures they yield, and in most cases, their visual appearance. Some three-dimensional modeling computer programs are capable of converting curved lines to straight lines and vice-versa, but in many cases the results of these conversions are sometimes surprising and might require considerable work before they can be used (Fig. 3.2.1 and 5.4.1).

3.2.1 Conversions of different types of lines. (Dialog box from Softimage 3D. © Microsoft Corporation. All rights reserved.)

Straight lines—as their name implies—do not have any curvature. Straight lines are defined by two endpoints only, and may have a slope but no change in angularity. In other words, the slope of curves is variable, the slope in straight lines is not. In three-dimensional modeling programs, straight lines are sometimes called polygonal lines because they can be used to build polygons and polygonal meshes. The three-dimensional modeling computer programs that use exclusively straight lines are capable of building models only with polygonal meshes (and not with spline-based surfaces). The three-dimensional modeling programs that use curves are capable of building models with both curved surfaces and polygonal meshes.

Many programs offer two different line drawing tools. One draws straight lines and one draws curved lines. While it is difficult for a straight line to turn into a curve (because straight lines just do not have a variable for change of angularity), it is easy for a curve to turn into a straight line (just by setting the change in angularity to nothing). For this reason, many three-dimensional modeling programs offer just one single—and powerful—tool that draws just curves of all kinds, including curves that look like straight lines.

Curved lines are usually defined by several points and deviate from a straight path without any sharp breaks in angularity. Curved lines are sometimes called curve segments and can be

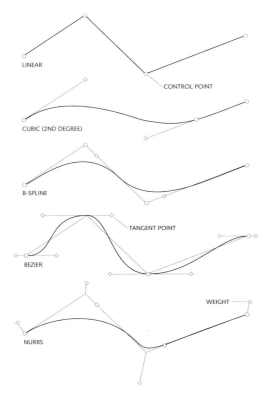

LINEAR

CONTROL POINT

CUBIC (2ND DEGREE)

B-SPLINE

TANGENT POINT

BEZIER

WEIGHT

NURBS

3.2.2 Five popular types of splines are illustrated here: linear splines, cardinal splines, b-splines, Bézier curves, and NURBS or Non-Uniform Rational B-Splines.

used to define curved surfaces and build meshes of curved surfaces.

Curves are also often called **splines** because they resemble the physical spline—a long narrow strip of wood or metal—used by a draftsperson or construction worker to shape or fit curves between various points. The spline, traditionally used in the design and construction of ships' hulls, is shaped by lead weights. By varying the number and position of weights the spline can be turned into a smooth curve that passes through the required points. Even though not all curves actually belong in the mathematical category of spline curves, some three-dimensional modeling programs use the name splines generically. That generalization is, of course, inaccurate.

There are many types of curves, and they can be catalogued based on their mathematical and geometric characteristics. In this text, however, we shall limit our summary to just five of the more popular types of splines used in mainstream three-dimensional modeling: linear splines, cardinal splines, b-splines, Bézier curves, and NURBS or Non-Uniform Rational B-Splines. Figure 3.2.2 illustrates these five types of curves.

All splines have in common the fact that they are generated from a defining polygon. Because of this fact splines are called **controlled curves**. The structures that control the splines are invisible—only displayed while we shape the spline—but contain important information that can be used to reshape the spline.

The controls found in splines of different types include the control line or control polygon or hull, the control points or control vertices, the tangent points, the knots, and the weights. Keep in mind that different software programs use different nomenclatures and slightly different implementations of the controls. Figure 3.2.3 shows some of the controls for modifying splines provided by different software programs.

Each of the spline curves can be quickly characterized by the way in which it is controlled by the **control points** or **control vertices**. A **linear spline** looks like a series of straight lines connecting the control points. A **cardinal spline** looks like a curve that passes through all of its control points. The **b-spline** looks like a curved line that rarely passes through the control points. A **Bézier curve** passes through all of its control points. A **NURBS** does not pass through its control points.

Another easy way of characterizing splines is by looking at their controls other than the control line and the control points. Control points can control the **curvature** or **tension** of a curved line mainly by how close they are to one another and, in some cases, by how close they or their tangent points are to the curve (Fig. 3.2.4). The Bézier curve differs from the three splines mentioned here so far mainly because it has **tangent points** in addition to the control points. Tangent points are used to fine tune the degree of curvature on a line without modifying the control points.

NURBS offer a high degree of local curve control by using weights and knots. These controls allow a portion of the spline to be modified without affecting other parts of the spline. One **weight** is attached to each control point, and they determine the distance between the control point and the apex of the curve. By default, all control vertices on a spline have the same weight factor, and that is called a **nonrational curve**. (B-splines, for example, are NURBS with equal weights.) When the values of the weights on the curve are modified then the curve is called a **rational curve**. Manipulating weights on a NURBS curve may improve the subtle shaping of a line but it usually also slows down the rendering of the final model. Another disadvantage of working with different weight values is that many systems will ignore the data when model files are exchanged. In many cases, results similar to using different weight values can be obtained by placing two control points very close to each other.

The **knots** on a NURBS determine the distribution and local density of points on a curve. The minimum number of knots required to form a curve segment is equal to the degree of a curve plus one plus the number of control points. The **degree** of curve refers to the high exponent in the mathematical formulas that generate curves. Each curve type (b-spline, Bézier, and NURBS) has a different mathematical formula, and each curve type may be created at different degrees (Fig. 3.2.5). As mentioned before, the higher the degree of a curve the more computation is required to create it. Curves of the first degree correspond to linear segments, curves of the second degree correspond to quadratic curves, and curves of the third degree correspond to cubic curves. The higher the degree of a curve the more control points and knots are required to form a curve segment.

3.3 Geometric Primitives

Virtually all three-dimensional modeling computer programs provide a collection of tools for creating simple shapes with a fixed structure known as **geometric primitives.** The number and type of geometric primitives varies from program to program, but the following list is a representative selection: cubes,

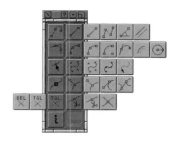

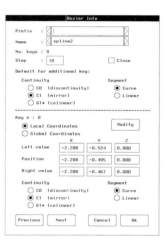

3.2.3 These tool palette and dialog boxes illustrate some of the spline controls and tools offered by different software programs. (a. Tool palette from Alias PowerAnimator. © Alias Research, Inc.; b. Dialog box from form•Z. © 1991-1995 auto•des•sys, Inc.; c. Dialog box from Softimage 3D. © Microsoft Corporation. All rights reserved.)

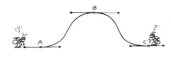

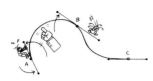

3.2.4 This sequence illustrates how control and tangent points affect the tension of a spline.

spheres, cylinders, cones, toruses, regular polyhedra, and two-dimensional polygons. Figure 3.3.1 includes many of the most common geometric primitives.

In some programs, the different geometric primitive tools will appear all as a single menu selection while in others each or some of the tools may appear separately. In all cases, however, the feature that relates all geometric primitives to one another is the fact that they are standard shapes that the modeling program can create and manipulate effortlessly and usually from a simple predefined mathematical description. In principle, all geometric primitives may be created as polygonal structures or as curved patches.

Geometric primitives can be used to represent simple shapes, or they can be used as the basis for more complex, composite three-dimensional shapes. In the former case, the shapes provided by the tool would require almost no modification except for changes to their position in space, size, and proportion in some cases. In the latter case, geometric primitives may be modified or used to build more complex objects with a variety of utility tools for trimming, attaching, and blending, among others. As most other tools, geometric primitives may be modified on-screen directly using the mouse, trackball, or electronic pen, or by typing the appropriate values in a dialog box.

Cubes

Cubes are usually modeled as six-sided, closed, three-dimensional objects. Since all sides of a cube have the same length, usually the only variable required for modeling cubes is the length of a side. Sometimes a number of subdivisions can be specified along each of the three axes. Cubes are almost always created as polygonal structures.

Spheres

Spheres, like cubes, are also modeled as symmetric, closed, three-dimensional objects. In order to be defined, all spheres require a variable of **radius** or **diameter**, and they can be modeled as a polygonal structure or as a patch of curves. When modeled as polygonal structures, drawn with straight lines, a sphere's definition requires a number of divisions along the longitude (top to bottom) or latitude (around). These divisions resemble the parallels and meridians on a globe, and their number has a proportional effect on the geometric smoothness of the final shape. When modeled as

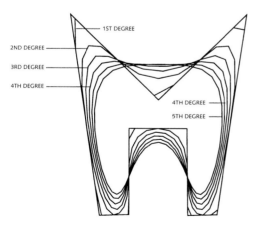

3.2.5 In general, the higher the degree of a spline the further away it is from the controlling polygon.

curved patches, spheres require a type of spline to be specified in addition to the information listed above. Spheres are also very popular as the starting point for freeform modeling (Fig. 3.5.1).

Cylinders and Cones

Cylinders and **cones** are commonly defined as polygonal objects and they may be shaped by the following variables: radius, height, number of longitudinal divisions, number of latitudinal divisions, and whether they are "capped" or not. The number of subdivisions used to build cylinders and cones define the amount of modeling detail of the these objects. Objects with a small number of subdivisions can be rendered quicker than objects with many subdivisions. When planning to render objects with image maps it is best to model them with a high number of subdivisions. Making small rendering tests is essential to determine the optimum number of subdivisions that should be modeled into any geometric primitive. **Capping** determines whether the round sides of cones or cylinders are open or whether they are closed.

Toruses

A **torus** is a three-dimensional, closed shape that resembles a donut. A torus is like a cylinder that has been bent and stretched so that the two bases touch each other. The variables required to construct a torus are almost the same as those required for building a sphere, plus one additional variable, which is the interior radius. A full listing of modeling variables for a torus includes: whether polygons or patches will be used, size of exterior radius, size of interior radius, number of latitudinal divisions, and number of longitudinal divisions.

Regular Polyhedra

Many three-dimensional objects belong to the category of **regular polyhedra**, or objects with multiple facets. A polyhedron

3.3.1 A sphere, cylinder, torus, and regular polyhedra including: a tetrahedron (4-sides), an hexahedron (6-sides), an octahedron (8-sides), a dodecahedron (12-sides), an icosehedron (20-sides), and a geodesic sphere.

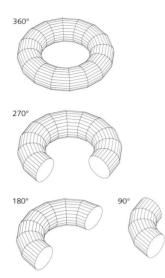

360°

270°

180°

90°

3.4.1 Toruses and other geometric primitives can be created by sweeping a two-dimensional outline around an axis. Slices of geometric primitive shapes created this way are usually easier and faster than the equivalent shapes created with the geometric primitive tool and then sliced with a trimming tool.

3.4.2 Controls to create a simple extrusion along a straight path. (Dialog box from Softimage 3D. © Microsoft Corporation. All rights reserved.)

(singular of polyhedra) refers to a three-dimensional object that is composed of polygons. Some of the most common regular polyhedra include the four-sided **tetrahedron**, the eight-sided **octahedron**, the twelve-sided **dodecahedron**, and the twenty-sided **icosahedron**. Regular polyhedra are usually modeled as polygon meshes and can be built by specifying a radius and a number of facets required.

Two-Dimensional Shapes

Two-dimensional shapes can be used to generate three-dimensional shapes by using derivative techniques such as extrusion or sweeping. Two-dimensional shapes usually include arcs, circles, spirals, triangles, squares, and other polygons.

Circles are two-dimensional, closed contours and require a radius or diameter, a number of control points, and a type of spline. **Arcs** are two-dimensional, open contours and require the same information that circles do plus the starting point and the ending point, both specified in degrees. **Spirals** are also two-dimensional, open contours and require a starting and an ending radius, a starting and an ending angle, a number of control points, and a height. **Polygons** (including triangles and squares) are two-dimensional, open contours, are almost always built with polygonal or linear splines, and can be defined by a number of sides and radius.

3.4 Sweeping

Sweeping is perhaps the most powerful derivative modeling technique, especially when one considers the complexity of the three-dimensional shapes created with it in relation to the simplicity of the input that is required for generating them.

The basic idea behind all sweeping modeling techniques consists of defining a two-dimensional outline that is swept along a predefined path. As the outline is swept it defines a shape in three-dimensional space. The resulting three-dimensional model depends largely on the complexity of the **seed outline** and the complexity of the path (Fig. 3.4.1). The three most popular sweeping techniques include extrusion, lathe or revolve, and freeform sweeps.

Simple Extrusion

In the conventional lingo of industrial design and manufacturing, **extrusion** stands for the process of shaping a material (such as plastic or metal) by forcing it with heat and pressure through a **die**. A die is a tool used for shaping or stamping different materials. The process of industrial extrusion is usually based on a stationary die just because of the limitations in handling both the hot materials and the heavy die. Meat grinders or pasta machines, for example, extrude the ground meat and the pasta through dies of different shapes.

Most three-dimensional modeling computer programs offer simple extrusion tools that—like their heavy industry counterparts—create three-dimensional shapes by starting with a two-dimensional outline and extruding or extending it along a straight path along one axis (Fig. 3.4.2). Simple extrusion happens along only any one axis. The two-dimensional outlines to be extruded can be created with geometric primitive tools or exported from other programs in highly portable file formats such as EPS (Encapsulated PostScript). Extrusion is sometimes called **lofting** because the two-dimensional outlines are duplicated and moved a level up.

Create Spiral

Starting Radius: 5.0
Ending Radius :   2.0
Starting Angle :   0.0
Ending Angle :   720.0
Depth   :   0.0
Step   :   8

Spline Type:
● Linear
○ Cardinal
○ B-Spline

Ok
Cancel

3.4.3 An extrusion along a complex path and a multitude of axes is also known as a sweep. (Dialog box from Softimage 3D. © Microsoft Corporation. All rights reserved.)

Freeform Sweeping

Some programs also offer the ability to extrude objects along paths of any shape and along any axis or combination of axes. An extrusion that takes place along several axes is sometimes called a sweep, sometimes called an extrusion on a path, or a **freeform extrusion** (Fig. 3.4.3). The results of freeform extrusion that is either scaled along the path or that is based on two paths are similar to those obtained with the skinning modeling technique decribed in Chapter 4.

Modeling by extrusion has been quite popular for centuries for creating the meringue and ornaments on pastries, cookies, and cakes. The pastry extrusion tool—or die—moves with a sweeping motion along a decoration path. The motions of the pastry tool usually extend on a surface in a single continuous action, such as that of a broom or a brush, and in a wide curve or range.

Lathe

One very popular sweeping variation is commonly referred to as a **lathe** or a **revolve**. This form of sweeping is so popular that it is almost always presented as a stand-alone tool, separate from the general-purpose sweeping tool. The surfaces created with this technique are usually called **surfaces of revolution**.

The software-based lathe tool simulates a real lathe, which

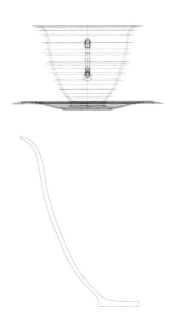

is a tool composed of a rotating base on which one places a cylinder of wood that is shaped by placing a steel blade on its surface as the base rotates around its vertical axis. A potter's wheel performs an almost identical operation on a slab of clay. The clay or wood are cut uniformly around the cylinder as a blade or sharp tool moves in and out following a predefined path. The software lathe sweeps a two-dimensional outline around one axis; the two-dimensional outline may be open or closed. A new three-dimensional shape emerges as the two-dimensional outline is swept along a circular or radial path; it usually remains perpendicular to the sweeping path as they are swept. The resulting three-dimensional object is defined by the areas enclosed within the revolved two-dimensional outline. Surfaces of revolution require an angle of rotation and a number of steps or facets. The number of subdivisions is usually determined by the number of points on the outline.

Surfaces of revolution that result from a 360-degree sweep are frequently closed, three-dimensional shapes. Sections—or slices—of three-dimensional shapes can also be created by sweeping less than 360 degrees. Two-dimensional outlines that do not touch the axis of sweeping will result in three-dimensional objects with holes (Fig. 3.4.4). In these cases, or when only a slice of a shape is created, the resulting shapes can be capped or uncapped.

The lathe modeling technique can also be used to recreate some of the geometric primitive shapes such as the cylinder and the cone (Fig. 3.4.1). Using the lathe for this purpose offers the advantage of increased control and economy of steps when trying to model a special version of a geometric primitive.

3.5 Freeform Objects

Some projects require the creation of **freeform three-dimensional objects**. The creation of these types of models is sometimes time consuming because they require that one sculpts them out of a planar or curved mesh (polygons or splines) in a way that is very similar to sculpting or modeling a piece of soft clay. Simple freeform objects usually require a lot of point-picking, pulling-and-pushing, and overall "massaging" of the surface mesh (Fig. 3.5.1).

Freeform modeling—also called freeform deformation—is used when other modeling techniques are too rigid for building a specific scene or when using a combination of other tools would get the job done but would also require additional production time and a larger production budget. Freeform objects are also sometimes used because of the creative preferences of the individuals who design the look of the three-dimensional scene.

Freeform modeling techniques can also be used in conjunc-

tion with other techniques—especially those described in Chapter 4. The technique of freeform modeling has a couple of variations including direct point manipulation, deformation with lattices, and terrains.

3.4.4 The cup pictured here was modeled by sweeping a two-dimensional outline 360 degrees around the Y axis. (Courtesy of Iris Benado.)

Direct Point Manipulation

The most common and easiest way of creating three-dimensional freeform shapes usually starts with an existing three-dimensional structure (polygonal or spline-based) that is to be "sculpted" and transformed into the desired freeform object. This **virtual sculpting** process is, in essence, quite similar to the process of modeling fresh clay with one's hands. The initial shape of the clay is fairly unimportant in terms of the desired final three-dimensional shape. But as our hands massage, push, pull, and rub the shapeless clay it is slowly transformed into a meaningful structure.

The direct point manipulation modeling process starts by identifying the points—or control vertices—in the wireframe structure that can be displaced in three-dimensional space. Most

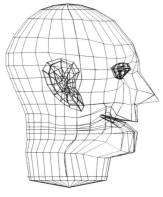

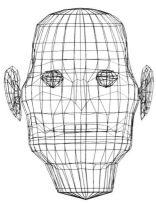

3.5.1 This wireframe head—except for the ears and eyeballs—was created with simple freeform modeling techniques by pulling and pushing the individual points in a sphere. Spheres are commonly used as virtual clay in freeform modeling both because they are easy to create and because they offer a good amount of points to work with. (Courtesy of Jonah Hall.)

three-dimensional modeling programs offer simple ways of picking a single point or a group of points. Direct point manipulation in the case of curve lines can be done directly to a point on the curve but also to a control or a tangent point. Usually the selection is done by just clicking and dragging one or several points. Once the points have been selected they can be dragged in any direction. Some programs offer excellent tools for picking and manipulating single points while similar capabilities in other programs leave a lot to be desired. Some of the most useful direct point manipulation options include the ability to select several points that are not contiguous, or the ability to lock the position of points in some parts of the object while other points are being manipulated. Figure 3.5.1 illustrates the process of freeform modeling.

Deformation with Lattices

Direct point manipulation can be a very efficient technique when only a few points need to be manipulated or when the user is really skilled at freeform sculpting. There is another freeform modeling technique that can be more appropriate for the task than direct point manipulation—especially in cases where a uniform global deformation is desired or when the user does not have the skill or the time to manipulate a large number of points one at a time. This technique is called **deformation with lattices**. (Lattices are sometimes called bounding boxes, not to be confused with the boundary boxes described later in this chapter.)

A lattice is a structure of points and lines that controls the points in the model. We can think of the lattice as a structure of grids that is connected to the points in the model with imaginary springs. Therefore, when the grids—or points on the grids—are moved, they drag the object's points with them (Fig. 3.5.2).

Every point on the lattice is connected to one or several of the model's points. The ability to control the deformation of the object by moving one or several grid points in the lattice depends directly on the number of lattice points. A small number of points on the lattice results in very rough or global distortion. Lattices with a large number of control points can be used to apply very subtle—or local—distortion on the object controlled by the lattice.

Simple Terrains and Functions

There is a great variety of techniques available for creating **terrains** that simulate or recreate natural or imaginary landscape surfaces. There is also a great variety of techniques that use **mathematical functions** for distorting those terrains.

The simplest technique for creating a terrain consists of

using a flat two-dimensional plane with XY subdivisions. Obviously, the more subdivisions on a plane the more detail will appear on the final terrain model. As mentioned earlier, the position of points on the plane can be modified by direct point manipulation or by lattice deformation. Using either of these techniques would be appropriate if the shape desired was to resemble a natural terrain. But if one is trying to create a more fantastic terrain then the basic plane could be deformed with a mathematical function. Figure 3.5.3 shows different terrains created by distorting a terrain with different functions.

Another technique for creating terrains consists of building a three-dimensional mesh based on two-dimensional contours that define an imaginary or real landscape. This technique for building terrains is very data intensive but also very efficient for creating accurate models of terrains. Because of their topological detail, terrains created with this technique are rarely distorted with mathematical functions. (Read Chapter 4 for additional information on creating terrain models from contours.)

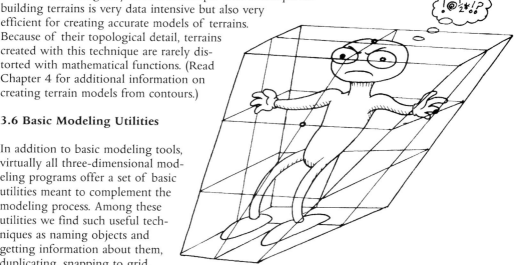

3.6 Basic Modeling Utilities

In addition to basic modeling tools, virtually all three-dimensional modeling programs offer a set of basic utilities meant to complement the modeling process. Among these utilities we find such useful techniques as naming objects and getting information about them, duplicating, snapping to grid, mirroring, displaying as a bounding box, calculating volumes, and creating text.

3.5.2 These drawings illustrate the effect of lattices on the shape of a three-dimensional object. Every time the lattice is moved the model is deformed since each of the grid points on the lattice is connected with imaginary springs to the object's points.

Getting Information and Naming Objects

Objects and components of objects in some cases can be named so that we can identify them faster. Many programs will automatically name objects as we create them with names like Cube 1, Cube 2, Cube 3, or Node 1 of 5, Node 2 of 5, etc. But in some cases where quick and unequivocal identification is required it is best to use unique names. For example, when one of fifty ellipsoids representing balloons is the target of a child's dart, naming it "target balloon" instead of "Ellipsoid 37" could be useful to quickly identify it during the explosion sequence.

Another useful feature for quickly assessing detailed information about a specific object—such as its position, dimensions,

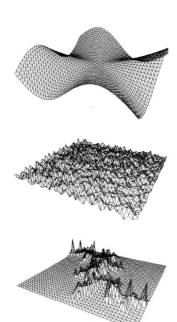

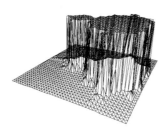

3.5.3 A plane terrain with a resolution of 40 x 40 units is deformed with different mathematical functions: a Starr function, a random function, and versions of the Julia and Mandelbrot fractal functions.

and orientation—is the Get Information feature that presents information about the active object in numerical form (Fig. 2.2.3).

Locking

Objects can be locked in a specific position, orientation, size, or spatial range. **Locking** an object or an object's element that is not supposed to move can help streamline the modeling process. In most cases, objects can be switched from the locked position to the unlocked position without losing or modifying any other attributes.

Duplicating and Instancing

Models can be easily duplicated without having to build them from scratch. **Duplicating** creates a single independent copy of the selected model or group of selected models. The copy can be created in the same location as the original or in a new position defined by an XYZ offset value. The duplicating utility can also create multiple copies of an object. The values needed to create multiple copies of an object typically include the number of copies, as well as the XYZ values for translation, rotation, and scaling (Fig. 3.6.1). Creating copies of an object creates more three-dimensional elements in the scene, increases the file size, and demands more computing time.

Instancing is an alternative to duplicating that is available in many systems. **Instancing**—also called **cloning** in some systems—creates multiples of an original object by using its numerical description and clonng it elsewhere in the scene. The multiples created with instancing are like "living clones" that continue to be related at all times to the original object. If the original changes shape or is scaled, its dependent instances are also transformed. Since instances of a model do not increase the size of a file they are convenient for creating large armies of objects that look alike and that display a consistent group behavior. Instancing, however, may not be appropriate if a project requires that each multiple undergoes a different shape transformation.

Setting a Face

Two-dimensional outlines drawn with freeform or curve tools are not really three-dimensional objects. When first drawn, two-dimensional outlines that are closed are just lines with a hole in the middle. Therefore, in order for two-dimensional outlines to be rendered properly it is necessary to turn them into planes. This process is called **setting a face** to an outline.

Snapping to the Grid

By forcing the objects or its components points, for example, to **snap to a grid**, three-dimensional modeling programs can help to simplify the construction of regular shapes or precise details within larger shapes (Fig. 3.6.2). Grids can usually be defined by the user. This includes the size of the grid unit, whether the points snap to the grid, whether the object's center or edges snap to the grid when the object is moved, and whether the snap to grid function is applied to all objects in the scene or only to some.

Bounding Box

When modeling a scene with multiple complex objects many computer systems may slow down because of the huge number of calculations needed to redraw the image of the models on the screen. Using bounding boxes to represent objects is a convenient technique for speeding up their display. **Bounding boxes** are usually rectangular and they are defined by the points most distant from the center of the model. Bounding boxes usually respond to interactive manipulation the same way a full three-dimensional model responds. If a particular computer system can display in real time the rotation of a three-dimensional model in wireframe or shaded form, it will do the same with a bounding box. Bounding boxes are not to be confused with lattices, which can be used to distort the three-dimensional objects contained within them. Bounding boxes and the lattices used to deform freeform objects look similar but behave differently.

Making objects invisible or ghosting them are two options similar to the bounding box. Making objects invisible removes them from the display but not from the information contained in the file. Objects made invisible with this method are usually not displayed regardless of the rendering method until made visible again—usually by just clicking a choice in a checkbox.

The ghosting option offered by some programs is similar to the bounding box. In some implementations of the ghosted display the model is represented with dotted lines, and the display of the ghosted model is only updated when the mouse button is released at the end of an interactive manipulation. In other implementations of ghosting it does not speed the display of images on the screen but instead facilitates working with complex models by making ghosted portions unselectable.

Mirroring

Mirroring a three-dimensional model is a useful technique when building an object composed of two identical (or almost identi-

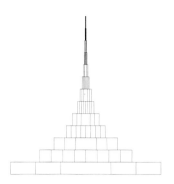

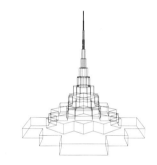

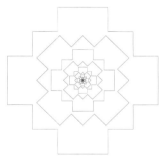

3.6.1 This object was created by duplicating 12 times the original shape at the bottom. Each instance of the original shape was mirrored by rotating 45 degrees and translating one unit on the Z axis.

cal) halves. The **mirroring** technique is implemented in a wide variety of ways by different software, each with particular requirements and subtle functional differences. Three-dimensional objects can be repositioned in space with the mirroring technique. In such cases the object is entirely moved to where its mirror image would be. In general, however, mirroring works by copying an object, placing the copy in the same location as the original, and finally repositioning the copy. This way the object remains in its original position and its copy is placed where the mirror image of the original object would be.

Mirroring works by either providing a scaling value of -1 along the axis on which the mirroring is to take place, specifying a two-dimensional plane (XY, XZ, or YZ) on which the object is to be mirrored, or by establishing an axis of reflection by clicking a line perpendicular to the object to be reflected (one end of the line represents the base point of reflection, the other end represents the beginning of the axis reflection). Mirroring is illustrated in Fig. 3.6.1.

Setting the Center of Objects

Most three-dimensional programs keep track of where the centers of objects are placed. By default these centers are automatically placed in the objects' geometric centers. These points become very important—especially later during the animation process because many operations are calculated based on the spatial position of the center of the object. These operations include scaling, rotation (global and local—the latter also known as pivoting), linking, and simulations of motion dynamics related to center of gravity. Being able to interactively reposition the center of an object is a powerful modeling and animation utility (Fig. 2.4.1).

Setting Text

The text tool is capable of automatically producing two-dimensional outlines or three-dimensional objects extracted from the two-dimensional outlines of fonts (or typefaces) installed in the computer system. The sophistication and variety of two-dimensional text outlines varies greatly from software to software, and so do all the additional features associated with letterforms, such as letterspacing, kerning capabilities, and point-editing features.

Most of today's three-dimensional modeling programs extract the text outlines from spline-based descriptions (often in the PostScript language) resident in the system software. Some three-dimensional programs extract this outline information from a font database—sometimes in curve format, other times in polygonal format—that is provided with the three-dimensional program itself. The shapes of the letterforms are usually smooth and detailed when the outline information is brought in as a series of curves. However, when the outline information is brought in as a series of polygonal lines, then the resulting shape may be jagged and unrefined, especially in the portions of the outline with the most curvature.

Most text tools work in conjunction with the keyboard. Any character that can be typed from the keyboard will show up in the three-dimensional environment as a two-dimensional outline. When an extrusion value is specified for the two-dimensional outline then the letterform can be three-dimensional. As with all objects modeled with extrusion, bevelling can be applied to letterforms modeled with extrusion-based text tools (Fig. 4.3.2). (See Chapter 4 for additional information on bevelling.)

Volume Calculation

The calculation of volumes and unfolding of planes are two modeling specialized techniques that can be useful when designing three-dimensional models that eventually get fabricated out of real materials.

Volume calculation tools allow users to find out the total volume and area of the inside, outside, or parts of any three-dimensional object. Knowing the exact volume of liquid that can be contained in a new bottle design can be very important to an industrial designer. Likewise, an engineer in charge of supervising the actual production of the bottle needs to know the volume of glass needed to fabricate the bottle. Some of the volume calculation tools can also be used to extract data related to the object's mass or its center of gravity and inertia. This information can be used later in the animation of models using motion dynamics animation software.

Being able to unfold the plans that bound a three-dimensional object can be quite useful for those cases when it is necessary to fabricate either a cardboard scale model or prototype of the three-dimensional object or the final object itself in more durable materials, such as plastic or sheet metal. Figure 13.8.1 shows three-dimensional objects that were built with a variety of modeling techniques and then unfolded into two-dimensional patterns.

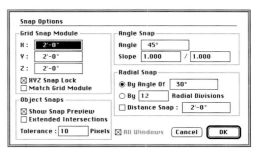

3.6.2 The snap to grid option. (Dialog box from form•Z. © 1991-1995 auto•des•sys, Inc.)

3.7 Groups and Hierarchical Structures

Three-dimensional objects can be grouped together in a limitless number of ways in order to create structures that define the ways in which these models are transformed, how they relate to one another, how they are rendered, and how they behave when animated. Groupings of three-dimensional objects are usually called **hierarchical structures**, because within these structured groupings some objects are always more dominant than others.

Objects within hierarchical structures have defined levels of importance and the objects within this hierarchy inherit attributes from the dominant objects. The object or objects at the top of the hierarchy are called **parents**, and the objects below are called **children**, and grandchildren: children inherit their parents' attributes. Hierarchical structures can also be visualized as an inverted tree structure where the highest level of importance in the structure corresponds to the trunk of the tree: the branches that come out of the trunk are the next level of hierarchy; branches that come out of the main branches are the next level; and so on until we get to the leaves, which are in the last level of the hierarchical structure.

In most cases, there is just one set of hierarchy diagrams per scene and these diagrams control all the modeling, rendering, and animation information about the objects. Some programs, however, provide several sets of hierarchy diagrams, and therefore hierarchy configurations, so that **modeling links** can be independent and different from the **rendering links** and the **animation links**. Modeling links, for example, make sure that the shape of all the children throughout the hierarchy changes when the shape of the child's parent is modified. Rendering links transmit the rendering attributes of the parent down the structure. Animation links automatically update the spatial position of the children when the parent is transformed.

The relations between objects in hierarchical structure are often complex and can be better visualized by a schematic representation in the form of a line diagram. These diagrams are often built with boxes representing items in the structure and lines representing their place in their hierarchy and their relations with other items.

As shown in Fig. 3.7.1 there are many possible ways to group several objects in a hierarchical structure. The best choice of hierarchy is usually one that takes into account the rendering and animation requirements of the scene. (See Chapters 10 and 11 for more details on how hierarchical structures affect the object's rendering and transformation attributes.)

The specific steps required to establish hierarchical relationships between objects obviously vary from software to software. But the basic concept has two variations. We can click on the three-dimensional objects themselves in any one of the views (perspective, top/bottom, front/back, and right/left). Or we can click on the boxes representing them in the diagram representing the links between them. With some programs one is required to first click on the object that is to be the parent and then the

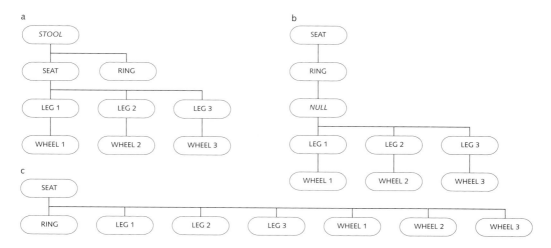

children. With other programs the object that is to represent the children must be clicked first and then the parent.

Even though hierarchical structures are more significant to the stages of rendering and animation, most often they are created during the modeling process. Hierarchies can also be efficiently used for positioning, scaling, or orienting groups of objects. Overall, hierarchical structures are fairly easy to understand. But one aspect of hierarchical structures that is not always obvious is the use of a null parent. A **null parent** is a node in the hierarchy that does not contain an object but holds several children together. A null parent is used, for example, when two or more objects are grouped at the same level in the hierarchy. Nulls are often represented with italics or as empty boxes in the structural diagrams. Figures 3.7.1a-b illustrate the use of a null cell that can be used to keep the four legs and the wheels all in one group so that they can be manipulated independently from the ring.

3.7.1 This diagram shows three possible variations of the hierarchical structure for all of the stool's components. The first arrangement (a) would be the most practical one if the stool were to roll on its round wheels, and if the seat, legs, and wheels were each to be rendered with a different material. The second option (b) would be best if the entire stool was made out of just one material. The third option (c) has the seat at the top of the hierarchy and everything else below the seat at the same level.

Review and Practice

Matching

____ Naming objects

____ Facets

____ Unfolding skin
____ Text tools

____ Cardinal spline

____ Hierarchy
____ Surfaces of revolution
____ Ungrouping
____ Bézier curve

____ Terrains

a. When used to model cylinders and cones it creates results similar to those that can be created with geometric primitive tools.

b. A curve that has tangent points in addition to control points.

c. Returns all objects to a stand-alone status.

d. Complex structures created with relatively little modeling work.

e. Their number defines the geometric smoothness of polygonal models.

f. Useful for quickly identifying models in a scene.

g. Capable of creating smooth letterforms.

h. A curve that passes through all of its control points.

i. Useful technique for creating two-dimensional blueprints that can be easily assembled into a three-dimensional scale model.

j. Capable of creating complex relations where children usually inherit most of the parents' attributes.

Answers Matching: a. Surfaces of revolution, b. Bézier curve, c. Ungrouping, d. Terrains, e. Facets, f. Naming objects, g. Text tools, h. Cardinal spline, i. Unfolding skin, j. Hierarchy.

BASIC MODELING TECHNIQUES

True/False

___ a.　Two-dimensional outlines can only be extruded along the Z axis.

___ b.　Regular polyhedra include three-dimensional objects that are symmetric and have 20 facets.

___ c.　Bounding boxes are used to speed up the display of three-dimensional objects on the screen.

___ d.　Five identical cubes can be created by instancing an original cube four times.

___ e.　Polygonal meshes are almost always defined with cardinal b-splines.

___ f.　The position of points in three-dimensional terrains can be easily disturbed with a variety of mathematical functions.

___ g.　Objects that have been locked into a specific XYZ position can be easily unlocked without them losing their other attributes.

___ h.　A torus is like a cylinder that has been twisted so that the bases touch each other.

___ i.　It is possible to model a three-dimensional spiral object by using a lathe tool that revolves a closed contour around an axis as it moves it away from the axis.

___ j.　It is always best to use b-splines in the modeling of any three-dimensional object regardless of the object's final application.

___ k.　NURBS offer a high degree of local curve control by using weights and knots.

___ l.　Mirroring can only take place by defining two reflecting planes on opposite sides of a three-dimensional object.

Key Terms

Animation links
Arcs
B-Spline
Bézier curve
Bounding boxes
Capping
Cardinal spline
Children
Circles
Cloning
Cones
Control points
Control vertices
Controlled curves
Cubes
Curvature
Cylinders
Deformation with lattices
Degree
Diameter
Die
Dodecahedron
Duplicating
Extrusion
Freeform extrusion
Freeform modeling
Freeform three-dimensional objects
Geometric primitives
Hierarchical structures
Icosahedron
Instancing
Knots
Lathe

Linear spline
Locking
Lofting
Mathematical functions
Mirroring
Modeling links
Nonrational curve
Non-Uniform Rational B-Splines
Null parent
NURBS
Octahedron
Parents
Polygons
Radius
Rational curve
Regular polyhedra
Rendering links
Revolve
Seed outline
Setting a face
Snap to grid
Spheres
Spirals
Splines
Surfaces of revolution
Sweeping
Tangent points
Tension
Terrains
Tetrahedron
Torus
Two-dimensional shapes
Virtual sculpting
Weight

CHAPTER 4

Advanced Modeling Techniques

Summary

This chapter covers some of the advanced modeling techniques used for building three-dimensional virtual objects and environments. These techniques include complex curved surfaces and blobby surfaces, trimmed surfaces, a variety of utilities like surface blending, and procedural description used mostly to model natural phenomena.

4.1 Freeform Curved Surfaces

Freeform curved surfaces allow a great degree of surface control. They are mathematically defined, and are also called **parametric curved surfaces** because each coordinate is a function of one or more parameters, such as a control hull, control points, tangent points, knots, and weights. **Freeform curved surfaces** and complex freeform surfaces are the generic names given to bicubic surface patches, Bézier surfaces, b-spline surfaces, and skinned surfaces. Each of these types of surfaces is based on different types of curves.

As explained in Chapter 2, curved lines are defined by several points and deviate from a straight path without any sharp breaks in angularity. Curves are used to define freeform curved surfaces and also to build meshes of curved surfaces. There are many types of curves, and the most popular types include: linear splines, cardinal splines, b-splines, Bézier curves, and NURBS (Fig. 3.2.2).

Each of the curved surfaces can be characterized by the way in which its curvature or tension is controlled by the control points. Curved surfaces defined by Bézier curves, for example, pass through all of its control points, and their degree of curvature is fine tuned with tangent points. Curved surfaces created with b-splines rarely pass through the control points, and those created with NURBS do not pass through the control points, but

4.1.1 Two curves were used to create patches of different resolutions.

rely on weights and knots for increased local curve control. (Read Chapter 2 for more information on curved lines.)

Cubic splines make use of curve fitting techniques and pass through all of the specified points. They also use parabolic blending and require numerical specification of both direction and magnitude of the tangent deviations. In the case of Bézier curves, the shape and order of the curve can be varied by the use of parameters. The first and last points are used to define the curve, which is defined by an open polygon. If any points are moved then the entire curve is altered because it is an average of all its vertices. B-spline curves offer more local control than Bézier curves.

Curved Patches

A curved patch is a small curved area that can be created from two or four curves. When a patch is created from two curves these are positioned opposite to one another (Fig. 4.1.1). When four curves are used they are usually positioned to define a rectangular area. Complex freeform surfaces are created by **merging** (two or more) **curved patches**. When curved patches that have the same number of rows and columns are merged the results are fairly predictable. But merging patches with different numbers of rows and/or columns requires the use of interpolation techniques that modify one of the two patches being merged (Fig. 4.1.2). This merging can also be controlled with great detail by specifying manually which points in the first patch merge into which points in the second patch. Having patches that merge into each other seamlessly is important to create a crisp rendering of the new patch, especially when the surface contains an image map on it.

Merging patches is one the most powerful modeling techniques that can yield detailed models with subtle shapes. However, the large number of points or vertices in a model created with patches is often a concern. This can be addressed by either making sure that the patches throughout the model have a small number of subdivisons, or by using a modeling utility that purges some of the points according to criteria such as the angle or distance to other points. Curved patches can be further manipulated and refined by using some of the utilities described both in this chapter and in Chapter 3.

Skinning

A unique way to create curved surfaces that fit predefined closed curves in three-dimensional space is called skinning. This technique creates three-dimensional objects by connecting a sequence of two-dimensional **cross sections**, also called **slices**

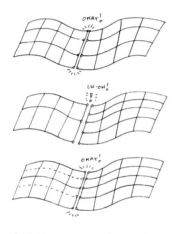

4.1.2 Merging two patches usually requires matching their number of columns and/or rows.

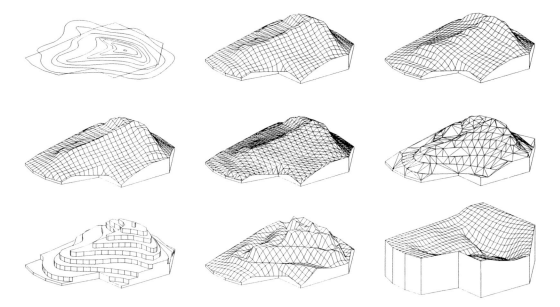

or **outlines**, with curves. Skinning is somewhat similar to freeform extrusion because the modeling follows a path, but it is different because the shape of the cross sections being skinned is pre-defined. Most skinning functions usually require that the two-dimensional outlines are closed and that they all have the same number of points. Some skinning functions, however, can skin outlines with different numbers of points by creating points as needed based on guessing what the best skinning would be. Topographic data that includes altitude information is commonly used to generate terrain models using the skinning technique (Fig. 4.1.3).

The technique of skinning is also called **cross section extrusion** or **serial section reconstruction** because entire objects can be reconstructed from cross sections or slices that can be obtained with a variety of methods. Skinning is particularly useful to create models of humans because these are easily described as series of two-dimensional contours. A variety of technologies, such as three-dimensional laser scanners and Magnetic Resonance (MR) scanners, for example, are used to gather precise data about the outside and inside shapes of human bodies (Fig. 4.1.4). The three-dimensional data used to create the stereo pair of a human thorax, illustrated in Fig. 4.1.5, comes from a volunteer who did 45-second breath holds in a magnetic resonance (MR) scanner. At each breath hold a series of scans of a single coronal slice were taken at ten different phases of the heart cycle. This was achieved by coordinating the scanning

4.1.3 Different three-dimensional objects can be created by connecting, or skinning, two-dimensional outlines (a) in variety of ways. A mesh based on both XY directions (b) looks slightly different than meshes weighted along the X or the Y axis (c and d). The outlines in e and f are connected by two triangular meshes of different resolutions, and by simple steps in g. The altitude of every other outline has been shifted up or down in h, and in i the altitude of the outlines has been inverted.

process—or data acquisition—with the electrocardiogram signal of the subject. This process was repeated about 50 times at different cross sections of the heart. The complete acquisition took about an hour, and it yielded 490 slices comprising ten groups of 49 slice-volumes at ten different phases of the heart cycle. The flowing blood appears as the brightest object in the images.

The contours that define a skinned object can also be traced manually on a digitizing tablet. This technique is especially useful to obtain three-dimensional skinned objects that have the irregularities typical of handmade objects. The amount of digitized cross sections needed to describe an object is in direct proportion to the complexity and detail desired in the final object. The sections on the X and Y planes represent a sample in the horizontal and vertical levels of the original object. Some objects are easier to describe by their horizontal cross sections, while others are easier to define by their vertical cross sections. The number of sections that are necessary to describe an object accurately can range from half a dozen to more than a hundred. A loss of data is apparent when the skinned objects are sampled at large intervals and the cross sections are too far apart from each other. Once the cross sections have been digitized it is sometimes necessary to edit the database in order to adjust individual sections within the three-dimensional object. Geometric transformations can be performed on the contours in order to change their relative spatial position.

Skin of Virtual Actors

There are many techniques for creating a surface that surrounds an **articulated skeleton** or a simple **articulated chain**. Two of the most common methods include assigning predefined three-dimensional models to a chain or specific segments of the chain, or creating a three-dimensional surface based on the chain itself.

Surface models that are attached to articulated skeletons always follow the motion of the chain segment, but they usually do not deform automatically. Attached models behave like hard shells around the skeleton and, in some cases, can be deformed with keyframe animation techniques by pulling individual points on the mesh. The procedure for **attaching rigid models** to an articulated chain is simple. It is usually done by clicking on one chain segment and one model at a time, just like creating any other hierarchical structure (read Chapter 3 for more information about hierarchical structures). However, three-dimensional rigid models that are assigned to a skeleton do not deform automatically with rotations of the joints.

Many software programs provide tools for generating a skin-like surface that wraps the skeleton or articulated chain (both of these are invisible to the rendering program unless cov-

4.1.4 A three-dimensional scanner can quickly gather precise modeling data. (Courtesy of Cyberware, Monterey, CA.)

ered with a three-dimensional model or surface). In some cases, the surfaces covering the skeleton are often called **skin surfaces** because they are continuous and flexible like skin. Skin surfaces deform in response to the movement of the skeleton that they cover. The technique chosen to define the skin or outer surface of an articulated figure defines the final appearance of the animated three-dimensional model. The realistic effect of skin that stretches with motion—especially at the joints—is often achieved only with a combination of animation techniques that may include motion dynamics of flexible bodies, and freeform shape animation in the form of flexible lattices.

Skin surfaces can be created around skeletons automatically or manually, and they are usually curved surfaces and not polygonal meshes. Skin surfaces can be generated automatically by creating an outline shape and letting the software extrude it along the skeleton (Fig. 4.1.6). Just like standard extrusion techniques, many automatic skin surface generators allow the animator to specify the number of times that the outline being extruded may be repeated along a segment of the articulated chain, and also whether the resulting shape will be capped or not. In most cases, the shape of the skin that results from **automatic generation** can also be edited manually.

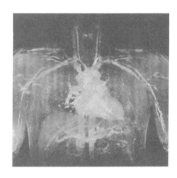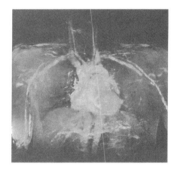

4.1.5 This stereo pair of the organs and structures inside a human thorax was created by reading the 49 slices comprising this volume into a volume rendering program. The images were processed with opacity settings to emphasize the bright flowing blood. The left image is a frontal volume rendering projection, and the right image was made by rotating the volume 10 degrees counterclockwise to the first image. (Data set by Dr. Paul Margosian et. al., Picker Inc., Cleveland, OH. Rendering software by ISG Technologies, Toronto, Canada. Data formatting and presentation by Irwin Sobel, HPLABS, Palo Alto, CA. Courtesy of Irwin Sobel.)

Skin surfaces can also be created manually with a variety of modeling techniques, and then be positioned around the skeleton (Fig. 4.1.6). **Manual creation of skin surfaces** offers two main advantages over automatic generation. More detail can be modeled with manual techniques, and skin surfaces generated manually can also be positioned more accurately over the skeleton in order to optimize the way in which the skin deforms. It is common practice to model more detail in the parts of the skin surface—usually the joints—that will bend under skeleton control. This can minimize unnatural stretching effects or extreme distortion of the skin (Fig. 4.1.7). Another advantage of using skin surfaces over rigid models to envelop the skeleton is that the skin surfaces automatically adjust to modifications in the scale of the skeleton. If a segment of an articulated chain is elongated then the skin that wraps it is adjusted accordingly.

Once the skin surfaces have been assigned to different segments of an articulated chain or skeleton they can be further refined and controlled by specifying their **deformation parameters**. These parameters allow animators to control the various

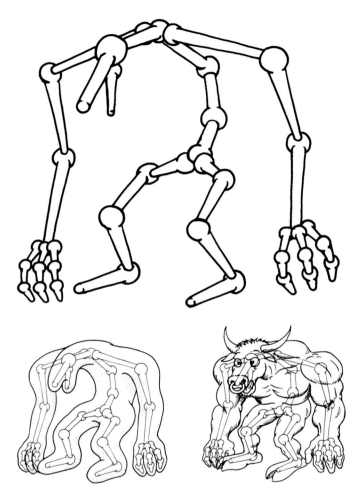

4.1.6 A skeleton with skins created automatically and manually.

properties bending skin, and to manipulate single vertices or groups of vertices on the skin's surface. The deformation parameters include the amount of bulging or rounding of a portion of the skin surface as a result of a joint bending. These parameters also control the weight that defines how the vertices will respond to deformation, the way adjacent regions blend with one another, and the assignment of vertices on the skin surface to a specific segment in the articulated chain (Fig. 4.1.8).

In some cases, the skin of three-dimensional models is not defined as a **continuous surface** but instead as a series of independent surfaces that are related to each other through a hierarchical structure. In these instances, the surfaces representing the skin should be arranged with care to minimize the amount of **gaps on the surface** of the animated model. Gaps on the sur-

ADVANCED MODELING TECHNIQUES

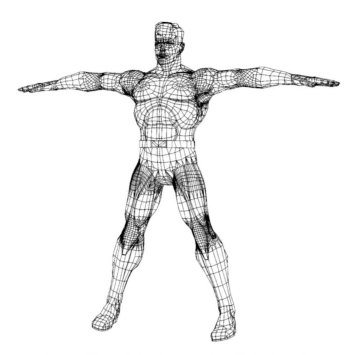

4.1.7 A figure with more modeling detail built at some of the joints. (Copyright Viewpoint Datalabs, used with permission.)

face of a model are obviously not an issue if the figure is designed in such a way that the surfaces are not connected—for example, a cartoon character with unconnected floating body parts. But in many cases, gaps on the skin surface tend to look like modeling mistakes. Two simple techniques that can be used to minimize the gaps on the skin of objects built with several surfaces consist of using filler shapes at the joints, and plain shape interpolation. **Filler objects** are usually of spherical shape and positioned at the joints that have wide rotation angles, which is where gaps in butting surfaces are most likely to occur. **Simple shape interpolation** can also take reasonably good care of small gaps that may develop on the surface of models during simple rotations. But simple shape interpolation offers far from perfect results because it also generates unexpected skin distortion when applied to gaps created with rotations that happen around several axes simultaneously.

Blobby Surfaces

Blobby surfaces are usually defined as spherical objects that change shape depending on how close they are to other blobby elements. The magnitude of the **attraction force** of blobby elements is usually defined by their volume, but their **area of influence** can also be set independently from their size. In an animation, **blobby surfaces** are dynamic and constantly regen-

4.1.8 The skin that represents the biceps muscle swells as a secondary action because it is linked to the bone rotation. (Courtesy of Acclaim Entertainment, Inc., Advanced Technologies Group.)

4.1.9 A rendering of characters created with blobby surfaces, a wireframe view of a single character, and the dialog box used to specify their blobbiness. (Images courtesy of Tim Cheung. Dialog box from Softimage 3D. © Microsoft Corporation. All rights reserved.)

erate as they move in and out of the areas of influence of other blobby elements (Fig. 4.1.9). When two or more of these touch one another they can fuse into a single object, just like two drops of oil or mercury merge into one another when they meet on a surface. The way in which blobby objects fuse into each other is determined by the explicit or random links that are established between each of the objects in a blobby system.

4.2 Logical Operators and Trimmed Surfaces

Logical operators are used to create models by adding and subtracting shapes in a variety of ways. The most common logical operators include **union**, **intersection**, and **difference**. The union operator is also known as **and**, intersection is called **or**, and difference is called **not**. The union and the difference of a sphere and a cross are illustrated in Fig. 4.2.1.

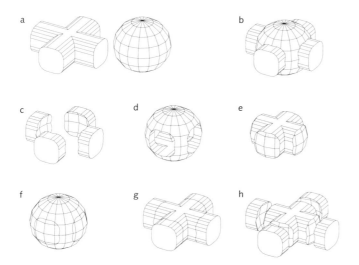

The logical operator of difference is usually referred to as **trimming**, and the surfaces created with trimming are called **trimmed surfaces**. The modeling technique of trimming is especially useful to create three-dimensional objects or **surfaces with holes**. The sequence illustrated in Fig. 4.2.2 shows this operator in action alongside with the union operator. The union of a cylinder and a box (a, b) results in a box with a rounded top. The difference between the rounded box and a cube (c) yields a rounded base with a rectangular trim. Finally, the difference between the base and a cylinder (d) results in a base with two round holes (e). Many implementations of trimming require at least one pair of intersecting three-dimensional objects as illustrated in Fig. 4.2.1. But others can trim surfaces or objects with just a line or a two-dimensional shape—the hole—that intersects the shape or that is projected through the object.

4.3 Advanced Modeling Utilities

Many modeling utilities like beveling, fitting, blending, and spline deformation are used to further manipulate surfaces, and to complement the advanced modeling techniques.

Beveling, Rounding, and Fillets

The edges between adjacent surfaces can be customized with great detail with a variety of beveling techniques. Simple **beveling** usually works by truncating the hard edge between adjacent surfaces—usually two or three—and replacing it with a slanted plane. The amount of beveling can be controlled by a distance, radius, or angle value between the edge being beveled to the

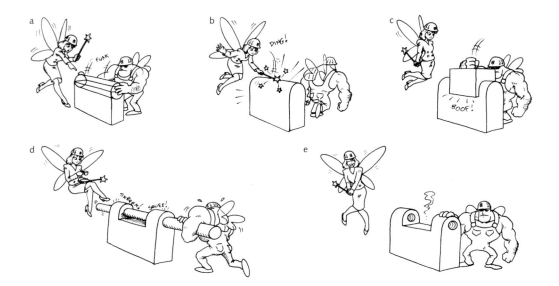

4.2.2 This sequence illustrates the logical operators of union and difference being used to model a complex three-dimensional object from four components.

place where the bevel is to be placed. **Rounding** is a delicate form of beveling that literally rounds the straight edges or points of an object. The degree of rounding is controlled by the number of segments or facets that are used to define the smooth transition between adjacent surfaces (Fig. 4.3.1).

Utilities for creating fillets also modify the junction of surfaces. **Fillets** create a custom trim that extends along the edge. This trim is more ornate than plain beveling or rounding. Fillets are like the decorative strips of molding that are often placed at the corners or edges of furniture, or like the functional molding that is used to protect the edge where walls meet the floor. Some software programs create fillets by trimming the surface, and others by sweeping a custom two-dimensional outline along the edge that is being modified (Fig. 4.3.2).

Aligning, Fitting, and Blending

Software programs with advanced modeling provide utilities that are especially useful for fine-tuning curved patches. Utilities like aligning, fitting, and blending manipulate the edges of curved patches—and also polygonal surfaces—to refine and clean up the shapes of three-dimensional models.

Aligning two patches usually works by selecting the two patches to be aligned and then moving and rotating them until they are aligned a certain way. **Fitting** utilities get rid of small gaps between surfaces. This is achieved by dragging the two surfaces that are not quite touching each other until their edges match each other perfectly. Fitting is almost always used prior to

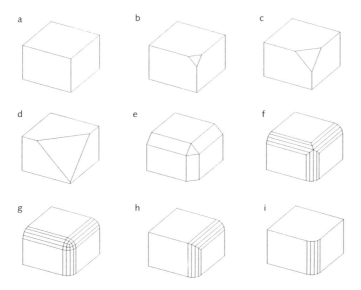

a b c

d e f

g h i

4.3.1 The first shape has no beveling or rounding (a). The next three shapes display a point bevel of different magnitudes (b-d). The second group of shapes includes a three-edge bevel (e), a three-edge rounding (f), and a three-edge and point rounding (g). The last two shapes are examples of a two-edge rounding (h), and a single-edge rounding (i).

merging two patches. **Blending** is a special way of merging two surfaces. Instead of merging two surfaces by first making them touch each other and then merging them, blending creates a new surface that extends from each of the two surfaces being blended. The new surface creates by blending connects the two surfaces, and the smoothness of the blending is controlled with a function curve or by manipulating the control points of the blended surface (Fig. 4.3.3).

Purging Points

Three-dimensional models created with curved patches often have a large number of points or vertices. This results in models that may be too complex for the requirements of the project and also increases rendering time and file size. **Purging** utilities are useful to automatically eliminate excessive vertices in complex three-dimensional models. This is usually done by identifying pairs of points that are too close to each other—based on a minimum distance—and deleting one of them. Manual point-editing is often used in conjunction with purging utilities to fine-tune and adjust the distribution of points in the model.

Deformed and Randomized Surfaces

In addition to using lattices for deforming the shape of three-dimensional objects, it is also possible to deform them with splines, patches, functions, or random numbers. (Deforming objects with lattices and functions is covered in Chapter 3.)

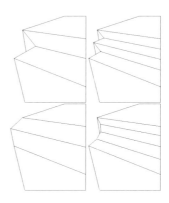

4.3.2 This figure shows the results of four different fillet styles applied to the corner and edge of a cube.

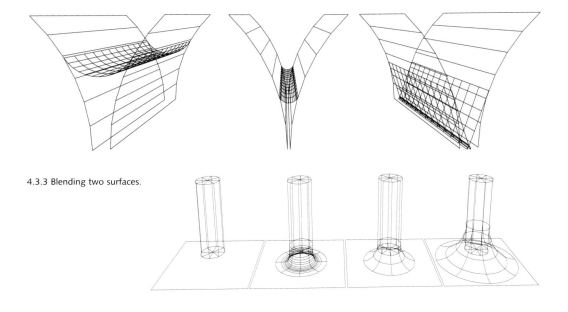

4.3.3 Blending two surfaces.

4.3.4 A dialog box for controlling patch deformation, and a sequence of icons that illustrates how different techniques work. (Dialog box and icons from form•Z. © 1991-1995 auto•des•sys, Inc.)

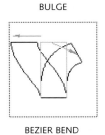

SHEAR

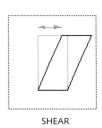

TAPER

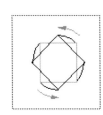

TAPER

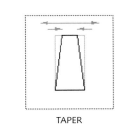

BULGE

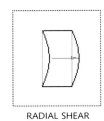

RADIAL SHEAR

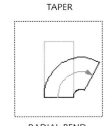

RADIAL BEND

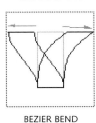

BEZIER BEND

BEZIER BEND
(PARALLEL)

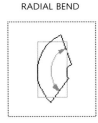

RADIAL BEND
(THROUGH CENTER)

ADVANCED MODELING TECHNIQUES

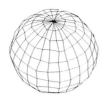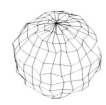

The technique of **deformation with splines and patches** consists of using a spline or a patch as the agent that deforms the object that is associated with them (Fig. 4.3.4). Deforming an object with a spline offsets the points in the object according to the shape of the spline. Deforming an object with a patch pulls the object to the shape of the patch in those areas where the object overlaps the patch.

Interesting deformations can be achieved by offsetting the vertices of three-dimensional objects with functions or random values (figs. 3.5.3 and 4.3.5). The technique of **random distortion** is especially useful in creating models of terrains that have so many irregularities that it would be difficult to model them with other techniques. Random distortion can also be used to animate the effect of shaking by displacing the points back and forth through time.

4.4 Procedural Descriptions of Natural Phenomena

Procedural descriptions of three-dimensional models—especially those found in nature—are effective alternatives to the regular and sometimes rigid shapes obtained with geometric modeling systems. With procedural description objects are not modeled by

sculpting their exterior shell. The modeling techniques of **procedural description** get their name from the fact that, with them, objects are modeled by simulating, for example, their natural growth process that is described in the form of procedures (Fig. 4.4.1). Fractal geometry and particle systems, for example, are two procedural description methods that create a modeling complexity that is difficult to obtain with geometric modeling. Both of these methods are well suited for the generation of natural-looking forms because they allow for randomness, recursion, and accidents of shape like those typical of natural shapes.

4.4.1 This raytraced scene, entitled *Crop Circle*, contains over 100 million primitives. It was specified using a new technique called "Procedural Geometric Instancing," which represents the field of wheat by hierarchically instancing a single wheat stalk. At instantiation, each stalk of wheat examines its position to determine if it should bend over or remain upright. (© 1994 John C. Hart, Washington State University.)

4.4.2a *Seasons of Life* illustrates how fractal procedures express the roughness and fragmentation of natural phenomena. (Courtesy of Midori Kitagawa De Leon.)

Fractal Geometry

Fractal geometry is especially effective for creating random and irregular shapes that resemble those shapes found in nature (Fig. 4.4.2a). This modeling technique was developed by Benoit Mandelbrot in the 1970s. It can be applied to existing three-dimensional meshes, or it can be used to generate entirely new models or parts of models. When applied to an existing model **fractal procedures** work by dividing the polygons in the object recursively and randomly into many irregular shapes that resemble those found in nature. The amount of subdivision is usually expressed in the form of a factor or **level of recursion** (Fig. 4.4.2b). Fractal geometry can also be used to create objects from scratch by using random seed values or as iteration of algebraic formulas (Fig. 4.4.3).

Particle Systems

Modeling with **particle systems** is based on employing simple shapes, usually small spheres or points in three-dimensional

space. These shapes, or particles, have **growth attributes**. When these attributes are simulated the particles have specific behaviors that result in specific particle **trajectories**. As the particles grow over time their trajectory defines a certain shape that results in a three-dimensional model. The growth process of many of the attributes of the particles, including their height, width, branching angle, bending factor, number of branches, and color, can be controlled or randomized. Figure 4.4.4 shows a scene that was modeled by simulating feathers of birds or petals of flowers by creating particles that grow densely on the surfaces of three-dimensional objects. In this project, colored maps were applied to the feathers, the bird is animated with a skeleton deformation technique, and all the feathers grow at their positions as the body moves. (Read Chapter 11 for more information about animating with particle systems.)

Procedural description, and particle systems in particular, are used to create a variety of natural materials and phenomena whose shape constantly changes throughout time. This includes, for example, snowstorms, clouds, flowing water, moving soil, and fire. When particles are used to recreate the motion of water, for

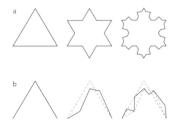

4.4.2b A fractal recursive subdivision is applied to a regular polygon (a), and to the detail of a three-dimensional mesh (b).

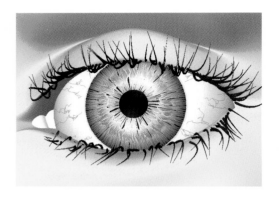

4.4.3 Rendering of an eye. (From "A Virtual Environment and Model of the Eye for Surgical Simulation," in the SIGGRAPH '94 Conference Proceedings. Courtesy of Mark Sagar, Department of Mechanical Engineering, University of Auckland, New Zealand.)

example, they each represent a drop of water with attributes like density, cohesion, transparency, and refraction. Particles have a life span during which they behave a certain way, and then fade away or merge with other particles (Figs. 4.4.5 and 4.4.6). Of all the procedural modeling techniques particle systems is the one that best recreates the dynamic shapes of natural elements. This technique produces large numbers of particles that do not have a specific shape and are usually spheres or dots. But the particles are grouped in shapes that change through time according to rules that define the behavior of elements such as water and fire.

Modeling Plants

Three-dimensional models of plants and trees created with procedural techniques offer increased modeling control and more efficient modeling than most other techniques. This is due to the large number of elements and surface detail contained in a plant, as well as the complexity of shapes. Polygonal modeling techniques are often less than adequate for modeling realistic plants. Curved surfaces are capable of modeling the shapes found in plants, but when done this way modeling plants quickly becomes time consuming.

Plant models can be built by encoding their characteristics in a series of rules or procedures that are used as the basis for a growth simulation. This method can also be used to animate the growth process of plant models in a scene. There are several ways to generate models of plants with procedural techniques. These techniques can be classified as either space-oriented or

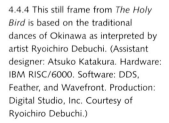

4.4.4 This still frame from *The Holy Bird* is based on the traditional dances of Okinawa as interpreted by artist Ryoichiro Debuchi. (Assistant designer: Atsuko Katakura. Hardware: IBM RISC/6000. Software: DDS, Feather, and Wavefront. Production: Digital Studio, Inc. Courtesy of Ryoichiro Debuchi.)

structure-oriented.

Space-oriented procedural techniques for modeling plants and animating their growth are based on the effect of the environment on them. **Structure-oriented procedural techniques** techniques, on the other hand, are based on the conditions that are internal to the plant, more specifically the growing process of the plant and the resulting structure that is characteristic of a plant species. Many of the procedural modeling techniques centered on the growth process of plants are often expressed in terms of the mathematical models formalized by biologist Aristide Lindenmayer during the late 1960s. These structure-oriented models describe the growth process of plants at the level of cellular interaction and are known as **L-systems**, short for Lindenmayer systems. L-systems are especially suited to represent structures that **branch in parallel**, just like a tree trunk splits into several branches at the same time (Fig. 4.4.7). Another characteristic of L-systems is that at each branching cycle the branching procedures generate **successor modules** that replace the **predecessor modules**.

4.4.5 This still from the animation *Flow* shows a particle system combined with a water mesh simulation system. (Rendering and animation by Gavin Miller, modeling by Ned Greene. Copyright Apple Computer, Inc.)

There are many variations of L-systems. Some are defined by parameters that represent exclusive conditions under which the L-system can bloom. Others are based on **stochastic** (or somewhat random) **values**. **Context-sensitive L-systems** are those whose performance is defined by the characteristic of the preceding module. The technique of **graftals** is an example of context-sensitive L-systems that allows the creation of complex images from small databases, a technique known as **database amplification**. Graftals are based on production rules and generation factors, they avoid random number generators, and can emply geometric or nongeometric objects— spheres, cylinders, or fuzzy objects with smooth edges.

4.4.6 Modeling of soil slippage. (Courtesy of Dr. Xin Li and Dr. Michael Moshell, Institute for Simulation of Training, University of Central Florida, Orlando, FL.)

Environmentally-sensitive L-systems are those defined by environmental characteristics, such as exposure to light and collision with objects. Pruning is an example of three-dimensional models based on a simulation of a growing plant whose shape is determined by an environmental variable (Fig. 4.4.8).

Some of the main techniques for controlling the simulation of a structure-oriented plant system include lineage and the interaction between the components of the growth process. **Lineage** is the transfer of attributes from one level of the plant to another at the time of branching. The interaction of the components of the growth process includes, for example, taking into account the watering conditions or the availability of nutrients that define the way in which plants grow. The plants modeled with procedural description are more faithful to the real plant based on the number of components that are considered into the derivation of the plant shapes.

4.5 Getting Ready

The following tips can help to simplify the successful modeling of complex three-dimensional objects.

Overlapping Edges and Gaps

Many three-dimensional software programs have trouble rendering objects with **overlapping edges** or overlapping facets. Clean up your three-dimensional models before you pass them over to those team members in charge of rendering them, or before you render them. Use modeling utilities such as aligning or blending to eliminate overlapping objects.

In critical situations automatic aligning tools may not be available to fix the misalignment of two elements and the resulting **gaps on the rendered surface**. In those cases it is often preferable to align the objects by typing their exact XYZ position on the keyboard in space instead of trying to drag them into position with the mouse.

Disable Polygons that Face Away

When building a large model that is to be rendered only from a single fixed point of view—front view only, for example—it is wise not to model the **surfaces facing away** from the camera and/or to disable the **back faces**. This technique is reminiscent of stage sets that are perfectly finished on the sides facing the audience but raw and unpolished on the sides that cannot be seen from the theater. Some programs allow users to turn off the rendering of individual polygons or groups of them. Other programs require to slice off the unwanted surfaces and discard them altogether from the three-dimensional scene. Either technique is useful for single-point of view renderings because it yields simpler models, more compact file sizes, and faster renderings.

Stay Away from Overmodeling

Creating too many elements, or **overmodeling**, is a bad habit

4.4.7 (opposite page) Black-and-white plants and lineage. (From "The Algorithmic Beauty of Plants," by P. Prusinkiewicz and A. Lindenmayer, Springer Verlag, New York, 1990. Copyright © 1994 by Przemyslaw Prusinkiewicz.)

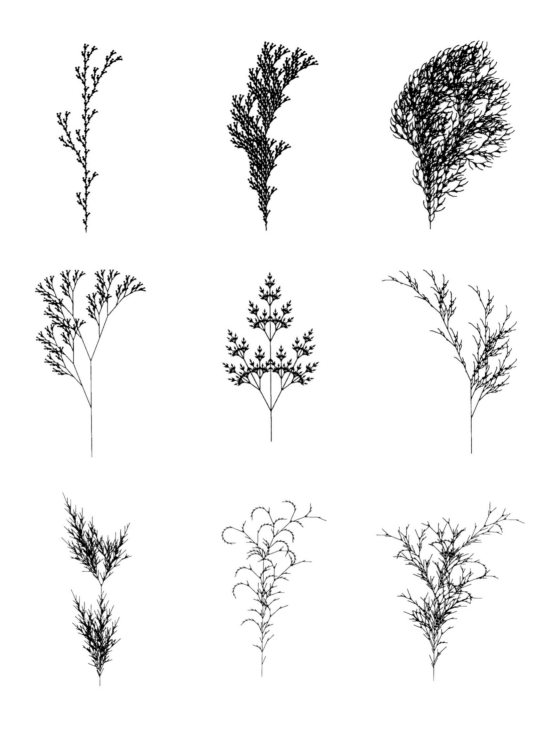

that usually has negative consequences in the stages of rendering and animation. Streamline the size of your models and data files by keeping the number of polygons, curves, or points on the curves down to an absolute minimum. If necessary, use purging or blending utilities like the one described in this chapter or edit your models manually. The numerous complications created by overmodeling are never obvious during the modeling process, but they become painfully clear later, during the animation and rendering of the models in the scene.

Consider the Hierarchical Structure

Even though hierarchical structures are more significant to the stages of rendering and animation, they are created most often during the modeling process. Three-dimensional objects within hierarchical structures have defined levels of importance. These levels not only define the ways in which the models are transformed during the modeling process, but also how they inherit rendering attributes, and how they behave when animated. There are many ways to group objects in a hierarchical structure, but the best choice always takes into account the rendering and animation requirements of the scene. (Read Chapters 3 and 10 for more information about hierarchical structures.)

Take Advantage of Modeling Mistakes

During the modeling process, one often encounters tools or functions that do not quite behave the way they are supposed to. This is particularly true of the so-called **derivative modeling techniques**, skinning and logical operators for example, that create objects from other already existing objects. The malfunction of the modeling tools is frequent when one tries to build unusual surfaces such as zig-zagged shapes, overlapping concave areas or a large number of acute angles. Modeling mistakes or accidents also happen when we try to get the tool to do something that it was not intended to do. For example, asking a skinning tool to first connect the two contours on opposite edges of the object and then proceed inward until all the contours are connected in this fashion insead of just skinning the adjacent contours serially and in sequence from one side of the object to the other. While the malfunctions of modeling tools are dissapointing at first—like any other defect or "bug" in a program—we can learn to look at them in a fresh way and seriously consider if the results can be used in a creative way to enrich the scene. Think of the ways in which the painters of the Abstract Expressionism of the 1950s used the shapes of accidental paint dripping and the unpredictable patterns of energetic brushstrokes to build their marvelous works.

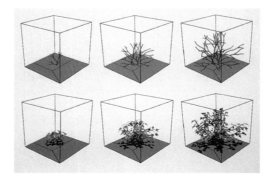

4.4.8 These images simulate the response of a tree to progressive pruning. The branches grow more densely near the edges of the volume—a cube in this case—used to clip the model. The leaves are defined as Bézier surfaces. Shown in red is the vigor of the reiterated branches on the appearance of the pruned tree. (Copyright © 1994 by P. Prusinkiewicz, M. James, and R. Mech.)

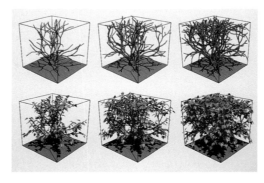

Review and Practice

Matching

_____ Beveling

_____ Fractals

_____ Degree of rounding

_____ Fillets

_____ Random distortion

_____ Lineage

_____ Patch

_____ Freeform surfaces

_____ Blobby surfaces

_____ Shape interpolation

_____ Trimming

_____ L-systems

_____ Skinning

_____ Skin surfaces

a. Useful to create three-dimensional objects or surfaces with holes.

b. Can be created from two curves that are positioned opposite to one another.

c. Can be used to animate the effect of shaking by displacing the points of the model back and forth through time.

d. Name given to a variety of curved surfaces including bicubic surface patches and Bézier surfaces.

e. Works by truncating the hard edge between two surfaces and replacing it with a slanted plane.

f. Useful in creating models that are described as series of two-dimensional contours.

g. Can be created manually with a variety of modeling techniques and then be positioned around a skeleton.

h. Mathematical models that represent structures that branch in parallel.

i. Modeling technique that employs starting shapes and generators.

j. Constantly regenerate as they move in and out of the areas of influence of similar elements.

k. Transfer of attributes from one level of a simulated plant to another at the time of branching.

l. Can be used to cover small gaps that may develop on the surface of models during simple rotations.

m. Controlled by the number of segments used to define the smooth transition between two adjacent surfaces.

n. Custom decorative trims that extend along the edge.

Answers Matching: a. Trimming, b. Patch, c. Random distortion, d. Freeform surfaces, e. Beveling, f. Skinning, g. Skin surfaces, h. L-systems, i. Fractals, j. Blobby surfaces, k. Lineage, l. Shape interpolation, m. Degree of rounding, n. Fillets.

Answers True/False: a. True, b. False, c. True, d. True, e. False, f. False, g. True, h. False, i. True, j. True, k. True, l. False, m. False, n. True, o. True, p. True, q. True, r. False, s. True.

True/False

_____ a. Many three-dimensional software programs have trouble rendering objects that have overlapping facets.

_____ b. Particle systems are particularly useful for modeling the human figure.

_____ c. Particle systems simulate the growth process and behavior of simple shapes.

_____ d. Structure-oriented techniques for modeling the growth of plants are based on the growing process that is characteristic of a plant species.

_____ e. Curved surfaces created with NURBS always pass through the control points but rely on weights and knots for increased local curve control.

_____ f. The most common logical operators include union, intersection, and distance.

_____ g. Skin surfaces that are generated manually can be accurately positioned over a skeleton in order to optimize the way in which the skin deforms.

_____ h. Procedural techniques offer much less modeling control than polygonal-based techniques for modeling plants.

_____ i. Control polygons are sometimes used to shape curved patches.

_____ j. The magnitude of the attraction force of blobby elements is usually defined by their volume.

_____ k. Geometric modeling systems are an alternative to the regular and sometimes rigid shapes obtained with procedural description.

_____ l. Most skinning functions usually require that the two-dimensional outlines are closed and that they all have the same number of points.

_____ m. Fractal subdivision of three-dimensional objects is usually regular.

_____ n. Three-dimensional scanners are used to gather precise modeling data about the outside and inside shapes of real models.

_____ o. An object deformed with a patch is pulled to the shape of the patch.

_____ p. Freeform curved surfaces can be characterized by the way in which their tension is controlled by the control points.

_____ q. Two blobby surfaces fuse with one another depending on their volume and the distance between them.

_____ r. Skin surfaces cannot be generated automatically because outlines cannot be extruded along a skeleton.

_____ s. Interpolation techniques can be used to modify one of two patches being merged when these have a different number of rows and/or columns.

Key Terms

Aligning
Area of influence
Articulated chain
Articulated skeleton
Attaching rigid models
Attraction force
Automatic generation
Back faces
Beveling
Blending
Blobby surfaces
Branch in parallel
Context-sensitive L-systems
Continuous surface
Cross section extrusion
Cross sections
Database amplification
Deformation parameters
Deformation with patches
Deformation with splines
Derivative modeling techniques
Difference, not
Environmentally-sensitive L-systems
Filler objects
Fillet
Fitting
Fractal geometry
Fractal procedures
Freeform curved surfaces
Gaps on the rendered surface
Graftals

Growth attributes
Intersection, or
L-systems
Level of recursion
Lineage
Logical operators
Manual creation of skin surfaces
Merging curved patches
Modeling plants
Outlines
Overlapping edges
Overmodeling
Parametric curved surfaces
Particle systems
Predecessor modules
Procedural description
Purging points
Random distortion
Rounding
Serial section reconstruction
Simple shape interpolation
Skin surfaces
Slices
Space-oriented procedural techniques
Stochastic values
Structure-oriented procedural techniques
Successor modules
Surfaces facing away
Surfaces with holes
Trajectories
Trimmed surfaces
Trimming
Union, and

RENDERING

5.1.1 The subtle use of lights, cameras, and materials can produce stunning results. (Courtesy of Blue Sky Productions, Inc.)

CHAPTER 5

Overview of the Rendering Process

Summary

Most of the visual characteristics of a simulated three-dimensional environment are determined through the **rendering process**. This chapter provides an overview of the steps in the process of adjusting the lights, setting the camera, and determining the surface characteristics of objects. The order in which topics are presented in the chapters related to rendering is somewhat different from the way in which it is usually done. The order of presentation was reversed here so that topics are presented from simple to complex. Cameras, which are rarely presented as an item, go first, then lighting, surface characteristics, and finally shading. However, since each of the chapters is relatively standalone, readers are welcomed to read them in their order of preference.

5.1 Lights, Camera, and Materials

The world of rendering by computer is populated by most of the attributes of our visual realm where the shapes of objects are revealed by light and obscured by shadow, where color creates moods of subtle tranquility or explosive happiness, where textures are as delicate and lyrical as fine sand or as dramatic and forceful as malachite, where the restless translucency of rain distorts the features of the world and the mirror of transparent water puts them back together. Rendering worlds of reality or fantasy with the computer can create results as artistic as with any other medium (Fig. 5.1.1).

When we use computers to render real or imagined scenes we can follow specific procedures, as we would if working with other media, that help accomplish all the tasks required before the rendering can be completed by the computer program. This fact is understood by artists who use media like painting, photography, or cinematography to depict scenes, to express emotions, or to tell stories with the elements of visual language. Each of these groups of professionals of the image has developed ways of doing things, basic techniques, orders of execution, and even complex procedures to do their jobs. In any case, most visual artists have to deal with some basic elements during the rendering process. These elements include composition, lighting, and defining surface characteristics such as color and texture.

Let's, for example, consider all the preparation that takes place before a professional photographer is ready to push the camera's trigger and actually take a photograph. The tasks that the photographer must complete will lead to the creation of an image. Likewise, when using three-dimensional computer software to simulate a realistic or imaginary scene, many tasks and variables have to be taken care of before the program can process the information needed to generate the image we have in mind. The tasks needed when rendering by computer are similar in theory to those tasks the photographer is involved with. But in practical detail, the tasks are carried out with very different tools and in a different environment.

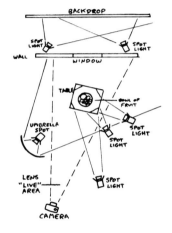

The photographer in this example is photographing an arrangement of fruit in a bowl placed on a small table in the middle of a large room with a bright landscape showing through the only window in the room. In this case the photographer has to start by selecting the models or "props" themselves. That includes the fruit, the bowl, the small table and the tablecloth. Those props may be procured from a variety of places that might include a farmer's market, a housewares store, and an antique shop. Keep in mind that the objects and the fruit have to be picked according to a certain criterion that specifies the way they are supposed to look. The table and the tablecloth, for example, might have to have a certain soft antique look. The bowl, on the other hand, might have to be made of dark translucent crystal and have a very elegant and simple design. Only the freshest of fruit can be used for this shot. Once all the objects have been brought to the studio then the photographer and her assistant will proceed to arrange the objects in a specific composition.

In three-dimensional computer graphics all of the objects used in the scene are simply called **models**. We have already learned in Section II of this book that three-dimensional models can be built with a variety of software techniques. Once the models have been built they can all be placed in the **virtual studio** that exists in the computer's memory and arranged in a specific way by using a combination of geometric transformations.

Let's return to the photographer who is in the process of placing the table near the panel in the middle of the room and the camera in front of it so that the window on the panel

appears behind the table (Fig. 5.1.2). The photographer also arranges the fruit in the bowl. She steps back, looks at the fruit through a professional photographic camera that is mounted on a tripod that is approximately three feet away from the subject, and returns to rearrange the fruit. At this point the photographer takes a snapshot with a hand-held camera loaded with instant film and a flash, just to get a quick preview of the composition. Because of the flash of intense light emitted by the flash the color in some areas of the instant photograph washes out, the overall illusion of depth is somewhat flattened, and the delicacy of some textures is lost. But the instant flash photograph does the job: it records the position of objects in space and the composition. It is also possible to create such quick snapshots with three-dimensional rendering software.

All the components of the still life are now in place, and it is time to start playing with the position, intensity, color, and focus of the lights. Since the shot is taking place inside the studio there is very little natural sunlight available. Therefore, the photograph-

5.1.2 The still life is arranged close to the fake wall in the photo studio so that the window and the painted backdrop showing through it appears behind the table.

er must recreate not only the sunlight but also some lights that must be focused on several areas of the fruit in order to delineate the shapes with more clarity and to accentuate the highlights and the shadows on the fruit to further the effect of depth.

Our imaginary photographer pauses for a minute, looks around the almost empty and dark room, and tries to visualize the effect of different types of lights on the fruit, the tablecloth, and the walls. After discussing some of the stylistic possibilities and production implications with her assistant, the photographer decides to start with one intense but indirect flood light for simulating the effect of warm natural light of a medium intensity. The flood light is placed between the still life and the camera, but away from the still life and into a concave portable reflective surface in the shape of an umbrella.

Then the photographer carefully maneuvers three small spotlights pointed at different fruits in the bowl. Since the three spotlights all have the same intensity the photographer has to move some of them closer or farther away from the fruit depending on the lighting effect desired. While the photographer is still arranging the three spotlights, her assistant is busy lighting the backdrop (with a landscape painted on it) that is placed behind the fake wall and visible through its window. The photographer's assistant decides to use two small flood lights with a slight blue coloration in order to simulate the exterior light of a cold rainy day. The two small floodlights are pointed at 45-degree angles from the back of the fake wall directly onto the backdrop (Fig. 5.1.2). Most three-dimensional rendering programs allow artists the selection and placement of light sources with the same amount of intuitive trial-and-error and precision as lighting with real lights.

During the placement of the lights, both the photographer and her assistant go back and forth to the camera to check through the viewfinder whether the lights are defining the image composition and mood that they had in mind at the onset of the process. At first the double checking of the lights done by the photographer is intuitive and purely visual. But before taking the final photograph it becomes necessary for her to measure light in a systematic and precise way. This measuring takes place by using a special device called a **light-meter**, which provides the photographer with a precise, numerical value that represents different characteristics of the incident light at any point in the three-dimensional environment.

It is also necessary, as part of the light measuring process, to double check and adjust those light readings against other numerical values involved in the process of photographing the still life. Those other numerical values might include, for example, the speed and chromatic characteristics of the photographic film, the chromatic value of the filter placed on the lens of the camera, and the chromatic value of the reflected light. This constant back and forth double-checking is not only necessary to stay on the desired track but is also an integral part of the creative lighting process.

During the visual checking done by looking through the view-finder, the photographer's assistant notices that the surface of one of the fruits looks somewhat dull and slightly flat, and that is not the way fruit is supposed to be portrayed in this image. The photographer and her assistant determine that this might be because the skin of the fruit became too dry while in storage at the store. They also agree that the best way to fix this—short of getting a replacement fruit—would be to apply a thin coat of oil to the skin of the fruit. The surface characteristics of all objects can be easily determined and fine-tuned with most three-dimensional rendering software.

Once all the lights and surfaces have been fine-tuned it is time to make slight adjustments to the placement and focusing of the camera. The photographer decides to replace the lens of the camera with another one that provides a wider field of vision. This way a larger portion of the scene will fit in the final image without the need to move the camera further away (Figs. 6.4.1–2). Finally, the scene is ready to be recorded. Three-dimensional rendering software provides tools for simulating lenses of different focal lengths as well as the effects, such as depth of field, associated with them.

5.2 Color

This section covers some of the most popular color models used in three-dimensional computer rendering. See Chapter 13 for more information on color resolution and color look-up tables.

Additive and Subtractive Systems

Those of us who learned about color theory when we were infants were given three jars with red, blue, and yellow paint, and told that we had to create other colors by mixing the paint from the three jars. We were told that the three primary colors are red, blue, and yellow (RBY). But that was only part of the story. Those three colors are indeed primary colors but only in a **pigment-based** color environment. The RBY **subtractive** color system is useful for understanding color relationships in a paper-and-paint environment.

Cyan, Magenta, Yellow, and Black

Another model that is used to explain and define colors that are pigment-based is the **Cyan**, **Magenta**, **Yellow**, and **Black**

(CMYK) color model. This model is widely used in the traditional graphic arts and digital printing.

Red, Green, and Blue

The colors displayed on a computer screen, however, occur in a **light-based** color environment. These colors are created by combining different amounts of the three primary colors in the **additive** color system: **Red, Green,** and **Blue (RGB)**. In the RGB model colors are defined in terms of their amounts of red, green, and blue. Combining—or adding—all the primary colors in the RGB system yields white, therefore the name additive system. Combinations of two primary RGB colors yield results that would not make sense in a pigment-based model. For example, the combination of red and green lights in equal proportions yields yellow light.

The RGB color model takes advantage of the technology used in computer monitors. It is therefore a precise and efficient way of describing color, and is used in all computer systems. RGB colors can be described by specifying numerical values that may range, for example, from 0 to 1, or from 0 to 255. The value of pure green is 0-255-0. The value of a greenish light blue could be 150-200-255, and a yellowish dark orange 120-80-30 (Fig. 7.2.2).

Hue, Saturation, and Lightness

Working with the RGB model can be confusing for many visual people. The **Hue, Saturation,** and **Lightness (HSL)** color model can be used as a more intuitive alternative for specifying color in a light-based environment. In the HSL model, colors are described in terms of their hue, saturation, and lightness. The HSL color model can be visualized as a three-dimensional space which simplifies the location and description of color. This space can be defined by two cones connected at their base. The vertical axis that runs between the two peaks is used to define the **lightness**, or darkness, of a particular color. The lightness of a color increases or decreases along the direction of this axis, with the lighter colors located at the top of this space, and the darker ones at the bottom. The **saturation** of a color increases along a line that starts perpendicular to the vertical axis of the space, and that ends at the outside surface. The colors on the outside surface are fully saturated while the colors close to the center of the space are washed out. The **hue** of colors in the HSL color space changes with the angular position of the color around the vertical axis. All the spectrum of hues can be found around the vertical axis, and their position can be specified in degrees.

Slicing the HSL space horizontally reveals many hues and

saturation values with the same lightness value. The grey colors—neutral and "colorless"—are found on the vertical axis. Absolute white and absolute black can be found in the peaks of the HSL space.

A popular variation of the HSL color model is the **Hue, Saturation,** and **Brightness (HSB)** color model. The main difference between the HSL and the HSB models is that the latter uses two cylinders—instead of two cones—for defining the chromatic space. A graphical representation of the HSB color space is shown in Fig. 7.2.3.

Color Conversions

When creating images with computers, it is often necessary to convert from one color space to another. This is mostly due to the fact that the creative process usually takes place in both light-based and pigment-based color environments. When we scan photographs or drawings we deal with pigment-based color. When we manipulate existing images or create new images on the screen we deal with light-based color. When we create a printout on paper of one of our images we deal, again, with pigment-based color.

In most cases this color conversion is done automatically by the computer software that we use. Obviously, the quality of these color conversions varies from program to program. If we are pleased with the color output of our computer system in general, we do not have to get involved in the color conversion process. If we are not satisfied with the automatic or default color conversion, however, it is important to get involved in the color balancing and correction, or enlist the help of a color experienced user.

Color Ranges

In the early 1930s the International Commission on Color (CIE is *Commission Internationale de l'Eclairage* in French) presented a color space that defined all the colors in the spectrum that are visible by the human eye. The **CIE color space** is a useful aid for understanding which colors we can see—for example, ultraviolet and infrared color frequencies are beyond the range of visible color (Fig. 5.2.1). The CIE color space is also very useful for visualizing the **chromatic ranges** of different media. It turns out that not all media and techniques we use for creating color are capable of creating exactly the same colors. This explains why so often the colors we see on the screen are different from the colors we see on the printout. Knowing which color ranges do not overlap between a variety of media and formats is helpful in devising solutions to work around this physi-

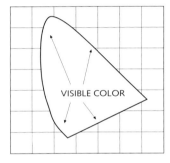

5.2.1 This simple diagram of the CIE color space defines all the colors in the electromagnetic spectrum. Those visible to the human eye are inside the inverted D-like shape, those beyond the range of visible color—like ultraviolet and infrared color frequencies—are outside of the shape.

cal limitations of color reproduction.

A common problem that one encounters when creating computer images for output on videotape is that the colors created with RGB computer monitors are too bright and saturated for display on standard television sets. Those working in RGB for eventual output to video have to clip the RGB colors that are outside the video color range in order to avoid distortions, such as color bleeding, from showing in the final video recording.

5.3 Steps in the Rendering Process

The rendering process consists of five major steps regardless of the computer system used. It is not required that these steps happen in a rigid order. In fact, some projects might require that the sequence of steps is slightly altered. Because of the complex and cumulative nature of the rendering process there is usually considerable bouncing back and forth between stages before the process is completed. But keep in mind that the implementation of general techniques in different programs might require slight variations in the sequence of steps described here. Figure 5.3.1 summarizes the main steps in the rendering process in the form of a flowchart. Each of the steps in the rendering process is covered in detail throughout Section III of this book.

The first step in the rendering process consists of getting the models to be rendered straight from the modeling module of the program or from some kind of peripheral storage like a hard disk.

Secondly, we maneuver the camera in XYZ space so that we look at the portion of the environment that we are interested in. We might reposition the camera, tilt it, change the focal point and the depth of field, and adjust the proportions and the resolution of the image. If necessary, we may further rearrange the objects in the scene.

Third, we design and implement the lighting scheme. This can be done by drawing and specifying the arrangement of the lights and their characteristics on paper or by visualizing it in one's head. We might define and place several light sources in the three-dimensional space of the computer software.

In fourth place we specify many characteristics of the surfaces of the objects including color, texture, shininess, reflectivity, and transparency. Specifying surface characteristics often requires a fair amount of attention to detail. Doing a good job during this stage will have a great impact on the quality, refinement, and energy of the final rendering result.

Finally, the fifth step consists of choosing a shading method and generating the final rendered image. Specifying the surface characteristics and choosing the shading techniques are two distinct steps but they are intrinsically related to one another and often overlap with each other.

5.4 Rendering Methods

There is a large variety of rendering methods that can be used to turn a wireframe view of a three-dimensional model into a shaded image. In addition to the skilled placement of light sources in a scene and the assignment of surface characteristics to objects, the final shaded image is largely dependent on the type of rendering method used. It is important to keep in mind that the users of rendering systems—especially turn-key systems—are dependent on the capabilities of the rendering method, or algorithm, used. This is partly because most rendering methods are usually supplied as "black boxes" that only accept geometry data and rendering variables—such as lighting, shading and surface characteristics—but cannot be modified by the user. Some rendering programs provide extensive technical notes explaining how they work, and such notes can provide useful insights about the ways in which the program renders. This information can prove invaluable when setting up a scene to be rendered. But in most cases it takes a fair amount of practice to get a feel for or to understand how a specific program renders. Knowing the strengths and weaknesses of a rendering program can be very advantageous for many stages of the three-dimensional creative process with computers, ranging from the sketching and storyboarding stage all the way through final output and recording.

Hidden Surface Removal

The hidden lines and surfaces of the object that are not visible from the point of view of the camera must be removed before the three-dimensional wireframe models can be rendered. Several algorithms have been developed to sort all the points, lines and surfaces of an object, and decide which of them are visible and which are not. Then, the **visible surfaces** are kept and the **hidden surfaces** are removed (Fig. 5.4.1). As explained in Chapter 8, the removal of hidden surfaces is determined by the relationship between the orientation of their surface normals, and the position and orientation of the camera. There are many methods for hidden surface removal, and they can can be separated into the general categories of object space and image space. A few hybrid rendering methods operate in both object and image spaces.

 Object space methods for hidden surface removal make the calculations in three dimensions. These algorithms require intensive computing but are unique because they generate data that can be used to improve the rendering of textures, shadows, and antialiasing. Ray tracing is an example of object space rendering methods, and it is the standard rendering method of many of today's rendering programs. Ray tracing follows the rays of

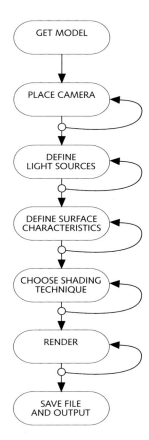

5.3.1 The steps of the rendering process.

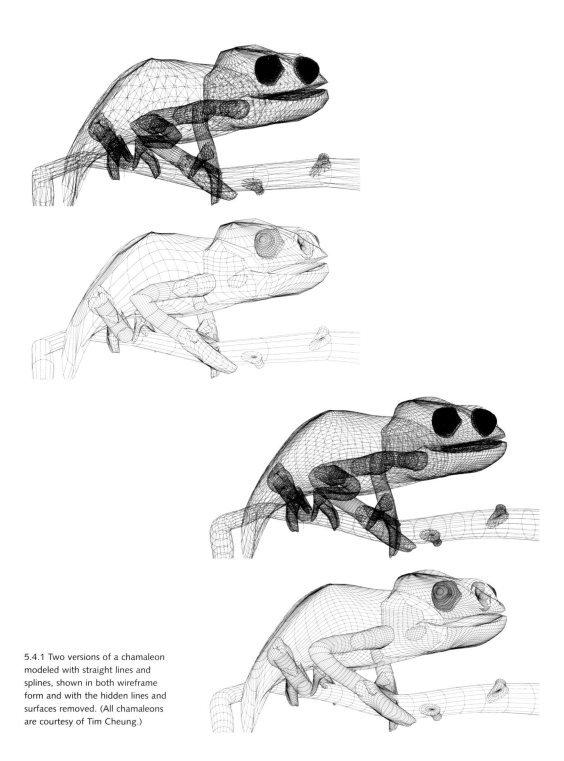

5.4.1 Two versions of a chamaleon
modeled with straight lines and
splines, shown in both wireframe
form and with the hidden lines and
surfaces removed. (All chamaleons
are courtesy of Tim Cheung.)

light—emitted by the light sources in the scene—as they bounce off or travel through objects, and eventually reach the camera.

Image space methods for hidden surface removal retain the depth information of the objects in the scene, but sort from a lateral position, and only to the resolution of the display device. Image space rendering methods render a three-dimensional scene by projecting the models onto the two-dimensional image plane (Fig. 6.2.1). Image space algorithms are generally efficient but discard some of the original three-dimensional information that can be used for shadowing, texturing, and antialiasing enhancement. Many of the image space methods for the removal of hidden surfaces were first developed in the early 1970s, and include Warnock's **area subdivision** (1969), Watkins' **scan line** (1970), and Newell's **depth sort** (1972). (The latter is generally considered a hybrid image/object space algorithm.) Multiple improvements and refinements to each of the original image space rendering procedures have continued to be made by several authors. Very few of today's programs that use image space rendering methods identify the specific type of method they use. But in general, there are no significant differences in quality between images created with different image space rendering methods of equal sophistication. However, some of the limitations of image space rendering methods include the fact that some work only with polygonal meshes but do not work well—or not at all—on models created with parametric curved surfaces.

5.4.2 A shaded chamaleon.

Z-Buffer

The Z-Buffer rendering method is an example of an image space rendering technique, but it also incorporates some concepts used in object space rendering. **Z-Buffer** rendering gets its name from the fact that all objects in the scene are sorted by their Z position, or depth, in the scene. This depth information is kept in a buffer, and made available to the rendering process as the hidden surface removal calculations are performed.

The Z-Buffer rendering method makes the hidden surface removal one object and one pixel at a time. This method determines whether an object is visible from the point of view of the camera at each pixel, and one pixel at a time. If the object is visible then its depth information (or distance from the camera) is checked, and this determines whether the object is the closest one to the camera up to that point in the sorting process. If that is the case, the object is shaded at that pixel, and this visibility test is repeated for the same object at all pixels on the screen. When the visibility of one object is completed, another object is chosen, and the visibility process is performed at all pixels all over again (Fig. 5.4.2). It is easily determined whether a new object is closer to the camera than the object tested earlier by

5.4.3 The ray tracing process.

checking the depth information of the new object. If the new object is closest to the camera, then its shading values replace the previous shading values at that pixel. The Z-Buffer rendering is completed when the visibility of all objects in the scene has been tested in all the pixels.

Ray Tracing

Ray tracing is a rendering technique that is capable of creating photo-realistic images of three-dimensional scenes. Ray tracing is one of the most advanced and accurate methods of rendering, in part because it calculates every ray of light in the scene by following them through the scene until they each reach the camera. Ray tracing creates images with very accurate reflections and refractions of light as well as detailed textures and shadows.

In general terms, **ray tracing** works by creating a ray for each pixel on the screen and tracing its path—one ray at a time—all the way back to the light source. A ray is an imaginary straight line that travels through three-dimensional space and collects rendering information. The values for the ray of light are calculated as it bounces off—or travels through—different surfaces in the scene with a variety of characteristics (Fig. 5.4.3). Ray tracing rendering techniques are based on the way in which rays of light in reality travel from the light sources to our eyes, bouncing off surfaces that affect their characteristics along the way. However, it would be impractical to trace all the rays of light emitted by a light source in a scene because many of them never reach the camera. It is for that reason that ray tracing programs trace the rays of lights **backwards**, from the camera to the light source, in order to minimize the amount of wasted calculations.

The main strength of the ray tracing rendering method comes from the fact that the image of a three-dimensional scene is calculated in three-dimensional space. The traced rays travel in three-dimensional space and often bounce from object to object. These rays are able to deal with processes—such as images being reflected on a surface, or the light being bent by a transparent object—that can best be simulated in a three-dimensional space. Unlike image space rendering methods, ray tracing is precise about simulating the behavior of light in three-dimensional space.

The primary controls in a ray tracing rendering are related to the depth of the ray tracing, the number of pixels in the image, and the number of light sources in the scene. The **ray tracing depth** is related to the number of times that a ray will be allowed to come in contact with surfaces in the three-dimensional space. Most subtle details in a ray-traced image are controlled by the depth of the ray tracing. Most ray tracing programs use different controls for the reflection rays, the transparency or refraction rays, and the shadow rays. Each of these types of rays calculate different components of the rendering of a three-dimensional scene. The depth of these three different types of rays is independent from one another. Figure 5.4.4 shows versions of a ray-traced image based on different combinations of tracing depth. The first image contains no reflections and the transparent surfaces are not rendered as such. The second image contains a fair amount of reflections on the reflective surfaces, and refraction in the transparent surfaces, but no shadows. The third images contain shadows, plus an increased amount of reflection and refraction. It is important to keep in mind that when using the ray tracing rendering method, a surface that is made very reflective becomes like a mirror and, as a consequence, looses many of its other surface characteristics.

Reflection rays travel through the scene in a straight way, and they bounce off the reflective surfaces they hit at the same angle at which they hit them. Once a point in three-dimensional space has been hit by a ray and the value of that surface has been calculated, then a **shadow ray** is shot from that point to the center of each light source in the scene. That point in three-dimensional space will only be visible if the shadow ray does not encounter another object before reaching the light source. In cases when the ray tracing process encounters transparent surfaces in the scene then **refraction rays** are generated, to calculate the amount of light refraction. In most ray tracing programs refraction is only enabled when the surface that is supposed to be refractive has a **thickness** defined by the distance between

5.4.4 These three versions of the same ray-traced image are based on different combinations of ray trace depth. The depth values of reflection, refraction and shadows are in the first image 1-0-0, in the second image 3-1-0, and in the third image 5-3-1.

Reflected Light =
Incident Light x
Surface Reflectivity

5.4.5 *Blue Glass* was produced by ray tracing a blue sphere and a grey sphere inside a hollow black sphere. A single point light source and the camera position are also inside the hollow sphere. The recursion depth is 14. The blue glass-like structures across the middle of the image are multiple reflections of the blue sphere as seen on the inside surface of the hollow sphere. Multiple reflections of the gray sphere appear above and below the reflections of the blue sphere. (Courtesy of Kevin Suffern, School of Computing Sciences, University of Technology, Sydney, Australia.)

the front face and the back face of the surface (Fig. 5.4.5).

The number of rays traced in a scene—regardless of their tracing depth—is related to the spatial resolution of a scene, which is determined by the total **number of pixels** in an image. A single ray is traced backwards to a light source through every pixel in the image. Therefore, an increase in the number of pixels will result in an increase in the number of rays traced, and also in the length of time that will be required to complete the rendering of an image.

The **number of light sources** in a scene also influences the number of rays that are traced through the scene and, consequently, the length of the ray tracing rendering calculation. This is due to the fact that ray tracing works by tracing backwards each ray of light that reaches the camera.

Due to the intense computations required by the ray tracing rendering methods many software programs provide simple ways to preview just a portion of the three-dimensional scene in the ray tracing mode (Fig. 5.4.6). Some programs also estimate the length of time that will be required to complete a rendering, and let the user know so that other tasks can be pursued in the meantime.

In most cases the color of the light that is reflected by a surface is calculated as the combination of red, green, and blue light. The color of the reflected light is based on the color of the surface, the color of the incident light that reaches the surface, and also on the reflectivity of the surface for each of the red, green, and blue components of light.

Radiosity

The rendering technique of radiosity provides an unparalleled way to calculate **diffuse interreflection** between surfaces. **Radiosity** rendering methods are based on the principles of illumination engineering theory and also on the principles of energy transfer. Radiosity rendering starts by dividing the environment into areas or clusters of polygons according to the way in which light affects them. Polygons in a radiosity calculation are typically catalogued into light sources, light-receiving surfaces, and light-blocking surfaces. By using iteration techniques, radiosity rendering calculates the amount of light that is transferred from one surface to another. This iteration or repetition is continued until the light energy is fully absorbed by the surfaces and/or it dissipates in space.

There are multiple variations of radiosity rendering, but in general the subdivision of the three-dimensional space is based on the amount of light that is emitted or transferred between surfaces. The cataloguing of surfaces that is necessary to perform radiosity calculations generates a data structures that look like **subdivision grids** when displayed on the screen (Fig. 5.4.7).

These data structures typically require large amounts of main memory (RAM), and of raw computing. Once a grid of subdivisions has been established then the energy that is emitted by each light source can be followed throughout the environment based on the geometry of the surfaces. The distance between surfaces and their angular position are two important factors used in establishing the amount of light energy that can be transferred. Before light dissipates in space, much of it bounces off between surfaces if they are parallel to each other. But less energy is transferred if the surfaces are perpendicular, and none is transferred if they face away from each other. Likewise, more energy is transferred between surfaces if they are close to one another than if they are further apart from each other (Fig. 5.4.8).

5.5 Getting Ready

Rendering can be a complex process because of the large number of factors that play a role in it. That is not to say that rendering is necessarily complicated. Most of the individual steps in the rendering process are actually simple. But when the steps are all taken into account and added up, then the result requires a thorough understanding of the process and some basic managing skills to keep track of all the subtleties and implications buried in our choices of tools and techniques. The recommendations presented here are meant to make the rendering process as successful and effective as possible.

Take Notes (and Don't Throw Them Away)

Even the simplest of three-dimensional scenes contains a large number of variables that define how the rendered objects will look when the rendering is calculated by the computer. It is always useful to write all or some of these numbers down in a notebook or a production log. It is also, of course, very important not to misplace this notebook and to have it handy at all times during the rendering process. Writing all the rendering information on a small piece of paper is not good practice, since we all tend to lose small pieces of paper.

   Sometimes while a scene is being rendered by the computer we want to review the information we fed into the program. In some cases, depending on the computer system we are using, it is possible to get this information even while the program is rendering. Obviously, in those situations it is not paramount to have a notebook at hand. But the book really comes in handy when our computer system cannot be interrupted for us to browse through the information we need while the program renders. It could be important to have a book in cases when our access to the computer is impaired by one of many reasons beyond our

5.4.6 The small square area in this image is previewed in the ray tracing mode while the rest of the image was rendered with faster and less accurate techniques.

5.4.7 In this radiosity rendering the three-dimensional space is subdivided with an overlaid mesh that simplifies the calculations into a sequence of small clusters of source, receiver and blocker polygons. (From "Partitioning and Ordering Large Radiosity Computations," by Seth Teller, C. Fowler, T. Funkhouser, and P. Hanrahan. University of Berkley Walk-Through Group, and Princeton University Computer Graphics Lab. Courtesy of Seth Teller.)

control: the system is being backed up and cannot be accessed, we might be travelling and the batteries of our portable computer suddenly lose charge, we are at our client's location and their telnet connection to our computer system just went down, or we are at the beach for the weekend, thinking about our project with just a bathing suit and a towel at hand.

Rendering Is Related to Modeling

As explained throughout Section II of this book, many of the decisions that one makes during the modeling process have a direct impact on the performance of the rendering software. In general, and under the same rendering conditions, models that were built properly render quicker than models that were built clumsily. In cases when we were in charge of building the models, it can be easy to diagnose the cause of rendering problems that might have their origin in inadequate modeling decisions.

But as you probably know by now, in some cases, due to production deadlines or lack of skills, we might not have modeled the objects that we are in charge of rendering. In those cases it is imperative that we find out what techniques were used to build the models, whether they were used properly or not, and whether the rendering requirements were taken into account during the modeling process.

Some modeling situations that can be the source of rendering headaches—this may vary from software to software—include: intersecting polygons, concave polygons, open polygons, surfaces with holes that have not been built properly, surfaces that are supposed to be aligned with each other but have small cracks between them, models with more control vertices or polygons than the rendering software can handle, models that were exported between modelers where some original modeling attributes got lost or altered during the translation process, and objects containing other objects that were not supposed to be there. Sometimes one can work around these modeling deficiencies by modifying the rendering variables or by switching to another rendering technique. But it is not uncommon to have to return to the modeling stage, fix the modeling problems, and then return to the rendering stage with a proper model file.

5.4.8 Lighting simulation of the main lobby of the Eli Lilly Library in Indiana University at Bloomington. The geometry was created with AutoCad Release 12 for the IBM RISC 6000. The rendered image was created with Greg Ward's Radiance version 2.2b, developed by the Lighting Group at Lawrence Berkeley Laboratory with the U.S. Department of Energy and the Laboratoire d'Energie Solaire et de Physique du Batiment at the Ecole Polytechnique Federale de Lausanne in Switzerland. (Courtesy of Reuben Mcfarland and Scott Routen, Artifex, Bloomington, IN.)

Rendering Is Related to Animation

There is a big difference between rendering just one view of a three-dimensional scene, and rendering hundreds of frames of that scene that are to be part of an animated sequence or an interactive walk-through. In general, when using the identical rendering technique—and regardless of the computer system that one is using—rendering just one view takes a lot less time than rendering many views of the same scene. This means that often we can overindulge in rendering sophistication when we are working on just one scene. We can set complex lighting arrangements, multiple texture layers and many levels of raytracing. If it does not look good we can try it again, twice, five or ten times until we get it right. But when we work on dozens or hundreds of frames we have to be realistic and choose rendering settings that can be completed by our system within our deadline or within a reasonable period of time. When choosing the rendering specifications for an animation, be cautious and consider the capabilities and rendering speed of your equipment. Test how long it takes to render one frame and multiply it by the number of frames that need to be rendered. Make sure that the frame you choose is representative of the rendering complexity in the animated sequence. It is common for the rendering specifications to vary throughout a sequence, for example, lights could be added or complex models could enter halfway through the scene.

Consider the Limitations of Your Computer System

It is extremely rare to work in an environment where hardware resources are not an issue. No matter how powerful our computers may be it is always possible to overwhelm them by submitting them to a taxing rendering. It is sensible to work within rendering specifications that are based on your system's capabilities. Unless you have an unlimited supply of funds to upgrade your computer system on a weekly basis it makes sense to work and be creative within your system's limitations.

Rendering Is Related to Output

Unlike finished three-dimensional models that can be changed without having to build them from scratch even after we thought them finished, finished renderings that we want changed have to be re-rendered all over again. Renderings are always created at a specific output resolution.

Before completing a rendering—especially one that is expected to require a lot of computer processing—it is wise to consider all the output options and choose the most appropriate one. Output issues, as explained in Chapter 13, almost always have to do with issues of color, spatial, and format resolution of the rendered image or rendered sequence. For example, ask yourself questions like: is it just one image that needs rendering, is it one hundred or one thousand? Will it be viewed on an RGB monitor or a television screen or will it be projected in a theater with a film projector? Read Chapter 13 for more information on output issues.

Check the Preferences Files

If you work at home or if you have a dedicated computer at work then you might be the only person using your rendering program or your entire computer system. In that case you probably know what is contained in both the System's Preferences File and the Rendering Preferences File. The settings contained in both files control many fundamental aspects of the rendering process. As shown in Fig. 5.5.1 the Rendering Preferences File may be altered in ways that absolutely cancel certain operations that you might have specified within other parts of the program.

Save Your Work Often

Save your work often, every fifteen minutes or so, and to make constant backups of your important data files.

Make Rendering Tests

One of the advantages of using a computer for rendering three-dimensional models is that we can preview our work as we develop it. This ability to preview is very useful throughout the rendering process, especially when the final rendering is a complex one. Making rendering tests at low resolutions or with simple shading techniques provides a good way to check as we go along that all of the basic rendering specifications, color for example, are being applied as we want. As we start applying more demanding rendering variables, like texture, it is useful to test again with a better shading model or higher color and spatial resolution. Finally, after we have specified in all objects the complex rendering attributes, such as refraction or motion blurr, then it might be time to make the last rendering test to visually check everything before the final rendering is produced. Remember that making rendering tests before the final rendering will save you a lot of work later trying to fixing mistakes that could have been avoided (and that might require a lot of com-

5.5.1 These dialog boxes illustrate the importance of checking the global preferences of the rendering program before starting the rendering of a model. (a. Dialog box from Softimage 3D. © Microsoft Corporation. All rights reserved; b and c. Dialog boxes from Infini-D 3.0. © 1991-1995 Specular International, Ltd.)

puter processing time to fix).

There are other strategies for testing the rendering specifications that, unlike previewing at low resolutions or with simple shading techniques, allow us to preview the scene or part of the scene in full detail. One strategy, which is supported by several programs, consists of selecting only some objects to be rendered. We might opt not to render some of the three-dimensional objects in the scene whose surface is too complex. Another strategy consists of turning off some light sources that are only of secondary or tertiary importance. Usually the number of light sources in a scene is proportional to the time that it takes the computer to render the scene. Finally, a third strategy, which is supported by many rendering programs that use raytracing rendering techniques, consists of rendering just one small area of the scene but with all objects, lights, and shading attributes turned on.

One of the best ways to understand both the potential and the limitations of a rendering program is by actually using the program. Additional insight can also be gained by reading the technical notes—when available—that explain how a specific rendering program works. But the best way to learn and really know how the rendering tools behave is by using them. Making rendering tests and comparing the results of different rendering tests while paying attention to the different variables that were used in each case is a good way to get a feel for what the numbers—or numerical values assigned to rendering variables—mean.

Learn the Strengths of Your Software and Use Them

After you read the three chapters in this section on Rendering (or even if you decide just to look at the illustrations) it will be obvious that every software for rendering has a unique approach to different aspects of rendering. In some cases the differences are as obvious as different names given to the same tool or different ways of presenting the information in the dialog boxes that we use for specifying values. But often the differences between rendering software are very significant, and it is often those important differences that are poorly explained in the manuals or not documented at all. In many cases it is up to you, the user, to find out some of the wonderful things that your software—and not the other programs—can do best. Explore this and take advantage of it.

Optimize Your Renderings

A professional artist of three-dimensional computer rendering and animation can be defined not only by the beauty and communication power of his or her images, but also by how often he or she completes projects within the deadline. Optimizing the rendering time of an image is directly related to completing projects within deadlines, and this is done by choosing techniques in a way that creates the results desired but in an efficient way.

Opportunities for optimizing the rendering can be found throughout the stages of modeling and rendering stages. Try keeping down the number of polygons or the geometric resolution of patches in a three-dimensional model. Try using texture mapping techniques when possible for simulating transparency, reflectivity, and roughness of a surface instead of ray tracing techniques especially in a complex scene. when ray tracing is a must, try to keep the ray tracing depth value down.

As mentioned in Chapter 7, use only the amount of light that is really necessary to create the desired mood. This principle should be kept in mind throughout the entire creative process, not only the final rendering but also the rendering tests created throughout. Making rendering tests before the final rendering is submitted to the computer is essential in avoiding rendering settings that might be wasteful. Try rendering critical portions of the scene before rending the entire scene. Consult Chapters 12 and 13 to learn about further optimizing possibilities by using two-dimensional techniques, and by previewing the final image in the final delivery medium and not only on the RGB monitor.

5.6 File Formats for Rendering

All three-dimensional rendering programs can save and retrieve rendered images—also called **picture files**—in their own native file format. Some rendering programs also have the capability of saving rendered image files in one or more standard file formats. This capability enhances the software's ability to share the image files with other application programs or across computer platforms. For that very reason we shall focus here briefly only on the file formats that can be used to exchange image files with other programs or with other computers. (Read Chapter 13 for additional information on image file formats.) Consult your software's manual for information about its own native rendering file format.

Image or picture files are not to be confused with model files. Image files contain only two-dimensional information and can only be manipulated in three-dimensional space by being mapped onto an object. In addition to their own native file formats, the majority of rendering programs offer one or all of the most popular picture file formats including: PICT, TGA, TIFF, EPS, and PICS, JPEG, and Quicktime. Each of these file formats has been designed with a specific goal in mind and, therefore, each is better suited for a particular task (Fig. 13.3.1). It is also possible to translate files from one format to another. Sometimes this can be accomplished within rendering programs that have internal picture file conversion capabilities. But especially when large amounts of picture file conversion are needed, it is common to use a specialized file conversion program like Adobe Photoshop, or one of several standalone utility conversion programs provided with the rendering software.

Generally speaking, in an everyday production environment and when translators for exotic file formats are not available or do not work, the following standard formats would be good choices. For example, the PICT format for file portability, the TIFF format for best halftone detail quality, the EPS format for high quality line drawings of wireframe renderings, and the Quicktime format for animated sequences in compressed form. In theory—and most of the time in practice too—these file formats are portable both across platforms and operating systems (Fig. 5.6.1).

The **PICT** file format is a very versatile format also popular with many drawing and photo-retouching programs. It saves data in a compact and efficient way, and is compatible accross computer platforms.

The **TGA** file format is very popular with video-oriented software and is very efficient and quite convenient for transferring files into the video environment. TGA is short for TARGA, the name of a family of graphics boards developed in the early 1980s that pioneered video input and output with microcomputers.

The **TIFF** file format (from Tagged Image File Format) is popular with prepress and publishing software and useful when the rendered image will be reproduced in a publication. The TIFF format preserves detailed grayscale information that can be very useful for generating the high-quality halftones (grids of dots of varying size) commonly required in publications. TIFF files tend to be large in size so many applications usually provide options or utilities for compressing and uncompressing them.

The **EPS** file format, or Encapsulated PostScript, is popular in prepress applications, and can be quite useful and effective when high-quality line wireframe drawings are needed. EPS files usually require significant amounts of memory for storage and transfer.

The **PICS** file format derives its name from the word "pictures," and is convenient when a series of images is required for animation purposes. A PICS file consists of several PICT files stored together.

The **Quicktime** and **JPEG** file formats are useful for saving both still images and animated sequences in a variety of levels of image compression and quality.

5.6.1 Two rings rendered with a procedurally-based environment map represent the union of art and technology. This image was saved in the Alias image file format on a Silicon Graphics computer running the UNIX operating system. It was then converted to the TGA format and transferred via an Ethernet network to a PC-compatible computer running the DOS operating system. It was then saved on a diskette and loaded into the Adobe Photoshop program running on an Apple Macintosh computer connected to a Matrix digital film recorder. You would never know that the file was transferred from format to format and from system to system just by looking at it!

Review and Practice

____ Efficient modeling

____ PICT

____ Hardware

____ QuickTime

____ Adobe Photoshop

____ Preference File

____ TIFF
____ Raytracing
____ EPS

a. Provides a range of levels of image compression and quality.
b. Its contents control many fundamental aspects of the rendering process.
c. File format useful for transferring rendered images to a prepress or desktop publishing software.
d. Rendering technique that is capable of rendering just one section of the scene for previewing purposes.
e. Useful file format when high-quality line drawings of wireframe renderings are needed.
f. It's speed often determines the speed of the rendering process.
g. Usually streamlines the rendering process.
h. Software often used for file format conversion.
i. One of the most versatile and popular file formats.

Answers Matching: a. QuickTime, b. Preference File, c. TIFF, d. Raytracing, e. EPS, f. Hardware, g. Efficient modeling, h. Adobe Photoshop, i. PICT.

True/False

___ a.   Native file formats are easily interchangeable between different rendering programs.

___ b.   Intersecting polygons may be the source of rendering problems.

___ c.   The QuickTime file format should never be used for animations created with raytracing rendering techniques.

___ d.   Rendering issues rarely affect the animation process.

___ e.   A file saved in the Encapsulated PostScript format is usually smaller than the same file saved in other file formats.

___ f.   Most rendering programs allow us to replicate many of the tasks typical of traditional photographer.

___ g.   Saturation in the HLS color system is represented by the vertical axis.

___ h.   Rendering tests are useful for previewing our work and one can avoid a lot of wasted time later in the rendering process.

___ i.   The rendering process is concerned with specifying lights and materials much more than placing the camera.

___ j.   Most of the rendering software is capable of saving rendered images in the form of picture files.

Answers True/False: a. False, b. True, c. False, d. False, e. False, f. True, g. False, h. True, i. False, j. True.

Key Terms

Additive
Area subdivision
Backwards
Black
Blue
Brightness
Chromatic ranges
CIE color space
CMYK
Cyan
Depth sort
Diffuse interreflection
EPS
Green
Hidden surfaces
HSB
HSL
Hue
JPEG
Image space
Light-based
Light-meter
Lightness
Magenta
Models
Number of light sources

Number of pixels
Object space
PICS
PICT
Picture files
Pigment-based
Quicktime
Radiosity
Ray tracing
Ray tracing depth
Red
Reflection rays
Refraction rays
Rendering process
RGB
Saturation
Scan line
Shaders
Shadow ray
Subdivision grids
Subtractive
TGA
Thickness
TIFF
Virtual studio
Visible surfaces
Yellow
Z-buffer

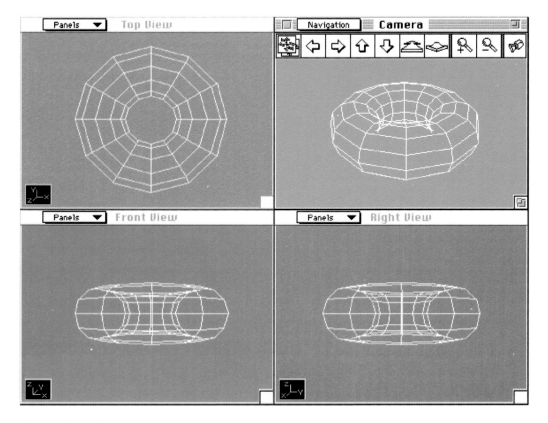

6.1.1 Most three-dimensional programs can display multiple projections of the camera view. Shown here are the perspective projection, and the top, front, and side orthographic projections. (Courtesy of Infini-D 3.0. © 1991-1995 Specular International, Ltd.)

The Camera

Summary

This chapter covers the techniques for setting the camera within a three-dimensional scene, and for controlling and adjusting all of its parameters. The most popular types of camera shots and lenses are also examined in this chapter.

6.1 Types of Cameras

When working in a real three-dimensional environment, the camera allows us to select and record portions of it. Without a simulated camera, however, an imaginary computer-generated world cannot be seen or shown, let alone recorded. Cameras are a small but essential detail in the rendering process. And while most of the steps in this process have to do with arranging and defining the objects in front of the camera, defining and positioning the camera itself marks the beginning of the rendering process.

In general, and for the sake of convenience, all three-dimensional rendering programs provide a **default or standard camera**. This camera is usually placed not to far from and aimed at the origin (or center) of the imaginary three-dimensional world. This camera is also usually equipped with an imaginary lens of medium focal length. The lens represents the scene in front of it using **perspective projection**, which projects all objects in the three-dimensional environment onto the image plane. This is done by projecting every point in space towards the camera until the projection intersects the image plane (Fig. 6.2.1). Other views of the default camera are commonly shown in the form of front, top, and side **orthographic projections** (Fig. 6.1.1).

The default camera can be modified or edited with mouse movements or through numerical input. Most three-dimensional rendering programs usually provide both methods. Figure 6.1.2

View Parameters

View Point:

Orientation	-60°	H	56'-5 13/16'
Altitude Ang	30°	Y	-97'-10'
Distance	130'-5 5/16'	Z	65'-2 11/16'

Clipping Planes: Center Of Interest:

Hither	12'-0'	H	0'-0'
Yon	166'-8'	Y	0'-0'
View Angle:	60°	Z	0'-0'

View Spin: 0°   [Cancel] [OK]

VIEW INFO

View Info for Camera

	Position	Orientation	Lens Type: Normal
H:	1.456	60.000	Focal Length: 50.000
Y:	-7.718	0.000	
Z:	5.220	30.000	[Cancel] [OK]

WINDOW OPTIONS

Window Options for Top View

Window Size: 640 x 480 - NTSC

Width: 640   Height: 480

Color Depth: Millions

Alpha Channel: None

☒ Dither Colors
☐ Display Background Image
☐ Force Visible Wireframes
☐ Show Invisible Objects

[Cancel] [OK]

Camera Settings

	X	Y	Z
Position	1.000	2.000	20.000
Interest	0.000	0.000	0.000
Roll	0.000		
Near plane	0.100		
Far plane	32768.0		☒ Hidden

Picture Format: Custom aspect   Ratio: 1.180

-------------- Lens --------------

Field of View 41.539

Depth of Field
◉ OFF
○ Custom

Near Focus	15.000	system units
Far Focus	25.000	system units
Max COC	20.0000	pixels
Max occurs at	40.000	system units

[Key]   [Cancel] [Ok]

6.1.2 The numerical values that define the position and characteristics of a camera can be edited through the use of dialog boxes like these. (a. Dialog box from form•Z. © 1991-1995 auto•des•sys, Inc.; b and c. Dialog box from Infini-D 3.0. © 1991-1995 Specular International, Ltd.; d. Dialog box from Softimage 3D. © Microsoft Corporation. All rights reserved.)

shows some dialog boxes for editing the numerical values that define a virtual camera.

Once the default camera has been customized it can be named just like any other object in the three-dimensional environment, and its parameters and position can be saved in a file independently from the geometry of the other objects in the world. This ability to save and retrieve the name of the camera and related information makes it possible to apply any **predefined position** with ease to the active camera in the scene. It is also possible to create other cameras in addition to the default camera, but when **multiple cameras** are present in three-dimensional space only one camera can be **active** at a time. An animated sequence or a collection of still images can be created with multiple cameras that become active one after the other as the camera moves around the scene.

In the wireframe display mode, cameras are usually represented with graphic icons that resemble cameras. When a scene with multiple cameras is rendered the secondary cameras placed in the field of vision can be seen, unless they are made **invisible**. In many programs, the cameras are visible by default, and when rendered they appear in the image as small three-dimensional objects that look like little cameras.

What a virtual camera sees in three-dimensional space is defined by the following parameters: type of shot, image aspect ratio, and type of lens. These characteristics can be set by typing numerical values on the keyboard, by clicking on the control buttons provided by some programs, or by directly manipulating the camera with a variety of input peripherals that include the mouse, graphics tablet, trackball, joystick, or dial box.

6.2 The Pyramid of Vision

The **pyramid of vision**, also called the **cone of vision,** can be defined as the portion of the three-dimensional environment that is seen through the camera. The pyramid of vision provides a simple way to understand some of the technical concepts involved in rendering. The pyramid of vision is defined by several parameters that are essential for controlling the position and characteristics of the camera. This numerical information includes: the point of view and the point of interest, the line of sight, the near and far clipping planes, the field of vision, the viewing angle, the focal length, and the depth of field (Fig. 6.2.1).

The pyramid of vision can be represented as a four-sided pyramid that grows out of the camera in the direction in which the camera is pointing. As mentioned earlier, the objects that are located inside of this pyramid can be viewed by the camera. These objects—or parts of objects—that happen to be outside of the pyramid of vision are not seen by the camera.

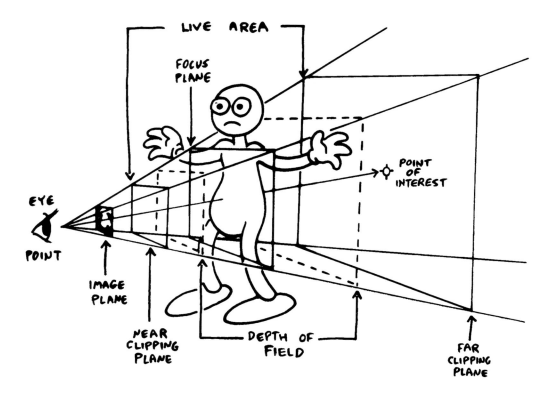

LIVE AREA
FOCUS PLANE
EYE POINT
POINT OF INTEREST
IMAGE PLANE
NEAR CLIPPING PLANE
DEPTH OF FIELD
FAR CLIPPING PLANE

6.2.1 The pyramid of vision.

Points of View and Interest

The **point of view (POV)**, or viewing point, is the location in the scene where the camera is placed. The **point of interest (POI)**, or center of interest, is the location in space where the camera is focused. The **line of sight** in the pyramid of vision is defined as a perpendicular line that travels away from the camera, from the point of view to the point of interest.

Clipping Planes

The clipping planes are perpendicular to the line of sight. The **far clipping plane**, also called the **yon plane**, defines the most distant area that can be seen by the camera. Think, for example, of a landscape with fog in the distance when we cannot see beyond the fog. In that case, the fog would be the far clipping plane in our field of vision (see Chapter 8 for more information on fog). The **near clipping plane**, also called the **hither plane**, represents the area closest to the camera that is visible to the camera. Think, for example, of your own eyelashes. Your eyes cannot see them because your eyelashes are placed before your own eye's near clipping plane and, therefore, outside your field of vision. The **viewing angle** defines the size relation between the near and the far clipping planes. The viewing angle also defines the width spread of the pyramid of vision, and consequently the focal length.

Field of Vision

The clipping planes truncate the pyramid of vision and define the **field of vision** or **image plane**. The objects contained in the pyramid of vision are projected onto the image plane to create the two-dimensional image of the three-dimensional environment. This projection process is quite similar to the way in which a real scene is projected by a photographic camera lens onto the film that is loaded inside of the camera. The relation between the width and the height of the image plane defines the **aspect ratio**, or proportion, of the image. **Media formats** such as film, video, or still photography each have their own characteristic aspect ratio. With the exception of a few square formats used in still photography—$2 \frac{1}{4}$ x $2 \frac{1}{4}$ in. for example—all computer-simulated cameras have a rectangular aspect ratio usually in a horizontal orientation, also called **landscape** style. **Field guides** are grids of concentric rectangles used to position the still elements and the action within the frame (Fig. 6.2.2). Some of the most common media formats and their aspect ratios are shown in Fig. 13.5.1.

Focal Length

The focal length of a camera controls the way in which three-dimensional objects are seen by the camera. The **focal length** in a virtual camera is defined by the relation between the near clipping plane and the far clipping plane. This relation defines the way in which the objects in a three-dimensional environment are projected onto the projection plane of a virtual camera—or the surface of the film in a real camera. The focal length in a photographic camera is determined by the curvature and shape of the lens. Standard camera lenses have a fixed focal length, except for zoom lenses that are capable of variable focal lengths by gradually changing, in real time, the distance between the near and the far clipping planes. Virtual camera lenses can have any focal length.

Depth of Field

The **focal plane** of a lens is the plane perpendicular to the camera that is resolved into a sharp image. Only one plane in three-dimensional space can be in perfect focus when seen through

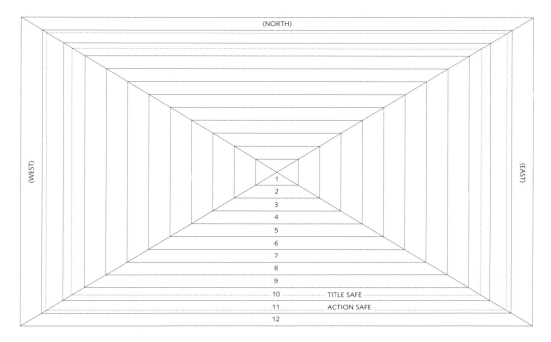

6.2.2 A field guide of 1:1.377 ratio (35 mm Academy format) consists of 12 concentric rectangles that help position the still elements and the action within the frame. The title safe and action safe areas for field 12 are shown with dotted lines.

any lens, but the areas that neighbor the focal plane are in focus. The **depth of field** is the portion of the scene in front of the camera that appears focused, and it is defined by the area between the near and the far focal planes.

6.3 Types of Camera Shots

Cameras, like other objects in three-dimensional space, can be placed in specific spatial locations in a variety of ways. The process of finding a position for a camera is called **interactive camera placement,** and sometimes **navigation** because we navigate through three-dimensional space looking through the camera. Stationary cameras that can be used to render still images can be placed with numerical input, interactive mouse movements, or predefined positions (dynamic cameras are described in Chapter 10). Navigation is essential for framing the objects, virtual actors, and scenery in an effective way. This process can take place during or before the rendering process in order to focus on specific areas of interest and tell the story more effectively.

When using the numerical input method cameras can be positioned and repositioned by specifying two absolute XYZ locations: camera position or point of view (POV), and camera point of interest. Cameras can also be positioned and repositioned using interactive mouse movements. This activates two of the basic geometric transformations: translation and rotation. All of the camera moves, even the most complex ones, can be expressed in terms of translations or rotations around one or several camera axes. But in some cases, the spherical or azimuthal coordinate system illustrated in Fig. 2.4.7 is used to specify the camera's position and orientation in terms of its angles around and above the horizon and its distance from the object. (See Chapter 2 for more information on geometric transformations.)

Navigating in some programs is often accomplished by clicking buttons and dragging tools that control the camera. Other programs offer a menu of complex camera motions that can be chosen and controlled by dragging the mouse. Another technique for focusing the camera in a specific orientation consists of choosing **predefined** points of interest. These are available from pull-down menus usually in the form of an absolute XYZ position, or absolute angle such as X=45° Y=30° Z=60°, or the name of an object in the scene, for example, point at the table.

There are several types of **stationary camera shots**. Each one has a specific name and an inherent **narrative and psychological effect**. Most of the stationary camera shots can be described in terms of their point of view, point of interest, the distance to the subject, and the type of lens used. (Animated camera moves are described in Chapter 10.) Both the point of view and the point of interest are used to define the traditional camera shots: point of view (POV), low angle, high angle, and reverse angle shot. The distance from the camera to the subject and the type of lens used defines the area of the scene that is captured by the camera. The camera shots based on the area of the scene that is framed within the image are illustrated in Fig. 6.3.1, and include: extreme close-up, close-up, medium close-up, waist, medium, knee, wide, long, medium long, and extreme long shots. Many software programs use the same names used in traditional cinematography to define camera shots, but some use a different nomenclature.

Point of View Shots

Point of view shots often place the camera at eye level looking straight into the action, because in many circumstances it is assumed that the active character is standing in front of the action. But generally speaking, a point of view shot cannot be pegged to an absolute spatial position, because by definition its location is always relative to where the active character happens to be. A **point of view shot** shows what the active character or narrator, or virtual cameraperson sees. This type of shot places the camera wherever the eyes of the active character happen to be and sets the orientation of the camera according to the direction in which the active character or narrator is looking.

Low Angle and High Angle Shots

In low angle and high angle shots, the camera is pointed at the action with a certain slant. The angle is usually defined in relation to the point of interest so that a **low angle shot** places the camera below the point of interest, looking up. Inversely, a **high angle shot** places the camera looking down at the point of interest, placed above it. The amount of slant in low and high angle shots is never implied and has to be defined explicitly in the form of an XYZ position or a specific angle measured in degrees. The range of low angle shots includes, for example, what a cameraperson would see if shooting lying down or in a kneeling position, or if shooting while standing up at street level and looking up at the action occurring on the roof of a house. High angle shots range from a cameraperson shooting over a crowd or perched on a ladder, to a camera mounted on a helicopter hovering over a crowd.

Reverse Angle Shots

Reverse angle shots are commonly used in conversations between two people where the sequence includes shots back and forth between the two faces. A **reverse angle shot** always happens as a response to a previous shot. A typical reverse angle shot sequence, for example, starts with the camera placed over the shoulder of character A so that character B speaks to the camera. The reverse angle shot is then placed over the shoulder of character B, and it shows character A responding to what character B said in the previous shot.

Close-Up Shots

A **close-up shot** places the camera at close range so that details in the subject can be appreciated. An **extreme close-up shot** is even closer to the subject than a close-up and presents delicate surface details such as the veins in the leaf of a plant or the pores and fuzzy hair of skin. A close-up shot usually fills the image with the subject in question and crops all other items in the picture, including the background (Fig. 4.4.3). A close-up of a face, for example, shows nuances of expression in all splendor. A close-up of a cut precious stone focuses on the delicate interplay of the facets and the refracted light. A **medium close-up shot** presents subjects close to the camera while leaving a generous amount of space between the subject and the edge of the frame to include a small portion of the background (Fig. 4.4.4). A medium close-up of the face of a character is often called a **head shot** because it focuses on the face, neck, and shoulders without being a close-up. Head shots typically focus on facial

Extreme close-up
Close-up
Medium close-up
Waist
Medium
Knee
Wide
Long
Medium long
Extreme long

6.3.1 Types of camera shots.

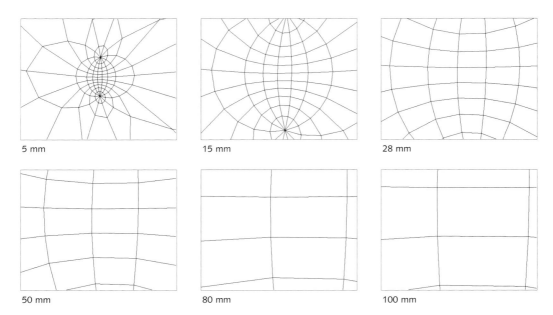

5 mm   15 mm   28 mm

50 mm   80 mm   100 mm

6.4.1 The focal length of a camera can be changed by modifying the distance between the point of view and the focal plane. The relation between the focal length of a lens is directly proportional to the magnification of the scene viewed through the lens. The inside of a sphere viewed through a normal lens with a focal length of 50 mm looks similar to the way we see reality with our vision. The same scene viewed through a wide angle lens with a focal length of 28 mm looks distorted and somewhat tense. This perspective projection is more extreme and all the diagonal lines are steeper. A 100 mm telephoto lens flattens the perspective due to its narrow viewing angle and the similarity between the areas of the near and far clipping plane.

expression and head movements (Fig. 11.3.3).

Medium and Wide Shots

A **waist shot** presents characters from the waist up. A waist shot focuses on the upper body language and gestures of the character, and includes a fair amount of the three-dimensional environment surrounding the character. Heads and faces are never cropped in a regular waist shot (Fig. 11.2.7). A **medium shot** frames characters from the hips up (Fig. 12.3.3). A **knee shot** crops the subjects at the knees, and is commonly used in shots of an encounter or conversation between two or three characters (Fig. 9.4.1). A **wide shot** presents enough of the scene to include the full bodies of five characters (Fig. 8.1.1).

Long Shots

A **long shot** focuses on the scenery and barely permits recognition of individual characters in the environment (Fig. 11.4.2). Wide and long shots are both used in animated sequences as establishing shots to introduce the place where a scene is supposed to be taking place. A **medium long shot** typically presents a landscape and focuses on features like the topography and the sky, the ambient lighting, the weather and the time of day. An **extreme long shot** presents environments seen from very far away, for example, the planet Earth seen from an orbiting spacecraft.

6.4 Types of Camera Lenses

Most three-dimensional rendering software provides an infinite range of camera lenses that can be used for practical and stylistic purposes. The **practical use** of switching camera lenses is to modify the size of objects in the image without having to move the camera. The **stylistic use** of employing different camera lenses is to create different moods in the scene by simulating different perspective projections. The emotional effect of a wide-angle lens, for example, is intense and can even be frightening because objects look distorted. The opposite emotion is aroused with a telephoto lens, one of tranquility and detachment because the objects in the scene are not distorted and most of the lines in the composition are horizontal and static.

Camera lenses, whether real or simulated, are perhaps the most important component in any camera system because they define the way in which the three-dimensional world is projected onto the **projection plane** of a camera. In photographic cameras, the photosensitive film is located exactly on the projection plane. The projection plane of computer-simulated rendering cameras can be positioned virtually anywhere in space.

Photographers refer to camera lenses in terms of their focal length because this characteristic controls the way in which three-dimensional objects are seen by the camera. Focal length, as explained earlier, is defined by the distance from the point of view to the focal plane. Most photographic camera lenses have a **fixed focal length**, except for the so-called zoom lenses that contain multiple lenses and are therefore capable of a range of **variable focal lengths**. Figure 6.4.1 illustrates the effect of changing the focal length of a virtual camera by increasing and decreasing the distance between the point of view to the focal plane. Lenses simulated with rendering software are not limited to the standard focal lengths of photographic lenses that are listed in Fig. 6.4.2.

The standard nomenclature for the focal length of lenses is expressed in millimeters (mm). There is a great variety of lenses, but the staple lenses used in traditional photography and cinematography include a normal 50 or 55 mm lens, a wide angle 28 mm lens, and a telephoto 135 mm lens. Each of the three standard lenses has characteristics that define the way images are projected onto the image plane and can be utilized for different situations. In general, lenses with a short focal length offer a wide angle of view and increased depth of field, but objects appear distant to the camera. Inversely, lenses with a long focal length have narrow angles of view and depth of field. The relation between the focal length of lenses and their angle of view is illustrated in Fig. 6.4.3.

The area of the scene that is framed within the image can

Type	Focal Length
Fisheye	7.5 mm
Extreme Wide Angle	18 mm
Wide Angle	28 mm
Medium Wide Angle	35 mm
Standard/Normal	50–55 mm
Medium Long	80 mm
Long/Telephoto	135–250 mm
Extra Long /Supertelephoto	500 mm or more

6.4.2 Types and focal lengths of the most popular lenses used in photography, cinematography, and video.

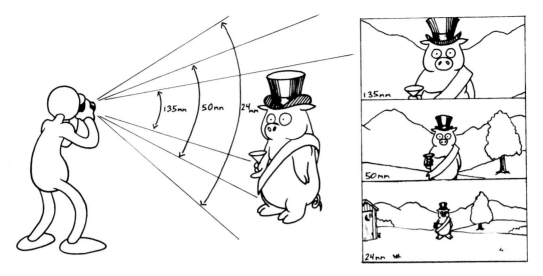

6.4.3 As the focal length of a fixed lens increases its angle of view decreases.

be defined by the type of lens used, by the distance between the camera and the subject, or by both. In the first case, when the type of lens is varied, it is assumed that the distance between camera and subject remains constant (Fig. 6.4.3). In the second case, when the distance between camera and point of interest is changed to include more or less of the image, it is assumed that the type of lens used remains constant. Only a small portion of the scene is contained in the frame when the camera is very close to the subject. As the camera is placed further away from the subject a larger area of the scene is contained in the frame (Fig. 6.4.4). When both the lens and the point of view are changed, the results are illustrated in Fig. 6.4.5. The subjects in the foreground of the image remain within a similar scale as long as the focal length decreases or increases along with the distance between the camera and the subject. The projection of the background elements, however, is significantly different.

Normal Lens

The **normal 50 or 55 mm lens** offers an adequate 46 degree angle of view with very little perspective distortion and with average depth of field. A 50 mm lens is useful for medium to wide shots.

Wide Angle Lens

A **wide angle 24 or 28 mm lens** supplies a generous 83 degree angle of view, outstanding depth of field, but also a small amount of distortion on the edges of the picture due to

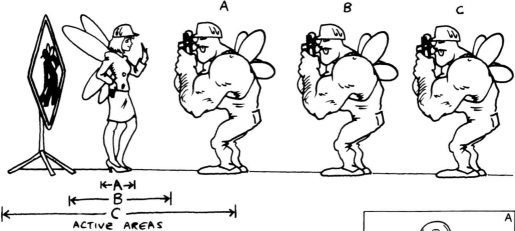

ACTIVE AREAS

the forced perspective projection typical of the wide angle of vision (Fig. 6.4.6).

Telephoto Lens

A **telephoto 135 mm lens** has excellent abilities for close framing. However, it flattens the perspective and has a narrow 5 degree angle of view and a small depth of field. On occasions the wide angle and telephoto lenses can be replaced or complemented with a zoom lens that allows for a variable focal length, for example, from 35 mm to 80 mm.

6.5 Camera Animation

The camera has a powerful storytelling effect because it leads the eyes and mind of an audience through a story. Animated camera moves can be based on both changes of position and orientation.

The **camera moves** that are based on a change of the **position** of the camera include a dolly, a truck, and a boom. A **dolly** is a translation of the camera along the horizontal axis. A tracking or **traveling shot** occurs when a dolly moves along with the subject and follows it. A **truck** move is a translation of the camera along the depth axis, and it usually goes in or out of the scene. A **boom** is a translation of the camera along its the vertical axis. A **crane shot** can be implemented with a combination of boom, truck, and sometimes dolly camera moves (Fig. 10.3.1).

The camera moves that are based on the change of the **orientation** of the camera include a tilt, a roll, and a pan. A **tilt** is a rotation of the camera on its horizontal axis. A tilt is also called a

6.4.4 Both the size of the image area and the depth of field increase when a camera moves away from a fixed subject.

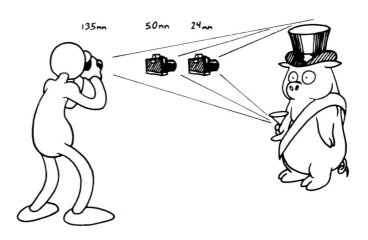

6.4.5 The pig in each of the three images is framed so that it occupies roughly the same amount of space in each image. But each view has been created with a different lens and distance between the camera and the rings. In the first example, a 24 mm wide angle lens is placed close to the pig. Due to the wide angle of view of the lens the shot is very panoramic and shows a large area of the scene. In the second example, a 50 mm standard lens includes less of the background in the three-dimensional environment, because its angle of view is narrower than the previous lens, but the pig occupies roughly the same amount of image area. In the third example, a 135 mm telephoto lens is placed far from the rings, but due to its long focus (or ability to concentrate on distant objects) the image retains as much of the pig as the previous lenses, but it includes little of the scenery.

pivot and is used to look up or look down. A **roll** is created by rotating the camera around its Z axis. Roll camera moves are common when simulating fly-throughs. A **pan** is a move created by rotating the camera around its vertical axis (Fig. 10.3.2). Panning is very effective for scanning the scene from side to side while the camera remains stationary. Sometimes, especially when simulating flying cameras, a tilt move is called a pitch—as in airplanes pitching—and a pan move is called a yaw. (A zoom is a camera move that is achieved not by moving the position or orientation of the camera but by animating its focal length.)

Read Chapter 10 for more information on camera moves based on changes of position and orientation, as well as camera animation based on zooming and motion paths.

6.6 Getting Ready

Set the Aspect Ratio Early

The aspect ratio of a virtual camera determines the relation between the width and the height of the final image. It is important to set the correct aspect ratio of the image early on in the creative process because many decisions like composition and lighting are closely tied to it. Changing the aspect ratio in the middle of a production may mean that all the placement of cameras, lights, and even objects in the scene may have to be done all over again.

Composition Tips

When composing still images it is useful to remember that the arrangement of elements within the image frame plays a fundamental role in expressing the emotion or telling the story behind the image. The following composition tips can be applied to any image, regardless of the subject. Whether a composition is simple or complex, there are some basic qualities and rules that contribute to **straightforward communication**. These include the clarity of foreground subjects, the number of image layers between the foreground and the background, the density of the background, the relation between the foreground and the background, the relation between the center of the image and the edges, and the relation between image zones and image proportions.

Keep the long straight lines in the composition parallel or perpendicular to the edges of the image to avoid unwanted tension and distraction. This includes, for example, the horizon or a tall tree in a landscape tilting to one side especially when the tree is close to an edge of the image.

It is usually distracting to cut off the head of a subject in a head shot or a portion of the object in a close-up shot. However, when done skillfully, cutting off portions of the main subject can help the viewer focus on details—such as the eyes or the mouth, for example—that may add emotion to the image.

Positioning the camera too close to an object may result in images with large unfocused areas occupied by these objects. This effect often overwhelms the rest of the image. Objects that are too close to the camera can be effectively used to create effects of intrusion or anxiety, but should only be used if those emotions are the right ones to present the main subject to the audience.

When image clarity is an important issue, it helps to place the main subject in a shot against plain backgrounds. Backgrounds with dense textures or with a multitude of objects and colors tend to take the attention of the viewer away from the items in the foreground.

6.4.6 Wide angle lens distortion. Screen shot from Myst® CD-ROM computer game. Game and screen shot © 1993 by Cyan, Inc.® All rights reserved.

Review and Practice

Matching

____ Aspect ratio
____ Navigation

____ Reverse angle shot

____ Low angle shot
____ Long shot

____ Boom
____ 135 mm lens
____ 50 mm lens
____ Wide shot

____ Cone of vision

____ Tilt

a. Rotation of the camera on its X axis.
b. Presents enough of the scene to include the full bodies of five characters.
c. Portion of the three-dimensional space that is seen through the camera.
d. Translation of the camera along its Y axis.
e. Offers an adequate 46 degree angle of view with very little perspective distortion and with average depth of field.
f. The process of placing a camera in three-dimensional space.
g. Places the camera below the point of interest and looks up.
h. Commonly used in conversations between two people.
i. Defined by the relation between the width and the height of the image plane.
j. Has excellent abilities for close framing, but it flattens the perspective.
k. Focuses on the scenery and barely permits recognition of individual characters in the environment.

Answers Matching: a. Tilt, b. Wide shot, c. Cone of vision, d. Boom, e. 50 mm lens, f. Navigation, g. Low angle shot, h. Reverse angle shot, i. Aspect ratio, j. 135 mm lens, k. Long shot.

True/False

____ a. A camera can be placed interactively by clicking on its icon and dragging it to a new location.

____ b. A zoom lens can only have two focal lengths: short and long.

____ c. The focal length of a lens is defined by its curvature and shape.

____ d. The default camera is never aimed at the origin and placed not too far from it.

____ e. A point of view shot often places the camera at eye level, looking straight into the action.

____ f. A virtual camera lens defines how the objects in a three-dimensional scene are projected onto the projection plane.

____ g. Point of view is another term for point of interest.

____ h. A wide shot includes about five people in the frame.

____ i. The far and near clipping planes are perpendicular to the line of sight.

____ j. A medium shot frames characters from the shoulders up.

____ k. In a zoom type of camera move, the camera's position and orientation remain unchanged.

____ l. A foggy environment cannot be simulated with a technique that involves the far clipping plane.

____ m. A close-up shot places the camera at close range so that details in the subject can be appreciated.

Answers True/False: a. True, b. False, c. True, d. False, e. True, f. True, g. False, h. True, i. True, j. False, k. True, l. False, and m. True.

Key Terms

Active
Aspect ratio
Boom
Camera lenses
Camera moves
Close-up shot
Cone of vision
Crane shot
Default or standard camera
Depth of field
Dolly
Extreme close-up shot
Extreme long shot
Far clipping plane
Field guides
Field of vision
Fixed focal length
Focal length
Focal plane
Head shot
High angle shot
Hither plane
Image plane
Interactive camera placement
Invisible
Knee shot
Landscape
Line of sight
Long shot
Low angle shot
Media formats
Medium close-up shot
Medium long shot

Medium shot
Multiple cameras
Narrative and psychological effect
Navigation
Near clipping plane
Normal 50 or 55 mm lens
Orientation
Orthographic projections
Pan
Perspective projection
Point of interest (POI)
Point of view (POV)
Point of view shot
Position
Practical use
Predefined
Predefined position
Projection plane
Pyramid of vision
Reverse angle shot
Roll
Stationary camera shot
Straightforward communication
Stylistic use
Telephoto 135 mm lens
Tilt
Traveling shot
Truck
Variable focal lengths
Viewing angle
Waist shot
Wide angle 24 or 28 mm lens
Wide shot
Yon plane

CHAPTER 7

Lighting

Summary

This chapter describes the main elements of lighting, presents a variety of simple and complex lighting strategies, and covers some of the basic techniques for controlling and adjusting the lights that illuminate the environment. Lighting is an important component of the rendering process not only because it reveals the three-dimensional world and sets the mood of the scene, but also because it may contribute significantly to the overall processing time necessary to render the scene.

7.1 Types of Light Sources

There are several basic types of light sources according to the way in which they irradiate light. Simulated light sources include: point lights, spot lights, linear lights, area lights, infinite lights, and ambient lights (Fig. 7.1.1). All of these types of light can be created and modified by the user. In addition most rendering programs automatically create one or several **default lights** in the three-dimensional scene. Default lighting schemes can usually be customized, and may consist of an ambient light source, or an infinite light that simulates the intensity and position of the sun, or a point light that is placed above and behind the camera or in any other XYZ position. Some default lights will automatically turn themselves off as soon as we specify any light source in the scene; others will remain on until turned off manually. Some rendering programs do not provide default lights, which means that if it is rendered without any new lights, the result will be like looking into a windowless room without any lights.

Point Light

A **point light** casts light evenly in all directions. For this reason

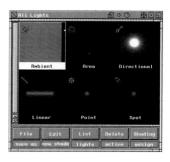

7.1.1 Different types of lights. (Dialog box from Alias PowerAnimator. © Alias Research, Inc.)

7.1.2 A spot light.

a point light is also called an **omni-directional** light (literally "in all directions"). Point lights are the simplest type of light source, and they can be placed anywhere in the scene. Point lights can be placed, for example, outside of the field of vision of the camera, behind an object in the scene, or even inside of objects. The effects of point lights placed inside of objects varies between software programs, but in many cases the light will shine through the walls of a transparent object as in the case of a light bulb. An incandescent light bulb is a simple example of a point light. A star, a candle, and a firefly are also point lights but require additional effects.

Spot Light

A simulated **spot light** is like a point light to which "barn doors" of the type commonly used in the performing arts ave been added. Spot lights cast light in a cone shape and only in one specific direction. Spot lights have some unique characteristics explained below that are not shared with other types of lights: a variable-angle cone of light, and a light fall-off factor. Flashlights, lamps with shades, jack-o-lanterns, and the light reflectors used in stage or movie productions are all examples of spot lights (Fig. 7.1.2).

Spot lights that are dimmed or turned up produce a very effective way of attracting the attention of the audience to a specific area or situation in a three-dimensional scene. A narrow soft-edged spot light can be especially effective for highlighting the action when the **illumination level** in the scene is low. A spot light in a dark scene can add a feeling of suspense or fear to the shot because the lighting effect might remind the audience of a search for something—or someone—that is hiding, or the process of trying to hide from someone—or something—that is looking for us.

Infinite Light

Infinite lights are so far from the elements in the scene that their light rays reach the scene parallel to each other. **Infinite lights** are also called **directional lights**, and behave like stars in the sky. But unlike stars, computer-simulated infinite lights can be placed anywhere in the environment, are massless, and their intensity can be modulated (Fig. 7.1.3). In many programs infinite lights have a constant intensity, and do not decay as they travel through space. The **sun** is a special case of infinite light source that can be accurately placed above the scene by typing the latitude and longitude of the location plus the exact time of day and date when the simulated scene is taking place (Fig. 7.4.1).

7.1.3 An infinite light.

Area Light

Some programs provide **area lights** in the form of rectangular areas of light. Area lights can be scaled to almost any size but are more efficient when kept small. Area lights are especially useful for lighting small areas uniformly like the way, for example, in which custom jewelry is photographed by professionals by being placed on a translucent light box or between two light boxes. Area lights can also be used to simulate the reflection of light coming into an interior space through the open windows.

Linear Light

The light of the fluorescent tubes used to light so many public spaces can be simulated with linear lights (Fig. 7.1.4). **Linear lights** have length but no width, and can also be scaled to any size. Using linear light sources should be exercised with care because their computation in some cases can be much more time-consuming than the combination of several points lights.

Ambient Light

The light radiated by the **ambient light** source is distributed

7.1.4 A linear light.

evenly throughout the entire scene. The term ambient light is often used very generically by different software programs, and technically speaking it does not always refer to an ambient light source. In some cases it refers to a point light source that is created automatically by the program for each scene.

Even though an ambient light source can be placed in a specific XYZ position in three-dimensional space, it is best to think of an ambient light as coming from all directions. The ambient light source often determines the general **level of illumination**, or shade, of a scene and almost always there is only one ambient light source per scene.

7.2 Basic Components of a Light Source

The main elements of all simulated light sources include: position, color and intensity, decay and fall-off, glow, and shadows. In addition, spot lights are also defined by their orientation and cone angle. These components are listed in Fig. 7.2.1. All lighting software makes it possible to edit separately each of the individual components of a light source. Some programs also allow to group several of these attributes and save them together in a file, called a **light shader**, that can be applied to any light source.

Position and Orientation

Both the **position** and **orientation** of a light source can be controlled with the standard navigation or geometric transformation tools provided by all rendering programs. In general, the tools for placing light sources in a simulated three-dimensional space are the same as the tools used for placing cameras: simple and combined translations and rotations.

In the wireframe display mode, light sources are usually represented with a variety of graphic symbols, for example, a light bulb for a point light, a lantern for a spot light, a sphere attached to a straight line for an infinite light, and so on (Fig. 7.1.1). But when a scene is rendered, the actual light sources themselves (not the light coming from them) can usually be seen, unless they are made **invisible** in which case they do not appear

7.2.1 Powerful tools for editing light sources. (Dialog box from Softimage 3D. © Microsoft Corporation. All rights reserved.)

in the final rendering. In many programs, the light sources are visible by default, and when rendered they appear in the image as bright spots or as small three-dimensional objects that look like the graphic symbols commonly used to represent the light source in the wireframe mode.

Color and Intensity

Simulated light can have virtually any **color**. In most rendering programs the color of lights is usually specified using a light-based or **additive color model**. The RGB (Red, Green, Blue) model and the HSB (Hue, Saturation, Brightness) model are both additive color models, and also described in Chapter 5. Some programs provide both color models to work with, other programs provide only one of them. In the RGB color model, a color can be specified by its individual red, green, and blue components. The numerical ranges used to specify color also vary from program to program. They can range, for example, from 0.000 to 1.000, 0 to 255, or 0 to 65,535 depending on the color resolution and precision of the system. Unlike pigment-based color models where the color mixture gets darker as more color is added, in the RGB color model the color of the light will become lighter as the amount of color mixed increases. The RGB values of ten different colors are listed in Fig. 7.2.2. Note that in a three-dimensional environment, the color assigned to objects is always influenced by the color of the light sources as well as the position of the object in relation to them.

Color	0-255 Scale	0-1 Scale
Red	255-0-0	1-0-0
Green	0-255-0	0-1-0
Blue	0-0-255	0-0-1
Cyan	0-255-255	0-1-1
Yellow	255-255-0	1-1-0
Magenta	255-0-255	1-0-1
Aquamarine	161-255-238	.631-1-.933
Cream	252-255-103	.988-1-.403
Rust	141-43-17	.552-.168-.066

7.2.2 The two columns of values represent the numerical values of color expressed in two different ways, using a scale of 0-255 and a scale of 0-1.

When using the HSB color system it is possible to specify the intensity of a light source independently from its color or hue. For this reason it is easier for most people to quickly define the color of lights with this color model than when using the RGB model. The Apple Color Picker, one of several tools for selecting colors visually within the context of the HSB color system, is illustrated in Fig. 7.2.3. Most three-dimensional rendering programs provide dimmers to control the **intensity** or **brightness** of a light source. Intensity values commonly range from 0.000 to 1.000 with maximum intensity represented by a number one and minimum intensity (or OFF) being represented by the zero when using the HSB color model. Some programs offer simple tools for boosting the intensity of a light source (Fig. 7.2.4). The intensity of the light source can be controlled independently from its color. But, since the intensity and the color of light mutually influence each other, almost any changes in the color of a light seem to affect its intensity. For example, if

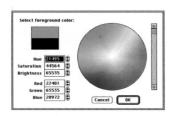

7.2.3 The Apple Computer Color Picker simplifies the visual selection of color within the ranges of the HSB (Hue, Saturation, Brightness) color model. Color can also be selected by inputting numerical values in HSB or RGB (Red, Green, Blue) formats.

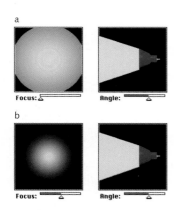

7.2.4 These two pairs of images compare two spot light beams with the same cone angle values, but the one on top (a) has sharp edges or almost no fall-off, and the lower one (b) has soft edges or lots of fall-off. (Graphs from Infini-D 2.6. © 1991-1995 Specular International, Ltd.)

we have two red lights with the same intensity but one of them has a dark red color and the other a light red color, the latter will appear to be a light with a higher intensity.

Decay and Fall-Off

The **decay** value of light controls the force of a light source and, as a result, how far from the light source the light travels. A weak light decays rapidly while a strong light decays slowly and travels far. In the real world the decay of light is always linked to the intensity of the light source that created the light, but in computer-simulated lighting decay is often independent from the intensity parameter.

In most programs the decay parameter defines the force of the light—regardless of its type—as it travels away from the light source. The light created from point lights decays equally in all directions. The light created from spot lights, however, decays as it moves away from the light source, but also as it moves from the center of the beam cone **toward the edges**. This type of decay is sometimes called **fall-off**. Decay and fall-off can be controlled with linear interpolation for slow fading effects, or with exponential interpolation for abrupt fading. The sharpness or softness of the edges of spot light beams are controlled with the fall-off value.

Cone or Beam Angle

The **cone angle** feature of lights is a characteristic that is specific to spot lights only. The cone angle of a spot light defines the diameter of the beam of light and also the surface area covered by the light. This parameter simulates the barn doors in real spot light lamps that control the **spread** of the light beam (Fig. 7.2.4).

Glow

It is possible with some programs to simulate a variety of glowing lights. The **glow** of a light is a circle of light that forms around the light source because the light is refracted and reflected by particles in the environment, generally ice, dust, or smoke. In some instances the glow of light is calculated based on the **bleeding** displayed by very bright light sources, insted of the refraction of light in a three-dimensional environment. The light bleeding effect is very common in situations when a photographic camera is pointed directly at a light source, and the resulting photograph has a bright spot with light bleeding around it. The difference between these two methods of creating a glow in computer-generated lights is that one (refraction) is based on three-dimensional calculations while the other (bleed-

7.2.5 Many light sources in this composite scene have glow. (Courtesy of Rafael Viñoly Associates.)

ing) is based on two-dimensional calculations.

The glow of a point light usually occurs as a **circle** or **halo** around the light source. The glow of a spot light occurs in the form of a **cone** of light. Circular and conical light glows are both defined by the decay of the light source. Linear decay results in a gradual fading of the glow effect while exponential decay results in a sudden vanishing of the glow. Conical light glow is further controlled by the spread or beam angle of the light source. The thickness or frequency of the particles in the environment that cause the light glow is controlled with parameters that simulate the size, orientation, motion, and opacity of the particles in the environment that cause the light glow (Fig. 7.2.5).

Lens flare is an effect that is related to light glow, and it simulates the refraction of light inside of a camera lens. Lens flare creates the rings or stars caused by the refraction of light inside camera lenses, and it is also a two-dimensional effect commonly available in many post-processing and compositing programs.

Global and Local Lights

Global light sources shine on all objects in the scene that are directly exposed to the light sources. The light sources in a scene are global by default. Rendering methods like radiosity are used when even those three-dimensional surfaces which are not directly exposed to a light source receive some light in the form of penumbra or **diffuse interreflections**. The illumination effect of global lights is largely dependent on their position and orientation in the scene, and their brightness. But objects directly exposed to global lights always reflect some of that light.

A different situation occurs with **local light sources**, also called **linked** or **selective light sources**. A local light source sheds its light on the objects linked to it, and this link can be exclusive or inclusive. An **exclusive link** between the light source and the objects limits the light projected by a local light source to fall only on the objects linked to it. In some programs an exclusive link may override the fact that a linked surface may not be exposed directly to the light source. This is as if the light source could magically travel through opaque objects that would ordinarily block light from reaching the linked object without affecting them. An **inclusive link** allows a local light source to always illuminate the objects linked to it as well as other objects in the scene that may be directly exposed to it.

Establishing links between light sources and three-dimensional surfaces can be an effective way to achieve complex lighting situations, but it can also increase the management complexity of a scene. Local light sources are implemented in different ways by different programs. For this reason local light sources should be used with restraint. From the point of view of an object that is linked to one or several local light sources, the object will only be illuminated by them and not any other light sources that may be active in the scene.

Shadows

In principle, all light sources cast **shadows**. But shadow-casting is a feature of lights that can be turned on or off. Since shadow-casting is also an optional attribute of objects and shading techniques, the final visual appearance of shadows is determined not only by the attributes of the shadow but also by the attributes of the shadow-casting object and the rendering method employed. Shadows can be defined by several parameters, including color

of the shadow, color of the penumbra, and softness of the shadow edge.

The portion of a shadow that blocks direct light altogether is called **umbra**, this is the inner part of the shadow. The area in the edges of the shadow that blends with other lights in the environment is called **penumbra**. The **softness** of the edge of a shadow is controlled in a variety of ways. With many rendering methods—excluding ray tracing—the soft edges of a shadow can be controlled by the distance between the light source and the shadow-projecting object. The shadow edges will be sharp as the light source moves further away from the object. The number of levels of shadow tracers influences the softness of a shadow when ray tracing is used. When using radiosity-based rendering the shadow edges are soft when the surfaces in the environment create a lot of diffuse inter-reflections (Fig. 7.2.6).

7.3 Lighting the Scene

Those who realize the importance of lighting can appreciate the importance of a systematic approach to lighting. Without light the entire contents of the world could not be appreciated visually. Without adequate lighting, shapes, colors, and textures can only be experienced halfway. Think, for example, of some of the elements of a beautiful face: the features, the proportions of the shapes and their curvatures, the evocative color of the eyes, the subtle coloration and the texture of the skin, and the weight and flow of the hair. A successful lighting arrangement can reveal all of these elements and present them in a harmonic way. But a poorly designed lighting scheme will fail to bring up the full experience and depth of the beautiful face. Strong shadow in the eyes, for example, may obscure or hide the eye coloring. Unbalanced shad-

7.2.6 *Cosmic Pinball* is a four minute motion simulator ride film that places the audience inside the game from the point of view of the pinball. (This Showscan production was produced by Ben Stassen of Talent Factory, and animated by Jos Claesen and Toon Roebben of TRIX, both in Brussels, Belgium. Courtesy of Wavefront Technologies, Inc.)

ows around the nose might distort its delicate balance. Lighting the face from certain angles might flatten the jawline or dilute the seductive meaning hidden in the shape of the lips.

Next we shall review some ideas about the placement of light sources based on concepts borrowed from traditional stage lighting. Amazingly enough, most stage lighting concepts can be easily adapted to the lighting of computer-simulated environments because in both situations the scene is totally dark unless we turn the lights on. We will approach lighting here from two points of view: the areas in the scene that require lighting and some of the basic positions of light sources.

From the point of view of stage lighting design there are some constant areas or aspects of the scene that require lighting. Throughout the ages many lighting methods and techniques have been developed for the different formats and genres presented on a stage, ranging from drama to comedy. The following categories of lighting summarize a variety of traditional lighting methods that can be adapted to the design and production of computer animation. These categories of lighting are: the main action area, the secondary action areas, the backgrounds, ambient or fill-in lighting, visible light sources, and moving lights.

Main Action Area

The **main action area** is the area in the scene where most of the action takes place. The main action area may consist of a small area, for example, if a molecular interaction is being rendered, or a large area in the case of a car chase in an underground parking lot. The main action area in a dialogue scene between two characters would be where the action takes place. In computer-generated scenes the main action area might be located in a quiet indoor space or extend over firewalls and colored rain. A couple of spot lights might be enough for a simple shot of a mostly static scene, but several of pointlights and spot lights might be needed to delineate the motion of ten fantastic characters dancing back and forth on the stage. A specific lighting arrangement of the main action area may require several variations in cases when the scene is shot from different points of view in order to emphasize different aspects of the subjects to cameras placed in different locations. In many situations the lighting of the main action area defines the overall mood of the scene. For that reason the light sources used to light the main action area are called **key lights**, and are often used in conjuction with the fill-in lights described below. In traditional stage lighting design it is not uncommon to divide the main action area into several sections, depending on the action that is to take place, and to assign each section a certain number of lights, for example, between two and five spot lights per section (Fig. 7.3.1).

Secondary Action Area

The **secondary action area** is the place in the scene into which some of the action eventually spills. For example, two characters in a scene that takes place in a living room spend most of their time sitting on the couch (main action area). But at some point one of the characters gets up and walks to the bookshelf (secondary action area), picks a book, and returns to the sofa. The lights illuminating the bookshelf and the book may be on at all times throughout the scene, or only turned up as the character starts walking to the bookshelf and dimmed down as the character sits back down. The number of lights needed to illuminate the secondary action area—especially in a small environment—is usually smaller than the number of lights required to light the main action area.

Background

The **background** in computer-generated environments, also referred to in computer simulations as the stage, the scenery or the surroundings. The background usually consists of the props surrounding the action areas. Scenery might consist of horizontal or vertical planes with texture maps—of bricks, for example—or convex surfaces with procedural maps of animated clouds or even a photographic background that has been composited. Scenery—especially backdrops with texture maps—is very sensitive to colored light. Very minor chromatic changes in the lights that illuminate the scenery will have significant effects on the color of the scenery.

Fill-In Light

The **fill-in light** is also called ambient light, and has the dual purpose of defining the overall color tone of the entire scene, as well as blending some of the other multiple lights in the scene. Fill-in light can be created with infinite light sources and also with spot lights. Depending on the lighting effect desired, fill-in lights can be soft and tinted or quite bright, but almost invariable fill-in lights do not project shadows.

Visible Light Sources

Visible light sources are those sources of light that can be seen by the camera and, therefore, the spectators. Visible light sources might include lamps, fireplaces, reflectors, candlelight, televisions, refrigerators, fireflies, and comets. These light sources are usually very important from the dramatic point of view because they usually play an important storytelling role. Often

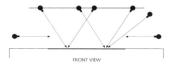

FRONT VIEW

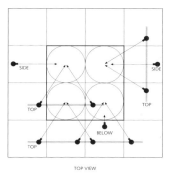

TOP VIEW

7.3.1 This diagram shows a lighting layout of the main and secondary action areas. In traditional stage lighting the size of each grid subdivision corresponds to a area that can be filled by a spotlight beam.

relevant events happen near visible light sources and that is why this type of light is commonly emphasized in the visual composition of a scene. Computer-simulated visible light sources can be simulated with point lights, and their effect can be accentuated by placing them inside of a sphere that is rendered with transparency and glow. The effect of a visible spot light can be accentuated by using a transparent cone to emphasize the cone of light of the spot light.

The sun or the moon, for example, are commonly represented as light sources. They can be easily defined as point lights, but also as ambient light sources. The point light sources recreating celestial bodies can have medium to high intensity and little or no fall-off. The color of these lights may have a tinted appearance a warm tint in the case of the sun, for example, or a slightly cold tint in the case of the moon. One advantage of using ambient light to simulate distant light sources is that the objects cast soft shadows if any at all. The light of many celestial bodies may include some flickering that can be recreated by animating the intensity or the glow of a point light source. This quality is especially apparent when the camera is pointed directly at the light source.

Moving Lights

Unlike a theater stage where most lights are fixed, all lights in a computer-simulated scene may be easily moved. But there is always a category of **moving lights** that move a lot or have motion as their main characteristic. Moving lights can be used to emphasize special aspects of the scene. For example, a very focused spot light that moves very subtly over one object to reveal a highlight or to emphasize its transparency, or a series of spot lights that are mounted on the camera and follow the action by trailing the camera. A number of moving lights falls within a subcategory of special lighting effects that can be used to emphasize certain dramatic moments or to impose very dominant moods. Fireworks, explosions, haze and fog, and lightning are all examples of special lighting effects.

Many lighting effects encountered in nature can be simulated with combinations of moving light sources (see Chapter 10 for more details about animation of light sources). Some of these lighting effects include, for example, the light emitted by lightning, fire, or natural explosions like a volcano, or the light reflected off the surface of moving water, or refracted through moving water like a waterfall.

Fire lighting effects that are off-screen can be achieved with a group of point lights and spot lights placed within an area that corresponds to the dimensions of the fire being recreated. The intense and constant lighting motion generated by a fire can be achieved with wiggly parameter curves for position, cone angle, and each of the RGB colors in order to achieve maximum irregularity. Other techniques to simulate fire are described in Chapter 10.

The lighting effects created by light travelling through colored glass—for example, the effect created in an interior space by exterior lights travelling through stained glass.—require a translucent image map, or a rendering technique like radiosity or raytracing that calculates the effects of light travelling through transparent or translucent surfaces.

7.4 Basic Positions of Light Sources

When compared to traditional stage lighting, computer-simulated lighting has the great advantage that lights can be moved around without having to worry about clamping them to spot light bars or poles. Computer-simulated lights have the ability to float in space. Most three-dimensional rendering programs use standard XYZ notation for positioning lights in three-dimensional space. However, some programs offer the **spherical coordinate system**—instead of or in addition to the Cartesian coordinate system—for placing lights. The spherical coordinate system, as mentioned in Chapter 2, specifies the position of objects in three-dimensional space in terms of their altitudinal and azimuthal angles (above and around) in relation to a center of reference. The position of the sun, for example, can be described in terms of its altitude and its azimuth (Fig. 2.4.7). The **altitude** is defined by the angle of the light in relation to the horizon. The **azimuth** is defined by projecting the angle of the sun onto the east-west axis. This technique is especially convenient in architectural projects where the position of the sun has to be defined for calculating both the amount of shadow cast by a building and its surroundings, as well as the amount of direct sunlight received by the structure at any time of the day (Fig. 7.4.1).

Once light sources are positioned they can be aimed at specific objects or areas in the environment in a variety of ways. Centers of interest can be specified **numerically** by typing XYZ values, **visually** by pointing the **light vector** displayed by some light sources at the object in question, or **procedurally** by choosing commands (provided by some programs) that will automatically point one object—usually a light source or a camera—to another.

In principle there is no limit to the **number of light sources** that can be placed in a three-dimensional scene. In computer simulated lighting, just as in real physical lighting, the only limitations to the number of light sources lighting a scene are of a practical nature. The budget and timetable of some projects may determine the number of light sources. Both in computer-simulat-

7.4.1 The position of lights—especially the sun or other stars—can also be specified using the spherical coordinate system. This dialog box provides an easy way to define the position of the Sun in relation to earth anywhere and anytime. (Dialog box from form•Z. © 1991-1995 auto•des•sys, Inc.)

ed lighting as in real lighting, to create, place, and fine-tune lights requires time and money. But lighting requirements—whether real or simulated—have a wide range of complexity. Compare the lighting requirements of an indoor large-scale sports event to those of the close-up photography of a diamond ring.

Lights can be placed in a variety of places in relation to the subject that needs lighting and the camera. Five basic positions of light sources and their corresponding variations as they focus on the subject are examined here: pair of spot lights at a 45 degree angle, front (below and subject's level), side (subject's level, above, and above and behind), back (above and side), and top. Figure 7.4.2 provides a visual summary of these basic lighting positions using only spot lights to accentuate each lighting effect. It is important to keep in mind that not all situations need all these lights present at all times. Use your judgement and preview in order to finalize a lighting arrangement.

45 Degree Pair

One of the most common lighting arrangements (in fact it is usually called ordinary lighting by stage lighting designers) consists of two spot lights placed above, in front, and to the sides of the subject. In this common lighting configuration the lights are both focused on the subject at a 90 degree angle in relation to each other. Both lights are rotated 45 degree around the vertical and horizontal axis. This ordinary **45 degree angle spot light pair** represents a simple and effective way to have a generous amount of light that reveals the features of the subject as well as some detail in the form of shadows.

Frontal Light

The **frontal light from below** is very effective for casting pronounced shadows both on the subject and the environment. Since we rarely encounter this type of light in natural surroundings frontal lights from below can look very artificial or overly dramatic. But they can also be quite effective for accentuating truly dramatic or scary moments.

The **frontal light at the subject's level** tends to flatten the subject because it usually eliminates most of the deepest shadows, but it can also be used as a low intensity fill light for blending other spot lights in the scene.

Lateral, Top, and Back Lights

A **lateral light at the subject's level** is useful for increasing the contrast between light and dark. The accentuated shadows created with lateral light can have a powerful dramatic effect and add

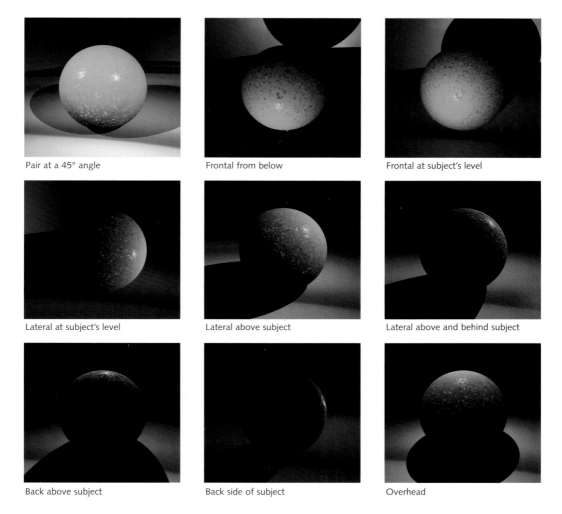

Pair at a 45° angle

Frontal from below

Frontal at subject's level

Lateral at subject's level

Lateral above subject

Lateral above and behind subject

Back above subject

Back side of subject

Overhead

a lot of depth to the scene. Lateral lights should be used with care because they can easily overpower other more delicate lights in the scene.

A **lateral light from above**—especially when used in pairs, one on the left and one on the right—creates an effect that is similar to the 45 degree spot light pair described earlier but with slightly more pronounced shadows. One advantage of creating pronounced shadows with lateral lights from above is that the shadows created by the main subject are usually projected on the floor and not on other objects in the scene, as would be the case when using frontal lights from below or lateral lights at the subject's level.

A **lateral light from above and behind** is an effective

7.4.2 The basic five basic positions of light sources and their corresponding variations as they focus on a head: pair of spot lights at a 45° angle, front (below and subject's level), side (subject's level, above, and above and behind), back (above and side), and top.

way for outlining the subject against the background. This position combines some of the advantages and limitations of all lateral, overhead, and back lights. It models the actor with contrasted shadows (lateral), and it also creates a halo of light on the top of the subject that clearly differentiates it from the background (back and overhead).

Both the side and top **back lights** create halos of lights on the subject's edges. Back lighting can be an effective way of creating depth in a scene.

The **overhead light** also creates a dramatic halo around the top of the subject. As with back lights, the overhead lights can also add depth and drama to the scene.

7.5 Lighting Strategies

There are as many philosophies of lighting as there are disciplines that require lighting. This would include at least the performing arts—dramatic theater, musical theater, dance, opera— which usually take place indoors, and cinematography, which may take place both indoors and outdoors. Lighting designers in each of these disciplines favor particular approaches to lighting, which in turn are based on the discipline's lighting needs. Of course, within each discipline there are many different points of view. We can learn a lot of interesting lighting techniques and creative points of view by examining specific movies, plays, operas, and musicals. (Next time you have the chance to attend one of these events, pay attention to the lighting arrangements and try to figure out the ways in which they affect the mood of the moment.)

Much of the mood in any three-dimensional scene is established with the choice of lights and their arrangement. Lighting can be bright and fresh, soft and intimate, multicolored and festive, or tinted and moody. Light on a scene can be even and peaceful or uneven and disturbing. The shadows created with light can be harsh and sharp or soft and slow.

Effective lighting design starts with the visualization of the effect of lights in a specific environment. Fortunately, three-dimensional rendering programs are capable of actually simulating for us specific lighting arrangements. But even when using a computer rendering program to visualize light, any lighting designer is likely to achieve a higher degrees of lighting sophistication, beauty, and efficiency if he or she spends some time visualizing in his or her mind the effects of the planned lights before trying them with the program.

Visualizing Light

An easy way to visualize lighting consists of starting with a dark space, turning the spot lights on, followed by the ambient light in small increments. By turning on the spot lights (or any other secondary light) first, one can focus on their lighting effect because much of the scene will still be quite dark. By turning on the ambient light (or the major point light) second, and in small increments, one can visualize the blending of secondary lights with the main light. This way the overall lighting effect shows through (or builds up) while retaining at all times the light accents. If necessary, those accents—usually in the form of spot lights or colored lights—can still be turned up or down after the ambient light has been defined, and adjusted to the requirements of the scene.

The lighting design can also be visualized by starting with a space that is already lit with ambient light. In this method the lighting accents are added towards the end of the process. While the final lighting result can be the same whether one starts visualizing a dark room or a lighted room. I find that the latter requires more concentration, greater visualization power, and perhaps a little more lighting skill.

White Light

Most of us assume, incorrectly, that all natural light—and artificial light to a lesser extent—is white. But light, in fact, is almost never white. Light is usually tinted. Few elements in nature (perhaps water) are as chromatically dynamic as light (Fig. 7.5.1). The color of light changes with the time of day, the weather, the landscape, and the location on earth. Just think of the chromatic differences, for example, between the light of a sunny winter afternoon in the Nordic fjords or a summer sunset in the stormy Caribbean or high noon in the clear spring skies of the Australian rocky desert. Nordic winter light might have a slight blue tint, while the light of a stormy Caribbean sunset might be the pink color of the *mamey* tropical fruit, and the spring Australian desert's light might have a slight yellow tint. The color differences in the three examples above might be subtle but very meaningful if one is trying to simulate environments like those with a three-dimensional rendering program.

The lighting effect created by a **lightning** storm can be recreated by inserting one or two white frames in the sequence just a couple of seconds before the sound of thunder is heard.

7.5.1 *Seafari* is a computer-generated motion ride that features a talking dolphin who guides the audience on an eye-popping undersea rescue mission while avoiding the razor sharp fangs of a gigantic sea monster. (© 1994 MCA/Universal. Courtesy of Rhythm & Hues Studios.)

After that a very strong light—placed in the area near where the lightning is supposed to have fallen—is suddenly turned up to a bright white color, and then dimmed in a flickering way.

Colored Light

We can achieve very startling lighting effects by using colored lights. The results are always reminiscent of the performing arts where performers are literally tracked around the stage with colored lights or dancing clubs where much of the festive atmosphere and visual chatter is created with constant sequences and patterns of colored lights. The visual power of colored lights is so great, however, that they must be used with prudence—especially when lighting spaces or situations where a festive atmosphere would be distracting.

A pleasing visual surprise that is very common in circus performance scenes happens when the projected lights of colored spot lights overlap with one another. This lighting resource owes its startling force to the unexpected colors that result from the mixture of colored lights. Audiences are somewhat familiar with the results of mixing primary **pigment-based colors** with one another. Most have experienced this first-hand in elementary school or earlier: red and yellow gives orange, blue and yellow gives green, and red and blue gives purple. Mixtures of **light-based colors** are startling because they follow the physical rules of **additive (light-based) color systems** as opposed to **subtractive (pigment-based) color systems**. It is always entertaining to puzzle your friends with a demonstration of the basic color mixtures in a light-based, three-dimensional rendering system: green and blue make cyan, blue and red make magenta, and (my favorite one) red and green make yellow.

The effect of colored light reflected off the surface of **moving water** can be recreated by placing spot lights with varying cone angles shining up through a surface that represents water and that has an animate shape (Fig. 7.5.2).

Tinted Light

Using tinted lights is a less dramatic but more subtle lighting effect than using colored lights. Using tinted lights is also a very common technique in the lighting of simulated three-dimensional spaces—especially in determining a mood for the scene.

Tinted lights can be an effective method for creating a cohesive atmosphere. Tinted lights have the same effect that a coat of overpaint or varnish has on the layers of paint closest to the canvas. They contribute to unify objects of disparate colors or surface finishes. Tinted lights are created by selecting a slight coloration for the light emitted by the light source. When using the HSB color model to describe a tint, the saturation values should be low so that the color is washed out, the brightness values should be high so that the tint is not too dark, and the hue values could vary depending on the coloration desired for the tint. When using the RGB color model, each of the three values (red, green, and blue) would be high so that the resulting color would be bright and not too saturated.

Animating Light

The position and attributes of light sources in a scene can be animated using the keyframe interpolation techniques described in Chapter 10. These techniques include the interactive specification of key poses, the editing of parameter curves, forward kinematics, and motion paths. A wide variety of lighting effects that affect the mood of a scene can also be created by animating the intensity of a light source as well as its color, cone angle, and fall-off. Moving lights in a three-dimensional environment, however, should be exercised with great restraint because poorly animated light sources can be a great source of visual distraction in any animated sequence.

7.5.2 This image was created with a lighting model that is based on optical phenomena such as the scattering and absorption of the light in the water. This model is capable of creating subtle details of the reflection and refraction of light on the water surface, the scattering and absorption of light in the water, and the shadows cast on the water surfaces. (Courtesy of Hideo Yamashita and the Computer Graphics Research Group of Hiroshima University.)

7.6 Getting Ready

Check the Default Light

Do not forget to check whether the rendering software that you use creates a default light automatically. If not, then you must define a light source before you render. The default light in most programs is an ambient light source that lights all the objects in the scene uniformly. Default ambient lights can be modified when the original settings are not suitable to the scene in question.

Invisible Light Sources

Do not forget to make the light sources themselves (the lamps, not the light) invisible after they have been defined and positioned in three-dimensional space. Otherwise, they will show—usually in the form of small boxes, arrows, or brilliant dots—in the final rendered image.

Missing Shadows

Sometimes an object that is meant to cast shadows does not do so even though the light source has been defined as a shadow-casting light. The answer to the problem might be the fact that the shadow-casting preference has been turned off either in the object itself or in the shading technique or in both.

Simulated Shadows

Transparent planes can be used to create shadows on objects in the scene, and even on photographic backgrounds that are composited, or blended, with a three-dimensional environment. In the latter case the transparent planes have to be aligned with elements on the background through a series of trial and error alignment tests. (For more information on image compositing read Chapter 12.)

Lighting is Related to Shading

It is difficult to talk about the effects of lighting in computer-simulated three-dimensional environments because so much of it is determined by the shading technique (or techniques) that are used to render a scene. But, at least for now, we will limit the discussion of lighting to the elements only directly associated with the process of lighting: the light sources, their lighting characteristics, and their positions in three-dimensional space. For more information on rendering read Chapter 8.

Minimize Rendering Time

Try to minimize rendering time by keeping the number of lights down to a minimum. Most scenes can be properly lighted with just a couple of well-placed light sources. Many inexperienced users tend to create more light sources than necessary to light a scene. A lot of rendering time can saved by studying the scene first and only placing those light sources that are essential to the lighting effect sought. Only special situations need large numbers of light sources.

Review and Practice

Matching

___ Scenery	a. Color systems that are based on lights and not on pigments.
___ Spot light	b. Their light rays reach the scene parallel to each other.
___ Overhead light	c. Value that controls the sharpness or softness of the edges of spot lights.
___ Point light	d. Position of a light source that can be very effective for accentuating "scary" moments.
___ Infinite lights	e. Can be seen by the camera and the viewer.
___ Ordinary	f. Value of light controls the force of a light source and, as a result, how far the light travels.
___ Additive	g. A type of light source that casts light in all directions.
___ Visible light sources	h. Used by many programs to define the color of lights.
___ Decay	i. Very sensitive to colored lights.
___ Penumbra	j. A type of light source that is also called directional light.
___ HSB	k. Can be used to add depth and drama to a scene.
___ Frontal from below	l. Name given to a stage lighting arrangement that consists of two spot lights at a 90° angle in relation to each other, and rotated 45° around both the vertical and horizontal axes.
___ Fall off	m. The area of the shadow that blends with other lights in the environment.

Answers Matching: a. Additive, b. Infinite lights, c. Fall-off, d. Frontal from below, e. Visible light sources, f. Decay, g. Point light, h. HSB, i. Scenery, j. Spot light, k. Overhead light, l. Ordinary, m. Penumbra.

True/False

_____a. All rendering software creates at least three default lights for each scene.

_____b. The softness of the edge of a shadow can be controlled by the distance between the light source and the object that blocks it.

_____c. Only the position, but not the orientation, of a light source can be controlled with the standard navigation tools.

_____d. A lateral light from above and behind can be used to outline a subject against the background.

_____e. The difference between two of the methods for creating a glow in computer-generated lights is that the method based on refraction requires three-dimensional calculations while the other one is based on two-dimensional calculations.

_____f. The final effect created by an arrangement of light sources is highly influenced by the shading technique used to render a scene.

_____g. The only true white light found in nature is found in the Mediterranean coast during the Spring season.

_____h. A very intense light can be created by turning each of the RGB values all the way up.

_____i. Both the Rectangular and the Spherical coordinate systems can be used to specify the position of light sources in space.

_____j. A sun light source can be positioned in a scene by typing its latitude and longitude coordinates plus a specific time and date.

_____k. The light of spot lights decays as it moves away from the light source and also as it moves from the center of the beam towards the edges.

_____l. The main action area in a scene is usually divided in lighting sections, and an average of two spot lights are assigned to each section.

_____m. The value 255 0 60 creates a light of bluish-green color.

_____n. The glow of a spot light is a circle of light that forms around the light source because the light is refracted and reflected by particles in the environment.

Answers True/False: a. False, b. True, c. False, d. True, e. True, f. True, g. False, h. True, i. True, j. True, k. True, l. True, m. False, n. True.

Key Terms

45 degree angle spot light pair
Additive (light-based) color system
Additive color model
Altitude
Ambient light
Area lights
Azimuth
Back lights
Background
Bleeding
Brightness
Circle
Color
Cone
Cone angle
Decay
Default lights
Diffuse interreflections
Directional lights
Exclusive link
Fall-off
Fill-in light
Frontal light at the subject's level
Frontal light from below
Global light sources
Glow
Halo
Illumination level
Inclusive link
Infinite lights
Intensity
Invisible
Key lights
Lateral light at the subject's level
Lateral light from above

Lateral light from above and behind
Lens flare
Level of illumination
Light shader
Light vector
Light-based colors
Lightning
Linear lights
Linked light sources
Local light sources
Main action area
Moving lights
Moving water
Number of light sources
Numerically
Omni-directional light
Orientation
Overhead light
Penumbra
Pigment-based colors
Point light
Position
Procedurally
Secondary action area
Selective light sources
Shadows
Softness
Spherical coordinate system
Spot light
Spread
Subtractive (pigment-based) color system
Sun
Toward the edges
Umbra
Visible light sources
Visually

8.1.1 *Kiss That Frog* is a rock video
based on the music of Peter Gabriel.
A rich array of shading techniques
was used to portray exotic creatures
in an environment that also contains
live action characters. (© 1993
MEGA/Real World. All rights
reserved. Courtesy of Angel Studios,
Carlsbad, CA.)

CHAPTER 8

Shading and Surface Characteristics

Summary

This chapter describes and explains the main techniques used for shading three-dimensional surfaces by calculating the effect of light on the objects in the scene. This chapter also presents how surface shaders and image mapping work. The characteristics of three-dimensional surfaces including reflectivity, color, texture, and transparency and different ways of defining them are also explained.

8.1 Surface Shading Techniques

The visual appearance of a simulated three-dimensional environment is determined mostly through the shading process. The shading process creates surfaces on the wireframe structures created during the modeling process. Surface shading is calculated based on the relative position and distance of the object from the light source, and it also takes into account the surface characteristics of the objects.

Shading is the moment in the rendering process when visible surfaces are assigned a **shading value**. This value is calculated based on the relationship between the surface normals and the light sources that reach the surface. The **surface normals** are vectors or straight lines with a specific direction, and they are located on the vertices or corners of each polygon of the surface. A large number of software programs convert all surfaces to polygonal surfaces for the purpose of shading. The surface normals are used to define the orientation of a surface, and they have a paramount role in the calculation of surface shading. (Surface normals are also used in some rendering methods to determine whether surfaces are visible or hidden.)

Each shading technique is based on different representations of light and surface. These shading representations are contained in mathematical models that process the variables associated with

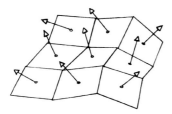

8.1.2 The shading of each polygon with faceted techniques is determined by only one surface normal per polygon.

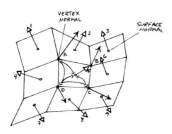

8.1.3 In smooth shading, the surface normals of four adjacent polygons are averaged to determine the four vertex normals of a single polygon. This process occurs four times in this illustration. Surface normals 1, 2, 4, and 5 are averaged to created vertex normal A. Surface normals 2, 3, 5, and 6 are averaged to create vertex normal B, and so on. Finally, the intensity values of the vertex normals are interpolated across the polygon.

shading in different ways. Some of the most popular surface shading techniques include faceted, smooth, and specular shading. Shading techniques are sometimes referred to by the last name of the individual who authored a specific version of the technique.

Oftentimes it is difficult to understand shading techniques in general because there are many different implementations of each of the basic shading techniques. Each rendering program offers its own version of the generic shading models, and sometimes the differences between implementations are significant. On occasion the basic shading models are mixed with each other or modified—for example, by adding new variables into the shading equation—resulting in **hybrid shading models** (Fig. 8.1.1). Therefore, when discussing shading techniques it is best to be specific and to discuss the implementation of a shading technique in a particular rendering program.

Faceted Shading

Faceted surface shading assigns a single and constant shading value to each visible polygon on the surface according to the angle of its normal in relation to the light source. This technique usually assigns a shading value to each polygon on the surface by measuring the amount of light that is received at the center of the polygon or in just one of the vertices. Most faceted shading models measure the amount of light received at the center of the polygon only. But some models measure the light received at the vertices of the polygon—usually three or four vertices—and the average value is applied uniformly to the entire polygon. Faceted shading, as indicated by its name, results in three-dimensional models with a faceted appearance that show each visible polygon in the model clearly distinguished from the rest. For this reason, faceted shading techniques are sometimes called polygonal shading, or constant value faceted shading. Most faceted shading techniques take into account parameters of ambient light only, but some also compute diffuse shading. Faceted techniques do not handle complex surface characteristics such as texture and transparency well—or sometimes not at all (Fig. 8.1.2). Faceted shading is the simplest type of shading and also the fastest because it uses only one surface normal per polygon to determine the shading for the entire polygon. The Lambert shading model is a popular form of faceted surface shading.

Smooth Shading

Smooth surface shading assigns a continuous shading value that blends throughout the visible polygons on the surface. The basic idea behind this technique is to average the surface normals of adjacent polygons, therefore creating a smooth transition of shading between polygons. This is often done by first sampling the amount of light reaching the surface normals in the center of polygons, then by creating a vertex normal that averages the values of the surface normals of adjacent polygons, and finally by blending the intensities of the vertex normals in a polygon (Fig. 8.1.3).

For this reason, smooth shading techniques create the appearance of smooth shading even with polygonal three-dimensional objects that have a small amount of modeling detail. Smooth shading is also called intensity interpolation shading. Some programs allow users to define the angle ranges for smooth shading to occur. Only when the angle between normals is less than the specified limit will this type of shading create a continuous blend throughout polygons on the surface. A popular shading model on which many smooth shading techniques are based is the Gouraud shading model. Smooth shading techniques do not compute the highlight values that are typical of reflective surfaces and, as a result, create only surfaces with a matte finish. Smooth shading techniques take into account ambient and diffuse lighting parameters, and handle some of the complex surface characteristics well.

Specular Shading

Specular surface shading techniques create surfaces with highlights that are found in reflective surfaces. The word specular means **mirror-like**. In addition, specular shading techniques create a smooth continuous shading across polygons by using normal interpolation techniques that are more detailed than those used by smooth shading methods. Specular shading is also called normal vector interpolation shading because it calculates the shading at every point on the surface of a polygon. This is done by interpolating the vertex normals, and shading every point on the surface of the polygon by computing the relation between the angle of its normal and the angle of the incident light. This process differs from smooth shading, which only calculates the shading values at the vertices of the polygons, and then blends them across the points on the surface of the polygon (Fig. 8.1.4).

Many shading models on which many specular shading techniques are based include the Phong, the Blinn, and the Cook shading models. Specular shading techniques take into account ambient, diffuse, and specular lighting, and they deal with detailed surface characteristics extremely well. This technique can create more accurate renderings than the other two shading techniques can, but it is also more computationally intensive.

8.2 Surface Shaders

A convenient way to think of all the variables that influence the

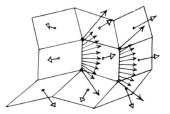

8.1.4 In specular shading, the vertex normals are interpolated across the surface of the polygon, and then shading is calculated at each point on the surface.

8.2.1 Surface properties can be edited by typing the numerical values or by dragging the appropriate sliders with the mouse. The surface pictured here corresponds to the second layer (from bottom to top) pictured in Fig. 8.2.4. (Dialog box from Infini-D 3.0. © 1991-1995 Specular International, Ltd.)

8.2.2 An editor of shading parameters. (Dialog box from Softimage 3D. © Microsoft Corporation. All rights reserved.)

rendering of a three-dimensional scene consists of grouping all of them in a shader. A **surface shader** is a collection of the surface characteristics and shading techniques that are applied to an object during the rendering process. Surface shaders are used to define the **surface finish** of the **simulated material** that a three-dimensional object is made of. The basic surface characteristics contained in most shaders include reflectivity, color, texture, and transparency. Surface shaders are used to determine the amount and color of light that is reflected by three-dimensional surfaces. Shaders also represent a flexible way to manage the large number of variables that are used to render three-dimensional objects. Ideally, shaders should be defined in such a way that different rendering methods can interpret the shaders according to their own rules.

The number of rendering methods available in different software varies between programs—some offer several rendering methods while others offer just a few. As explained in Chapter 5, each rendering method has a particular approach to rendering three-dimensional objects. Some rendering methods may ignore variables that are not necessary for their calculations. This would be the case, for example, with a rendering program that is based on the Z-buffer method and that uses faceted or constant shading ignoring the transparency values contained in a shader. Ideally, even when a specific rendering method ignores some shader values it would still use the values that are relevant to it.

Other rendering methods may require values that are particular to them but meaningless to other rendering methods. That would be the case, for example, with the reflection depth values that are meaningful only to a ray tracing program and not to other rendering techniques.

The concept of shaders has slightly different meanings in different programs. In general, it means a collection of surface characteristics and shading techniques. Sometimes rendering programs provide all the information that is usually contained in a shader but scattered throughout several dialog boxes. In such cases, the surface characteristics and shading techniques applied to a three-dimensional object cannot be found and edited all together in the same place. Instead the user has to look for them in different menus and work with multiple dialog boxes. While this approach may be less convenient than working with shaders that can easily be edited and applied to different objects, the end result in most cases is the same, as long as all the shading variables are available.

Sometimes shaders include only surface characteristics that can be applied to the three-dimensional objects independently from the shading techniques used to render them (Fig. 8.2.1). When shaders include only the characteristics of the surface material and not the shading technique to be used for rendering they are often called **surface libraries** or **material databases**. Shaders are usually applied to entire objects or groups of objects, but they can also be assigned to parts of an object, for example, a group of polygons. In general, surface shaders use some or all of the following information to determine the shading of a surface: shader name, shading technique and parameters, surface characteristics and parameters, and rendering method and parameters. Shaders can be edited by typing numerical values, by dragging sliders, or by modifying function curves. The ranges of shader values are often between zero percent and 100 percent, from 0 to 255, or from 0 to 1. Figures 8.2.2 and 8.2.3 show interfaces for defining shader information.

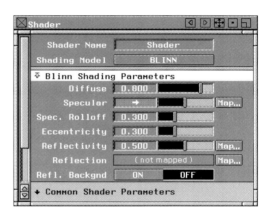

8.2.3 An editor of surface shaders. (Dialog box from Alias PowerAnimator. © Alias Research, Inc.)

Specifying surface characteristics often requires a fair amount of attention to detail. Doing a good job in the simulation of surface materials has an impact on the quality, refinement, and energy of the final rendered image. Specifying the surface characteristics and choosing the shading techniques are two distinct steps, but they are intrinsically related to one another and often overlap with each other.

When defining surface shaders and when applying them to three-dimensional surfaces it is important to consider the lighting characteristics that the shaders will be used under. Lighting conditions have a powerful effect on the appearance of shaders to the extent that the same shader can look very different under two different lighting conditions.

Surface Layers

One of the great advantages of using surface shaders or surface libraries is that complex surface characteristics can be defined in the form of **surface layers**. This method builds the surface characteristics of a three-dimensional object by adding layers and compounding their effects to determine the final look of the surface (Fig. 8.2.4). This method is similar to the way, for example, in which painters during the Renaissance created their paintings by first priming the surface with a white mixture, and then applying, one at a time, multiple coats of opaque and transparent paint and varnish. On occasions the **underpaint** coats contained colors that were not directly visible but that influenced the translucent colors from upper layers in particular and the overall color effect in general. At the end of this process the dry surface was burnished to compact all the layers of paint and varnish, and also to create a smooth and shiny outer surface. There is a great variety of techniques for layering surface shaders, just like there are many other techniques for painting. Fig. 8.2.5 shows an interface to compose complex surfaces with layers.

8.3 Image Mapping

Image mapping is a very important component of the surface shading process, it is also a rich technique that deserves to be examined separately. The basic idea behind **image mapping** consists of taking a two-dimensional image and mapping it on the surface of a three-dimensional object. There are many mapping techniques, for example, projecting or wrapping, and each creates a distinct result. But the real power of image mapping lies in the fact that two-dimensional images can be used to very efficiently simulate not only the texture of a three-dimensional surface, but also other surface attributes such as reflectivity, transparency, and roughness.

Image mapping techniques are often used as shortcuts for simulating surface characteristics. In fact, the exact same image can be mapped in different ways onto a surface for simulating attributes such as reflectivity, color, texture, and transparency (Figs. 8.3.1).

Images maps can modulate the surface characteristics by linking the brightness or color of a pixel in the image map to the characteristics of the point in the surface where that pixel is mapped. For example, the brightness of a pixel in an image map can control the reflectivity of the point on the surface where the pixel is mapped, or its color, or its transparency. Different image maps can also be combined to control different aspects of the surface characteristics of an object. The types of image maps covered in this chapter include reflection and environmental maps, color maps, procedural maps, bump and displacement maps, and transparency maps. The nomenclature used here to describe image maps is quite generic and is used in many three-dimensional software programs. The reader should be cautioned, however, that once in a while the same name is used by different programs to indicate different types of image maps.

Creating the Map

Two-dimensional images that can be mapped onto three-dimensional surfaces include painted images, photographic images, and

8.2.4 The surface in the top layer is composed of the four separate layers below it.

abstract patterns. As explained below, each of these images is best suited for a specific purpose. Image maps can be created directly with computer paint systems, and brought into the rendering program in a variety of file formats. **Digital painting** software—commonly called paint systems—provides many of the tools found in the studio of a traditional painter, such as brushes and sticks of different types, paints of different colors and densities, and papers with different degrees of texture and absorbency (Fig. 8.3.2). These painting tools and media are simulated by the computer system. But in many cases these simulated tools behave like their physical counterparts, especially when a **pressure-sensitive** graphics tablet is used instead of a mouse. Painted images that are to be used as maps can be created from scratch with the computer paint system, or can be based on a sketch or photograph that is scanned into the program.

Images that can be mapped onto three-dimensional surfaces can also be captured directly into the computer system with a variety of input devices. This includes recording a live image with a **digital camera**, or scanning an existing photograph or painting with a flatbed or laser **digital scanner**, or loading an image file that was previously scanned and saved on a **CD-ROM**.

Both scanners and digital cameras transform the visual information into numerical information that can be easily proc essed by the computer software. This conversion is done by converting the **continuous visual information** that we find in reality, a color photograph or a painting into a series of **discrete numerical values**. This conversion is based on an **averaging** of the values found in the original image. The scanning process starts with a **sampling** of the color values in the image. The number of samples taken from an image directly determines the spatial resolution of the image map.

Projection Methods

There are many ways of projecting image maps onto three-dimensional surfaces. Some projection methods are simple and others are complex, some create realistic effects and others create surprising results. Choosing a **mapping projection method** should be based on creative considerations without ignoring production concerns. Some projection methods may express the ideas behind a rendered image better than others. Some of the most useful projection methods include flat and cubical, cylindrical, and spherical.

The **flat projection** method applies maps onto surfaces in a flat way. This projection method is ideal for applying image

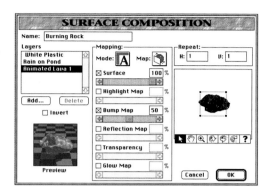

8.2.5 An editor for the composition of surface layers, mapping projection, and interactive map placement. (Dialog box from Infini-D 3.0. © 1991-1995 Specular International, Ltd.)

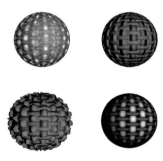

8.3.1 The same two-dimensional image is used as a map to control different surface attributes including color, texture (bump and displacement), and transparency.

8.3.2 Digital painting techniques were used in addition to sophisticated rendering and image compositing to create this image of the Columbia Pictures identity. (Produced by Kleiser-Walczak Construction Co. for First Light, Inc. and Columbia Pictures. Animated by Jeff Kleiser, Diana Walczak, and Ed Kramer. Courtesy of Kleiser-Walczak Construction Co.)

maps onto flat surfaces because the results are totally predictable, and the potential for distortion is minimal as long as the three-dimensional surface is parallel to the projection plane. In principle, flat projection can occur on any plane—XY, XZ, and YZ—with identical results as long as the three-dimensional surface is parallel to the projection plane. But flat projection can also be used on curved objects to simulate the effect of slide or film projectors because this method projects a flat image in a perpendicular way onto whatever is in front of it (Fig. 8.3.3a). Another useful application of flat projection is the creation of **backdrops** and simple **dioramas** that include three-dimensional objects and characters placed in front of a painted or photographic backdrop.

The **cubical projection** method is a variation of the flat projection method that repeats the map on each of the six sides of a cube. This projection method is particularly effective with cubes but only as long as one of the planes of the cube is parallel to the projection plane. Cubical projection can also be used on curved or irregular objects to achieve unexpected results (Fig. 8.3.3b).

The **cylindrical projection** method applies maps onto surfaces by wrapping the sides of the map around the shape until the two ends of the map meet behind the object (Fig. 8.3.3c). This projection technique is useful to map textures around elongated objects like a carrot or a glass bottle. Cylindrical projections are designed to wrap around the object and to cover its entire surface, but wrapping of cylindrical projections can be customized so that the opposite sides of the map do not meet and cover only a portion of the object. This is controlled by specifying the **angle of mapping** around the object with a degree value. A cylindrical projection can also be customized by determining whether the top and bottom of the object are to be left uncovered or whether they are to be covered with a cap. A cap in a cylindrical projection uses the same texture wrapped around the object unless specified otherwise.

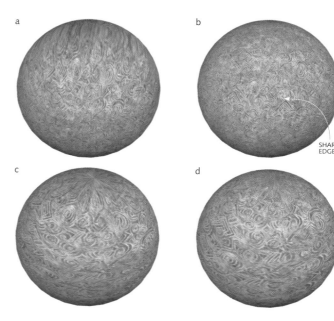

8.3.3 An image map is applied to a sphere with different projection methods: flat or straight projection (a), cubical projection (b), cylindrical projection (c), and spherical projection (d). Notice the sharp edge where the two surfaces meet in the cubical projection, and how the capless cylindrical projection slightly stretches the map towards the poles.

The **spherical projection** applies a rectangular map by wrapping it around a surface until the opposite sides meet, and then pinching it at the top and bottom and stretching it until the entire object is covered. This technique is useful for projecting maps onto round objects, such as a basketball or a football. Spherical projections wrap the map around the entire three-dimensional object unless the projection is customized to cover just a portion of the object. This can be controlled—as it is in cylindrical projections—by specifying an angle of mapping (Fig. 8.3.3d).

The **wrapping** projection method—as it is called in some programs—allows textures to be projected onto three-dimensional objects in a straight way, but also be stretched until the four sides of the map are pressed against each other. This projection type is useful for placing texture maps over objects that may require stretching throughout the map for a good fit, for example, terrains or complex surfaces. This technique is also effective for applying textures to small portions of three-dimensional objects in the form in which decals are applied to model airplanes (Fig. 8.3.4).

Positioning the Map

There are a variety of techniques that facilitate the placement of

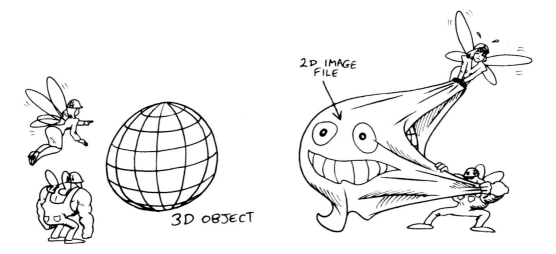

2D IMAGE FILE

3D OBJECT

8.3.4 Wrapping projection is useful for fitting image maps with maximum coverage onto three-dimensional objects.

texture maps on three-dimensional surfaces. Ideally, maps should cover the entire three-dimensional surface unless a specific project requires a different approach. Texture maps are always **rectangular images** that are applied to polygonal or curved surfaces, and they can be defined by tagging their four corners. The nomenclature for identifying the corners of a texture map is simple whether the surface is made of polygons or curved patches (Fig. 8.3.5). The upper left corner of the map is designated as the origin (0, 0), the lower left corner is (0, 1), the upper right corner is (1, 0), and the lower left corner is (1, 1). In some cases, the lower left corner is designated as the origin, and the upper right corner is designated (1, 1).

Ordinarily a texture map is pinned by default to the origin of a surface, wherever the origin may be (origins can be located, for example, in one corner of the surface or in its center). This procedure is straight-forward in cases when the three-dimensional surfaces are simple, and when the maps are supposed to cover the entire shape. However placing texture maps on three-dimensional surfaces requires some fine-tuning when the surfaces are complex, when the proportions of the map and the surface differ, or when special effects are sought. It is important to keep in mind that the tools for positioning of the texture maps over three-dimensional surfaces vary greatly between programs.

Some programs allow interactive placement of texture maps over three-dimensional surfaces. Texture maps can also be positioned very accurately over three-dimensional surfaces by inputting **numerical values**. With this method a map can be moved with precision over the surface. In the cases of polygonal objects, **XY coordinates** are used to **offset the map** over the surface. The default position of maps aligns them at (0, 0). If the map is offset by (.5, .5) then it will be moved horizontally and vertically halfway across the surface. Figure 8.3.6 shows a map that is translated, or offset, over an object that can also be translated and rotated interactively.

In general, the **parameter space** used to position image maps on curved patches is based on the rectangular coordinate system used when maps are applied to polygonal models. But points on curved surface are defined in terms of their **UV coordinates** instead of their XY values. The parameter space of a curved surfaces is defined by a U (or u) horizontal value that stretches from 0 to 1, and a V (or v) vertical value that also ranges from 0 to 1. The value of U is commonly 0 on the left edge of the parameter space, and 1 on the right edge. The value of V is 0 at the top of the parameter space, and 1 at the bottom. All the points located within this rectangular parameter space are defined in terms of U,V coordinates. The rectangle is twisted and bent to match the shape of curved patches or quadric surfaces, which are built from a curve that is swept in three-dimensional space around an axis, like a surface of revolution. In quadric surfaces, the U axis represents longitude and it runs approximately the circumference of the revolution, the V axis represents latitude and runs along the curve that is used to define the surface.

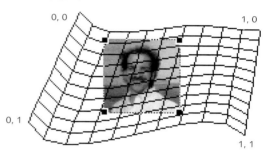

8.3.5 The parameters for placing maps interactively on a surface range from (0, 0) to (1, 1).

Positioning image maps with UV coordinates is a very precise method that allows to match specific pixels on the mapped image with specific vertices on the surface of the three-dimensional object. When mapping textures on curved surfaces it is common to use UV parameters. Similar accurate placement techniques are also available for positioning image maps onto polygonal structures. Image textures that are mapped with UV techniques usually stretch in a way that follows with little distortion the shape of the three-dimensional object. This is due to the extreme control of image pixel-to-object vertex matching offered by UV mapping. Textures mapped with UV techniques are like elastic surfaces, a silk stocking, for example, that stretch over three-dimensional objects.

In addition to all the controls for accurately placing a two-dimensional image map on a three-dimensional surface, there are other techniques for controlling the map once it has been placed on the surface. These techniques include scaling and tiling. **Scaling** image maps can be used when the maps need to cover more or less of the surface of an object. Image maps that are too small to cover the entire object can be scaled up. Likewise, image maps that are too large to be seen in their entirety when placed on the surface of the object can be scaled down. Scaling of

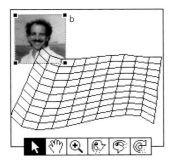

8.3.6 An image map is first placed at (0, 0), which happens to be in the center of the object (a). Then it is offset to (-1.8, -1.9) so that it is aligned near one of the corners of the surface (b). Finally the map is tiled (c) with a UV tiling factor of (5, 5). (b. Graph from Infini-D 3.0. © 1991-1995 Specular International, Ltd.)

image maps can also be used in cases where the software automatically scales a map of any dimension to fit the object but the desired effect requires that the map only covers a portion of the object.

Tiling an image allows to create patterns based on repeating a tile or single rectangular image map. A large number of three-dimensional software programs can repeat an image in a variety of arrangements along the vertical and horizontal axes. Some tiling permutations commonly available are: plain repetition without any image flipping, repetition with horizontal flipping on every other tile only, repetition with vertical flipping only, and repetition with both horizontal and vertical flipping (Fig. 8.3.6).

Map Blending

Map blending techniques determine the way in which surface layers, including image maps, blend with the surface of the object as well as with other surface layers. The blending of an image map with other surface characteristics can be controlled in a variety of ways. Some map blending techniques include: overall blending, blending by types of illumination, blending with alpha channel, and blending with matting techniques. **Overall blending** allows to control the degree by which the image map blends uniformly with all the attributes of the surface. Overall blending is usually expressed in percentages of visibility, ranging from blending where only the map is visible to blending where only the surface is visible (and the map is totally invisible). Intermediate stages of overall blending allow for different degrees of blending. Blending by type of **surface illumination** controls the degree by which the maps blends with the surface by splitting it in terms of ambient, diffuse, and specular areas of surface illumination.

Blending with **matting techniques** allows to control the degree of blending using different parts or aspects of the image map as a mask. A **mask** is an image that masks or protects a surface, or portions of it, and determines the degree by which different portions of the image map blend with the surface. Masks can be high-contrast or continuous. **High-contrast masks** have sharp edges and solid areas while **continuous masks** have soft edges and different shades of gray. Blending with matting techniques can be done by using all the pixels in the image map to mask out the surface, or by using only the black or white pixels in the map as a mask. Overall blending controls can be used in conjunction with matting techniques for creating a wide variety of blending possibilities (Fig. 8.3.7).

Blending or compositing with an alpha channel allows to control the blending of the surface and the image map according to an additional image file that is used as a mask in the matting process. An **alpha channel** is a black and white image file that is linked to an image map. Alpha channels can be saved with an image file in the form of a fourth channel in a standard RGB image file. An alpha channel can be used to determine the degree of blending of the image map with a surface based on the intensity of brightness values of the pixels in the file used as alpha channels. Some programs assign total blending (or total transparency) to the black pixels in the alpha channel, and lack of blending (or total opacity) to the white pixels. Other programs assign total blending to the white pixels and total opacity to the black pixels in the alpha channel. The pixels with gray values are always assigned different degrees of blending. (Read Chapter 12 for more information on matting techniques and the alpha channel.)

8.4 Surface Reflectivity

Light can be reflected off reflective surfaces in different ways depending on the proportion of the types or components of surface reflectivity. The basic three types of surface reflectivity are: ambient, diffuse, and specular. These types of surface reflectivity refer only to **reflection of light**, and are also called **areas of illumination** of a surface. A fully reflective object that also reflects the environment surrounding it can only be simulated with the ray tracing rendering method described in Chapter 5, or with the reflection mapping techniques described later in this chapter.

Different combinations of surface reflectivity types can be used to simulate the surfaces of different materials. **Matte surfaces**, for example, can be simulated by using a combination of ambient and diffuse reflections. **Metallic surfaces** can be simulated with ambient and specular reflections. **Plastic surfaces** are typically simulated with a combination of ambient, diffuse, and specular reflections (Fig. 8.4.1d). Most shading software programs provide accurate controls to vary the sharpness and decay of the specular reflection in both metallic and plastic surfaces.

Ambient Reflection

The type of surface reflection that reacts to the intensity and color of the ambient light sources only is called **ambient reflection**. A unique characteristic of ambient reflection is that its intensity is independent of the distance between the reflective surface and the light source and also of the angle of the surface in respect to the light source. This means that light scatters evenly in all directions and that, as a result, all the polygons in three-dimensional models that are shaded with just ambient reflection end-up with the same intensity. As a result the three-dimensional models appear as a completely flat silhouette when only this

a

b

c

d

8.3.7 Blending with matting techniques can be used to reveal or cover portions of the image layers on the surface of an object. In this example the final result (a) was obtained by layering an image map (b) and its own alpha channel (c) onto a blue sphere, and revealing the dark blue surface of the sphere only through the black pixels in the alpha channel. A similar result can be obtained with a simpler image map without an alpha channel (d) and using the white pixels in the map to reveal the dark blue surface underneath.

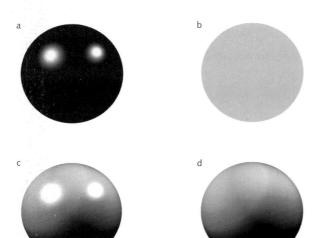

a

b

c

d

8.4.1 These images show a simple object rendered with four different combinations of surface reflectivity. The first image is rendered with ambient reflection and an ambient light source only (a). The second image is rendered with diffuse reflection only, one spotlight and one point light (b). The third image is rendered with specular reflection only, one spotlight and one point light (c). The fourth image combines the three types of surface reflectivity and the three light sources (d).

type of reflection is used to shade them. But when ambient reflection is used in conjunction with other types of reflection it contributes to the overall intensity of the object. (Fig. 8.4.1a).

Diffuse Reflection

A surface with **diffuse reflection** reacts to incident light in different ways depending on the position and orientation of the light source in respect to the surface. Naturally, a light source that is very close to a surface with diffuse reflection will reflect more than a light source that is far away. But the most important factor in diffuse reflection is not so much the distance between the light source and the object but the angular position of the light source in relation to the object. Diffuse reflection is greater in areas of the surface that face the light source in a perpendicular way. The amount of light reflected with diffuse reflection decreases as the angle between the incident light source and the reflective surface becomes more oblique. Areas of a surface with diffuse reflection that are not reached by the light reflect very little or not at all (Fig. 8.4.1b). The size of the surface area that faces the light source is also a factor in the intensity of the reflected light when using diffuse reflection.

Specular Reflection

Surfaces with **specular reflection** appear very shiny because they reflect light the way a mirror does. Specular reflection light does not scatter evenly throughout the surface. Instead it is reflected in a focused and concentrated way, a characteristic known as **highlight sharpness**. In determining the amount of light reflected by surfaces with specular reflection the position of the light source alone in respect to the surface is not as critical as it is in diffuse reflections. Instead, the apparent intensity of light reflected off surfaces with specular reflection depends mostly on the relation between the angle of the reflected light and the angle of the camera that is looking at the object. The intensity of the reflected light is greater when these two angles coincide. As the two angles move farther apart the intensity of the reflected light decays sharply, a characteristic known as **highlight decay** (Fig. 8.4.1c).

Reflection Maps

The visual effects of reflection can be used effectively to render shiny materials such as glasses, metals, or plastics, and varnished surfaces. When applied to objects that are not ordinarily reflective in the real world, reflectivity attributes can be effective to simulate virtual realities. Realistic reflection effects can be best obtained with ray tracing rendering, which simulates with precision the amount of reflectivity on a three-dimensional surface. Another strategy for creating reflective surfaces is based on reflection maps.

A **reflection map** consists of a two-dimensional image that is applied to a three-dimensional surface with the purpose of making the surface—or portions of it—reflective. A surface with a reflection map reflects the image of the three-dimensional models that are placed in front of the surface. The brightness values in a reflection map are used by the software to determine which parts of the surface are reflective and which are not. The dark values in a reflection map are used by some programs to determine which parts of the object will be fully reflective, but sometimes the light values in the map are used for the same purpose. Either way, the final results are the same.

Reflection maps are usually monochromatic and not in full color because the brightness values drive the simulation of reflectivity. Chromatic information in reflection maps is irrelevant and can also be misleading to the individual who fine tunes the subtle degrees of reflection in the map. Reflection maps can be projected onto three-dimensional surfaces with any of the standard projections used in texture mapping.

8.4.2 An environment map is mapped onto an irregular sphere with 100 percent reflectivity, and 90 percent specular highlights.

Environment Maps

Environment maps, like other types of image maps, are used to compute the color of light reflected by the surface of the map. **Environment maps** can be thought of as a special type of reflection map because they reflect not only the objects surrounding the mapped object, but also the environment surrounding the reflective surfaces (Fig. 8.4.2). But the main characteristic of environment maps is that they are projected on all the objects with reflective surface characteristics in the scene and not just on

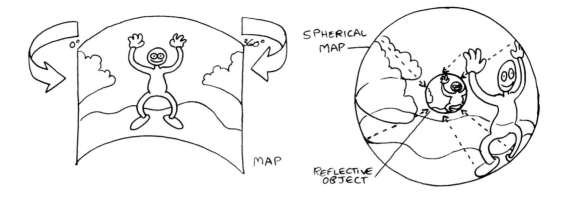

8.4.3 In spherical environment mapping, a flattened image of the environment is created and then mapped inside a spherical space that contains the reflective objects.

one particular object. (Reflection maps are usually applied to only one three-dimensional surface at a time.) The reflections of the surroundings on a group of objects can also be calculated with ray tracing rendering, but environment maps are often a cost-effective way to achieve similar results that are appropriate and sufficient in a large number of rendering projects. This technique is a favored alternative for creating the appearance of global reflections when ray tracing rendering methods are not used. When both ray tracing and environment mapping are active simultaneously most rendering programs calculate the two parameters. However, in such cases, priority is usually given to the ray-traced reflections by placing them closer to the objects, and in front of the environment map reflections.

Environment maps create an image of the environment that surrounds the object as seen from the object itself. The appearance of the reflection of the environment is achieved by preparing a simplified version of the three-dimensional environment in the form of two-dimensional images and then projecting those images onto the object with reflective surfaces as if they were the environment being reflected. Environment maps can be created with a variety of techniques. Two popular choices include a technique that resembles the spherical projection method and a technique that is an interesting variation of cubical projection of maps. In both cases though, an image of the environment is first mapped inside the spherical or cubical space that contains the reflective object, and only then is the environment mapped onto the object or objects inside of the space (Fig. 8.4.3 and 8.4.4). Other environment mapping techniques that include procedural generation of environments are described below.

Spherical environment mapping is based on a flat image that is first projected on the inside of a sphere that represents the environment. The sphere is defined as a longitudinal space that goes from 0 to 360 degrees, and a latitudinal space that

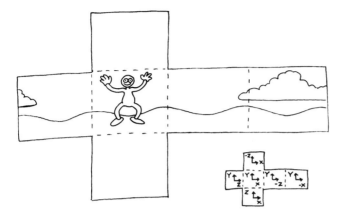

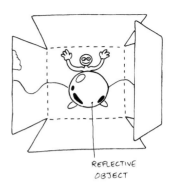

8.4.4 In cubic environment mapping, a six-panel view of the environment is created and then mapped inside a cube that surrounds the reflective objects. The small diagram indicates the orientation of each of the six two-dimensional views of the simulated environment.

ranges from -90 to 90 degrees. Once the image representing the environment has been applied to the sphere it is then projected onto the object or objects that need environment mapping and that are placed inside the sphere. When an image is mapped inside a spherical environment, its left and right edges of the image end up butting against each other, and its top and bottom edges are crimped. It is necessary to keep these mapping distortions in mind when preparing the image map for environmental spherical mapping. It usually works best when the left and right edges of the image map match perfectly with one another, this way their projection can be seamless. It is also useful to keep the top and bottom areas of the image map uncluttered in order to avoid extreme distortion when the images on the top and bottom of the spherical space are somewhat compressed when crimped (Fig. 8.4.3).

The process of assembling an image suitable for **cubical environment mapping** is somewhat more demanding that preparing a spherical environment map. This is largely due to the fact that an environmental map based on the modified cubic projection is created by assembling six views of a scene. These six different views of a three-dimensional scene must represent a simplified view of the environment as if seen from inside an object that is placed at the center of this environment. The six views of the environment include four side views, a top view, and a bottom view. The four side views are created by looking from the center of the environment towards the outside in angular increments of 90 degrees. In addition, each of the four side views must capture a full 90 degree view of the environment, so that when the four side views are assembled in sequence next to each other the result is a full 360 degree view of the environment (Fig. 8.4.4). The six panels required for a cubical environmental map can be painted from the imagination of an artist, or photographed in a real environment. These six panels can also be created by rendering six different 90 degree views of a computer-generated three-dimensional space. The images used in an environment map can also be generated with procedural techniques. Simple **color ramps**, for example, can be generated procedurally in the form of smooth gradations or blendings of color, and are commonly used to represent clean skies or the chromatic effects of the sunrise or sunset on horizon lines. Clouds and an assortment of lighting effects can also be created procedurally and be used as environment maps (Figs. 5.6.1 and 8.4.5).

Environment maps can be animated to represent the motion that may happen around objects with mapped surfaces. The activity in a busy café can be simulated, for example, by mapping on a reflective sugar bowl a movie of people walking, drinking coffee, and interacting with each other. Another example of an animated environment map would consist of a movie of people dancing on the floor of a discotheque. This sequence could be mapped on the rotating silver sphere that is used to deflect light in all directions, or the eyeglasses being worn by an observer.

Some programs provide tools for accurately placing the environment map on the surface. This interactive preview is commonly done in low resolution or in the wireframe mode, and it can save a lot of rendering tests that are otherwise necessary to find out how an environment map falls on a three-dimensional surface.

Some programs provide rich procedures for generating environment textures of skies that take into account not only the position and brightness of the sun and whether the sky is cloudy or not, but also atmospheric parameters such as the curvature of the planet, and the densities of the air and dust particles. (Shading that takes into account atmospheric characteristics is related to the volume shaders mentioned later in this chapter).

8.4.5 The cloud dialog box. (Dialog box from Alias PowerAnimator. © Alias Research, Inc.)

Glow or Incandescence

Surface **glow**, sometimes called **incandescence**, is a surface characteristic that is associated with reflectivity. Incandescence makes objects glow in ways that resemble a variety of naturally glowing objects. Incandescent objects may appear as if they have an internal light source, like a fiber optic transmitting light for example, or as if they generate a glow because of their extremely high temperature, such as molten lava, for example (Fig. 8.4.6). This surface characteristic also resembles the opalescence of some gems that results from the reflection of iridescent light. Glow can be created as a uniform color across a surface or with an image map that determines which areas of the surface display glow. Glow or incandescence, however, is not related to the light sources in the three-dimensional scene, and it does not turn the glowing object into a light source either. A surface glow is quite different from a light glow, and objects with surface glow do not cast light on the surrounding objects.

8.5 Surface Color

Surface color is one of the most obvious of all surface characteristics. Color attributes are easier to identify and remember than most other surface characteristics. Surface color contributes to the personality of a three-dimensional character or the mood of a scene. When assigning a specific color to a three-dimensional surface it is important to keep in mind that the final color of the surface will also be greatly influenced by external factors such as the angle and color of the lighting applied to the surface, and even the color of the surrounding objects when rendering techniques such as radiosity or ray tracing are used.

Surface color can be defined with a variety of color models, many of which are covered in Chapter 5. Additive or light-based color models, like RGB or HLS, are used to define the colors in images displayed on computer monitors. Subtractive or pigment-oriented systems, such as CMYK, are used to define the colors in computer printouts. When defining surface color it is important to keep in mind the **color shifting** that occurs when a computer-generated image is moved from an additive color environment—like an RGB monitor—to a subtractive color environment—like a printout on paper (see Chapter 13 for more details on minimizing color shifting).

Color Maps

A great variety of subtle or loud color effects can be created by mapping two-dimensional images onto the surface of three-dimensional objects. Like other types of image maps, **color maps** are used to compute the color of light reflected by the three-dimensional surface on which the color map has been placed (Fig. 8.3.1). Color maps are also called **picture maps** because they often involve photographic images. Color maps are often used to represent the images and labels that we find on packages and containers such as a cardboard cereal box, a glass wine bottle with a paper label glued on, or a plastic shampoo bottle with lettering printed directly on the plastic surface.

When color maps are applied to three-dimensional models of cardboard cereal boxes, for example, six different images are usually mapped with flat projection onto each of the six panels in the box. In cases such as this, when the label or printed graphics

8.4.6 These images show the effects of shading the incandescent object (in the center) with and without a surface glow.

cover the entire surface of the packaging, there is no need to use other types of maps in conjunction with the color map.

It is common to use the cylindrical projection method when color maps are applied to three-dimensional models of glass containers. This projection method allows the label to be mapped onto the side of the bottle or jar. If the label being simulated is of a rectangular design and made of an opaque material, there is usually no need to use other types of maps in addition to the color map. But a transparency map may be necessary to define, for example, a label made of translucent paper, or an opaque label with a shape other than strictly rectangular. In the latter case, a label with a triangular shape, for example, has to be contained within a rectangular color map because virtually all three-dimensional shading programs require that image maps be rectangular. In such case, a transparency map would also be used to specify the triangular area of the label as opaque, and the excess or unused areas within the rectangular map as fully transparent. (For more information on transparency maps read Surface Transparency at the end of this chapter.)

Color maps can also be applied to three-dimensional models of plastic containers, like a shampoo bottle, for example. This type of container often requires that the lettering be printed directly on the plastic surface of the container, without a paper label being involved. In such cases, it is common to use the cylindrical projection method and a transparency map in addition to the color map. The transparency map is used to determine the opacity and transparency of different areas in the color map. The lettering and other graphic elements would be opaque, and the background (or areas in the map without lettering or graphic elements) would be transparent so that the plastic surface of the bottle can show through the transparent areas in the color map. Displacement maps (described later in this chapter) can be used to simulate the slight relief of the lettering and graphics that are silkscreened on containers with thick ink, enamel, or varnish.

Color maps can be projected onto surfaces by using any of the standard mapping techniques described earlier in this chapter. Interactive positioning of color maps is useful for accurate placement of labels and lettering on three-dimensional surfaces. Some systems provide a wireframe mode for positioning labels, which is usually much faster than any rendering test would be.

8.6 Surface Texture

It is possible to create very interesting visual effects by applying textures onto the surfaces of three-dimensional objects. Surface textures can be modeled so that they have true dimensionality. Modeling surface characteristics, however, is usually time-consuming and also results in inefficient three-dimensional models that require a lot of rendering time. This can be especially wasteful when objects with **modeled surface textures** are too far from the camera for the surface detail to be appreciated. Surface textures can also be simulated with a technique originally known as texture mapping, which today can be more accurately described as image mapping. This method, pioneered in the mid-1970s by Ed Catmull, affects the intensity and chromatic values of a surface, but it does not affect its smoothness.

The great variety of **texturing** techniques can be grouped in visual and spatial textures. **Visual textures** are flat simulations of three-dimensional texture and do not affect the geometrical surface of the object; they look textured but they are not. For example, a visual texture representing bricks is like brick **wallpaper**, and different from a real wall of bricks with relief textures that can be felt by touch (Fig. 8.6.1). A practical benefit of using visual textures—in addition to their inherent aesthetic value—is the they make possible the creation of complex and rich textures with a minimal investment of polygons. Some of the most useful visual textures include color and procedural maps, as well as environment, bump, and transparency maps.

Spatial textures exist in three-dimensional space and affect the spatial integrity of the smooth surface of an object. Spatial textures are closer than visual textures to the concept of a real tactile texture. Spatial textures can be created by modelling a detailed mesh of planar polygons. But this approach is time consuming and impractical. More effective methods for creating spatial textures include using bump and displacement maps, or the fractal modeling techniques described in Chapter 4.

8.6.1 The visual maps in this image include weathered metal surfaces with rust, corrosion, bumps, and raised patterns. (Screen shot from Myst® CD-ROM computer game. Game and screen shot are © 1993 by Cyan, Inc®. All rights reserved.)

Bump Maps

Bump maps provide an effective way to simulate roughness or bumpiness on a flat surface. **Bump maps** alter the orientation of the surface normals during the shading process. Changing the orientation of the surface normals of polygons before shading then causes the light to be reflected in several directions simulating the way light would be reflected from an object with rough surfaces. This results in the appearance of a textured surface with modulations that resemble the pattern contained in the image file used as a bump map (Fig. 8.3.1). The darkest values in the image map may represent the valleys, and the lightest values simulate the peaks in the simulated texture, or vice versa. The surface, however, remains flat, and the peaks cannot project a shadow.

Bump maps are an effective technique for creating complex and realistic textures especially in objects that are not too close to the camera or that also have a slightly irregular shape. Bump maps, however, create undesirable results when applied to objects that are too close to the camera and with their edges visible. This is due to the fact that bump maps do not create any texture on the profiles of objects. This flaw is accentuated when the bump map has a wide range of brightness values that create the impression of a lot of bumpiness and that may contrast a lot with the smooth profile of the object.

Spatial textures exist in three-dimensional space and affect the spatial integrity of the smooth surface of an object. Spatial textures are closer than visual textures to the concept of real tactile textures.

An alternate method for creating visual textures, developed by Jim Blinn and refined by several authors, simulates the imperfections on a smooth surface not by affecting the surface itself

8.6.2 A terrain created by displacing the XYZ locations of a surface with an image map.

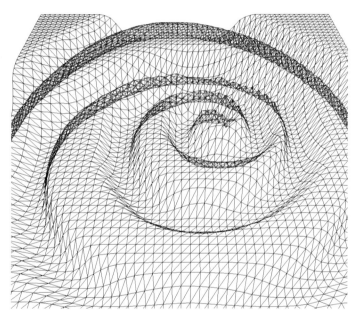

but by altering the surface normals of the object. Altering the surface normals before shading the object causes the light to be reflected in several directions, therefore simulating the way light would be reflected if the object would be really textured.

Bump maps are often used in combination with parametric waves to represent the motion of water. This motion is usually limited to the linear or concentric undulations created on the surface of the water by wind or objects that touch a point on the surface (Fig. 10.2.9b). Parametric waves used as bump maps can also be used as displacement maps to create a more three-dimensional effect.

Displacement Maps

Displacement maps provide a unique way to use an image map to actually modify not only the shading but also the geometry of the surface being mapped. **Displacement maps** alter both the orientation of the surface normals, and the three-dimensional position of the surface itself. This results in a truly textured surface that has three-dimensionality as well as two-dimensional patterns mapped on it (Figs. 8.3.1 and 8.6.2).

Displacement maps are often used to create three-dimensional terrain that includes mountains and valleys. Terrains can be built with displacement maps that are based on photographic images of aerial views where the different elevations are coded with different colors or shades of gray. Three-dimensional terrains can also be built by generating two-dimensional images with fractal techniques and using them as displacement maps. Whether photographic or fractal, the two-dimensional images are usually applied to a three-dimensional surface in the form of a black and white displacement map and also as a color map.

Two-Dimensional Procedural Texture Maps

As mentioned earlier, the two-dimensional images that can be mapped onto three-dimensional surfaces can be painted by hand, captured with cameras, or created with procedural techniques. **Procedural creation** relies on mathematical functions or computer programs to create images that are usually abstract. Mathematical functions that create pseudo-random or rhythmic patterns of color are popular ways to create two-dimensional procedural texture maps (Fig. 8.6.3). Two-dimensional images that are created with procedural techniques can be mapped onto three-dimensional surfaces following the standard procedures for image-mapping.

Some software programs provide tools to extract two-dimensional image maps from three-dimensional procedural texture maps. This handy function works by taking a snapshot of the surface texture on the object with solid texture and saving it as an image file that can be mapped onto other objects. This option is especially useful when rendering speed is a consideration, and in many cases image files are mapped faster than procedural textures. However, they also require more storage space since image files—especially those that are high resolution—tend to be large files.

8.6.3 Examples of procedural two-dimensional textures. The first two textures from top left to bottom right (a-b) were generated with procedures based on functions with different levels of complexity, detail, twisting, and contrast. The next four textures (c-f) were created by blending the two original textures with the same function curves, and the following operators: A+B, A-B, A x B, and A/B. The remainder of the textures (g-l) were created with the A/B operator, and a different combination of function curves each time.

0-0-0	50-0-0	100-0-0	0-50-0
0-100-0	0-0-50	0-0-100	25-0-25
50-50-0	50-0-50	0-50-50	50-50-50
100-100-0	100-0-100	0-100-100	100-100-100
0-50-100	0-100-50	100-0-50	100-50-0

8.6.4 Variations of a solid wood texture cross-section created with different values of swirling, grain density, and cutting. These previews are used to quickly visualize how a solid texture looks like before it is sent to a detailed rendering. Examine the first example with values of 0-0-0, the third example with maximum swirl values of 100-0-0, the fifth example with maximum grain values of 0-100-0, the seventh example with maximum cutting values of 0-0-100, and the sixteenth with overall maximum values of 100-100-100.

Three-Dimensional Procedural Texture Maps

Many of the textural qualities of objects found in nature can be easily simulated with texture maps created with three-dimensional procedures. Three-dimensional procedural texture maps are **solid textures** that exist on the surface of an object as well as inside the object. These textures are based on mathematical functions or short programs that create abstract patterns. But unlike two-dimensional procedural textures that are projected only on the surface of an object, three-dimensional procedural texture maps distribute the three-dimensional patterns throughout the object being textured. A small chunk of marble is a good example of how three-dimensional solid textures behave. On the outside marble has a very distinct texture defined by the colors and surface characteristics of the minerals that it is composed of. But the texture of marble does not only occur on its surface, it continues inside of the stone because the minerals that define the marble are all throughout the stone. The texture of marble cannot be peeled off like a two-dimensional texture map could. When the stone is chipped or cut, the surface texture changes revealing the inner mineral composition and continued texture of the stone.

Many natural and synthetic materials can be recreated with procedural solid textures. This is done by providing different values to a variety of procedural parameters, such as color, roughness, frequency, scaling, orientation, cohesion, and density. These values can be typed directly on the keyboard or controlled interactively with sliders. Some natural materials that are offered as pre-packaged standard options in many software programs include a variety of stones, such as marble and granite, wood, corroded metal, leather, and even smoke and clouds (Fig. 8.6.4).

Software programs have slightly different ways for defining three-dimensional solid textures, and each produces a unique result. Figures 8.6.5–7 illustrate how marble solid textures are defined by different software. In the first example, the variables used are Color 1, Color 2, X Weight, Y Weight, Z Weight, Turbulence, and Cohesion (Fig. 8.6.5). In the second example, the variables are Color 1, Color 2, Color 3, Color 4, Color 5, Spacing, Angle, Strength, Iteration, and Power (Fig. 8.6.6). In the third example, the variables used are Filler_color, Vein_color, Vein_width, Diffusion, and Contrast (Fig. 8.6.7). In the last example, other general three-dimensional solid texture variables associated with marble definitions include some noise parameters and the minimum and maximum levels of recursion depth.

Many procedural texturing techniques are based on the idea that some degree of controlled randomness is useful, even necessary, to define the characteristics of specific textures. This randomness is often specified in the form of a **noise** function that generates stochastic (or pseudo-random) values, and feeds them to the procedure as the solid texture is calculated. Much of the parametric randomness contained in procedural textures is best defined with noise functions. One way to define the turbulence in marble-like surfaces, for example, is with patterns whose magnitude decreases with frequency. This means that as the marble texture patterns become tighter—as their frequency increases—their area on the surface becomes smaller.

Placing solid procedural textures is usually done by typing numerical values that offset the texture across the model that the solid texture is applied to. Some software programs preview how the solid texture looks on a shape (Fig. 8.6.8). Procedural solid texture maps do not use the standard projection techniques. Solid textures exist throughout the object (outside and inside), and there is no need to project them.

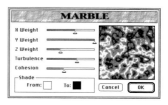

8.6.5 Dialog box for a three-dimensional marble texture. (Dialog box from Infini-D 3.0. © 1991-1995 Specular International, Ltd.)

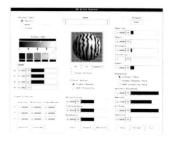

8.6.6 A three-dimensional texture dialog box. (Dialog box from Softimage 3D. © Microsoft Corporation. All rights reserved.)

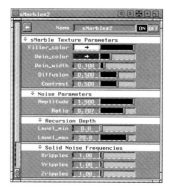

8.6.7 A three-dimensional texture dialog box. (Dialog box from Alias PowerAnimator. © Alias Research, Inc.)

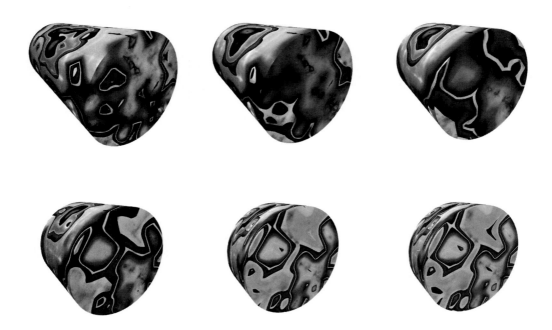

8.6.8 Slicing a cylinder reveals how solid textures exist throughout objects.

8.7 Surface Transparency

Transparency and translucency effects are useful to render materials such as glass or water, and also to visualize fantastic transformations of matter—for example, a short animation that shows how opaque charcoal turns into a transparent diamond. **Surface transparency** is represented by simulating the behavior of light on transparent materials. Realistic transparency effects are best simulated with the ray tracing rendering method (described in Chapter 5), which usually provides accurate controls for transparency and for light refraction.

Transparency Maps

Another strategy for simulating transparency consists of applying transparency maps to the surface of a three-dimensional object. A **transparency map** consists of a monochromatic two-dimensional image that is applied to a three-dimensional surface with the purpose of making all or some of the surface transparent. The basic idea behind a transparency map is that the rendering program looks at the **brightness values** of the pixels in the map and uses them to determine whether the surface will be transparent, opaque, or translucent.

Some programs use the black values in the transparency map as the indicator for full transparency, while other programs use the white values to activate full transparency. In either case a gray transparency map results in a translucent surface (Fig. 8.7.1). Creating a transparency map in full color is somewhat of a waste of time because the majority of shading programs only pay attention to the grayscale brightness values when dealing with transparency maps. Furthermore, preparing transparency maps in color can be distracting and can also make it more difficult for users to focus on the brightness values.

An interesting situation occurs when transparent surfaces are rendered with both reflection maps and reflectivity settings in the ray tracing rendering method. Most rendering programs combine the ray-traced reflections with the effect of the reflection map, but the ray tracing of reflected three-dimensional objects takes precedence over the reflection mapping.

8.7.1 Ray tracing of an irregular sphere with 80 percent transparency, a 2.5 refraction index, 90 percent specular highlight, a six-level transparency tracing depth, and no reflection.

8.8 Environment-Dependent Shading

There is a large variety of shading attributes that are determined by the characteristics of the three-dimensional environment in which the rendered objects are placed. Some of the most common tools for controlling environment-dependent variables include antialising, motion blur, and depth-fading.

Antialiasing

When the spatial resolution of an image is too low, its details are often lost. This phenomenon is called **spatial aliasing**, and it occurs when the details in the image are smaller that the size of the individual pixels used to represent the image. Aliasing, as spatial aliasing is usually referred to, is usually seen in the form of **jagged edges** of objects, especially those with diagonal and curved profiles. Aliasing effects can be found not only in computer generated images but also in images generated with other media, such as painting or photography, for example, when the brush strokes or the film grain are larger than the image details. Aliasing can also be thought of as the image distortions that result from a limited or insufficient sampling of the original visual data.

8.8.1 The same detail of a three-dimensional scene rendered with three different levels of antialiasing (none, low, and high).

The best way to eliminate aliasing is to increase the **spatial resolution** of an image, which means to increase the number of pixels in the image. However, this approach may also dramatically increase the time that is required to render a three-dimensional scene, because the number of rendering calculations is related to the number of pixels that must be created in an image. Alternative methods for eliminating aliasing effects are called **antialiasing** techniques. These are usually based on **oversampling** and **interpolation** techniques. These techniques determine the color value of a pixel by first examining the value of the surrounding pixels, then averaging those values, and finally using that average to determine the value of the individual pixel.

There are many antialiasing algorithms, and some are more efficient and accurate than others. Some antialiasing techniques can dramatically increase the quality of an image but sometimes at the expense of performance. For this reason, when choosing degrees of antialiasing, users of three-dimensional rendering systems must consider all the factors in a specific production—such as deadlines, budget and quality desired—and apply their best judgement (Fig. 8.8.1).

Motion Blur

When recording reality with a video or a film camera we observe that objects that move too fast in front of the camera appear blurred. This phenomenon is called **motion blur,** and it occurs naturally in film or video recordings where the shutter speed is too slow to freeze an object in motion. Motion blur is a form of **temporal aliasing** that results from samples that are too far apart from each other to capture motion details. The speed of shutters in photographic still cameras is measured in the amount of seconds or fractions of a second that the camera shutter remains open. Usually speeds of 1/250th of a second are necessary to freeze fast-moving objects. The speed of shutters in motion film or video cameras is usually measured in terms of the number of frames that are recorded per second. Most motion cameras have fixed speeds of 24 frames per second (fps) for 35 mm film, and 30 fps for video. Only high-speed motion cameras are capable of high shutter speeds that can freeze the motion of objects. This is achieved by recording a large number of frames per second and, therefore, slowing down the motion of the objects.

Motion blur can add a touch of realism to computer animation because it reminds viewers of the blurring effect that occurs when we record directly with a camera fast-moving real objects (Fig. 8.8.2). But motion blur does not occur naturally in computer animation, it must be added. Motion blur is commonly defined by specifying a shutter speed expressed in seconds or frames per second, and also the rate at which moving objects are sampled while the shutter is open.

For animation that is recorded at 30 fps, for example, a camera shutter that remains open for two frames has a speed of 1/15th (or 2/30ths) of a second. In most shading programs, motion blur is not directly calculated based on the absolute speed of the object but instead based on a minimum number of pixels that the object moves within the two-dimensional space of the image plane of the camera (Fig. 8.8.3). Motion blur is applied as a process that takes place after the calculation of the position of the three-dimensional object in the three-dimensional scene. Even though motion blur softens hard edges, it is not used to compensate for the lack of detail found in aliased images.

8.8.2 Motion blur enhances the animation of a match whose body language was emphasized to achieve the desired motions and attitudes. (© 1994 The Clorox Company. Courtesy of Rhythm & Hues Studios.)

Fog

Most rendering software provide atmospheric or environmental shading tools for simulating the effect of **fog** in a three-dimensional scene. The presence of fog makes the three-dimensional images fade into the color of the fog according to their position relative to the camera (Fig. 8.8.4). Objects that are far away from the camera and deep into the three-dimensional scene blend more with the fog. For this reason this technique is sometimes called **depth-fading**. In most cases, fog and depth-fading are just two different names given to the same function. But in some programs, fog and depth-fading are actually two different functions.

There are many algorithms for calculating fog, and some produce more realistic effects than others. In general, the functionalities of fog tools control the starting and ending distance of the fog, its color, and sometimes its transparency. The starting and ending distances—also called minimum and maximum distances—of the fog specify the distances from the camera to the plane where the fog starts and ends. Objects that are closest to the ending distance blend more with the fog. The color of the fog can be specified with a variety of color models, and in many cases the color of the fog is related to—even determined by—the **background color**, a global shading parameter. The transparency of the fog defines the degree in which the objects placed behind the fog are visible. Opaque fogs, for example, may entirely block everything that is placed behind them, while

8.8.3 The motion blur of an object increases with it speed, and also as the object gets closer to the camera.

somewhat transparent fogs allow the objects behind them to partially show through (Fig. 8.8.5).

Many fog functions provide a **visibility** parameter that is usually related to the depth, or thickness, of the foggy area. Visibility can be easily determined by subtracting the starting distance of the fog from the ending distance.

Both fog and depth-fading techniques can be used to create images that incorporate the principles of aerial perspective refined by Leonardo da Vinci in the 16th century. **Aerial perspective** techniques are used to depict depth in a two-dimensional image by simulating the atmospheric effects of light, temperature, and humidity on objects situated far away from the observer. Aerial perspective was developed to complement the realism of images represented with the principles of linear perspective. (Linear perspective techniques are implemented in the determination of visible surfaces that occurs during the rendering process.)

Many software programs provide fog and depth-fading functionalities, but often these two words represent different versions of an effect. This is the case, for example, with software programs that support the functionalities provided by the RenderMan programming language. The difference between fog and depth-fading basically lies in the way in which each of these operators adds the background color to the light that is reflected by three-dimensional surfaces. Both operators add the background color to the reflected light based on the distance between the surface and the position and orientation of the camera. But in depth-fading the color of a surface is entirely the background color if the surface is beyond the maximum distance, while in fog the reflected light always retains some of the color originally reflected by the surface.

Fog can also be simulated as a cluster of fog particles with uniform density that is placed in front of the camera. Small clusters of fog, smoke, or steam can be created with the solid procedural textures described earlier in this chapter.

Fog belongs to the category of volume shaders, a type of shaders that go beyond light and surface shaders. In the RenderMan environment, for example, **volume shaders** define the characteristics of materials in three-dimensional space that affect light as it travels through them. Our atmosphere, for example, contains gases and even solid and liquid particles that affect light before it reaches our eyes and after being emitted by light sources or being reflected by surfaces. The characteristics of the light or imaging ray that travels through the volume can be defined based on attributes of the volume, such as density, color, and motion. Other examples of light or other types of imaging rays traveling through volumes include underwater scenes and even the inside of the human body (Fig. 4.1.5). A procedure

SHADING AND SURFACE CHARACTERISTICS

related to volume shaders is described earlier in this chapter in the section about environment maps.

In addition to fog that extends only horizontally, some programs offer the capability of simulating distant layers of fog placed at different altitudes. This is usually achieved with an image map that has a painting or a photograph of the horizontal layers of fog. This image map is used to calculate the color of light reflected by objects behind the fog plane or by a color map that is used as a backdrop.

8.9 Getting Ready

Rendering in a Network

Computer networks offer several strategies for increasing the speed of your renderings. But keep in mind that the final performance depends not only on the specifics of the network, but also on the network rendering features of

8.8.4 The fog behind the clock tower fades the surface of the water and the horizon line. (Screen shot from Myst® CD-ROM computer game. Game and screen shot are © 1993 by Cyan, Inc®. All rights reserved.)

your software and computer. The two most common strategies for sending your rendering to other machines on the network are distributed rendering and remote rendering.

Distributed rendering consists of sending portions of a rendering job to different computers on the network, for example, rendering the top half of a scene on one machine and the bottom half on another machine. Distributed rendering requires software that is able to split a rendering job into several sections, and then put the results back together. **Remote rendering** occurs when the rendering of a three-dimensional model—that may reside in your machine—takes place in one of the other machines on the network. Many companies today have **rendering farms** that consist of many computers solely dedicated to network rendering. These rendering farms may be located in the same building as the rest of the company. They may also be located in other buildings, other cities, or in other countries— where rendering labor may be more economical.

Depending on how a computer network is configured, renderings can be sent to other computers with or without the permission of their respective users—also called owners. But regardless of your network configuration or technical skill, keep in mind that it is considered impolite in network etiquette to submit renderings to somebody's computer without his or her express permission. Find out what the rules are regarding remote rendering in the network you use. Not only can you be slowing down another machine on the network by sending your renderings there, but your own system may be performing below the norm because other users are rendering "in the background" on your machine. But by all means, take advantage of remote rendering whenever possible; it is a great time-saver.

Streamline Your Shading Data

Shading parameters, such as the number of surface layers or the number of image maps applied to surfaces, should be kept to a minimum especially in productions where rendering time is of the essence. Very often, the best rendering results are achieved with just a few well-chosen shading parameters. Too many shading parameters not only prolong the time needed to render a scene, but also might not significantly contribute the visual quality of the final image. It is the responsibility of an artist, especially those working within production environments, to find a balance between the essential aesthetic needs and the practical limitations of the project, such as the rendering speed of the computer system, people's schedules, the budget, and the delivery deadlines. In general, an overabundance of shading parameters burdens not only the computers that must render the scene but also all the individuals involved in the production, including the client.

Consider the Final Output Media

Before producing your final renderings consider for a moment what the final output media is. As mentioned in Chapter 5, there can be significant color shifts when recording an RGB computer-generated image onto media with other chromatic ranges. This becomes especially critical when recording still images or animated sequences onto NTSC videotape due to its limited range of color and its stringent color balance requirements.

Rendering Glass

Many rendering programs today provide users with predefined shading parameters or surface shaders for a variety of often used materials. There is a wide range of recommended shading parameters to simulate glass. Most software manuals—or digital libraries of shaders—suggest to start by selecting a specular shading technique. Depending on the color, thickness, transparency, and roughness of the glass being simulated, both the reflectivity and the transparency of the object should be set very high—values above 90 percent are not uncommon. The refractive index can be set slightly above normal to create a small amount of distortion, or it can be boosted to simulate the increased light-bending qualities of handmade glass, for exam-

Within the image: MAXIMUM FOG LINE, MINIMUM FOG LINE

ple. Specular highlight values can be sharpened and focused. In cases where the software provides separate controls for the ambient, diffuse, and specular areas of illumination, the specular reflection can be boosted up above 100 percent to overcompensate for the high values of reflectivity and transparency; ambient and diffuse reflection can be turned off altogether. Finally, the transparency and reflection depths of a ray-traced rendering must be set to a minimum value of 4 in order to capture the subtle distortions that give refraction its tantalizing qualities.

8.8.5 The shading of objects within the foggy area in this diagram gets influenced by the color of the fog.

Review and Practice

Matching

_____ U parameter

_____ Image mapping

_____ Ambient reflection

_____ Reflection maps

_____ Spatial aliasing

_____ Cubical projection

_____ Matte surfaces

_____ Map blending

_____ Color maps

_____ Volume shaders

_____ Mask

_____ Specular shading

_____ Surface normals

_____ Surface shader

_____ Fog

_____ Spherical projection

_____ Motion blur

_____ Aerial perspective

_____ Faceted surface shading

a. Image that protects a surface or portions of it.

b. Collection of surface characteristics and shading techniques that are applied to an object during the rendering process.

c. Cluster of particles with uniform density that is placed in front of the camera.

d. A horizontal value that stretches from 0 to 1 in the parameter space of curved surfaces.

e. Determines the way in which surface layers are combined with the surface of the object as well as with other surface layers.

f. Vectors located on the surface of a polygon.

g. Defines the characteristics of three-dimensional spaces with a variety of materials that affect light as it travels through them.

h. A two-dimensional image is projected on the surface of a three-dimensional object.

i. Usually monochromatic because the brightness values determine the simulation of reflectivity.

j. Occurs when the computer-generated image is sampled at a lower resolution than the original data.

k. A form of temporal aliasing that results from samples that are too far apart from each other to capture motion details.

l. A method that repeats an image on each of the six sides of a cube.

m. Wraps a rectangular map around a surface until the opposite sides meet, and the top and bottom are stretched and pinched.

n. Techniques used to depict depth in a two-dimensional image by simulating the atmospheric effects of light, temperature, and humidity on objects situated far away from the observer.

o. Assigns a constant shading value to each visible polygon on the surface.

p. Can be simulated by using a combination of ambient and diffuse reflections.

q. The type of surface reflection that reacts only to the intensity and color of the ambient light.

r. Calculates the shading at every point on the surface of a polygon by interpolating the vertex normals.

s. Often used to represent the images and labels that we find on packages and containers.

True/False

_____ a. Smooth shading techniques average the light reaching the surface normals of adjacent polygons to determine the value of a vertex normal.

_____ b. The amount of light reflected with diffuse reflection decreases as the angle between the incident light source and the reflective surface becomes more oblique.

_____ c. Color maps are often called picture maps because they often involve photographic images.

_____ d. Most faceted shading techniques take into account parameters of ambient light only, but some also compute specular shading.

_____ e. Many specular shading techniques are based are the Phong, the Blinn, and the Cook shading models.

_____ f. Displacement maps can be used to simulate the slight relief of the lettering and graphics that are silkscreened with thick ink on containers such as shampoo bottles.

_____ g. Objects that are closest to the ending distance of the fog blend more with the fog.

_____ h. The color of the fog is determined by the background color.

_____ i. Images that are mapped with UV techniques are like elastic surfaces that stretch over three-dimensional objects.

_____ j. Complex surface characteristics can be defined in the form of surface layers.

_____ k. Different image maps cannot be combined to control different aspects of the surface characteristics of an object.

_____ l. Only photographic images can be mapped onto three-dimensional surfaces.

_____ m. Texture maps are always rectangular images that can be applied to polygonal or curved surfaces.

_____ n. The parameter space used to position image maps on curved patches is defined in terms of UV coordinates.

_____ o. Blending with matting techniques makes it difficult to control the degree of blending using different parts or aspects of the image map as a mask.

_____ p. Specular surface shading calculates the shading at every point on the surface of a polygon.

_____ q. Faceted shading is the fastest shading method because it uses only the surface normal to determine the color for the entire polygon.

_____ r. Plastic surfaces are typically simulated with a combination of ambient, diffuse, and specular reflections.

_____ s. Ambient reflection light is reflected in a focused and concentrated way and does not scatter evenly throughout the surface.

_____ t. Volume shaders define attributes such as density, color, and motion that may affect light as it travels through regions of three-dimensional space.

_____ u. The minimum and maximum distances of the fog specify the distances from the camera to the planes where the fog starts and ends.

_____ v. Bump mapping creates three-dimensional bumps that are visible on the profile of three-dimensional objects.

_____ w. Motion blur is commonly used to compensate for the lack of detail found in aliased images.

_____ x. The shading process creates surfaces on the wireframe structures created during the modeling process.

_____ y. Specular shading techniques take into account ambient, diffuse, and specular lighting.

Answers Matching: a. Mask, b. Surface shader, c. Fog, d. U parameter, e. Map blending, f. Surface normals, g. Volume shaders, h. Image mapping, i. Reflection maps, j. Spatial aliasing, k. Motion blur, l. Cubical projection, m. Spherical projection, n. Aerial perspective, o. Faceted surface shading, p. Matte surfaces, q. Ambient reflection, r. Specular shading, s. Color maps.

Answers /False: a. True, b. True, c. True, d. False, e. True, f. True, g. True, h. True, i. True, j. True, k. False, l. False, m. True, n. True, o. False, p. True, q. True, r. True, s. False, t. True, u. True, v. False, x. True, y. True.

Key Terms

Aerial perspective
Alpha channel
Ambient reflection
Angle of mapping
Antialiasing
Areas of illumination
Averaging
Backdrops
Background color
Brightness values
Bump maps
CD-ROM
Color maps
Color ramps
Color shifting
Continuous masks
Continuous visual information
Cubical environment mapping
Cubical projection
Cylindrical projection
Depth-fading
Diffuse reflection
Digital camera
Digital painting
Digital scanner
Dioramas
Discrete numerical values
Displacement maps
Distributed rendering
Environment maps
Faceted surface shading
Flat projection
Fog
Glow
High-contrast masks
Highlight decay
Highlight sharpness
Hybrid shading models
Image mapping
Incandescence
Interpolation
Jagged edges
Map blending
Mapping projection method
Mask

Material databases
Matte surfaces
Matting techniques
Metallic surfaces
Mirror-like
Modeled surface textures
Motion blur
Noise
Numerical values
Offset the map
Overall blending
Oversampling
Parameter space
Picture maps
Plastic surfaces
Pressure-sensitive
Procedural creation
Rectangular images
Reflection map
Reflection of light
Rendering farms
Remote rendering
Sampling
Scaling
Shading value
Simulated material
Smooth surface shading
Solid textures
Spatial aliasing
Spatial resolution
Spatial textures
Specular reflection
Specular surface shading
Spherical environment mapping
Spherical projection
Surface finish
Surface illumination
Surface layers
Surface libraries
Surface normals
Surface shader
Surface transparency
Temporal aliasing
Texturing
Tiling
Transparency map
Underpaint

UV coordinates
Visibility
Visual textures
Volume shaders

Wallpaper
Wrapping
XY coordinates

ANIMATION

CHAPTER 9

Basic Concepts of Animation

Summary

Using computers for the creation of animated images offers animators new creative possibilities as well as potent production tools. This chapter reviews some of the basic concepts of animation including fundamental techniques such as keyframing and in-betweening, the components of storytelling and storyboarding, the communication of emotions and thought processes through an animated character, and the planning and management of a computer animation project.

9.1 Principles of Animation

To animate means to give life to an inanimate object, image, or drawing. Animation is the art of movement expressed with images that are not taken directly from reality. In animation, the illusion of movement is achieved by rapidly displaying many still images—or frames—in sequence. Computer animation is a process that begins with the development of a story through scripting and storyboarding, continues with extensive preproduction planning, and ends with the production of an animation on film, video, or digital media. The story behind the animated images is critical to the success of the project, regardless of whether the topic is a short animation of an abstract logotype or the animation of a cartoon character.

    The first animated flipbooks and films were created at the turn of the 19th century. But most of the principles of animation were developed during the first two decades of the 20th century and perfected with the hand drawn cartoon animations of the 1930s and 1940s. Some of the computer animation techniques used to create **sequences of still images** are based on the techniques of traditional cel animation, but most are unique computer-based simulations of three-dimensional worlds and characters in motion.

Cel Animation

The most common technique of traditional animation is called **cel animation**. This technique starts with sequences of individual pencil drawings on paper. These drawings are recorded successively on an animation stand to create a preview of the motion or **pencil test**. Once refined the pencil drawings are traced with ink on individual acetate overlays or **cels**. These cels contain the foreground shapes that move over the background. The **foreground** may contain, for example, drawings of cartoon characters, letterforms, or scanned photographs, the **background** usually consists of painted or photographic images. Once finished the transparent cel overlays are placed over the background and recorded one frame at a time.

In addition to cel animation, there are other traditional animation techniques that include stop motion photography, mechanical effects, and motion control systems. Oftentimes these animation techniques are used in conjunction with computer animation, live special effects and compositing techniques such as front and rear projection.

Keyframing and In-Betweening

One of the fundamental techniques used in animation is called **keyframing**. This technique is used to define an animated sequence based on its key moments. The drawings that correspond to the key moments in an animated sequence are called keyframe drawings or **keyframes**. Another animation technique called **in-betweening** is used once the keyframes have been established and drawn. In-betweening consists of creating all the transition or **in-between** drawings that fill in the gaps between the keyframes. In traditional animation, the in-betweening process is done by laboriously creating each in-between drawing by hand. In computer animation, in-betweening is usually done with a technique called **interpolation**. A variety of computer interpolation techniques can be used to create as many in-between frames as needed by using simple information, such as keypoints in a keyframe or interpolation curves. (See Chapter 10 for more information on interpolation.)

Units of Animation

Animations are made of thousands of frames, but the smallest unit of animation is the **frame**. One frame consists of a single still image, and for that reason one frame of animation is sometimes called a still frame or simply a still. The number of frames that constitute one second of animation depends on the output media on which the animation is delivered. One second of animation at normal speed video equals 30 frames; on film one second equals 24 frames, and on an interactive real-time computer it may range from 8 to 60 frames. The number of frames of animation per second is also called the **rate of display** or rate of projection, and is usually indicated with the letters **fps** (frames per second).

A **shot** is a string of frames recorded by a single camera without interruption. A shot can consist of just a few frames, or it can go on for several seconds or even minutes. The style of the great majority of today's computer animations certainly relies more on the juxtaposition, or **montage**, of short shots than on a few long shots. A **sequence** consists of a succession of camera shots that are connected to each other because they develop the same aspect or moment of the action. Several sequences of shots usually add up to a scene. A **scene** can also be described in a more traditional way as continuous action in one place or as a unit of traditional storytelling (a scene is a division of an act).

Timing of the Action

Telling a story with computer animation is based on timing the actions to the story and on designing motions that convey the desired effect. The **timing** of a computer animation is based on how the visual action—usually the actions of the characters—are timed to the story. There are many ways for the visual action to relate to the story. The action may be ahead or behind the story, or it may be shown in parallel.

The action may be **ahead of the story** in cases when, for example, an animated character reacts to a sound located off-camera by turning its head. The character's action is ahead of the story because it indicates to us that something will happen before we know what it is. The action may be **behind the story** when the audience knows before the character what is going to happen next. The action is behind the story, for example, in a long shot where the audience can see that a piano is falling from the roof of a building right over a character who is unaware of the impending and disastrous action. Timing the action to be slightly ahead or behind the story is a good technique for keeping the interest of the audience. The effect of actions that are ahead of the story may be suspense and expectation, because the audience wants to find out the outcome of the story and they try to guess what's next. The effects of the actions that are behind the story are commonly used in comedy, and audiences enjoy it because they can watch the character find out—often the hard way—what they already knew. **Interrupted action**, also called a **fake hold**, can be used to give the audience a moment to catch up with action that is ahead of the story, or to savor action that is behind the story.

Parallel action occurs when the audience is shown actions that take place at the same time but in different places. Parallel action is often shown as a series of shots that cut back-and-forth between each location. Parallel action may show, for example, a man having lunch at a restaurant with his friend, while their respective wives are having lunch and talking about their husbands in a restaurant that is located around the corner from where their husbands are. Parallel action can be used to indicate a change of events or a turning point in the storyline. The action in an animation can also be interrupted to hold the interest of the audience for an unexpected action that is about to occur.

The skillful timing of the action in an animated project—or in any visual storytelling for that matter—can have a major positive effect in the audience: to hold their interest by having them constantly trying to guess how the story will evolve. This sense of curiosity and **anticipation** of the action is essential to all successful visual stories. Equally important to a good story is the **follow-through** of the action. Good follow-through keeps the interest of the audience by allowing them to either confirm their expectations or suspicions or to surprise them with an unexpected turn of events. In any case, the visual follow-through of the action gives the audience a chance to digest and enjoy the plot of the story.

The Visual Grammar of Motion

The motions of a character help to tell the story and also define the personality and emotions of the animated character. (In cases when the computer animation is based on abstract shapes and not on characters, the motion of the shapes and the timing of the action becomes the main conduit for storytelling due to the lack of facial expressions and body gestures.) Motion is also a great tool for directing the **attention of the audience** to a specific place in the image. For example, a slight motion in the background of a calm scene will immediately draw the eyes of the audience to that area. Motion is so effective for guiding the eyes of the audience that it should be carefully choreographed. The **readability of motion** will result in action that flows, while confusing motion will result in unfocused action.

Different combinations of timing, speed, rhythm, and choreography result in different types of motion including: primary and secondary motions, overlapping motions, staggered motions, and motion holds. These types of motions apply not only to the objects and characters in the environment but also to the camera. The virtual camera plays an important role in computer animation because its motions—as well as its position, point of interest, and focal length—have a powerful storytelling effect (see Chapter 6 for more information on camera animation).

To choreograph motion is to compose and arrange the motion of all objects or the parts of objects in a sequence of actions. Choreographing motion starts with planning the action and breaking it down into manageable blocks. This becomes very useful when animating characters with many parts that move at the same time and is also helpful to refine simple movements. **Simple motion** may consist of just one object or part of the object moving in a single direction while **complex motion** may consist of several objects or their parts moving in a variety of directions, speeds, and rhythms. In computer animation, most environments with multiple models, and most models—particularly characters—with multiple joints imply complex animation.

Complex motion consists of primary or dominant motions and secondary motions. The **primary motion** in a shot is the motion that captures the audience's attention. The primary motion in a character is the motion that carries the action forward. The primary motion in an interior shot, for example, could be personified by two loud patrons in a bar who laugh hysterically while the rest of the customers watch. The **secondary motion** in a shot is the motion that echoes or complements the primary motion. The arms slowly moving closer to the body of a spinning ice skater, or the snapping fingers of a jumping dancer are both samples of secondary motion. Secondary motion often starts as a reaction to a primary motion and through time becomes the new primary motion.

Motions in a sequence—whether just primary motions or a combination of primary and secondary motions—are rarely independent from one another. Motions often alternate and overlap. **Overlapping motion**, also called staggered motion, occurs when some motions start before others conclude. Our world is full of overlapping motion: people walking, birds flying, the wind blowing, even soup boiling in a pot. For this reason, animations that want to replicate or echo natural motion must be based on the principle of overlapping motion: as one motion dies a new motion should start to bloom.

A **motion hold** happens when a character interrupts or concludes one motion and pauses. The function of a motion hold is to give the audience a chance to catch up with the development of the story or to indicate that a new action is about to happen. The most effective way to create a motion hold is by interrupting the primary motion while continuing with a small motion. Motion holds should never result in an absolute and total interruption of the action because that results in mechanical motion or destroys the continuity and flow of the action. Secondary motions such as the turning of a head or blinking of the eyes can help carry on a motion hold.

The relation between primary, secondary and overlapping motions, and motion holds becomes an important concern when animating a group of moving objects and especially when animating articulated figures with hierarchical groupings of objects. A useful strategy for planning and refining complex motion in computer animation is based on the idea of animating the **layers of motion** one at a time. An animated scene can have several layers of motion. In a scene with primary, secondary, and overlapping motion it usually makes sense to animate first the layer of primary motion, then add layers of secondary motion, and finally go back and forth between layers in order to adjust all the overlapping motions. Animated objects or characters can also have several layers of motion, and the most practical way of animating them consists of starting with the primary motion and the secondary motions next. When animating an articulated figure with keyframes this implies establishing the poses for each keyframe starting at the top of the hierarchical structure and working down to the details only after the dominant motions have been worked out. In a scene that consists, for example, of one singer and a five-character chorus it would be convenient to start animating the primary motion of the lead singer. One could continue with the dominant motions of the chorus singers. Then the secondary motions of the lead singer could be determined, followed by the secondary motions of the chorus singers. At this point fine-tuning the overlapping motions would be easy because all the primary and secondary motions would already be contained in the scene.

Animating motion in layers is convenient because it breaks down a complex challenge into smaller and more manageable parts. It is also convenient and almost necessary in complex animated sequences because in many of them the keyframes in different motion layers are placed in different moments along the time line. Keyframes in an animated sequence with complex motion are usually abundant and scattered throughout the scene in an overlapping fashion.

Techniques for Motion Control

There are many computer animation techniques for controlling the motion of three-dimensional objects and characters. Some of these **motion control techniques**—inverse kinematics, for example—work well within the context of keyframe animation, and others, including motion dynamics, require animation methodologies that are borrowed from scientific simulations. But increasingly, however, computer animations are developed within a **hybrid framework** that combines many different motion control techniques and production methodologies into a single project. An important task of computer animators consists of selecting the most appropriate technique or set of techniques for **implementing the motions** designed for a specific project.

Some of the most common computer animation motion control techniques for the arrangement of keyframes include interactive or manual, kinematic, motion dynamics, procedural, and hybrid techniques, all of which are covered in Chapters 10 and 11.

The simplest, most direct—and potentially most time consuming—of all motion control techniques consists of manually arranging the objects in a scene. This approach has its roots in traditional hand drawn keyframe animation where all the information in the keyframes was originally drawn by hand, and is based on the idea of defining keyframes, specifying the ease function, and letting the software interpolate the in-between frames. The technique of **manual arrangement** of the objects in a scene is always done interactively, and works best when the animator is experienced and has a good eye and a good hand for animation.

Kinematic techniques for animating objects and characters are based on changing the position and orientation of models in three-dimensional space. In **forward kinematics,** the angles of the joints are manipulated to achieve a specific motion, while in **inverse kinematics** the limbs or objects are moved to a position and the software calculates the joint rotations that are necessary for the in-between positions to be created. Inverse kinematics techniques are especially useful for animating complex models with a large number of joints. Inverse kinematics calculates the motion of entire skeletons by specifying the final angle positions of just some of the key joints that define the motion. **Motion capture** techniques provide the kinematic information to the software by recording the positions or angles of joints of live actors or objects in motion. Kinematic techniques is general can greatly simplify the animation of models that have to move in a realistic way, for example, a tiger running.

Animation techniques based on the physical laws of motion, called dynamics, can generate realistic motion of objects by simulating their physical properties and nature's laws of physical motion. **Motion dynamics** techniques control the motion of three-dimensional objects by applying forces to the joints and actually simulating the motion that would result in the physical world if such forces were applied to a real object with specific characteristics. Motion dynamics techniques take into account variables such as an object's weight, mass, inertia, flexibility, and collision with other objects, as well as the environment's friction, gravity, and other forces that may influence the motion of objects.

Procedural or **rule-based motion** techniques animate the objects in the scene based on a set of procedures and rules to control motion. The animation of flocks is an example of procedural motion control. Rule-based motion techniques are often scored with a special-purpose programming language so that they can be easily edited and previewed.

Overview of the Computer Animation Process

The process of creating a computer animation has several basic steps that can be grouped in three stages: preproduction, production, and postproduction. Most computer animation projects follow these steps, but in practice this process can adopt many different forms and variations.

Preproduction involves all the conceptualization and planning that takes place before a computer animation project is produced. This stage in the process includes nonvisual tasks such as screenwriting and planning the management of the project, as well as visual tasks such as storyboarding and developing the overall look of the project.

The **production** stage in the process of three-dimensional computer animation involves a series of standard steps: modeling, animation, and rendering. First the characters, objects, and environments used in three-dimensional computer animations are **modeled**. This can occur with a wide range of computer-based techniques such as using virtual modeling tools to sculpt objects, or using a three-dimensional digitizer to capture the shape of a physical model directly into the computer program. Once the virtual actors and objects are modeled, they can be arranged on the stage and be **animated** with a wide variety of techniques. Animation techniques range from keyframing animation where start and end positions are specified for all objects in a sequence, to motion capture where all positions are fed to the objects directly from live actors whose motions are being digitized. The results of the animation can be previewed in the form of digital flipbooks displayed on the screen. Once the objects are modeled and animated then they can be **rendered**. Computer rendering is the process of representing visually the animated models with the aid of a simulated camera, lights, and materials. (In some cases, the rendering characteristics are specified before the animation is laid out. But the rendering itself, the calculation of the finished computer-animated images, always happens after the modeling and animation parameters have been defined.)

Once the images have been rendered, a variety of **postproduction** techniques can be applied to the images before they are recorded. For example, computer-generated images can be digitally composited or mixed with other computer-generated images or with live action. Computer animation can also be distorted, retouched, processed or color corrected using postproduction techniques. In order to minimize time and budget complications **motion tests** are often produced to preview the computer animation sequences before the final production takes place. When computer animations are completed they are usually recorded on videotape or on film so that they can be shown later on a TV screen or in a movie theater. Each of the film or video formats has different requirements and characteristics. For example, the standard rate of display of animated images recorded on videotape is 30 frames per second, on film it is 24 frames per second. Increasingly, computer animation is delivered in a **digital format** that may be played back in real time as part of a multimedia interactive game.

9.2 Storytelling

Stories are the most common and most powerful vehicle we use to talk about life. Not just one life but many lives. Life in general, and our own lives in particular. Past, present, and future lives. Real, imagined, and assumed lives. Inspiring, intriguing, tormented, or impossible lives.

Stories communicate facts. Stories provide answers to questions. Stories make us feel different emotions. Stories sometimes even provoke actions that shape reality. Whether they are linear or nonlinear, whether they depict an event with cartoon characters or a colorful dance of abstract shapes, stories are the essence of animation.

Being a good storyteller requires many talents and skills. But why should anybody interested in computer animation have to learn about storytelling? Because animations are more than just moving images. Animations tell stories and communicate emotions that are initially drafted in screenplays, and later in storyboards and character sheets.

In most cases, the work of animators involves the **visual interpretation** of a story. Animators translate the personality of characters into motions, whether the story is a complex epic drama between nations, or the simple courting of a lady sphere by a male square. Animators, and other visual people involved in the production of animations, often start to sketch their visual interpretations of a story by reading and discussing a screenplay.

The Screenplay

A **screenplay** is a written document that tells a story by using descriptions, dialogue, and some production notes. Unlike a novel, which is written to be printed and read, a screenplay is not an end-product in itself. Instead the screenplay is written as intermediate works, as a vehicle for the story to be retold with images in the form of an animation, a movie, or a play. For this reason, screenplays tell stories in ways that can be **translated into moving images**. One screenplay page is usually equivalent to one minute of action on the screen.

Screenplays can differ by the amount of dialogue they incorporate, the number of characters they present, or the detail of their descriptions of imagery. But what all screenplays have in common is a subject and a clearly defined treatment of the subject that is adequate for the intended audience.

The **treatment of the subject** in a screenplay is defined by the point of view that the storyteller wants to convey to the audience. Treatments can be, for example, dramatic, comic, or lyrical, action-packed or introspective. Considering the **intended audience** can make it easier to define the treatment for a screenplay's subject. This includes not only the philosophical or political treatments of the subject, for example, but also the visual treatment. This concerns animations because some screenplays may require very simple or specific computer animation techniques to achieve the desired effect or emotion. The **subject of a screenplay** is defined by what the story is about, who the characters are, and what happens to them throughout the sequence of events. Because the subject of a story is often presented through the actions of a character, it is important to develop the personality of all the characters before the story is told.

A screenplay's subject can be presented in the context of a variety of dramatic and narrative structures. The **structure** of a story holds all the parts of the story together. There are no rigid rules about the best way to structure a story, and stories can be told with a wide variety of styles and techniques. But stories that are told in the context of a **linear** medium—such as film or video—consist of a beginning, a middle, and an end, and the action in a story always moves from one event to another.

The **beginning of the story**—also called exposition or setup—usually introduces the main characters, establishes the dramatic premise, and sets up the events and situations that will develop the story. The **middle of the story**—also called confrontation or climax—usually contains the moments when the main characters confront the conflicts that when resolved will lead to a resolution. The **end of the story**—also called resolution or *dénouement*, from the French *untying a knot*—usually contains the outcome of the dramatic sequence of events in the story.

Several variations of the traditional structure of a story are possible. For example, the structure can be altered so that the story starts with the resolution, continues with the setup, and concludes with the confrontation. But in every instance stories are always told in terms of **events** or **plot points** that made the story evolve in a particular way. These events are the moments in the story when the action takes a different turn. These moments and events help develop the story and keep the action moving.

Nonlinear Storytelling

Storytelling in most visual media happens in a linear way because images, sounds, and text follow each other in just one single predetermined order. But a variety of possible sequences may be possible in an **interactive project** because users can make different requests and also follow a variety of paths. Interactive projects may have multiple endings and even multiple beginnings each time they are played. Storytelling for interactive media requires unique techniques because of the **nonlinearity** of the media.

Creators of an interactive project have in **flowcharts** a powerful tool for planning the project, and for determining the many paths that the story may follow. Flowcharts are diagrams that clearly lay out all the **branching** options that may occur in the **flow of events** of interactive dialogue. The branching structure in an interactive system may be simple if few options are offered or complex if the options are multiple. Each branching node in a flowchart is controlled by a choice made by the individual or individuals interacting with the system. When a choice is made at a branching node the flow of events advances to another **hierarchy level** in the flowchart. On occasions the sequencing of events in an interactive project may also be sketched out in the form of a traditional storyboard. The **interactivity** of a computer system is based on the **dialogue** established between the system itself and the individuals using it.

Individuals using interactive systems can make their choices through standard input peripherals such as mice, joysticks, and keyboards, or unique ones such as gloves and bodysuits with ultrasonic and light sensors that determine the position, orientation, and physical gestures of a person. Interactive media systems are usually built around one or several computer systems that are able to control the flow of information stored in a variety of media, formats and systems, including still and moving images, sound, and text. Hence the name of interactive multimedia.

Flowcharts describe in an abstract manner the overall structure and dynamics of an interactive project. But **scripts** actually control the flow of events in an interactive project; they are the practical implementation of a the ideas contained in a flowchart. Scripts are computer programs that collect and evaluate information about the choices made by the system's users, and then direct the program in the appropriate direction. Scripts trigger events that may include displaying an image or playing a sequence of images or sounds.

Interactive media are not made to be just watched or read, instead they are made to be used by people. For this reason, the functionality of an interactive system should always be checked with extensive **user testing**. The feedback and suggestions of users usually uncover the moments in the flow of events that may be confusing, or important functionalities that may be missing, or user's requests that crash the program and freeze the system. Only after a thorough user testing process can interactive nonlinear storytelling projects be released to the public.

One of the aspects that is paid special attention during the user testing process is the **computer-human interface**, or interface for short. An interface is the collection of techniques that facilitate the dialogue between an individual and an interactive computer system. The **interface design** of a project has to do with the graphical conventions such as the shape of icons, typography, and color, but also with the sequencing of events, selection techniques, and interplay of sound, text, and images.

9.3 Storyboarding

Screenplays are converted into storyboards as they are readied for visual production. A **storyboard** is a visual interpretation of the screenplay and contains many images and production notes. A storyboard consists of a series of panels that contains in visual form the scenes and shots specified in the screenplay. There is no standard medium for storyboards, but they are usually drawn on boards, on plain paper, or on paper preprinted with guides. When using preprinted storyboard paper one has to be certain that the proportion of the drawing area corresponds to the proportions of the format that the animation will be recorded on, for example, video, 35 mm film, or 70 mm film. Many of the characteristics of a storyboard, including its **dimensions**, are determined by whether the main function of the storyboard is to develop the concept, to present the concept to a client, or to guide the actual production of a piece.

A **conceptual storyboard** is used to develop the basic visual ideas such as the actions of the characters, the camera positions, the timing of motions, and the transitions between scenes. Conceptual storyboards are often loose, sketchy, and informal, and may contain lots of abbreviated notes. These storyboards are often drawn on napkins and sketchbooks, and sometimes on letter size or A4 size plain paper.

The **presentation storyboard** is used to show a detailed visual summary of the project to individuals with a decision-making authority, such as clients or supervisors. Presentation storyboards usually include important scenes of the project executed with great attention to detail, in color and on high-quality materials. The visuals are usually large enough so that several people in a meeting room can look at them from a distance, and small enough to fit inside a portfolio. The notes included in presentation storyboards should always be very legible and descriptive without getting too technical.

The Production Storyboard

A **production storyboard** often guides the production of an animated project. This type of storyboard can be the document that everybody involved in the production process refers to in order to clarify detailed questions. For this reason, they are always very detailed and precise, and they include drawings and written information about every shot in the story. It is very important to work out many of the technical details in an animation before a production storyboard is created. Otherwise information contained in the storyboard may change a lot, rendering the storyboard useless for production purposes.

The **written information** in production storyboards may include detailed descriptions of the motion, the camera, the set, the lighting, and other rendering specs, the timing, and the transitions between the shots. Production storyboards also include soundtrack information such as transcripts of the dialog and narrator's voice-over, and descriptions of the music and sound effects.

Each still frame that represents a shot in the storyboard is usually numbered with a **shot number** or with a **scene-and-shot-number**. The timing information for each shot is usually noted right below the visual representing each shot. Absolute timing values, or **elapsed time**, indicate the exact time at which the shot starts and ends in terms of hours, minutes, seconds, and frames. For example, a one and a half second long shot in the middle of the storyboard for a short video animation may start at 00:01:37:15 and end at 00:01:39:00. Relative timing values or **running time** simply indicate the total length of a shot, usually in seconds and frames, for example, the same shot may be one second and 15 frames (1" 15 fr.) long.

The **drawings** in the storyboard depict the images seen by the camera. Sometimes the motions of the camera are further clarified by using directional arrows to indicate them visually over the drawing. The points of visual interest in the composition and the direction of the paths of visual interest are sometimes also overlaid on the still drawings in the storyboard.

The passage from one shot or scene to the next is called a **transition**. Some of the most common transitions between shots specified in a storyboard include a cross-dissolve, a fade-in, a fade-out, or a soft-cut (these are explained in Chapter 12). Plain cuts between shots are usually not indicated in storyboards because it is assumed that most of the transitions are cuts. Some of the aspects of the camera specified in a storyboard include the type of shot, the type of move, the point-of-view or POV, and the type of lens (See Chapter 10 for more information on camera animation).

Production storyboards can be drawn in formats that can be easily pinned to a wall or carried in a binder or briefcase. Sometimes these storyboards are drawn so that the visual and written information on each shot is contained on a single piece of paper. This way a sequence of shots in a storyboard can be easily rearranged if necessary while production is underway. Other times these storyboards are drawn on letter size or A4 size paper so they can be carried by different members of the animation team.

Titles and Credits

In addition to the animation itself, many production storyboards commonly contain detailed information about the titles, the opening and closing credits, and any other text, letterforms, or graphic information that may appear in the animation. The titles of a computer animation can be simple or elaborate, but they are always storyboarded in detail. Simple titles typically consist of two-dimensional letterforms superimposed on the animated opening sequence. Two-dimensional letterforms are usually created with a **character generator** or an electronic **paintbox**, and not with a three-dimensional modeling program. The latter is used in cases when the titles are of three-dimensional nature or when they are part of the animated environment. The credits almost always consist of two-dimensional letterforms. Some major credits may be superimposed on the opening sequence, but most appear at the end of the animation as **rolling credits**. (See "Creative and Production Teams" later in this chapter for more information about the proper way to credit those who participate in an animated project.)

When designing the placement of text and graphics on the screen it is important to make sure that they are readable and that they will not be cut off by being too close to the edge of the frame. **Field guides** are graphs with concentric rectangles that can be used to specify the exact position of text and graphics within the frame (Fig. 6.2.4). The **title safety area** in the field guides clarifies what constitutes a placement of the titles and graphics that may not always be within the frame due to slight differences in vertical and horizontal positioning of the image among television sets or film projectors.

9.4 Character Sheets

Much of the story in an animated film is communicated through the actions of characters. For that reason a great deal of time and energy is dedicated to the character development stage in a project. **Character sheets** are drawings used to define the main emotions and attitudes of the characters in the form of body positions and facial expressions. Character sheets are also used as templates by all the individuals involved in the **development of the character** that includes both drawing and building models. But before the final character sheets are completed it is also necessary to create hundreds of studies and sketches on paper and a simple modeling material such as clay.

Character sheets usually present two different aspects of a

character: its anatomy and its personality. In traditional animation, the anatomy of a character is related mostly to the way the character looks. But in three-dimensional computer animation the **anatomy** of a character is related to its external shape and internal structure (Figs. 9.4.1 and 9.4.2).

External Shape

The **external shape of a three-dimensional character** defines how the character looks—its visual appearance. Oftentimes the shape of a character implies much of the character's personality or the way it moves. For example, think of the difference in motion implied by a fat and heavy body shape with a small round head as opposed to a long and thin body shape with a large cubic head. Or think of the difference in personality that would be projected by a character with a slender frame shaped with a rich assortment of soft curved spaces gracefully connected to each other, as opposed to a disjointed character with a hunched frame covered with unevenly distributed sharp and irregular thorn-like shapes. Of course appearances can be deceiving, and the personality of a character or its motion is not defined just by its shape. But also keep in mind that much of **casting**—or the assignment of dramatic roles to actors—is partly dependent on the desired appearance of the character to be represented.

Animated characters, just like humans, animals, plants, and minerals, come in all shapes. One of the most fun aspects of developing a computer animation is designing the shape of the characters. Character design usually starts as sketches done on paper, and it takes into account the **production technique** that will be used to animate the character. For example, a computer animation developed with limited computing resources may favor characters with simple shapes, while a project developed with unlimited resources may employ human-like characters. The design of a character also takes into account the type of story that is being told and the type of emotions that it contains. For

9.4.1 The external shape of these two charming characters is soft and playful. Their silhouette and internal structure is simple and straight forward. Their lack of facial expressions concentrates the expression of their vivacious and mischevous personality on their body language. (Agency, Nickelodeon; Producer, Agi Fodor; Creative Director, Scott Webb; Production Company, Blue Sky Productions, Inc; Director/Designer, Chris Wedge; Producer, Alison Brown; Technical Director, Oliver Rockwell; Animator, Chris Wedge; Music, Pomposello Productions; Hardware, Sun, SGI, Hewlett Packard workstations; Software, CGI Studio, Softimage. Courtesy of Blue Sky Productions, Inc.)

example, characters may be caricatures or realistic representations of human beings; each treatment will tell the story in a slightly different way and will also have different animation requirements. Characters may be shaped with stylized forms and ball-joints, or with a single continuous skin. When designing a character one must consider the modeling tools available to do the job, the time constraints, and all the implications of a simple or complex model in the rendering and animation stages. On occasion it is useful to make studies of the character in clay. Three-dimensional clay models complement the character drawings and help to better visualize the overall shading, facial expressions, and body gestures of the characters.

The shape of characters can be used to accentuate an aspect of the character's personality. For example, a big bouncy nose can accentuate the silliness of a character, an overly long tail can be an excuse for its clumsiness, or a slender waist can help focus on its grace and agility. However, it is always the relation between all the parts of a character—and not just a single shape—that expresses the character's personality. When designing characters it is important to consider not only the shape of its body, but also the shape of its clothing. Keep in mind that the realistic animation of cloth may require complex animation techniques.

Internal Structure

Since motion is a fundamental component of animation, the **internal structure of a three-dimensional character** is of the utmost importance in a computer animation because it defines how a character moves. The structure of a three-dimensional character is often determined by its hierarchical **skeleton** and by the functionality of its **joints**. This is convenient since most three-dimensional computer animation systems provide a variety of techniques for manipulating skeletons and joints as if there were muscles moving them. The skeleton and joints of a three-dimensional character are like the frame and joints of a puppet—they define the ways in which it can move. The puppeteer animates the puppet by pulling strings. The computer animator brings the virtual characters to life by manipulating data, and by applying functions and transformations to the skeleton and joints. Hierarchical skeletons are defined in more detail in Chapters 3 and 10.

The complexity of a character's skeleton and joints controls the timing of its motions. A skeleton with a simple structure usually results in simple motions while complex skeletons may yield complex motions. For example, a character that can move its shoulders independently from the lower torso will be capable of more complex—and expressive—motion than a character that can move its shoulders only in conjunction with the lower torso. Likewise, motions animated with a set of joints that have

a few rotating constraints may
be more convincing than the
motion created with joints that
have very limited angles of
rotation.

Personality

It is usually easier for audiences
to follow a storyline when the
personality of the characters is
well developed and consistent.
Audiences get to know a character not only through its dialogue but also through its body
postures, facial expressions,
hand gestures, and walking
rhythm. It is usually easier to identify with a character that we
know, because we can figure out what the character is thinking
and predict the action. The personality of an animated character
is obviously defined by its dialogue lines, but also by many subtle visual elements such as its internal structure, its shape and silhouette, its facial expressions, and its way of moving.

9.4.2 These two characters are opponents in a duel that will probably end
in the anhilation of one of them.
Their external shapes are realistic, and
the internal structure that governs
their motion is complex. Their facial
expressions are limited in range, but
intense: pain and fear, determination
and coldness. (Courtesy of Acclaim
Entertainment, Inc., Advanced
Technologies Group.)

The shape and **silhouette** of a character define its personality due to the inherent visual characteristics of shapes. Shapes
with a lot of contrast tend to be more exciting than shapes with
no contrast, the latter can even give an aura of dullness to the
character. Fragile shapes can emphasize a fragile personality or
reveal the contrast between a fragile appearance and a strong
personality. Heavy and imposing shapes can accentuate the bul-
lyness of a character or emphasize the contrast between a huge
frame and a gentle spirit. The skeleton of a computer animated
character also helps to define how the character moves and
therefore influences its personality.

Facial expressions often reveal much of a character's personality. Character sheets include just the key facial expressions
that define the personality of a character. But it is often necessary to develop hundreds of key facial expressions that will give
the character its personality—and that will also be used as
keyframes. These facial expressions can be stored in a library of
expressions and be used throughout the animation. Part of the
research for defining those facial expressions consists of observing and drawing the expressions of others as well as making
faces in front of a mirror and drawing or modeling them.

The motion or timing of a computer animated character is
essential in defining its personality as well as its emotional state.
Timing includes tempo and rhythm. The **tempo**, or pace, of a
motion can have different rates of speed, and these variations in

the speed of the character's motion can be very expressive. For example, a slow tempo may express seriousness, fatigue, caution, or intimacy. A flowing tempo may project trust, elegance, or moderation. A lively tempo may express happiness or nervousness. The rate of speed of a character is based on its skeleton but also related to its shape. **Speed** of motion can be constant, change slowly or change very rapidly. A friendly and trustworthy character may move at a constant speed while a treacherous and mean character may have sudden changes in the speed at which it moves. The speed of animated objects and characters can also be used to indicate their weight, mass, and power. A fast moving object implies lightness only if it can stop relatively quickly. A fast moving objects that requires a long time to stop implies lots of inertia and, therefore, great mass, and weight. The speed of animated objects can also be a good indicator of the amount of stretching and squashing to be expected if and when the object collides and bounces off some other thing in the scene.

The **rhythm** of a character's motion is the repetition or recurrence of motions performed by a character, or the pattern of motion projected by the character. The rhythm of a character's motion can be flowing or broken, regular or irregular. Motion rhythm can combine long motions with short motions, strong and weak beats, in different ways. For example, think of the differences in personality derived from the rhythm characteristics of three characters as they walk down the road (Fig. 9.4.3).

The first character in Fig. 9.4.3 barely raises its feet off the ground as it walks but keeps its arms close to its stiff torso, and its neck leans forward with the eyesight fixed on the ground. The resulting overall motion—and personality—is quite dull and uneventful. The second character walks with extreme energy. The head is free and high with a radiant smile on the face. With each step each shoulder moves back and forth echoing the motion of the opposing foot, the relaxed waist rotates gently from side to side, and the hands hang loose from the arms bouncing back and forth like the shoulders. The motion of the second character speaks for itself, and its personality seems animated and confident. The third character limps as it walks with short tense steps. Every three or four steps the character stops, nervously turns its head from side to side and looks around with quick eye movements. Its arms are held close to the chest as if seeking some protection.

Expressing Emotion and Thinking Process

The storyline drives all the events in a computer animation, but the **emotions** expressed by the character help define the mood of the story. Emotions are a powerful medium for conveying the fine points of a story or for reinforcing some of the character's

9.4.3 The personality differences of three characters walking down the road are expressed in their motions and body posture.

traits. In addition to feeling emotions, and expressing or hiding them, characters actively think throughout the story. The **thinking process** of characters provides many clues and insight about their fate and the possible developments of the story.

One of the reasons why audiences follow with interest the development of a story is because they empathize—or identify—with a character or because they anticipate the action. The emotions, thoughts, and intentions of characters are a perfect vehicle to generate empathy and anticipation in an audience.

Motions and actions in keyframe animation are often built as a series of poses and gestures that will be used as keyframes to create the motion. When establishing these **key poses** it is important to keep in mind that the goal of the pose is to **express an emotion** and action, and not to just be a beautiful pose. Key poses should not be built with the same criteria that we create, for example, a sculpture. Sculptures are made to be looked at from different angles and throughout long periods of time. Sculptures turn time and emotion into a still pose that we can contemplate. But key poses in an animation are transitory because they are just moments in continuous motion. When composing key poses for keyframe animation it is important to pay attention not only to the visual arrangement of the pose itself but also to the idea or emotion that is being expressed through motions. In computer animations that are based on cartoon characters, **exaggerated gestures** are often used to punctuate dramatic deliveries.

When composing keyframes it is useful to consider the visual line of action. The **visual line of action** determines the position and sequence of the motions in the scene that will guide the eye of the audience to different parts of the image.

9.5 Production Issues

Most computer animation projects require the collaboration of many individuals with different skills, talents, personalities, and working habits. Computer animation projects are **team efforts** where **collaboration** is a key ingredient for success. The production of any computer animation requires lots of **planning** and constant **supervision** due to the number of individuals involved and also to the short production cycles, limited budgets, and the unpredictable and changing nature of cutting edge technology.

The Digital Computer Animation Studio

The creation and production of computer animation takes place in environments where most of the tools and processes are computer-based. There are many ways to configure a **digital studio** depending on the type and volume of work that needs to be done and the number of people working in the studio. All digital animation studios include: personnel, software, and computer systems with a specific configuration of processing power, storage, networks, and input and output peripherals.

The **personnel** of a computer animation studio or production house includes creative, technical, and administrative positions. The number of individuals employed is in direct proportion to the size and volume of a particular project or a studio. Small studios may be as small as 5 individuals, medium-sized studios may have around 20 employees, and some of the large studios can go as high as 100 employees. Large studios sometimes include creative and technical personnel from areas other than computer animation, such as traditional character animation, live action film, optical compositing, sculpture and model-making. Later in this chapter you can find a listing and descriptions of some of these technical and creative positions.

A large number of computer animation facilities use **turn-key software**. This type of software is commercially available from a variety of vendors, and ready to use on virtually all computer platforms. Turn-key software systems can range in price from under $1,000 to over $100,000 depending on their capabilities, sophistication, and speed. Small turn-key systems are usually sold as a single unit, but the large turn-key systems are usually sold as a collection of stand-alone modules that can be purchased in different configurations. When selecting a turn-key software it is important to consider its upgrade policies, and its upward and downward compatibility. Turn-key software is upgraded periodically. Upgrades consist of adding new functionalities, optimizing existing features, and fixing problems— also called software bugs. In general, software upgrades are offered to owners of the upgraded software at a nominal fee, but on occasion the extent of the software upgrade is such that the software is considered a new product. In the latter case, the upgraded software is sometimes offered to owners and new buyers at the same price. **Upward compatibility** exists when files created with previous versions of the software are compatible with new software upgrades. **Downward compatibility** exists when files created with a new software upgrade are compatible with earlier versions of the software.

Much of the sophisticated computer animation software is often produced with a combination of commercially-available software and also with custom or proprietary software. **Proprietary software** is developed in-house to provide tools and techniques that are not available in commercial turn-key systems. Proprietary software can also be used in conjunction with turn-key software, for example, it can be used to preprocess motion-capture data before it is sent to the turn-key animation module. Proprietary software is often quite costly because it requires a team of specialized and dedicated programmers to develop, maintain, and upgrade.

The **processing power** of a computer animation facility is determined by the power, speed, and number of computer dedicated to compute the animation. The power and speed of a single computer system is dictated by the configuration of the computer's central processing unit, co-processors, clock, bus, and internal memory. The exact configuration of a computer used to create animation depends on the budget available but also on the type of task assigned to that machine, for example, modeling, or rendering, or compositing.

Today's production of computer animation is dominated by microcomputers and super-microcomputers. The **microcomputers** used today for computer animation usually have a generic 32-bit processor, graphics co-processors, and clock speeds approaching 100 MHz. Popular microcomputers include the 486 or Pentium-based PCs, or Apple Computer's PowerPCs or Quadras. Today's **super-microcomputers**, or workstations, used for computer animation are based on one or several 32 or 64-bit custom graphics processors, and they run at clock speeds of at least 100 MHz. Popular super-microcomputers include a variety of models from Silicon Graphics (SGI), Hewlett-Packard, and Sun Microsystems, among others. Microcomputers have traditionally been considered low-end, and super-microcomputers have been considered high-end. But there are multiple instances today where the quality of computer animations produced on microcomputers rivals the projects created on personal workstations. This trend started in the mid-1980s and is expected to continue as the processing power of microcomputers continues to increase. However, in absolute terms, workstations still deliver more processing power than most microcomputers, this is particularly true of the multiprocessor graphics workstations (such as the SGI Power Series) or the computing-servers (such as SGI's Predator and Challenge models).

The type of **peripheral storage** used in a computer animation facility is also based on the volume, quality, and complexity of the work done at that facility. The frames of a computer animation are stored in digital form as they are generated and until they are recorded on film or video. Online storage is necessary so that it is possible to preview an animation in progress, or to retouch and to composite some frames in the animation. The size of a single frame of high-quality computer animation may range from 4 to 50 megabytes depending on its spatial, temporal, and chromatic resolution. The online storage capacity of a production facility may be measured in megabytes or millions of bytes, gigabytes or billions of bytes, or terabytes or trillions of bytes.

The main function of a computer **network** is to bring the information to the processors from the storage and the peripheral devices, and vice versa. Networks usually have one or several computers—called **network servers**—whose main purpose is to assist the other computers on the network to fetch and send data. The **bandwidth**, or transmission capacity, of a network is a crucial issue that determines the functionality of that network. Some popular network bandwidths include **T-1** or **DS-1** (Digital Signal Level One) at 1.544 megabits per second, Xerox's **Ethernet** at 10 megabits per second, **FDDI** (Fiber Distributed Data Interface) at 100 megabits per second, and **ATM** (Asynchronous Transfer Mode) at 154 megabits per second. Networks are commonly used in production environments to share files, and also to keep as many computers on the network as possible busy at all times. Very high-bandwidth networks are starting to be used for transferring computer animations between studios in different cities and even different countries.

The **input capabilities** of a computer animation studio are used for a variety of purposes that include two- and three-dimensional information. Flatbed scanners or digitizing cameras are used mostly for scanning images that may be used as texture maps or backgrounds during the rendering process. Film digitizers are used for digitizing entire live action sequences that are composited digitally with the computer animation. Three-dimensional scanners are used for digitizing the shape of scale models or the actions of human actors to be used as motion templates for an animation.

The **output capabilities** of a computer animation facility include a variety of devices to record motion tests and the finished animations. High-resolution electronic film recorders are used to output computer animation onto film. Digital disk recorders are used to output animation onto a variety of video formats. Digital disk recorders are also a popular form of peripheral storage because they can record video in digital format and also playback computer animation at standard video rates on video output devices.

Creative and Production Teams

Most computer animation projects require one or several teams of individuals with a variety of skills and talents. Computer animation teams are put together in different ways depending on the nature and needs of the project. Often there are several teams involved in the creation of a single project, especially when the project is complex and requires the participation of several companies. In some cases, a single team may handle both the creative and production responsibilities, but oftentimes these two stages of a computer animation project are implemented by two separate teams: the creative team and the production team. The members of both of these teams are often credited in the closing credits that may be shown at the end of an animated piece.

The **creative team** is usually represented by the design studio, communications company, or advertising agency that developed the concept and the visual treatment. This team is typically responsible for creating a script or screenplay and a storyboard. The main responsibility of the **production team** is to execute the ideas provided by the creative team and to deliver a finished animation. The production team may be based in one or in several production and postproduction companies or groups within the same company.

The creative and production teams for a short computer animation project, a **television commercial** for example, may include the following positions:

Creative Team
    Creative Director
    Art Director
    Copywriter
    Producer
    Account Executive

Production Team
    Animation Supervisor
    Senior Animator
    Junior Animators
    Producer
    Production Manager
    Technical Assistant

The production team may also include a visual effect supervisor, and an editor if the project involves a significant amount of live action and compositing.

The production of long computer animations, for example, a **feature film**, may require a relatively small creative team but an extensive production team with specialized groups. The creative team may consist of a little over half-a-dozen individuals including the following:

Creative Team
    Director
    Scriptwriter
    Production Designer
    Visual Effects Director
    Art Director
    Storyboard Artist
    Producer

A large production team is one solution to better handle both the tight production schedules and the volume of work contained in a feature film computer animation. A production team for this type of project may include several groups and positions, but under some circumstances many of the positions may be assigned to a single individual.

Production Team

Visual Effects Group
    Visual Effects Producer
    Visual Effects Director
    Visual Effects Supervisor or Assistant Director
    Visual Effects Editor
    Visual Effects Assistant Editor
    Visual Effects Coordinator
    Stage Technicians

Computer Animation Group
    Computer Animation Supervisor
    Computer Animation Shot Supervisors
    Computer Animators
    Computer Animation Production Coordinator

Computer Technical Support Group
    Computer Graphics Department Manager
    Computer Graphics Software Developers
    Computer Graphics Technical Assistants
    Computer Graphics Systems Support

Digital Postproduction Group
    Digital Supervisor
    Digital Artists
    Digital Transfer Operator
    Digital Coordinator
    Scanning Supervisor
    Scanning Operators
    Scanning Software
    Rotoscoping Supervisor
    Rotoscopers
    Plate Photography Coordinator
    Optical Photography Supervisor
    Plate Photographers
    Effect Photographers
    Negative Cutter

The **visual effects** group is responsible for the overall production of all the special effects in the project, including the computer animation. Usually the director of visual effects decides what creative treatment and production techniques will be used in every single shot that requires special effects. A visual effects producer develops a production guidelines, as well as a budget and a schedule for the project. A visual effects supervisor is in charge of making sure that these production guidelines, budget, and deadlines are followed by the different production groups and sub-group.

The **computer animation** group is responsible for the production of the computer animation sequences. The computer animation supervisor primarily makes sure that all the visual effects guidelines are understood and implemented by the animator. The computer animation shot supervisors are in charge of subgroups that are responsible for completing a single shot or a series of shots. The computer animators develop the imagery and motion tests until the sequences are approved by the visual effects director. The computer animation production coordinator makes sure that everybody has what they need to do their job; this individual also schedules equipment, personnel and meetings.

The **computer technical support** group maintains the computer systems in working order and develops custom software that may be required for special production requirements. The **digital postproduction** group is responsible for scanning, retouching, and compositing all the different layers of visual effects, computer animation, and live action.

In addition to the creative and production teams, the administrative team oversees many of the financial, legal, and marketing issues related to the production of a complex computer animation project. An administrative team typically involves the following positions:

Administrative Team
    Executive Producer
    Production Assistant
    Production Manager
    Director of Postproduction
    Director of Finance
    Production Accountant

The members of the administrative team also work with the group directors in the creative and production teams to make sure that the production budgets, deadlines, and strategies are adequate to complete the project successfully.

Production Strategies

Planning the **production strategy** for any computer animation project starts with a review of the type of production, the technical complexity, and the basic resources, such as budget, schedule, personnel, and computer systems.

Computer animation projects can differ a lot from each other depending on the **type of production** they are. An experimental animation, a commercial production, an animation for broadcast television, or a feature film production all have very different purposes and project dynamics. Think of the differences that exist between the two extremes: the production of a one-person experimental computer animation and the production of a computer animation for a feature film. An experimental computer animation seeks to explore techniques, topics, or treatments that are not commonly used in mainstream productions. Most experimental works are not developed to be crowd pleasers so the director, who often is also the screenwriter and animator, has great freedom to experiment even though production resources in experimental production are usually limited. This fact may have a negative impact on the technical sophistication and amount of computer systems and personnel that may be employed, but also may have a positive effect in the form of a relaxed production schedule and creative freedom. The technical complexity of experimental computer animations varies greatly from project to project, but in all cases, the technical challenges in a computer animation have to be chosen carefully so that the production may be completed successfully with the available resources. A feature film computer animation is usually produced to tell a story that may be appreciated by a mainstream audience. Most productions of this type are quite complex and require a careful plan even though the resources are usually significant. This allows for ambitious technical challenges, but it also implies great pressure to deliver a product that will sell and will generate returns to investors.

The **technical complexity** of a computer animation may range from the very simple to the extremely complex. A computer animation project that is technically simple may involve a few objects that are animated with just a single or a few simple motion techniques. For example, many television station identifications or news program openers created with three-dimensional animation may be complex from the choreographic point of view but technically simple from the point of view of the motion techniques used. These animation typically involve keyframe animation enhanced with beautifully crafted models and outstanding rendering. A special effects segment produced for a live action feature film that includes computer animation typically requires several motion techniques such as keyframing, inverse kinematics, and motion dynamics. In this type of project the computer-generated motion has to be in perfect synchronization and alignment with the live action, the live special effects, and the traditional cel animation.

The best way to deal with technical complexity is by planning thoroughly before any production starts. The stage of preproduction planning starts with **meetings** with the producers or directors of the project. The goal of these initial meetings is to gather project information related to the technical strategies that may be necessary to generate the desired results. Producers and directors can provide a lot of information—such as visual style, budget, and deadlines—that affects technical complexity. Once the sequences to be animated are storyboarded it is commonly necessary to meet with the technical directors that will be responsible for clarifying complex technical issues, providing technical support, and for developing new tools that may be necessary to complete the project. The goal of having these meetings and developing the storyboard is to narrow down the possibilities and to develop a precise plan of action. This plan must contain a **technical implementation** for each shot in the computer animation as well as a crystal-clear creative approach that will guide the production.

The process for choosing one technical implementation—or specific set of techniques—over all the others usually requires finding a balance between the optimal method to achiever the desired result and the lowest cost to do so. This balance should take into account not just one shot but all the shots in the project. The technical implementation for each shot starts with an analysis of the elements in the shot and the ways in which they interact with each other. This analysis results in a **written description** of the plan for the shot which covers the elements of the shot, the interactions between them, and the specific techniques that will be used to create them.

A computer animation project is defined to the greatest extent by the **resources** allocated to it. One of the main tasks, for example, of a director of visual effects or supervisor of computer animation consists of making sure that the **budget** allocated to the project by the Producer and Director is adequate to produce the desired results. Equally important is that the production **schedule**—also set by the Producer or Director of the project—is based on realistic deadlines and that it provides sufficient time to achieve the desired results. Both the budget and the schedule of a production drive much of the daily dynamics of the production because they determine the number and expertise of the **personnel** that can be hired, and the amount and power of the **computer resources** that can be used.

The amount of time that is necessary to complete a computer animation depends on the type of production and its technical complexity. The typical duration of the production of a simple commercial computer animation is between one and two months, and such production may employ just a couple of animators and computers. A short production with complex technical requirements and compositing—for example, a television commercial—can last between two to three months, and may require half a dozen animators and computers, and a couple of supervisors. A longer computer animation production that involves dozens of shots and that requires a lot of interaction with both line action, special effects, and compositing—for example, a feature film—may take over one year to complete. This type of production may involve a production staff close to 100 individuals and a "farm" of dozens of computers. The technical challenges of experimental computer animations vary greatly. Some are produced during the course of a year by a couple of animators working after hours and a couple of borrowed computers. Other experimental computer animations, those with better funding, may be completed in six months and employ half a dozen individuals working on several computers.

Once completed, computer animations have a wide range of durations. There is no standard length of time that determines what is a short or a long piece of computer animation. But usually anything over 30 minutes is considered long. Thirty minutes is not such a long time, especially when one considers that the average length of a feature film is 120 minutes. But the huge amount of work and computer time that are required to produce a 30-minute segment of computer animation qualify it to be called a long work. Short-length computer animations under one minute long are commonly created for experimental pieces, student projects, T.V. commercials, T.V. station identification sequences or program openings, and film titles. Computer animation productions that fall in the medium-length category include episodes in an animated series, a collection of special effects to be inserted in a feature film or TV series, sequences for an amusement park motion ride or other types of location-based entertainment, or special creative projects funded by industry or government. Long productions of computer animation—over thirty 30 long—are rare, and include mostly feature films.

9.6 Animation File Formats

Most computer animation programs are able to save the animation parameters and data in a **stand-alone** animation file that is independent from the files containing the modeling and the rendering information. However, unlike many modeling and rendering programs that are capable of saving data in both native and portable file formats, most animation programs only save the animation information in native file formats that are proprietary and incompatible with other programs. Furthermore, many simple computer animation programs can only save the animation parameters embedded the modeling file or in the rendering file. Needles to say, this results in a rigid working environment.

9.7 Getting Ready

The preproduction stage in all computer animations is very important to the success of the final animated piece because computer animations are team projects that require extensive planning. This is especially true of computer animations that may have a tight deadline or that may be produced by a variety of companies or groups within the same company. Failing to do adequate planning for a computer animation project or failing to follow the production schedule often results in a negative and serious impact to the budget of a production and the credibility of those involved.

Check Your Three-Dimensional Models

The success of a computer animation project depends to a large degree on whether the three-dimensional models are well built or not. Take the time to make sure that the three-dimensional models that will be used in your animation are well built. This may avoid many problems later in the animation process. Checking the quality of a model may not be an issue if you built the model yourself and made sure that it was solid when you first built it. But if you are working with models built by others—as is often the case in commercial productions—then schedule some time before you start animating the models to examine them on your own or with the individual who modeled them if possible. Some of the items to check include: the hierarchical structure of all the parts in the model, their overall grouping, and their centers of rotation.

Check the Preferences File

The default settings stored in the preferences file or dialog box are important because they control directly and indirectly the result of many operations, functions, and tools of three-dimensional animation programs. Some of these settings include, for example, the animation rate of frames per second, the aspect ratio of the still image, and whether to load external files—such as texture maps or custom procedures—that may affect the final look of the animation project.

Make Motion Tests

One of the advantages of animating with a computer is that we can preview the motion as we develop it. The ability to create motion tests in the wireframe mode or with simple shading techniques at low resolutions provides invaluable feedback when developing complex motion sequences. Wireframe motion tests are useful mostly to check the choreography of a scene and the timing of the motions. But low resolution shaded motion tests are often required when we want to check, for example, the effect of light and shadow on the models as they move. Moving light sources may often cast undesirable hard-edge shadows on some objects or leave others looking too bright and overexposed. Virtually all computer animation programs allow for the creation of motion flipbooks that can be played back directly on the computer's screen. In cases when this is not possible, motion tests are recorded onto videotape and played back with a videotape player.

There are many strategies for testing different aspects or parts of the motion, some are useful for previewing scenes with many objects, others for previewing scenes with complex motion. One strategy for checking the speed of the motion—and supported by many programs—consists of animating all the objects in the scene as bounding boxes. It is also possible to render some objects in full shape and other as bounding boxes. Another strategy for focusing on the motion of just one or two objects in a crowded scene consists of turning off—or making invisible—all the other objects in the scene. Secondary objects in the scene can also be rendered in the wireframe mode with dotted lines or lines of a different color from the lines in the primary objects. A third strategy that is useful for analyzing the motion of objects in detail consists of playing the flipbook back in slow motion. This technique is often useful for discovering small mistakes such as single objects—fingers, for example—that should be moving within a hierarchy and are not, or small objects that may be colliding with each other.

Keep Digital Backups

The preferred method for recording computer animations consists of accumulating a good number of still frames in peripheral memory and then dumping or recording them onto film or videotape. This batch mode of recording animation is usually more efficient than recording still frames one at a time as soon as each is rendered. But in any case it is highly convenient to keep all the files that contain the digital still frames, even after they have been recorded on film or videotape. Keeping a **digital backup** of the animation can be invaluable if anything should happen to the master videotape or the original film negative before the project is delivered. Discarding the computer animation still frames as soon as they are recorded onto film or videotape is a situation that should be avoided at all costs. If this were done and the master videotape or original film negative were damaged then large portions of the project would have to be rendered all over again.

Save Your Work Often

Save your work often, every 15 minutes or so, and to make constant backups of your important data files.

Review and Practice

Matching

_____ Plot points

_____ Network server

_____ Sequence

_____ Frame

_____ Visual line of action

_____ Production Coordinator
_____ Visual Effects Supervisor
_____ Storyboard

_____ Elapsed timed
_____ Inverse kinematics

_____ ATM

_____ Character sheets

a. Series of panels that contain a visual interpretation of the screenplay.

b. Specifies the absolute length of a sequence in hours, minutes, seconds, and frames.

c. Used to define emotions and attitudes with body positions and facial expressions.

d. Makes sure that all the group leaders follow the storyboard and the agreed production strategies.

e. Its main purpose is to assist other computers to fetch and send data.

f. The smallest unit of animation.

g. Event in storyline that keeps the action moving.

h. Useful for animating models by specifying the final angle positions of some of the key joints in the model.

i. Network bandwidth of 154 megabits per second.

j. Makes sure that all the computer animators have the equipment, programs, and technical support they need to do their jobs.

k. Succession of camera shots that are connected to each other because they develop the same aspect of the action.

l. Guides the eye of the viewer by determining the position and sequence of the motions in the scene.

Answers Matching: a. Storyboard, b. Elapsed time, c. Character sheets, d. Visual Effects Supervisor, e. Network server, f. Frame, g. Plot points, h. Inverse kinematics, i. ATM, j. Production Coordinator, k. Sequence, l. Visual line of action.

True/False

_____ a. The subject of a screenplay is defined by the conclusion of the story.

_____ b. The detail of the three-dimensional models does not affect the production of a computer animation.

_____ c. The personnel of a computer animation studio or production house includes creative, technical, and administrative positions.

_____ d. The angles of rotation of a character's joints may define the complexity of its motion.

_____ e. Experimental computer animations always tell stories that can be appreciated by a mainstream audience.

_____ f. Motion dynamics animation techniques are especially useful for animating complex models with a large number of joints.

_____ g. Key facial expressions may be stored in a library and be used throughout the animation as keyframes.

_____ h. High-bandwidth networks can be used for transferring computer animations between studios in different countries.

_____ i. Computer animation productions for feature films are often composited with live action and live special effects.

_____ j. One second of animation at normal speed NTSC video equals 30 frames.

_____ k. There is only one dramatic structure that can be used in storytelling.

_____ l. Keyframes in an animated sequence with complex motion are usually placed at the same points throughout the scene.

_____ m. Interpolation is a technique that creates in-between frames based on start and end points.

_____ n. A production storyboard is usually drawn on a sketchbook and includes detailed renderings of each shot.

_____ o. Directional arrows can be used in a storyboard to clarify the camera motions in a shot.

_____ p. Animating motion in layers is convenient, because it breaks down a complex challenge into smaller and more manageable parts.

Answers True/False: a. False, b. False, c. True, d. True, e. False, f. True, g. True, h. True, i. True, j. True, k. False, l. False, m. T, n. False, o. True, p. True.

Key Terms

Ahead of the story
Anatomy
Animated
Anticipation
ATM (Asyncronous Transfer Mode)
Attention of the audience
Background
Bandwidth
Beginning of the story
Behind the story
Branching
Budget
Casting
Cel animation
Cels
Character generator
Character sheets
Collaboration
Complex motion
Computer animation
Computer resources
Computer technical support
Computer-human interface
Conceptual storyboard
Creative team
Development of the character
Dialogue
Digital backup
Digital format
Digital postproduction
Digital studio
Dimensions
Downward compatibility
Drawings
DS-1 (Digital Signal Level One)
Elapsed time
Emotions
End of the story
Ethernet
Events
Exaggerated gestures
Express an emotion
External shape of a three-dimensional character
Facial expressions
Fake hold
FDDI (Fiber Distributed Data Interface)

Feature film
Field guides
Flow of events
Flowcharts
Follow-through
Foreground
Forward kinematics
Fps (frames per second)
Frame
Hierarchy level
Hybrid framework
Implementing the motions
In-between
In-betweening
Input capabilities
Intended audience
Interactive project
Interactivity
Interface design
Internal structure of a three-dimensional
    character
Interpolation
Interrupted action
Inverse kinematics
Joints
Key poses
Keyframing
Keyframes
Layers of motion
Linear
Manual arrangement
Meetings
Microcomputers
Middle of the story
Modeled
Montage
Motion capture
Motion control techniques
Motion dynamics
Motion hold
Motion tests
Network
Network servers
Nonlinearity
Output capabilities
Overlapping motion
Paintbox
Parallel action

Pencil test
Peripheral storage
Personnel
Planning
Plot points
Postproduction
Preproduction
Presentation storyboard
Primary motion
Procedural motion
Processing power
Production
Production storyboards
Production strategy
Production team
Production technique
Proprietary software
Rate of display
Readability of motion
Rendered
Resources
Rhythm
Rolling credits
Rule-based motion
Running time
Scene
Scene-and-shot-number
Schedule
Screenplay
Scripts
Second
Secondary motion
Sequence
Sequences of still images

Shot
Shot number
Silhouette
Simple motion
Skeleton
Speed
Stand-alone
Stories
Storyboard
Structure
Subject of a screenplay
Super-microcomputers
Supervision
T-1
Team efforts
Technical complexity
Technical implementation
Television commercial
Tempo
Thinking process
Timing
Title safety area
Transition
Translated into moving images
Treatment of the subject
Turn-key software
Type of production
Upward compatibility
User testing
Visual effects
Visual interpretation
Visual line of action
Written description
Written information

10.1.1 A sequence with three keyframes and two interpolations—one quicker than the other.

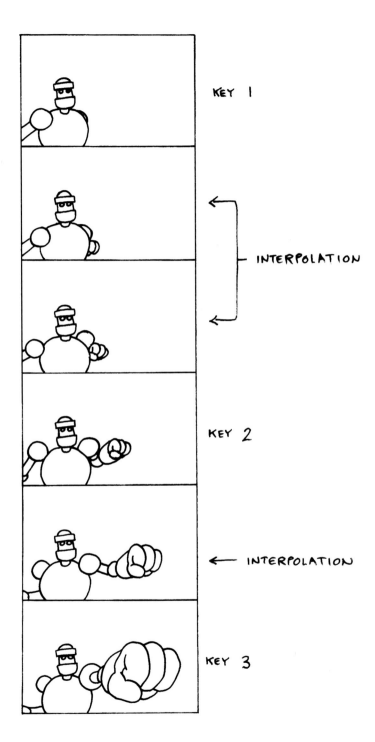

KEY 1

INTERPOLATION

KEY 2

INTERPOLATION

KEY 3

CHAPTER 10

Basic Animation Techniques

Summary

This chapter starts by reviewing the principles of keyframe interpolation as applied to animating the position and orientation of objects in three-dimensional space, as well as their shape and attributes. A variety of three-dimensional computer animation techniques that are based on keyframe interpolation are also reviewed. This includes the spatial animation of models, cameras, and lights with interactive placement of the keyframes and with forward kinematics; the shape animation of three-dimensional models with lattice deformation or morphing techniques; and the interpolation of attributes like the surface characteristics of models, the depth of field of cameras, and the color of lights. The chapter concludes with an explanation of hierarchical animation.

10.1 Principles of Keyframe Interpolation

The **keyframe interpolation** technique is used in computer animation to create sequences of still frames. This computer animation technique calculates the **in-between frames** by averaging the information contained in the keyframes. Interpolation techniques can be used to calculate the position of objects in space, as well as their shape and other attributes. Keyframe interpolation provides as many in-between frames as needed—depending on the length of the sequence being interpolated—but the spacing of the in-between frames varies depending on the type of interpolation used. The most common type of interpolations include linear interpolation and curve interpolation.

A **keyframe** is defined by its particular moment in the animation timeline as well as by all the parameters or attributes associated with it. These parameters include, for example, the position of an object in space, its shape and its surface characteristics (Fig. 10.1.1). Interpolations are a simple but powerful way to express and control the relation between the time that it takes

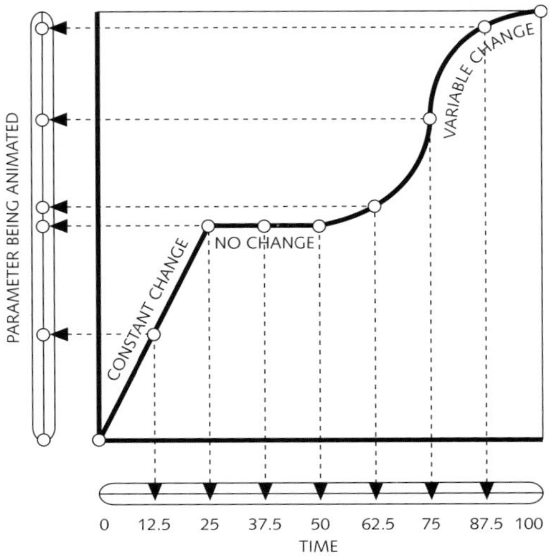
PARAMETER BEING ANIMATED
CONSTANT CHANGE
NO CHANGE
VARIABLE CHANGE
0 12.5 25 37.5 50 62.5 75 87.5 100
TIME

10.1.2 The slope of an interpolation path results in changes of speed or the parameter being animated.

to get from one keyframe to another and the amount of change in the parameters or attributes. The **speed** or **rate of change** is defined by the amount of time that it takes to get from one keyframe to another and by the amount of change in the animated parameters.

Interpolations are commonly expressed in the form of a graph that summarizes the relation between time and the parameter being animated. Time is usually represented by the horizontal axis, and the parameter in question is usually represented by the vertical axis. The **slope** of the path in the graph represents the speed or rate of change. A flat path, for example, indicates no change—zero speed—a diagonal path indicates constant change, and a curve path represents variable change. The steeper the slope of the path the greater the rate of change (Fig. 10.1.2). Interpolation graphs are generated automatically by most computer animation software as soon as the animator specifies the animation parameters on one or several objects in the scene. It is usually possible to edit these graphs interactively.

Linear Interpolation

Linear interpolation is the simplest and most straightforward computer animation technique for calculating in-between frames. **Linear interpolation** simply averages the parameters in the keyframes and provides as many equally spaced in-between frames as needed. However, linear interpolation techniques may produce mechanical results when applied to subtle motions, unless significant amount of work and animation skill are used to fine tune the results.

Linear interpolation is based on constant speeds between the keyframes, but produces abrupt changes in speed on the keyframes where one constant speed ends and a different constant speed starts. **Constant speed** is represented by the straight lines in the graph. Linear interpolations cannot handle subtle changes in speed because the in-between frames are created at equal intervals along the path (Fig. 10.1.3).

Curved Interpolation

Curved interpolation, also called an **interpolation ease**, is a technique for calculating in-between frames more sophisticated than linear interpolation. Curved interpolation averages the parameters in the keyframes taking into account the variations of speed over time, known as **acceleration**. When curved interpolation is represented in graphical form the increase in speed, also called an **ease in**, is represented by a line that curves up. An **ease out**, or decrease in speed, is represented by a line that curves down. Therefore the distribution of in-between frames along the path depends on whether the rate of change increases or decreases. Curved interpolation can also include motion with constant speed, and that is represented with straight lines (Fig. 10.1.4).

Working With Parameter Curves

A graph representing curved interpolations is also called a **parameter curve** or a **function curve**. As mentioned earlier, parameter curves are generated automatically by most computer animation software as the animator positions the objects in space and defines their animation parameters for each keyframe. Working with parameter curves provides animators with an additional method for modifying the animation by manipulating just the paths contained in the graphs and without having to manipulate, for example, the position of objects in three-dimensional space. Working with parameter curves is commonly used to edit and fine tune subtle aspects of an animated project.

As mentioned in Chapter 3 some of the most popular types of curves include linear splines, cardinal splines, B-splines and Bézier curves. Each of these types of curves is shaped in a characteristic way by their control points, or control vertices. Therefore, the exact shape and functionality of function curves depends on the type of curve used (Fig. 10.1.5). A linear spline, for example, consists of a series of straight lines that connect all the control points. The animation generated by linear splines is based on constant speed between keyframes and abrupt changes of speed at the keyframes where two different constant speeds meet. The animation generated with a cardinal spline is very dependent on the placement of the keyframes in the interpolation graph because the control points in a cardinal spline force the curve to pass through all of them. The tight fit of cardinal curves to the control points often results in harsh closed curves which translate into rough eases. The animation created with B-splines usually contains very smooth interpolation eases because the shape of the curve is loosely controlled by the control points but not forced to pass through them. Parameter curves calculated with Bézier curve functions offer the most flexible—and complex—path control because the shape of the curve is controlled by the position of both the control points and the tangent

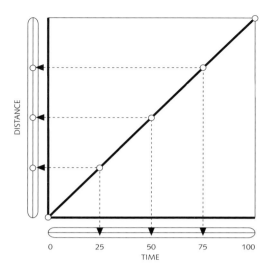

10.1.3 A linear interpolation graph.

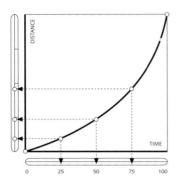
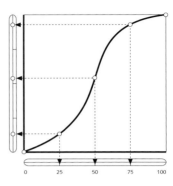

10.1.4 Three graphs for curved interpolation. Notice how the distance travelled over time by the animated model varies with the slope of the curve.

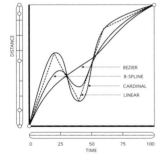

10.1.5 Four types of function curves with the same control hull have been overlapped to show the different animation results.

points. Bézier curves facilitate the creation of flexible curves with a wide range of characteristics that often translate into the animation. Bézier curves, for example, can be made to blend into a straight line very slowly and softly or suddenly. Another advantage of using Bézier curves for defining interpolation graphs is that their slope can be modified with just the tangent points, therefore avoiding the insertion of additional control points (keyframes) to shape the curve and the motion.

Parameter curves can represent either a linear interpolation, an ease in, or an ease out. But complex interpolations that include these three interpolation types are called **ease functions**. These complex interpolations can be defined interactively by specifying the type of curve function that the keyframe control points in the graph should use to calculate the interpolation. Ease functions are also defined by dragging a slider that represents the proportion of ease in, linear, and ease out in the function (Fig. 10.1.6). Ease functions can also be specified by inputting numerical values that range from 0 percent to 100 percent or from 0 to 1 (Fig. 10.1.7).

Interpolation of Position and Orientation

Interpolation techniques can be used to calculate the position and orientation of animated objects in three-dimensional space. This includes not only the models in a scene, but also the cameras and the light sources. As mentioned in Chapter 2, the position and orientation of an object in three-dimensional space can be modified by changing the values in the **transformation matrix** that controls the translations, rotations, and scaling that are applied to the objects in the scene. When keyframe interpolation techniques are used the values in the transformation matrices of moving objects are specified at the keyframes, and the in-between values are interpolated. Most computer animation programs provide animators with direct ways to edit the transformation matrix of an object through the parameter curves.

Interpolation of Shape

Interpolation techniques can also be used to animate the shape of three-dimensional models. The basic idea behind **shape animation** consists of transforming one key shape into another one by letting the interpolation techniques calculate all the in-between positions of the points and lines that define the shape of the model. A variety of shape interpolation techniques are illustrated in Fig. 10.2.6.

Interpolation of Attributes

The **attributes** or characteristics of models, cameras, and lights,—other than spatial position and shape—can also be animated with interpolation techniques. In the case of three-dimensional models, it is common to animate their surface characteristics, such as color, texture, or transparency. Focal length and depth of field are two characteristics of cameras often animated. In the case of light sources, it is common to animate attributes such as color, intensity, cone-angle, and fall-off values. Several interpolations of attributes are exemplified in the next three sections in this chapter.

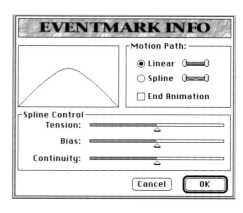

10.1.6 Sliders and a function curve to control ease in and ease out. (Dialog box from Infini-D 3.0. © 1991-1995 Specular International, Ltd.)

10.2 Model Animation

Keyframe interpolation techniques are very effective for animating the position, shape, and attributes of three-dimensional models. The spatial animation of simple models can be easily controlled through the parameter curves or through motion paths placed in the three-dimensional scene. (The techniques used to animate hierarchical models are covered at the end of this chapter and in Chapter 11). The shape animation of models can be implemented with a variety of techniques that include freeform shape interpolation, three-dimensional morphing, and external control structures such as lattices and functions. Finally, very spectacular results can be achieved by animating the surface characteristics of models with interpolation techniques.

The most common method for specifying the **spatial animation** of three-dimensional models when using keyframe interpolation is to interactively arrange their position and orientation. This method is based on the idea of defining keyframes by placing the models in three-dimensional space and applying the geometric transformations to them, refining the motion with the ease functions, and letting the software interpolate the in-between frames. This idea is, in fact, the essence of all keyframe animation, traditional and computer-based.

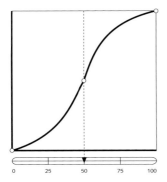 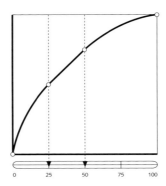 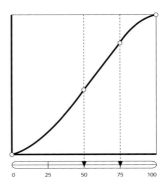

10.1.7 Ease parameter curves specified with different numerical values: 50% ease in and 50% ease out (a); 25% ease out, 25% linear, and 50% ease out (b); 50% ease in, 25% linear, and 25% ease out (c).

Interactive Specification of Keyframes

The **interactive specification of key poses** can be enhanced when the animator previews his or her work on several camera views simultaneously so that the subtlety of the motions can be examined from different points of view. It should be clear by now that the interactive specification of key poses can be done by either dragging the objects interactively with the mouse, pen, or track ball, or by editing the **parameter curves** as described earlier. In both of these cases, it is necessary to preview the motion in order to check that the parameters specified are producing the desired results.

Forward Kinematics

Another technique that can be used to specify motion through key poses, especially with jointed figures, is called **forward kinematics**. This technique consists of determining the motion and final position of a model by first specifying the angles of its joints (Fig. 10.2.1). This can be easily accomplished by typing the numerical value for each joint angle directly into the appropriate fields or dialog boxes provided by the software (Fig. 2.2.4). Forward kinematics is a simple technique that requires a great deal of manual work, and it should not be confused with the technique of inverse kinematics that is described in Chapter 11.

Forward kinematics can be used very creatively in situations when all the joint angles are known in advance and are repeated many times. Once such case is exemplified by an interactive program—like a videogame—where the positions of the characters are finite, repeated many times, and known in advance. In forward kinematics the joint angles must be laboriously input through the keyboard or another input peripheral, and the motions have to be such that the angles are easy to establish or calculate before the motions are actually performed (Fig. 10.2.2).

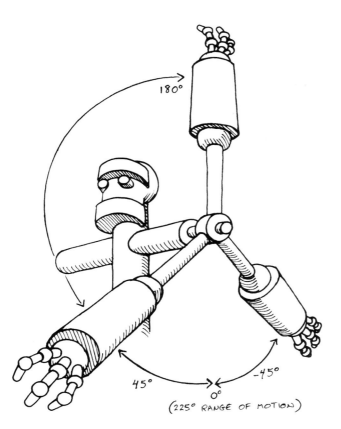

180°

45°   -45°

0°
(225° RANGE OF MOTION)

The project illustrated in Fig. 10.2.3 shows the results of a computer program that seeks to create interactive animated characters that dance with some sort of emotional expressiveness and a minimum number of joints. In this case, the joints were universal, four for each limb and one for each waist, neck, and head. (Even with such a small number of joints this figure has two separate joints at the base and the top for the neck because the head position is so important for emotional expressiveness.) The figure was driven by a combination of forward kinematics expressed in the form of key actions, body constraints, and a small amount of somewhat random noise. In this example, the actions are taught to the animated character in advance, and the transitions between actions are adjusted so that the motion looks natural. Establishing the proper joint angles before the motions occur is important since most of the personality of the character and the mood of the dance step is expressed through body language.

The model of the dancer is built with ellipsoids. Some of the motion contraints include a few simple joint constraints—the

10.2.2 This articulated model can be used to input and visualize joint angles to animations based on forward kinematics techniques. (The Monkey™ is courtesy of Digital Image Design.)

head, for example, cannot turn all the way around. Obstacles in the path are avoided by turning away from them, and the supporting foot at floor level propels the character. Predefined actions such as a dance step can be stored in the form of a table of ranges for each joint involved in the action. The values used to specify the rhumba dance in Figure 10.2.3 are listed here:

```
{
    { 5 5 5 }       {-5 -5 -5 }     { n1 n2 n3 }Nod
    { 15 5 0}       { -15 -5 0 }    { b a    }  Rchest
    { 0 0 0 }       { 0 0 0 }       { a a    }  Rshoulder
    { -90 0 0 }     { -70 0 0 }     { a a    }  Relbow
    { 0 0 0 }       { 0 0 0 }       { a a    }  Rpelvis
    { -25 5 -15 }{ 0 -10 0 }        { a a a  }  Rhip
    { 50 0 0 }      { 0 0 0 }       { a a    }  Rknee
    { 0 0 0 }       { 0 0 0 }       { a a    }  Rankle
    { 0 10 0 }      { 0 -10 0 }     { a a    }  Waist
    { -15 -5 0 }    { 15 5 0 }      { b a    }  Lchest
    { 0 0 0 }       { 0 0 0 }       { a a    }  Lshoulder
    { -70 0 0 }     { -90 0 0 }     { a a    }  Lelbow
    { 0 0 0 }       { 0 0 0 }       { a a    }  Lpelvis
    { 0 -20 0 }     { -10 20 -25 }{ a a a }     Lhip
    { 0 0 0 }       { 20 0 0 }      { a a    }  Lknee
    { 0 0 0 }       { 0 0 0 }       { a a    }  Lankle
} 'rhumba define_action
```

The lowercase letters represent a variety of functions, including a random noise generator function (n) applied to the head to simulate the character looking around as she dances. The arm joints at the chest (Rchest and Lchest) are controlled by functions in the X and Z axis that result in an elliptical motion of the shoulders. The noise function is also used to give the standing still figure of the dancer a subtle restlessness and apparent

10.2.3 Still frames from *Danse Interactif*, a real-time procedurally animated interactive dance performance. These four images from the Rhumba Sequence represent the cycle the animated dancer goes through in completing the move. (Courtesy of Ken Perlin, New York University, Media Research Laboratory. © 1994 Ken Perlin.)

shifting of weight back and forth from one side to the other.

Motion Paths

The technique of **motion paths** provides an additional method for defining the motion of objects in three-dimensional space. This technique is somewhat similar to working with parameter curves because it also involves a path. But the actual motion path is drawn as a single path in the three-dimensional environment instead of being drawn as several two-dimensional interpolation graphs.

Three-dimensional motion paths are easy to work with because they allow the animator to define motion that may involve translations and rotations in a very quick way. Working with motion paths allows us to think of motion in terms of "go from here to there, and follow this path." This technique is especially useful to define with precision the motion of flying and swimming models because they both move by following a three-dimensional path. Motion paths are particularly useful for defining the motion of flying cameras, and they can also be used to animate objects that move by sliding over a surface. This would include, for example, sail boats and snow skiers (Fig. 10.2.4).

Motion paths are also useful to sketch or layout the motion of traction vehicles like bicycles and tractors, and also of legged creatures like ants and humans. In these cases, the motion path can be used to define the basic motion of the models, and the rest of the motion can be added later. A legged creature animated with just a motion path would probably look stiff and unrealistic. The additional motion of the wheels in traction vehicles and the limbs in legged creatures can be created in both cases with simple interactive placement of keyframes or with advanced animation techniques like inverse kinematics or motion dynamics.

Motion path animation is defined in several steps and it starts with a curve being drawn in three-dimensional space, usu-

10.2.4 The motion paths of two skaters are made visible here.

ally with a curve modeling tool. Then the model to be animated is selected and **linked to the path**. The timing parameters of the path are then defined. This is usually done by typing the values of the frames in which the motion path animation is to start and end. When a motion path animation is first defined a linear interpolation with constant speed is often applied as a default value in most software programs. But the speed and acceleration in the motion path can be refined after previewing the results by editing its timing parameters with an interpolation graph.

The alignment of a three-dimensional model to the path as the model moves through the path is an important detail in motion path animation. Most software programs will keep the object linked to the motion path so that the front of the animated object is always facing in the direction of the path (Fig. 10.2.5). This is also called keeping the direction of the object tangential to the path. In order to do this, most computer animation programs need to know which is the **front of the object** at the time when the object is linked to the motion path. In most cases, objects will be animated down the path in the position in which they were linked to the path. But some programs will only animate objects along the path in the position in which they were originally created.

Freeform Shape Animation

Simple shape animation can be created by interpolating the shape of two objects on a point-by-point basis. When this interpolation is done between two versions of the same three-dimensional model it is usually called freeform shape animation, and when it is done between two different models it is called morphing.

Freeform shape animation can be created first by placing two versions of a three-dimensional polygonal or spline-based model in each of two contiguous keyframes, and then modifying the shape of one of the two models by pulling the points in the planar or curved mesh that define it. The in-between frames that constitute the shape transformation will be interpolated by the computer program.

The freeform shape animation process starts by identifying the points—or control vertices—in the model that will be animated. This is usually done in the wireframe mode. A single point or a group of points are selected and dragged to a new position. Each point in one model will be interpolated to only one point in the other model. Sometimes some or all of the points in a three-dimensional object may be locked so it is useful to check if the points in a model are locked before attempting to animate them with freeform shape animation techniques.

Freeform shape animation can be very useful in the creation of squash and stretch effects. **Squashing** and **stretching** are commonly used in animation to emphasize the motion of objects in response to the forces of compression and expansion. Squash and stretch effects help characterize the mass and weight of moving objects as well as the material it is made of.

Three-Dimensional Morphing

Three-dimensional morphing is a very effective technique for creating shape animations that do not require as much time consuming detail work as freeform shape interpolations. **Three-dimensional morphing** works by animating all the points of one object into the positions occupied by the points of another object (Fig. 10.2.6). The results of three-dimensional morphing animation are usually fascinating, but there are two important technical requirements that must be satisfied before this technique works to its fullest. First, the best results are obtained when each of the three-dimensional models has the same **number of points**. This fact implies that a fair amount of pre-planning—especially during the modeling stage—is necessary for this technique to be practical. Many software programs will not even attempt three-dimensional morphing unless this condition is satisfied. Second, it is also necessary to specify the **order of correspondence** between the points in each of the three-dimensional models. Many software programs allow for the interactive linking of points between objects. This is helpful to make sure that the morphing results do not include morphing accidents—like objects that wrap inside out, overlapping surfaces or holes in the models—that may be distracting. In some cases, however, these results may be appropriate effects to tell a particular story.

Freeform Lattices

Freeform shape animation can create striking results, but it requires a great deal of skill and time for manipulating large numbers of points one at a time. Using **external control structures** to regulate the shape animation of objects can be a better

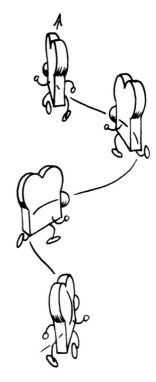

10.2.5 This camera always looks down the motion path as it moves.

10.2.6 This still frame from the film *The Mask* is an example of three-dimensional morphing. (© 1994 New Line Productions, Inc. All rights reserved. Courtesy of New Line Productions, Inc.)

a   b

c   d

10.2.7 A circular sine function was used to distort a sphere.

choice, especially in cases where a uniform shape deformation is desired. Two popular animation techniques that use external control structures include freeform lattices and wave functions.

A **freeform lattice** is a three-dimensional grid of points and lines that controls the points in a three-dimensional model. The control points in the freeform lattice are connected with imaginary springs to the points in the model. As the control points in the lattice are moved they push or pull the points in the object (Fig. 3.5.2). The ability to create shape animations by moving one or several points in a freeform lattice is directly related to the resolution of the lattice. A lattice with only a small number of points yields rough shape animations, while lattices with larger numbers of control points can be used to apply more subtle local distortions on the model controlled by the lattice.

Wave Functions

A great variety of mathematical functions can be applied to a three-dimensional model with the purpose of changing its shape. Animating with functions can be an economical way to create animations because little work is required once it has been determined how to apply the function to the object (Fig. 10.2.7). For most animations that involve traditional storytelling, animating with functions provides an effective way to create the foundation of a motion that can be complemented with other techniques. Functions are also very effective for animating secondary motion or objects in a scene. This is easily accomplished by applying the function to just one branch of the hierarchical structure. However, most functions tend to be of limited use and are rarely used as the primary technique in a computer animation project. This is because the motion generated with functions—while interesting and exciting from the mathematical point of view—is usually too simple or monotonous to be used by itself, and also because developing new functions requires—for most productions—a significant amount of time, skill and energy.

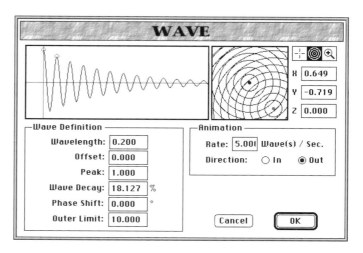

Many computer animation programs allow animators to define two-dimensional function curves of almost any shape and use them as control structures to animate the shape of objects. These control curves are often called **wave functions** since their shapes resemble the outline of a wave. (A similar wave function for creating procedural textures is described in Chapter 8.) The distortions created by applying wave functions to three-dimensional models are sometimes unpredictable, and a trial and error approach is often required. Some of the characteristics of this technique, however, are quite simple and easy to control (Fig. 10.2.8). The wave type variable determines the way in which the wave propagates from its center throughout the three-dimensional model. Functions can be easily looped and used to simulate the recurring motions, for example, of water waves. **Circular waves** are an excellent technique for recreating the motion of the water waves on the surface of a lake, and **planar waves** can recreate the effect of waves on the surface of the sea. **Spherical waves** can be used to recreate an explosion.

10.2.8 These dialog boxes show the implementation of a wave function in two different software programs. (a. Dialog box from Infini-D 3.0. © 1991-1995 Specular International, Ltd.; b. Dialog box from Softimage 3D. © Microsoft Corporation. All rights reserved.)

Animation of the Surface Characteristics

Several techniques used to render the surface characteristics that define the exterior appearance of objects and characters in still images are covered in Chapter 8. But these surface characteristics can also change throughout time. Changes in color, transparency, texture or reflectivity always indicate not only a change in the exterior appearance of objects or characters, but also a change in their inner emotions, chemical composition, or state of mind. Changes in the surface characteristics of objects or characters

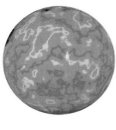

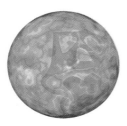

10.2.9 A sequence of animated surface textures where a shiny semi-precious stone turns into carved wood.

can be very useful elements of visual storytelling because they always happen as reactions to other actions or as responses to a variety of stimula.

In our world, some of the changes in surface characteristics happen very rapidly—in a matter of seconds—while others require several months or even years to occur. Both the blushing of a face or the maturing of an apple, for example, involve changes in color and visual texture, but one happens in seconds while the other requires weeks. In both of these cases, the **timing of the transformations** of color and texture is crucial to the understanding of the action. If the reddening of an apple takes place throughout a long period of time we know that we are watching a **natural transformation**, but if it happens in a matter of seconds we assume that some **fantastic transformation** process is under way. Likewise if an audience watches the blushing occur in a matter of seconds they will know that they are watching somebody express feelings of shame, excitement, or modesty. But if the reddening of the face takes place throughout several days then the audience would assume that transformation to be not the quick display of a sudden emotion but perhaps the reaction of the skin to an allergy or disease.

Animating the surface characteristics of objects or characters can create realistic or fantastic effects of material transformation and also communicate subtle or sudden changes of events in a story. The animation of surface characteristics is easily done with interpolation techniques. The process is simple but powerful. It starts by applying a set of surface characteristics to the objects in question in the keyframe at the beginning of a sequence. Then the same set of surface characteristics can be applied to the objects in the last keyframe of that sequence, and then modified with the parameter curves that represent each of the surface characteristics or by typing in new values.

The parameter curves that represent color, transparency, reflectivity, and shading characteristics can be easily edited because those surface characteristics are usually controlled by a single numerical value or by a simple set of values, like RGB values, for example. The textures of a surface are usually controlled by as many as 20 variables and, consequently, as many parameter curves. Animating the two- and three-dimensional textures of surfaces usually requires increased setup time, additional rendering tests, and more trial and error than some of the simpler surface characteristics. Figure 10.2.9 illustrates the animation of a variety of surface characteristics. See Chapter 8 for more information about surface characteristics and their variables.

In addition to animating the standard shading attributes of a three-dimensional surface, it is also possible to create spectacular effects by mapping sequences of animated images on a three-dimensional surface and by animating the parameters of a three-dimensional procedural texture. **Mapping a sequence of images** is done by assigning two-dimensional picture files that are applied as maps to three-dimensional objects (Fig. 13.3.4). The sequencing can be done on a one-on-one basis (one two-dimensional image per frame of three-dimensional computer animation) or by following a script where some two-dimensional images may be applied in different sequences and loops to frames in the three-dimensional animation.

10.3 Camera Animation

The camera plays an important role in computer animation because its motion and the changes in some of its attributes can have a powerful storytelling effect. As explained in Chapter 6, the point of view of a camera and the type of camera shot are both defined by the position and orientation of the camera. All camera motions require a change in position and orientation of the camera. (The placement of cameras and their basic attributes are explained in Chapter 6.)

The motions of the virtual cameras used in computer animation are based on the camera moves defined in traditional cinematography. Most software programs use the same camera names used in traditional cinematography, but some use a slightly different nomenclature. All the possible camera moves can be expressed in terms of translations or rotations around one or several camera axes.

In addition to changing the position and orientation of virtual cameras, their focal length and depth of field are some of the attributes that can be easily animated.

Position Camera Moves

The position of a camera can be easily defined by typing an **absolute position** value specified in XYZ world coordinates in the field or dialog box that controls the camera position. This technique can be useful to define keyframes where the camera must be in a precise location. A more intuitive way to define the position of a camera consists of using one or several camera moves that are usually available as pull-down menu items in most computer animation programs.

The camera moves that are based on a change of the **position of the camera** include a dolly, a truck, and a boom. A **dolly** is a translation of the camera along the horizontal axis. A tracking or **traveling shot** occurs when a dolly moves along with the subject and follows it. A **truck** move is a translation of the camera along the depth axis, and it usually goes in or out of the scene. A **boom** is a translation of the camera along its the vertical axis. A **crane shot** can be implemented with a combination of boom, truck, and sometimes dolly camera moves (Fig. 10.3.1).

Orientation Camera Moves

The orientation of a camera can also be easily defined by typing an absolute position value specified in XYZ world coordinates in the field or dialog box that controls the camera orientation. This technique can be useful to define keyframes where the camera must be looking in a precise direction or at a specific point in space. A more intuitive way to define the orientation of a camera consists of using one or several camera moves that are usually available as pull-down menu items in most computer animation programs.

The camera moves that are based on the change of the **orientation of the camera** include a tilt, a roll, and a pan. A **tilt** is a rotation of the camera on its horizontal axis. A tilt is also called a pivot and is used to look up or down. A **roll** is created by rotating the camera around its Z axis. Roll camera moves are common when simulating fly-throughs. A **pan** is a move created by rotating the camera around its vertical axis (Fig. 10.3.2). Panning is very effective for scanning the scene from side to side while the camera remains stationary. Sometimes, especially when simulating flying cameras, a tilt move is called a pitch—as in airplanes pitching—and a pan move is called a yaw. (A zoom is a camera move that is achieved not by moving the position or orientation of the camera but by animating its focal length.)

Camera Motion Paths

The technique of motion paths is especially useful to lay out complex camera moves—crane shots, underwater shots, and flying cameras in particular—consisting of several individual moves. As explained earlier, the motion path technique works by animating an object—the camera in this case—along a path defined in three-dimensional space. The paths are drawn with a simple curve modeling tool and edited just like any other object in three-dimensional space would be edited. Motion paths can be created with any type of curve but it is recommended to use B-spline or Bézier curves since both offer superior control for shaping the curvature of the path.

Once a camera is linked to the motion path and once the timing parameters of the path are defined, then it is possible to refine the motion of the camera. The speed and acceleration of a camera moving down a motion path can be fine-tuned with a timing interpolation graph. The constant speed that is commonly used as a default value in motion path animations can be enhanced with variable speeds, ease ins and ease outs (Fig. 10.3.3).

The position and orientation of a camera that is animated

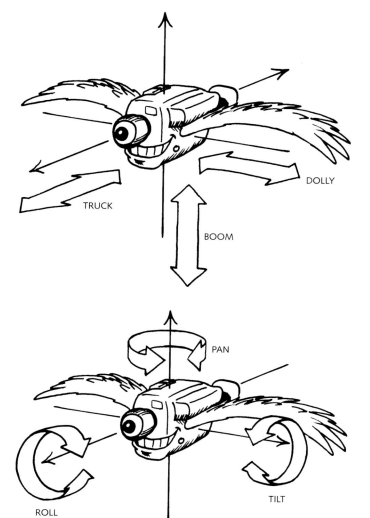

10.3.1 A dolly, a truck, a boom, and a crane camera moves.

DOLLY

TRUCK

BOOM

10.3.2 A tilt, a roll, and a pan camera moves.

PAN

ROLL

TILT

along a motion path can also be fine tuned by adding standard camera moves, by adjusting the camera's point of interest, or by controlling the banking of the camera with an external object. A convenient feature of motion paths in many computer animation programs is that they can be converted to explicit transformations. This means that a motion that was originally defined by a path in three-dimensional space with just a timing interpolation graph can be converted to motions defined by the standard interpolation graphs for each of the geometric transformations along every axis. This conversion can help refine the motion by editing the interpolation parameter curves. Adjusting the point of interest of a camera as it moves along the motion path can be used to simulate the **sideways scanning** done by most live creatures as they move down a path (Fig. 10.3.3). The **banking motion** of flying or underwater cameras as they take the curves in a motion path can sometimes be easily set by linking the camera to an invisible object below or behind it. The purpose of this invisible object is to simulate weight or drag, and its animation can complement the motion of the camera.

Focal Length and Zoom Camera Moves

The focal length of a camera controls the way in which three-dimensional objects are seen by the camera. The **focal length** in a virtual camera is defined by the relation between the near clipping plane and the far clipping plane. This relation defines the way in which the objects in a three-dimensional environment are projected onto the projection plane of a virtual camera—or the surface of the film in a real camera. The focal length in a photographic camera is determined by the curvature and shape of the lens. For that reason, the unit to measure focal length even in virtual cameras is millimeters (mm). Standard camera lenses have a fixed focal length, but **zoom lenses** are capable of variable focal lengths by changing the distance between the point of view and the focal plane (Figs. 6.2.2 and 6.4.3). Some computer animation programs allow for the focal length to be animated independently or in conjunction with the near and the far clipping planes. This provides great flexibility when trying to clip—or remove—an object in the field of vision by placing it ahead of the near clipping plane or beyond the far clipping plane while maintaining a constant focal length.

A **zoom** is also a special type of camera move where the camera remains still but the framing of the image changes by gradually and continuously modifying the camera's focal length. In a zoom camera move, both the position and orientation of the camera remain untouched. With a zoom move it is common to migrate from one type of camera shot to another, for example, from an extreme close up to a waist shot, or from a long shot that shows the scenery to a wide shot that focuses on a group of characters.

Depth of Field

The focusing properties of a lens are determined by its **depth of field**. The **focus** of a lens defines the plane that is perpendicular to the camera and that will be resolved into a sharp image. Only one plane in three-dimensional space can be in perfect focus when seen through any lens—our eyes included. But the areas that are slightly ahead and slightly behind the **focal plane** are also in focus, not perfect focus but close enough so that almost nobody can tell the difference. The depth of field is bound by the near and the far focal planes, both of which are close enough to the focal plane to still be in focus (Figs. 6.4.1 and 6.2.3).

In a real camera, a specific depth of field is determined by the combination of the focal length of the lens used, the **lens aperture** measured in f/stop units, and the distance between the camera and the subject, also called **focal distance**. As a general rule the smaller the lens aperture—which is inversely proportional to the f/stop numerical value—the greater the depth of field. Unlike photographic cameras, virtual cameras are capable of imaging in perfect focus all the objects in a three-dimensional environment. This means that issues of focussing and depth of field can be ignored when creating an image with three-dimensional computer graphics techniques. In fact, many software programs do not support depth of field or allow animators to turn it off altogether. But using the depth of field when rendering an image can contribute to the realism of the results. Depth of field should not be confused with the depth-fading rendering technique covered in Chapter 8.

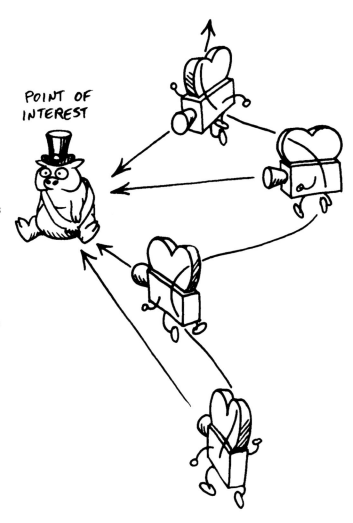

10.3.3 The point of interest of the camera is constantly adjusted as it moves down the motion path.

10.4 Light Animation

The position and attributes of light sources in a computer animation project can be animated using keyframe interpolation techniques. The position and motion of light sources can be defined with the same interpolation techniques described earlier in the section on Model Animation. These techniques include the interactive specification of key poses, the editing of parameter curves, forward kinematics, and motion paths. A wide variety of lighting effects that affect the mood of a scene can be created by animating the intensity of a light source as well as its color, cone angle, and fall-off. These and other attributes of light sources are described throughout this section and also in Chapter 9.

Defining and scripting the animation of light sources can often be a challenge to both art directors and computer animators. This is partly due to the lack of a standard system for scripting light animation. But writing down the description of light animations in a shot is often used as a preliminary step before the light animations are actually input into the software. These written descriptions are meant to give all those involved in the production a clear idea of what lighting effects are sought and what techniques may be required. The following is one such description:

> The length of the transformation scene is ten seconds. It takes place in an interior space with a round table with four chairs around it in the center of a room. There is a window on the wall that is opposite to the wall with a closed door in the middle of it. There is a wooden sculpture of a bird on the table. The scene starts with the room lights turned off. There is a fire outside and its crackling sound can be heard, but the flames are barely visible through the closed window shades. Suddenly a strong wind current throws the door open, and a whirling light flies into the room and glows more intensely as it circles over the table for two or three seconds. The light hovers over the table, floating up and down for another couple of seconds. The light sparkles, and as the sparks land on the table and the wooden sculpture, both glow gently for a couple of seconds and then, suddenly and unexpectedly, they vanish.

A written description of the light animation is usually complemented—or followed—by a simple diagram that annotates the changes in the position or attributes of light in a way similar to a music score. This visual diagram can be a useful reference when actually scripting the animation of lights with the software program.

Moving lights in a three-dimensional environment should be exercised with great restraint because poorly animated light sources can be a great source of visual distraction in a shot. In principle, light sources should not be moved or animated unless we are trying to achieve a very specific change in the mood of a scene. Subtle emotional effects can be achieved, for example, by slowly increasing the intensity of a very narrow soft-edged spotlight that is focussed on the face of a character. An effect like this one can be especially effective when the **illumination level** in the scene is low. Spot lights that are dimmed or turned up are a very effective way of attracting the attention of the audience to a specific area or situation in a three-dimensional scene. Both point lights and spotlights can be turned on or off or gradually turned up or dimmed throughout an animated sequence. Turning lights on and off is easily achieved with linear interpolation, while dimming is done by easing in or out.

Light sources can also be animated when we are trying to achieve a specific lighting effect that is built on moving lights. Few light sources move in our world, and those that do have very specific characteristics. Animating the position and attributes of lights can simulate natural lighting effects, theatrical lighting effects based on artificial light sources, or both—natural lighting and artificial lighting often interact. **Natural lighting effects** are based on moving light sources like celestial bodies, the elements and natural phenomena, and a few animals.

Celestial Bodies

The light of **celestial bodies**—such as the sun or the moon—usually moves very slowly because those light sources are far from us. An exception to this rule is, of course, shooting stars and comets. The moving light of celestial bodies is usually perceived in the form of **moving shadows** because we can rarely tell that the sun or the moon are moving by just looking at them in real time. (Stop-motion animation can compress real time by recording still frames in a delayed fashion, for example record one still frame of the moving sun every minute.) Surreal lighting effects can be achieved by animating celestial bodies at speeds that do not correspond to their real speeds. The moving light created by a shooting star is a perfect example of a light animation that involves changes in both spatial position based on the speed and distance of the shooting star, and attributes such as the brightness and color determined by the moment when the asteroid enters the atmosphere of the Earth.

The light of celestial bodies can be recreated with infinite light sources or with point light sources that have medium to high intensity and little or no fall-off. The color hue of the light of celestial bodies is constant but it may have, for example, a warm tint in the case of the sun or a slightly cold tint in the case of the moon. Short of procedural or parametric techniques the flickering effect of shooting stars can be implemented by creating an irregular pattern in the parameter curves that control the animation of the color or the fall-off of the light source.

Natural Phenomena

The elements and various **natural phenomena** display a wide

10.4.1 An example of natural phenomena lighting. (Courtesy of
Rhythm & Hues Studios.)

range of lighting behavior that involves motion. This type of
natural lighting effects includes, for example, the light emitted
by lightning, fire, or natural explosions such as an erupting volcano; the light reflected off the surface of moving water or
refracted through moving water like a waterfall; and the light
interrupted by the motion of objects that could be caused by
wind in front of a light source (Fig. 10.4.1). The animation of
these types of lighting effects can be done with a variety of
techniques depending whether the light sources were defined
with procedural techniques or as a collection of point lights and
spot lights. In the former case, the animation of the light source
would simply be done by animating the parameters that were
used in the first place to define the procedural light (the characteristics of procedural lights are reviewed in Chapter 7). But in
many situations, creating lighting effects with procedural techniques is not possible either because the software does not provide that option or because it would be computationally too
expensive. In those instances, the lighting effects of moving natural phenomena can be simulated with a variety of tricks borrowed from traditional stage and movie special effects.

Lighting tricks like these may seem crude when compared to
the conceptual elegance of motion dynamics simulations. But they
are often cheaper than simulations to produce and almost always
as·effective—at least from the point of view of the audience.

A trick that is quite common in stage lighting for simulating
the light emitted by a small fire or a fireplace consists of using a
couple of pulsating spot lights to project light through overlapping stripes of colored gel that are constantly waved by a fan
(Fig. 10.4.2). The irregular motion of the yellow, red, and
orange stripes creates a pattern of transmitted light that can be

very effective when projected on the subjects in the scene. This lighting trick commonly used in both opera and theatre can be easily simulated in computer animation with just a small group of spot lights and point lights and their parameter curves instead of using gel strips, a fan, and spot lights.

Computer animation can also be used to recreate the lighting effects created by light travelling through falling water, for example, the effect created in an interior space by moon light or street lights travelling through rain. This trick may include arrays of small three-dimensional models that are animated off-screen between the simulated light source and the scene. In the case of rain, for example, the array of small three-dimensional models could include two or more layers of small cylindrical and translucent shapes that constantly move next to the light source. The two layers of translucent shape patterns can be built in the form of cylinders that rotate around the horizontal axis between the light source and the scene. The resulting top to bottom motions simulates falling water (Fig. 10.4.3). Two or more layers are necessary to avoid a simple pattern of light that is repeated at small intervals. The arrangement of the shapes in each of the layers should also be as irregular and different as possible in order to avoid a repeating motion pattern that is easy to identify. This lighting effect can be maximized by rotating the two cylindrical layers at different variable speeds. The density of the shapes on the rotating layers can yield a variety of effects that range from drizzle to a waterfall. There are alternate versions of this trick for instances when the extreme length of a scene may give audiences enough time to recognize the lighting pattern and get bored. One alternative to the rotating cylinders of shapes consists of a very long strip with a **translucent image map**—instead of translucent three-dimensional shapes—that is translated from top to bottom between the camera and the scene.

Another variation of the rotating cylinders can be used to simulate the **obstruction of light** caused by objects such as dry leaves being swept in front of the light source. This lighting effect can be achieved by animating groups of flat leaf-shaped models with a pseudo-random factor so that the effect is repeated each time with a slight variation. A primary motion may keep the

10.4.2 Fire effects can be simulated by projecting light through stripes of colored gel moved by a fan.

leaves spiraling in front of the light source, and a secondary motion may keep them rotating around their center or flipping as they rotate. The rotation of several of these groups of leaves can be looped to provide a continuous effect. The effect of the leaves blocking the light can be enhanced by applying a transparency map that makes the leaves transparent on the edges.

The effect of light reflected off the surface of **moving water** can be recreated by placing spot lights with varying cone angles shining up through a surface that represents water and that has an animate shape. The lighting effect created by a lightning storm can be recreated by inserting one or two white frames in the sequence just a couple of seconds before the sound of thunder is heard. After that a very strong light—placed in the area near where the lightning is supposed to have fallen—is suddenly turned up to a bright white color and then dimmed in a flickering way. The motion of artificial lights during an earthquake, for example, is an interesting convergence of artificial lighting and a natural phenomenon such as those described in Chapter 11.

Fireflies

Only a few animals are capable of emitting natural light as they move. Many of us have been fascinated by the blinking patterns of light created by **fireflies** as they fly through the night. Other animals—such as the fluorescent fish that live in the depths of the oceans—are also natural moving light sources. However, for better or for worse, the opportunities in the life of a computer animator to simulate fireflies or other fluorescent animals are, to say the least, very rare.

The light emitted by fireflies can be simulated with point lights or with spot lights that have a very wide cone angle and a narrow spread angle. Firefly light has a large amount of fall-off because it does not travel very far, and its color can be animated within a narrow range of fluorescent green hues. The blinking pattern of firefly light can be replicated by drawing parameter curves for color, fall-off, or cone angle so that they are interrupted with abrupt jumps. The parameter curve in Fig. 10.4.4 represents the abrupt jumps in cone angle values that represent a blinking light. The small zig-zag variations along the vertical axis represent flickering, and the abrupt jumps and sharp 90 degree angle changes in direction represent blinking. The flat horizontal lines represent a constant darkness achieved by a cone angle value of zero.

Artificial Lights

Theatrical or **artificial lights** can be still or in motion and can be based on point lights or spot lights. Artificial still point lights

10.4.3 The effect of light being projected through rain or a waterfall can be achieved by rotating two cylindrical layers of translucent shapes at variable speeds between the light source and the scene.

include, for example, a bare light bulb. Man-made moving spot lights include, for example, the light reflectors used in stage or movie productions—and so commonly associated with Hollywood—the light projected in darkness by moving vehicles, or the light projected by flashlights or other appliances such as open refrigerators, copy machines, and televisions that are turned on in darkened environments.

Animating lights that resemble artificial moving lights should also be done with restraint, and only when a specific lighting effect is required. Animating spot lights in a dark scene can add a feeling of suspense or fear to the shot because the lighting effect may remind the audience of a search for something—or someone—that is hiding, or trying to hide from someone—or something—that is searching.

10.5 Hierarchical Animation

Three-dimensional objects can be limitlessly grouped together in order to define the ways in which these objects relate to one another and behave when animated. Groupings of three-dimensional objects are called **hierarchical structures**, and within them some objects are always more dominant than others.

Hierarchical diagrams are often represented as an inverted **tree structure** where the highest level of importance in the structure corresponds to the trunk of the tree. The main **branches** that come directly out of the trunk represent the next level in the hierarchy; branches that come out of the main branches are at the next level and so on, until we get to the leaves, which represent the last level in the hierarchical structure. The objects within the hierarchy inherit attributes—including motion—from the dominant objects just like children inherit the attributes of their parents. It is also possible to animate just a selected branch in the structure without having to animate the entire structure. The relationships between objects—or parts of objects—in a hierarchical structure can be easily visualized with a schematic representation in the form of a line **hierarchy diagram**. These diagrams often consist of **boxes** that represent the items in the structure, and **lines** that represent the place of the items in the hierarchy and their relations with other items. In most cases, there is just one set of hierarchy diagrams per scene, and these diagrams control the animation of all the objects.

Levels of Precedence

Objects within hierarchical structures have well-defined **levels of precedence** or importance. The object or objects at the top of the hierarchy are called **parents**, and the objects below are called **children** and **grandchildren**. The most dominant object in a

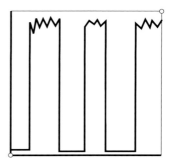

10.4.4 Parameter curve of the cone angle values of the light emitted by a firefly.

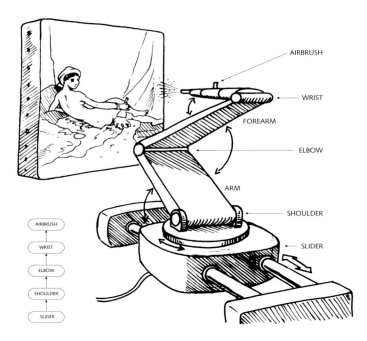

AIRBRUSH

WRIST

FOREARM

ELBOW

ARM

SHOULDER

SLIDER

AIRBRUSH

WRIST

ELBOW

SHOULDER

SLIDER

10.5.1 This spray-paint robot arm is an articulated figure with three joints. The shoulder has two degrees of freedom, and the elbow and wrist each have only one degree of freedom. The box at the bottom of the diagram represents the root of the hierarchical structure.

hierarchy is usually called the **root** of the hierarchy, and objects that are placed in the same branch of the hierarchy or at the same level in the hierarchy are often called **siblings**. A **null parent** is a node in the hierarchy that does not relate to any specific part in the model but that controls several child objects together. A null parent is used, for example, when two or more objects are grouped at the same level in the hierarchy. Nulls are usually represented as empty boxes in the structural diagrams. Figure 3.7.2 illustrates the use of a null node.

Hierarchical structures sometimes include objects that are assembled into an articulated figure. Other times they include objects that are not physically connected to one another, and often they include both. **Articulated figures** are made of objects that are connected to others. Articulated figures with hierarchical groupings of objects are an essential tool for the creation of computer-based character animation. In the majority of articulated figures, the connection between the objects is such that they touch each other so the connection happens in the form of a joint. There are many possible ways to group several objects in a hierarchical structure, but the hierarchy of parts in a model should always be driven by the motion requirements. Figures 10.5.1 and 10.5.2 show an articulated and a non-articulated model each with their corresponding hierarchical diagrams. The hierarchy in both examples is quite simple since there is minimal branching.

Joints and Degrees of Freedom

The type of **joints** used in computer animation are defined by the number of degrees of freedom that they have. **Degrees of freedom** are used to express the ability of a joint to rotate around and/or to translate along one or several axes. One degree of freedom, for example, corresponds to the ability of a joint to rotate around one axis, while a joint with three degrees of freedom is capable of rotating around three axes. Our knee, for example, is a joint with only one degree of freedom, and our shoulder has three degrees of freedom (go ahead, try it, you can rotate your arms around the X, Y, and Z axes). Joints can be catalogued according to their degrees of freedom from a simple one-dimensional **twist joint** or **bend joint** to a multidimensional **universal joint** that can rotate in all directions. In addition to the number of degrees of freedom, joints are also defined by a **rotation range**, which restricts the rotation of the joint between a minimum and a maximum value (Fig. 10.5.3). A joint can have a different rotation range for each of its degrees of freedom. These **motion constrains** imposed by rotation ranges are especially useful when animating articulated figures with the inverse kinematics techniques described in Chapter 11.

10.5.2 A merry-go-round is a good example of a hierarchical structure with multiple levels, where the motion of the objects in the parent levels determines the motion of those objects in the children levels.

The centers of objects—often called **centroids** or pivot points—play an important role in the hierarchical animation process because many operations are calculated based on their spatial position. These operations include all the geometric transformations as well as simulations of motion dynamics related to the center of gravity. By default most three-dimensional programs place the centroids in the geometric center of the objects. Most software programs also allow animators to interactively reposition the centroids of objects.

All computer animation that supports hierarchical structures offers some sort of hierarchy or **skeleton editor** for the purpose of creating links between objects and setting **joint information** such as stiffness and ranges of rotation. Skeleton editors are usually based on a graphical diagram and dialog boxes with information for each item in the diagram or a spreadsheet that lists all the items in the diagram. One of the most popular methods for establishing **links** between objects allows animators to build the links by clicking directly on the three-dimensional objects in any one of the camera views. Another method establishes hierarchical relationships by clicking on the boxes in the diagram that represents the links between the three-dimensional objects. The programs that build the hierarchy from top to bottom require that the object that is to be the parent is clicked before the children in the hierarchy. The programs that build the hierarchy from bottom to top require that one selects the children first and the parent last.

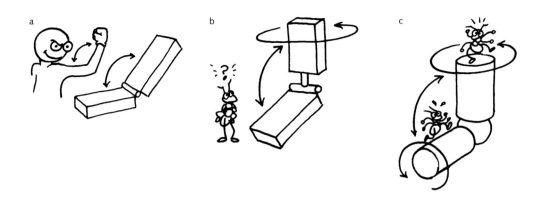

10.6 Getting Ready

Choose Appropriate Motion

Audiences learn a lot about the emotions and intentions of animated characters by the way they move. Make sure that the motion applied to the models matches the purpose of the scene. Motion should also match the level of rendering realism in the scene. For example, realistic renderings make more sense if realistic motion is applied to the models, while sketchy motion is usually more appropriate for simple renderings.

Avoid Still First Frames

One or several still frames at the beginning of an animated sequence usually look like a mistake, for example, when the camera starts rolling before the actors are ready. Unless the sequence calls for several frames of a motion hold, avoid starting your animations with still models. Instead, you can improve the sense of motion flow and continuity between scenes and shots by starting them with objects that are in motion, regardless of how subtle that motion may be.

Preview the Motion

Virtually all computer animation programs allow for the creation of motion flipbooks that can be played back directly onto the computer screen. A **digital flipbook** consists of a sequence of image files displayed in an area of the screen, ranging from a small window to the full screen. Digital flipbooks are always played back at their final output speed, for example 24 or 30 frames per second. In cases when digital flipbooks are not available, it is possible to preview the motion tests by recording them onto a videotape, and playing it back on a videotape player.

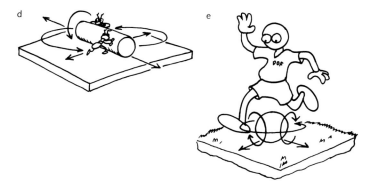

10.5.3 A variety of joint types with different degrees of freedom: one degree (a), two degrees (b), three degrees (c), four degrees (d), and six degrees (e).

Preview With Multiple Camera Views

It is helpful to use multiple active camera views when setting the keyframes in a three-dimensional animation. The camera perspective view is useful for previewing the motion from a specific point of view. But the other camera views, including the front view, side view, and top view, are useful for checking details, such as overlapping objects.

Unlock Objects Before Animating

Remember to unlock the objects in the scene that were previously locked in a specific position, orientation, size, or spatial range, during the modeling process. In most software programs, locked objects will not be animated according to the animation score and/or parameter curves.

Follow the Storyboard

It is important to stick to the storyboard because other individuals may be working at the same time on the same sequence as you are. If you decide to interpret the storyboard liberally you may create animated sequences that will not match the previous shot or the one that follows, or even other aspects of the production, such as the soundtrack. Consult the production coordinator when you have an idea for improving the portion of the storyboard that you are working on. Maybe your idea can be carried on but only after other team members have been consulted.

Review and Practice

Matching

_____ Cardinal
_____ Interpolation
_____ Focal length

_____ Depth of field

_____ Ease
_____ Freeform lattice

_____ Truck

_____ Texture

_____ Zoom

_____ Morphing

_____ Degrees of freedom
_____ Tracking

_____ Linear

_____ Null parent
_____ Motion path

a. Used to create three-dimensional transformations of shape.

b. An external structure for controlling motion.

c. Used to express the ability of a joint to rotate around one or several axes.

d. Interpolation that produces equally spaced in-between frames.

e. Defined by the areas that are contiguous to the focal plane.

f. Needs to know where the front of the object that is linked to it is.

g. Technique used to create sequences of in-between frames by averaging keyframe information.

h. Node in the hierarchy that does not relate to any specific part in the model but that controls several objects.

i. A variation of a dolly camera move that moves along with the subject.

j. Interpolation that takes into account variations of speed over time.

k. A camera move that goes in or out of the scene.

l. Animating it usually requires more set-up time than animating color because of the number of parameter curves involved.

m. A camera move achieved by slowly changing the focal length of a camera.

n. A spline that matches the control points very tightly.

o. Defined by the relation between the near and the far clipping planes.

Answers Matching: a. Morphing, b. Freeform lattice, c. Degrees of freedom, d. Linear, e. Depth of field, f. Motion path, g. Interpolation, h. Null parent, i. Tracking, j. Ease, k. Truck, l. Texture, m. Zoom, n. Cardinal, o. Focal length.

True/False

_____ a. Keyframe interpolation techniques can produce a maximum of 30 in-between frames between two keyframes.

_____ b. Tilting camera moves are very effective for scanning a scene from side to side.

_____ c. Animated spotlights can add a feeling of suspense to a scene.

_____ d. The speed of the animation of the surface characteristics can determine whether the effect is realistic or fantastic.

_____ e. A crane camera shot may include translations along the X, Y, and Z axes.

_____ f. Ease functions contain only ease ins and ease outs but not linear interpolations.

_____ g. Freeform shape animation creates better results when the two models involved are created with geometric primitive modeling tools.

_____ h. The sideways scanning of a moving camera can be simulated by adjusting its point of interest as it moves along a motion path.

_____ i. The intensity of an animated light source will flicker or blink when controlled by a parameter curve that has a zig-zag pattern.

_____ j. The motion of celestial bodies is easily perceived through the motion of their shadows.

_____ k. The rate of change of interpolations is always constant.

_____ l. The connection between parts in articulated figures usually happens in the form of a joint.

_____ m. Poorly animated light sources can be a great source of visual distraction.

_____ n. Motion paths can be used to sketch the motion of objects with other motion techniques added later.

_____ o. Curved interpolation techniques can only be applied to three-dimensional models and cameras but not to light sources.

_____ p. The depth of field is defined by the focal length, the f/stop, and the focal distance.

_____ q. The levels in a hierarchical structure are organized with branches.

_____ r. Many of us have been fascinated by the blinking patterns of light created by fireflies as they fly through the night.

_____ s. Motion paths can be converted to explicit transformations that can be edited with the standard interpolation parameter curves.

_____ t. A degree of freedom corresponds to the ability of a joint to translate along one axis at a time.

_____ u. Forward kinematics techniques derive the angles of the joints in a model from the final position of the model.

_____ v. The intensity of a light source can be dimmed with an ease function.

_____ w. Keyframes have parameters of time spatial position, shape, and surface attributes.

Key Terms

Absolute position
Acceleration
Articulated figures
Artificial lights
Attributes
Banking motion
Bend joint
Boom
Boxes
Branches
Celestial bodies
Centroids
Children
Circular waves
Constant speed
Crane shot
Curved interpolation
Degrees of freedom
Depth of field
Digital flipbook
Dolly
Ease functions
Ease in
Ease out
External control structures
Fantastic transformation
Fireflies
Focal distance
Focal length
Focal plane
Focus
Forward kinematics
Freeform lattice
Freeform shape animation
Front of the object
Function curve
Grandchildren
Hierarchical structures
Hierarchy diagram
Illumination level
In-between frames
Interactive specification of key poses
Interpolation ease
Joint information
Joints

Keyframe
Keyframe interpolation
Lens aperture
Levels of precedence
Linear interpolation
Lines
Linked to the path
Links
Mapping a sequence of images
Motion constrains
Motion paths
Moving shadows
Moving water
Natural lighting effects
Natural phenomena
Natural transformation
Null parent
Number of points
Obstruction of light
Order of correspondence
Orientation of the camera
Pan
Parameter curve
Parents
Planar waves
Position of the camera
Rate of change
Roll
Root
Rotation range
Shape animation
Siblings
Sideways scanning
Skeleton editor
Slope
Spatial animation
Speed
Spherical waves
Squashing
Stretching
Three-dimensional morphing
Tilt
Timing of the transformations
Transformation matrix
Translucent image map
Traveling shot
Tree structure

CHAPTER 11

Advanced Animation Techniques

Summary

Most of the advanced animation techniques covered in this chapter are quite different from those techniques based on the traditional keyframe approach. These techniques are used to simulate complex or realistic motion of objects and characters. Many of these techniques, in fact, start by "capturing" the motion of real actors and applying it to animated characters. This chapter also presents the **hybrid environment** in which some of the latest advanced animation techniques are almost always used in combination with others. The concept of working in layers or channels of motion is stressed throughout the chapter. One of the main reasons for using hybrid animation techniques is the fact that natural motion is too complex to be recreated with just one technique. For example, the motion of three-dimensional models can be controlled in detail if we provide their positions and angles to an inverse kinematics program, but their motions may not be physically correct. Likewise the motion of models will be if their motion dynamics are simulated based on the forces applied to them, but it will be difficult to obtain a specific motion especially as the models become more complex.

11.1.1 The end effector of an articulated chain representing an arm is usually the hand or a fingertip.

11.1 Inverse Kinematics

Inverse kinematics techniques are useful for animating complex models with a large number of joints. Unlike their counterpart, forward kinematics, **inverse kinematics** techniques determine the motion of entire skeletons based on the final angles of some of the key joints that define the motion. As explained in Chapter 10, forward kinematics techniques calculate the motion and final position of a model by first specifying the angles of its joints. That is, in essence, the inverse approach to inverse kinematics.

The inverse kinematics animation techniques require that the three-dimensional models to be animated are built as hierarchical

11.1.2 An inverse kinematics sequence without motion or position constrains may result in endless motion variations when the end effector is repositioned.

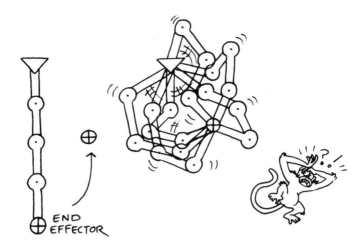

structures. Inverse kinematics techniques are most commonly applied to articulated figures that are defined as hierarchical skeletons constructed with links that are connected by joints, each with different motion constrains. Hierarchical skeletons are composed of many articulated chains that are grouped together in a hierarchy. Skeletons are also related to the skin surface surrounding them and the models attached to them. This hierarchical relation varies between programs, but in most cases, the root chain or different parts of the chain are the parents of the skin or models attached to them (read Chapter 4 for more details on skin).

Inverse kinematics techniques can greatly simplify the animation of models with multiple joints that have to move in a complex and somewhat realistic way. Trying to animate a running tiger, for example, with interactive specification of keyframes could turn into a long and tedious process of trial and error, especially if the tiger was running on an uneven terrain that had obstacles scattered along the way. But the same process could be simplified using inverse kinematics because this animation technique uses the position of the limbs or joints in an articulated figure to animate the entire figure into the desired configuration. The components of the inverse kinematics process include a hierarchical structure or chain, joints, motion constrains, and effectors. Articulated figures with hierarchical structures allow simultaneous movement of all its parts but always following the specified hierarchy. The hierarchy in an articulated figure prevents all of its parts from scattering in all directions when a transformation is applied to the figure. Hierarchical structures are covered in more detail in Chapter 10.

An articulated chain is composed of a chain root, a certain number of joints, and an effector. The **chain root** is usually the first joint in the first segment of an articulated chain. The chain

root is often the parent of all the segments and joints in the articulated chain. The **effector**—also called **end effector**—in a hierarchical chain is the joint in an articulated figure that is used to determine the positions of a moving chain with inverse kinematics. When the effector in a chain is moved then the inverse kinematics are invoked and the rotations of the joints are automatically calculated. In the case of an arm reaching to push a button, for example, the end effector of the motion would be located in the hand or an extended fingertip (Fig. 11.1.1). The end effector of most arm motions is, in fact, usually placed in the hand or the fingertips.

A **joint** is defined by the articulation point where two segments of the articulated chain meet. Some inverse kinematics programs allow the joints in the chain to be rotated in any direction unless motion constrains have been placed on any specific joint. This means that the joints in the hierarchical chain can rotate in any direction during the calculation of new positions with inverse kinematics. This brings us to the fact that a hierarchical chain can follow the motion of an end effector in many different ways whenever motion constrains are not set (Fig. 11.1.2). Other programs, however, define the articulated chains as planar and will only allow the joints in a chain to rotate around one axis (usually their Z axis when looking at the chain sideways).

One of the big advantages of animating complex articulated figures with inverse kinematics is that if the figure has the proper joint motion constrains the motion of a single end effector can be used to determine how all the joints in the figure must rotate. The entire figure follows the motion of the end effector. But inverse kinematics techniques can save work during the animation process only as long as the joint **motion constrains** have been placed in a way that makes sense and leads to the desired motions. In most situations, animating a complex

11.1.3 Throwing a ball with inverse kinematics. Only the starting and ending positions need to be specified.

articulated figure with inverse kinematic techniques is often more efficient than using forward kinematics (Fig. 11.1.3). In some cases though, forward kinematics offers more direct and immediate control of the joint positions at any point during the animation process (Fig. 11.1.4).

Assigning motion constrains to each joint is necessary to contain the motion of a hierarchical chain so that only one configuration results when the end effector of the chain is dragged to a specific point. Figure 11.1.5 illustrates the results of animating a hierarchical chain with different rotation and position motion constrains but the same end effector. Motion constrains are often expressed in terms of degrees of freedom and rotation

11.1.4 Throwing a ball with forward kinematics. All joint angles need to be specified.

angles. They are covered in more detail in Chapter 10.

The hierarchy of skeletons that represent a complex articulated figure can be broken to facilitate the animation of a figure with a part or limb that should not follow the motion of the chain root. That would be the case, for example, of a character whose feet must remain on the ground or whose hands must remain attached to an object even as the chain root—usually located somewhere in the torso or hips—moves. In a **broken hierarchy,** some or all of the limbs do not descend from the chain root but instead have their own root. In a broken hierarchy, a hand, for example, is not directly controlled by the torso through the shoulder. In cases like this, it is necessary to somehow keep the split articulated chains together during the motion, and stretch the surface skin at the point where the two chains meet. This facilitates independent motions of each chain as well as a continuous skin surface.

Inverse kinematics is a powerful technique for building secondary motions on top of primary motions. When animating a hierarchical model like a human body (Fig. 11.1.6) it is best to animate down the hierarchy before dealing with the details. This means that primary motions such as those of the torso would be specified before secondary motions such as those of the head or arms. Inverse kinematics can be an effective technique for laying

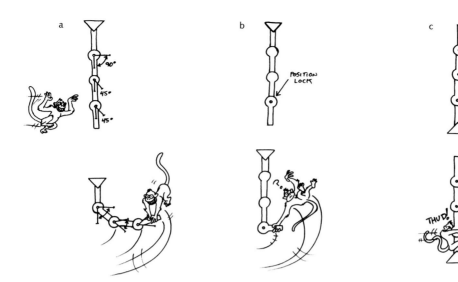

out actions by specifying key poses at each keyframe. This approach can be complemented with the techniques presented in the Channel Animation section of this chapter.

11.2 Motion Capture

Real-time **motion capture** is an advanced animation technique that allows animators to capture live motion with the aid of a machine and then apply it to computer animated characters. Motion capture is different from traditional keyframe animation because it captures all the motions of live actors as they move. Motion capture can also be used to create the **basic tracks of motion** that can later be enriched with other animation techniques. Much of the **secondary motion** in an animation based on motion capture techniques—such as the detailed animation of hands, fingers, and facial expressions—is usually added on top of the basic tracks of primary motion (Fig. 11.2.1).

Motion data that is captured and saved as XYZ joint positions can be manipulated directly and also applied, for example, to an inverse kinematics skeleton. Some motion capture methods are better suited for **live control** of animated characters, while others are more adequate for situations that require complex motion sequences with **multiple layers of motion**. Except for when the motion capture data is used to control live motion, the data collected with motion capture systems is subjected to different amounts of cleanup and refinement in the computer animation system. This is because the **raw motion** captured often contains too much noise that has to be cleaned out, or because it is not sufficient to generate by itself the motion required in the

11.1.5 Three inverse kinematics sequences of a simple hierarchical chain, they all follow the same end effector but each has different motion constrains including a single rotation constrain (a), a single position constrain (b), and multiple position constrains (c).

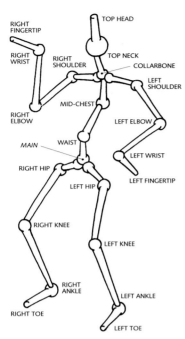

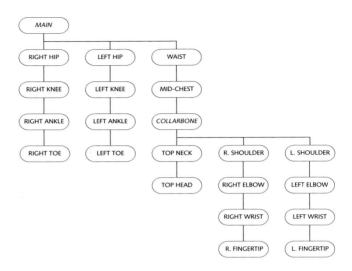

11.1.6 A simple articulated model and its corresponding hierarchical diagram.

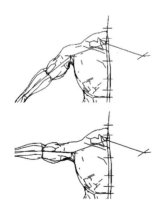

11.2.1 Two stages of the primary motion of an an arm, and the secondary motion of a shoulder. (Courtesy of Acclaim Entertainment, Inc., Advanced Technologies Group.)

animation sequence.

A major attraction of motion capture techniques is that they may be used to produce animation in a cost-effective way, but only after all the initial setup has been worked out. Depending on the nature of the project motion capture techniques make it possible to automate large portions of the character motion, and they can also eliminate some of the keyframe-based manual work.

Motion capture techniques began to be practical in the early 1980s when researchers experimented with potentiometers attached to human bodies for measuring the angles of joints. Light emitting diodes (LEDs) and mechanical armatures were also used early on to measure both the position and orientation of joints. Most of the early applications of motion control were limited to animating live simple cartoon characters or heads and faces, but not full body animation. These live animations would often be composited with live action. In many cases, a variety of helmets and armatures have been used to capture the motion of the face and body of an actor. Today, even though motion capture animation techniques are still being refined, there is an increasing variety of character animation based on motion capture techniques. Many off-the-shelf computer animation packages offer hookups for a range of motion capture gear that can bring motion data directly into the animation system. The prejudice about motion control being a technique that is used only by those who do not know how to animate the "old-fashioned way"—entirely by hand—is also slowly giving way to more progressive points of view.

Motion capture implies one or several real actors that generate motions for one or several animated characters (Fig. 11.2.2). Preparing both of the **real actors** and the animated charac-

ters—or **virtual actors**—for the process of motion capture involves two somewhat independent series of steps: setting up the capture points on the human actor, and setting up the hierarchical structures that will control the virtual actor. The exact positioning of the sampling points depends on the type of motion desired. But in all cases, it is necessary to establish a correspondence between the **sampling points** in real actors and the joints in the animated characters. Illogical correspondances between sampling points and joints in the animated characters can lead to unexpected and amusing results. Imagine the motion of an animated character whose neck joints are animated by the motion collected by the sampling points in its tail!

Motion capture is often used to capture primary motion so sampling points are often distributed throughout head, torso, and limbs. Secondary motions such as facial expressions and hand gestures are often added with other animation techniques to the captured primary motions. It is also important to make sure that the hierarchical structures of both real and virtual actors are structured so that the captured motion will result in the desired effects. Computer animation projects have a wide range of requirements in terms of the minimum number of both sampling points and joints in the figure. It is not necessary that the hierarchical struc-

11.2.2 Still frame from the *Duel* computer animation showing two virtual characters animated with motion capture techniques. (Courtesy of Acclaim Entertainment, Inc., Advanced Technologies Group.)

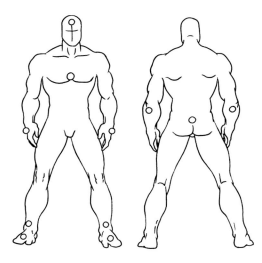

11.2.3 Motion capture system with 11 motion sensors.

tures be identical, but when the hierarchies of real and virtual actors are structured in different ways the resulting motion will not be a direct translation of the captured motion. In these cases, the resulting motions will be **filtered** and modified. (The special modeling requirements of computer animation that is based on motion capture techniques—including continuous skin-like surfaces and clothing—are described in Chapter 4.)

A few high-end motion capture systems can be purchased with all the components integrated, functioning, and ready to be used. This includes, for example, the computer having enough external ports to accept data input from many motion sensors. It also includes having a transmission rate that is fast and wide enough to be able to process data input from many motion sensors sampling at rates that are adequate. But when assembling low-cost motion control systems from parts that are purchased separately it is often necessary to keep several issues in mind in order to have a functional system. These issues are related to the placement of the motion sensors on the actors, the stage used to capture the motion, and the type of motion capture technology.

The **number of motion sensors** used in a motion capture gear—or suit—varies from a high of 70 in a very high-performance custom system to a low of a dozen sensors in lower cost units. The exact **placement of the sensors** depends on many factors, such as the number of sensors available, the type of motion sensor technology being used, the type of motion that is being captured, the type of data—rotation angles or XYZ position—being sent to the computer animation program, and the type of motion constrains implemented in the computer animation software. Regardless of their number, motion sensors are attached to the body of the actor with adhesive or elastic materials, or a combination or both.

Figure 11.2.3 illustrates a minimum configuration with 11 sensors for motion capture. Two sensors are placed in the upper body: one on the forehead just below the hairline, and one in the center of the chest right on the sternum. The sensors in the limbs are placed one on the back of each forearm below the elbow or close to the wrist, one on the back of each hand, one in the front of each shin just above the ankles, and one on the top of each foot. A sensor in the lower back or pelvis just below the waist is used to determine the position and direction of the body with respect to the floor. In this configuration, several important joints are not covered so their motion has to be derived with inverse kinematics techniques. Much of the subtle motion of the torso and the neck is also lost due to the small number of sensors placed on the body of the actor.

Figure 11.2.4 illustrates the implementation of a motion capture system with 20 sensors. Compared to the previous configuration illustrated in Fig. 11.2.3, this one is able to capture a larger number of joint motions and also a greater degree of detail in the motion of the torso and the head. A motion capture configuration like this one assumes that much of the secondary motion will be added later on top of the initial motion capture. This configuration of motion sensors includes one sensor on the forehead, one on the chin, one on the back of the neck, one on the sides of each shoulder, one on the back of each forearm close to the elbow, one on the back of each hand, one on each side of the back, one on the sides of each hip, one in the lower back or pelvis, one on each knee, one in the front of each shin, and one on the top of each foot.

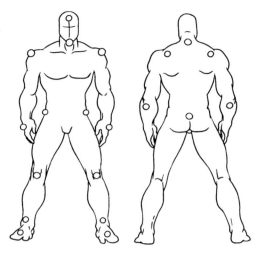

11.2.4 Motion capture system with 20 motion sensors.

Real-Time Motion Capture Technologies

There are several technologies used for capturing motion in real time. Each of these technologies has advantages and disadvantages that make each more suitable for different applications of motion capture. Some of the factors that distinguish each technology from one another include their data accuracy, sampling rate, the freedom of motion they allow the live actors, the number of sampling points, the number of actors whose motions can be captured simultaneously. The number of sampling points were covered in the previous section. Useful sampling rates start at 30 samples per second or higher. When simple motions are being captured a small capture area can be adequate, but larger areas are preferred for capturing two or more actors interacting with each other. That way the motions do not have to be interrupted and the editing of motion is minimized. The basic technologies for motion capture include: prosthetic, acoustic, magnetic, and optical.

Prosthetic motion capture technologies provide very accurate angular rotation data and are based on **potentiometers**, which are devices capable of measuring electromotive force based on the amount of energy that passes through the device as a result of the motion of a joint. However, a problem with prosthetic motion capture is that potentiometers are usually bulky and restrict the type of motion that can be performed by the individuals wearing them. Prosthetic motion capture technologies have been around for a long time and are still widely used in medical applications that measure or simulate the motion of

11.2.5 Two actors wearing optical sensors for motion capture, engaged in a simultaneous two-person capture. (Courtesy of Acclaim Entertainment, Inc., Advanced Technologies Group.)

11.2.6 *Moxy*, the virtual host of a television program, was animated with a live motion capture and motion control system. (Produced by Colossal Pictures in association with the Cartoon Network. © 1993 Cartoon Network, Inc. All Rights Reserved. Courtesy of Colossal Pictures.)

patients with limited motion range.

Acoustic motion capture technologies are based on **transponders** that determine their position in space by sending radio signals from each sample point. **Magnetic motion capture** techniques are based on **receivers** that detect magnetic fields. Both acoustic and magnetic motion capture technologies require stages that do not create noise that may interfere with the data capture in any significant way. This may include, in the former case, hard polished surfaces around the stage that may generate an inordinate amount of echo. In the latter case, this may include metallic structures in the vicinity of the stage—including metal studs inside of walls and ceilings—that may create or bend magnetic fields. In the case of some motion capture systems based on magnetic technology, it is also necessary to construct a harness above the stage in order to hold the wires connecting the motion sensors to the computer system, and to keep them out of the way of the motion of the actors.

Optical motion capture technologies utilize lights, cameras, and reflective dots to determine the position of the joints in three-dimensional space. Optical capture of motion is convenient because the actors are virtually free to perform any motion that they are capable of. Optical technologies have also excelled at the simultaneous motion capture of more than a single actor. Figure 11.2.5 illustrates a high performance optical system that employs between 50 and 70 sensors and several cameras. It is capable of capturing the motion of two actors simultaneously. An obvious problem with optical technologies for motion capture is the fact that some of the sampling points may be hidden intermittently by the motions of the actors, especially when two or more actors are being sampled at the same time. A common solution to this occlusion problem is to increase the number of cameras used to look at the sample points. This solution can provide detailed motion, but it also increases the complexity of the motion capture process.

Rotoscoping

Rotoscoping is a form of delayed motion capture. Rotoscoping captures motion by tracing, manually or automatically, still frames of a live action scene. The schematic information that results from this tracing is used to guide the motion of animated figures. Rotoscoping is also a popular cel animation technique used for combining hand-drawn animated images with live action. The handdrawn images are created by tracing element of the live scene or by using them as a spatial reference. Then the handdrawn images are recorded in sequence, and the resulting animation can be combined with the live action sequence using matting and compositing techniques.

Live Motion Control

In some applications related to live entertainment, the motion of live actors is both captured and applied to the animated characters in real time. In these cases, the motion is captured live, and the characters are animated and matted into live video in real time. In many of these instances, the animated characters are cartoons (Fig. 11.2.6). For that reason, the goal of the motion capture process is not to capture detailed and realistic motion but, instead, to capture theatrical motion that can bring a cartoon character alive (Fig. 11.2.7). In these cases, motion that looks too natural and not exaggerated is inappropriate because it often makes the cartoon character look stiff and spiritless. The motion that works best for most live cartoon characters is exaggerated and spirited. For this reason, it is common to have experienced puppeteers, actors, and dancers manipulate the input devices that generate the motion to be applied to the character. These professional performers are able to transmit emotion and expression through motions captured by a cold input peripheral. In situations where a sophisticated sensing system is lacking, it is common to have one or more individuals manipulating one or several input peripherals for controlling the motion of the character. These peripherals may include one for the lips, one for the XYZ displacement, one for joint rotations, and one for the camera position.

11.2.7 Two performers do a live animation of *Moxy*, the animated character. One of them is in charge of creating the voice of the character, and the other creates the motion of the head and hands with a simple motion capture system. (Produced by Colossal Pictures in association with the Cartoon Network. © 1993 Cartoon Network, Inc. All Rights Reserved. Courtesy of Colossal Pictures.)

Editing the Captured Motion

The result of the motion capture process is several tracks of motion that control different aspects of the animation. Each track is assigned to a channel, and usually each channel controls the motion of an object in the three-dimensional scene (additional information on channel animation can be found later in this chapter). The motion data in the channels are usually displayed by most computer animation software in the form of function curves (Fig. 11.2.8). Once all the data sets of captured motion are ported into their respective channels then the data can be attached to different joints. At that point it is possible to apply an inverse kinematics system to the skeleton.

But before the motion capture data can be used, all the animation trees have to be clearly structured so that the motion subtleties in the form of multiple XYZ rotations will not be applied to the wrong joint. Blending several channels of motion requires using high-end tools so that the existing information is not wiped out. Several channels of motion are used to layer motions such as lip-syncing, hand motions, and rule-based facial expressions.

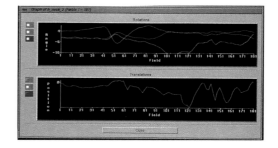

11.2.8 A motion editor program showing the rotation and translation data channels for one bone in an articulated skeleton. (Courtesy of Acclaim Entertainment, Inc., Advanced Technologies Group.)

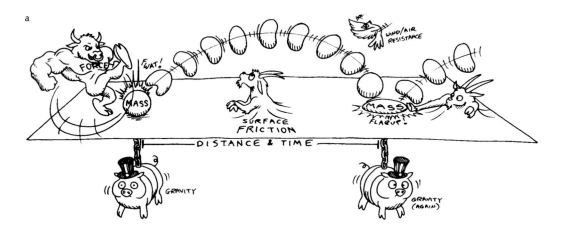

a

11.3.1 The dynamics simulation of flexible (a) and rigid objects (b) takes into account the mass of the objects, the forces that propel them as well as the forces of gravity and friction, and the distance and time travelled by the object.

11.3 Motion Dynamics

Motion dynamics animation techniques generate realistic motion of objects by simulating their physical properties and the natural laws of physical motion. Motion dynamics techniques take into account the characteristics of an object, such as weight, mass, inertia, and flexibility, as well as external forces such as friction or gravity, and even collisions with other objects. Just like the other techniques covered throughout this chapter, motion dynamics can be combined with other advanced animation techniques such as inverse kinematics and simple keyframe animation.

A **dynamic simulation** calculates the motion of objects through time by providing the software with some of the physical properties of an object—mainly its mass—as well as some information about the forces applied to the object (Fig. 11.3.1). The **mass** of an object is established by the product of the **volume** of the object and its **density**. Forces have a specific **strength** or **intensity**, and a **direction**. In simple terms, a dynamic simulation calculates the **acceleration** experienced by an object with a certain mass when a **force** is applied to it. The motion of objects is calculated by using the effects of acceleration on the object over distance and time to define the **velocity** and positions of the object through time.

Dynamic simulations are calculated based on a particular length of real time and then sampled at a specific rate of frames per second. Ideally, when the computer animation is recorded onto videotape, the dynamic simulation should be sampled at a minimum of 30 frames per second. Dynamic simulations are run

mass = density x volume

ADVANCED ANIMATION TECHNIQUES

b

by default on all of the elements that are present in the three-dimensional environment. Cameras and lights have to be turned off the simulation so that they are not affected by it. Otherwise the cameras can be moved by the simulated forces, and the moving lights can influence the final simulation.

Physical Properties of Objects

Mass is the physical property of an object that most influences a dynamic simulation. As mentioned above the mass of an object can be easily determined based on the volume and density of an object. The volume of three-dimensional objects can be automatically calculated by most computer animation programs, so the density of an object is oftentimes the only value that animators are required to provide in order for the software to calculate the mass of the object. Other characteristics of the object can also contribute to the realism of its motion. **Elasticity** and **stiffness**, for example, can be used to define the rigidity or flexibility of an object especially at the times of collisions (Fig. 11.3.2). **Rigid objects** do not bounce far from a collision, and their surfaces do not move much—if at all—after the collision. A solid ball made out of steel is an example of a rigid object that is extremely stiff and, as a result, does not deform when it hits most surfaces. But the steel ball bounces off the surface because it is somewhat elastic. **Flexible objects**, on the other hand, may bounce far away from the collision point. The surfaces of flexible objects also deform as a result of the collision and may keep moving moments after the collision took place. Objects made of

$$force = mass \times acceleration$$

11.3.2 During a collision rigid objects are rigid, and flexible objects are elastic.

hard rubber and gelatin, for example, well illustrate the range of flexibility based on characteristics of elasticity or stiffness. A solid ball made of **hard rubber**, for example, is a flexible object that is very elastic. As a result it bounces hard when it hits a surface, but it does not deform much because it is quite stiff. A solid sphere made out of **gelatin**, on the other hand, is not elastic at all. As a result it bounces little—or not at all—when it hits a surface, and it deforms greatly because it is not stiff at all.

The ability of flexible objects to absorb the impact of a collision by deforming their shape is usually controlled in dynamic simulations by applying the forces to a **flexible lattice** that controls the vertices in the object. With this technique the bending and deformation of the surface of an object is filtered by the way in which the lattice points control the vertices of the object. Some computer animation systems simulate stiffness with functions that simulate the effect of having **springs** between the vertices on the surface of the object. Springs have a natural rest position that they always return to after being stretched. Springs will move back and forth between the **stretched position** and the **rest position** until the initial balance is restored (Fig. 11.3.3).

In some cases, the stiffness of rigid objects and the force of a collision are such that the real object is incapable of absorbing the force of impact and breaks or shatters. A dynamic simulation of an object breaking is much more complex than the simulation of objects that do not break because, in essence, the results of the collision would have to be applied to thousands of fragments instead of to just one object. In addition, issues of structural composition, brittleness, randomness, and chaos theory would have to be calculated to make the dynamics simulation as realistic as possible. In most productions—except those of a scientific nature—it would make more sense to fake the shattering of an object instead of simulating the motion dynamics of the event. One way to approximate the shattering of an object as a result of a collision consists of applying several forces to an object and approximate its values by trial and error until the resulting motion looks like it was the result of a dynamic simulation. This method, however, requires at least two models of the same object. One of the models is whole and is used until the collision takes place. The second model is shattered prior to the collision but all its parts are kept together, and it is used only after the collision. For example, an object can be thrown into a collision course with a specific linear force. But when the object reaches the collision point then the initial force is cancelled, the initial model is replaced with the shattered model, and one or several new point forces are applied to the second model in order to throw it away from the surface.

11.3.3 The motion of the synthetic actress on the trapeze is calculated using motion dynamics animation techniques. The animation of the clothes is also calculated using a physics-based simulation of motion. (© 1992 Nadia Magnenat Thalmann, MIRALab, University of Geneva, and Daniel Thalmann, Computer Graphics Lab, EPFL, Lausanne.)

Types of Forces

There are many types of forces that can be simulated with

2:00:11

11.3.4 In this simulated snapshot of a severe storm, the yellow-gold regions represent small cloud drops and ice particles, and the blue region represents large water drops. The surface grid lines in the image are 10 km apart and the darkened area indicates the horizontal integration domain surface of the storm, 100 km in the east-west direction by 54 km in the north-south direction. The very dark region on the surface below is an artificial storm shadow obtained by darkening the surface whenever there is cloud, ice, or rain directly above. (Image from "Study of a Numerically Modeled Severe Storm." Principal investigators: Robert Wilhelmson, Harold Brooks, Brian Jewett, Crystal Shaw, Louis Wicker, and Ncsa/University of Illinois at Urbana-Champaign. Visualization: Matthew Arrott, Mark Bajuk, Jeffrey Thingvold, Jeffery Yost, Colleen Bushell, Dan Brady, and Bob Patterson. Produced by the Visualization Service and Development Group at NCSA/University of Illinois at Urbana-Champaign. Courtesy of the National Center for Supercomputing Applications.)

motion dynamics techniques. Some of the basic forces include linear forces, point forces, and conical forces. These basic forces can be used in combination with one another to create more complex forces. A **linear force** is unidirectional, it has one intensity value, and is traditionally represented with a vector. Linear forces include the forces of wind and gravity, punching, or throwing. A **point force** or **radial force** travels like rays in all directions and is best illustrated with the forces released by a bomb that explodes in all directions. A **conical force** resembles a collection of linear forces that spreads out of a single point resembling the shape of a cone. When these forces impact a surface they are strongest at the center of the impact area and weaker at the edges. The forces created by a fan, for example, are conical forces.

Simple forces can be combined with each other to produce variations of complex forces. Figures 11.3.4 and 11.3.5 illustrate the complex turbulent forces that are behind severe storms. In this case, the evolution of small clouds into giant storms was simulated with the aid of computer animation techniques. The simulation of the storm development can be a useful tool for understanding their behavior, and even to predict when a severe storm may appear based on the conditions that usually lead to the development of similar storms. The equations that are used to simulate storms, or other time-dependent events, can be solved first by specifying the initial values of wind velocity and direction, temperature, pressure, and moisture at selected locations within a specified three-dimensional rectangular region of the atmosphere. This region is often called the **simulation domain**. The changes in these values are then computed every few seconds over a time span of several hours. Due to the extremely large amount of data that is necessary to achieve a realistic simulation of this kind it is not uncommon to perform the computations on a powerful computer system such as a supercomputer or a parallel processor. Performing the same type and number of calculations on one of today's microcomputers—or even a low-end super-microcomputer—could take several weeks and would be very impractical.

Forces can be applied locally or globally. **Local forces** only affect just one object or one joint, while **global forces** affect all the objects in the three-dimensional environment. The force of the Earth's **gravity** is a good example of a global linear force. The force of one ball pushing just another ball on a billiard table is an example of a local force. Forces can also impact, attract, or resist objects. **Impacting forces** push objects away from the source of the force, like wind does. **Attracting forces**

ADVANCED ANIMATION TECHNIQUES

pull the objects in like magnets. **Resisting forces** offer resistance or opposition to objects moving through the three-dimensional environment. Examples of resisting forces that can slow motion down include friction and viscosity. **Friction** happens when one surface rubs against another. All spaces, unless they are a vacuum, have some amount of **viscosity** or **environmental density** that facilitates or impedes the motion of objects. In underwater scenes, for example, moving objects encounter more resistance from the density of water than they do from the density of air.

The image shown in Fig. 11.3.6 is a good example of a motion dynamics simulation created for a TV commercial. The animation of the car was created with a combination of techniques including the deformation of a flexible lattice that controls the vertices in the surface by applying wind forces to it. Each of the points on the lattice had a specific value of mass assigned to it, and they were all connected with simulated springs (Fig. 11.3.7).

The wind forces applied to the lattice were timed so that they would start at different points in time, and were focused on different areas of the lattice so that the motion would look as if driven by natural wind forces. The forces were applied in a variety of ways including linear, conical, and turbulent forces, all of which had intensity and directional parameters that were animated throughout the sequence. The forces had variable intensities so that they were strongest at the center and weaker at the edges.

11.3.5 The orange-red ribbons represent the tracer particles in a storm simulation that rise through the depth of the storm in the updraft, and the blue ribbons represent tracers that eventually fall to the ground in the downdraft. The length of the ribbons corresponds to the entire tracer path throughout the storm. The spatial resolution of the wind, pressure, and temperature data used in the simulation was 2 km horizontally and .75 km vertically. (See Fig. 11.3.4 for a complete listing of credits.)

The project pictured in Figs. 11.3.6 and 11.3.7 is also a good example of a motion dynamics simulation that included **shortcuts in the simulation** to fit both the production deadlines and a limited budget. Early in the production process of this animation it was determined that it would not be possible to use collision detection techniques to keep the flying surface from colliding with the body of the car or from penetrating its space. This was due to both the number of points on the lattice and the number of forces applied to it. These conditions could translate into a situation that would exceed both the deadlines and budget allocated to the project. Instead, the simulated layer was kept away from the car by applying radial forces to it from below as if it were blowing in an upward direction. But the shortcuts used in this simulation were balanced by performing the computation of the wind forces at intervals shorter than one frame. This was necessary due to the fact that in one cycle of this dynamics simulation the spring forces attached to each vertex on the mesh only affect the immediate neighboring vertices. For the forces to spread to several vertices and—as a result—for

11.3.6 The main visual effect in this commercial project included the creation of a computer-generated surface that looks like a cloth covering the photographic image of a Lexus car. This surface is animated so that it ripples and flies away as if pushed by the wind. The image of an old car model was texture-mapped on the three-dimensional surface. The new car model is revealed after the computer-generated surface is lifted and flies away. (Animated by Mark Henne. Courtesy of Rhythm & Hues Studios.)

the cloth to ripple with detail it was necessary to simulate several cycles between frames so that the rendered images contained rippling that propagated throughout several vertices in the mesh.

Collision and Collision Detection

The motion that results from a collision can be calculated in a variety of ways. The simplest approach consists of aiming the collision forces at the center of the object, and assuming that the mass is distributed evenly throughout the object. Other approaches can be used to simulate richer and more realistic motion, but this is also much more time consuming to calculate. One of these approaches starts by determining the accurate position of the **center of mass** of the object, as opposed to using the geometric center of the object as the center of mass. The **distribution of mass** is also calculated. Symmetric objects usually have a balanced distribution of mass, but irregular objects with an uneven distribution of mass such as meteorites tend to have unpredictable motion. When forces are applied to objects on parts other than the center of gravity they tend to produce motion that is not linear. These forces are call **torques** because the motion they produce is in the form of rotations or torsions with varying amounts of **rotational velocity** and acceleration, and changing orientations.

One of the most interesting and useful applications of motion dynamics animation techniques consists of detecting collisions between the objects that are being animated. Real objects react naturally to a collision by deforming and changing the direction and speed of their motion, and even breaking. Simulated three-dimensional models, however, will naturally ignore other objects that penetrate their space unless collision detection techniques are used. Using **collision detection** techniques can add a lot of processing time and expense to a scene because they must constantly check the position and dynamic properties of objects in order to avoid overlapping objects. A simple, inexpensive alternative to collision detection for small animation projects that do not involve motion dynamics techniques consists of previewing the animation—in the form of a motion test, for example—and detecting the collisions visually. The correct positions of the overlapping objects can then be approximated manually, and the sequence can be previewed again with simple keyframe animation techniques. Some of the problems posed by visual detection of object collision include that it may require a lot of time in scenes with a multitude of objects.

Automatic collision detection is convenient because it frees the animator to do other tasks that are more important than detecting collisions visually. Automatic collision detection is also usually faster and more accurate than visual collision detection. There are many techniques for automatic collision detection and a number of them are provided by turn-key commercial software. A common method for doing a first pass collision detection test consists of using rectangular **bounding boxes**, and sometimes bounding spheres or surfaces. This method can save thousands of calculations by simply determining whether the boxes intersect at any point. If the bounding boxes intersect then a second stage collision detection test can be performed with the objects themselves to determine whether they intersect. A third stage collision detection test usually consists of checking the polygons of one of the intersecting objects against the polygons, or even edges, of the other intersecting object. In cases when the collision detection test is positive, then a response to the collision can be animated with motion dynamics techniques.

The approach for collision detection that relies on brute

11.3.7 The resolution of the dynamic mesh used to model the Lexus car cover was a total of 6,000 points arranged in a grid of 60 columns by 100 rows. This high resolution was necessary to represent the detailed mapping of the surface required by the project. (Animated by Mark Henne. Courtesy of Rhythm & Hues Studios.)

computing force consists of testing all the objects in the environment against each other. In an average computer animation production, this approach only makes sense when the motion in the scene is such that most of the objects are expected to bounce into each other. But a simpler and more economical method for collision detection can be implemented by identifying the **obstacles** that the moving object is likely to encounter along the **collision path**.

11.4 Procedural Animation

Procedural or **rule-based motion** techniques animate the elements in the scene based on a set of procedures and rules that control motion. Rule-based animation has a wide range of applications that include the animation of natural phenomena, flying birds, growing plants, fantastic life forms, and humans dancing or gesturing. (See Chapter 4 for more information on modeling plants with procedural techniques.)

Particle Systems

One of the most popular forms of procedural animation is exemplified by the animation of particle systems. Animation with **particle systems** recreates the motion of particles that follow some generally defined motion. In the majority of computer animation programs, the particles themselves do not have a specific shape but can be used to control other objects or attributes. When particles are used to recreate the light of fireworks, for example, they represent a point of light with a variety of attributes such as intensity, flickering, and tail tracking values (Fig. 11.4.1).

Particle systems are used to represent dynamic objects that have irregular and complex shapes, each with its own behavior. Particles have a life span during which they are created, behave a certain way, age, and die. Particles can also be used to control the motion of three-dimensional models—such as snow, water, or even a flock of birds—and to animate the growth process of plants by encoding their characteristics in a series of rules that can be used as the basis for a simulation (these methods are described in Chapter 4).

Flock Animation

There are many different strategies to generate flock animation. In most cases, the behavior of the birds in the flock is contained in a series of rules that constitute the computer model that simulates the flock animation. These rules control all the variables involved in the behavior of the flock. These rules include, for example, whether the flock has multiple leaders or a single leader and, if so, in which patterns does the rest of the flock follow the leader. Some of the basic variables provided by most computer software to control the motion of flock animation include the way in which the members of the flock move towards a target, how they avoid obstacles, and how they relate to other members in the flock as the flight conditions change throughout time.

Animating a flock of birds with rule-based techniques is a more practical alternative than using keyframe animation. Flocks can be simulated with particle systems so that each particle in the system represents a bird. Each bird in the flock moves according to the laws behind the physical simulation, its own perception of the environment formalized by the rules of the system, and by a series of parameters defined by the animator. The overall motion of a flock can be represented as the result of the behavior of each individual bird and the interactions between them. A common strategy to recreate the flying behavior of each bird is based on rules that simulate some of its perception and the action of flying. Once the model is expressed in terms of rules then several birds can be simulated and allowed to interact with each other.

A significant difference between particle systems and flock animation based on particle systems is that in flock animation the particles are replaced by three-dimensional models; they have orientation, and they also have more complex types of behavior.

The behavior of flocks is determined by the internal conditions of each bird in the flock, and also by the external conditions that affect the flight of each individual bird and the flock as a whole. Birds in the flock present many forms of behavior and goals. Common behaviors and goals of flocks include, for example, avoiding collisions with other birds in the flock or objects in the environment, matching the speed of nearby birds, and staying together. Each of these behaviors requires a specific acceleration and direction.

When the goals of dozens of birds are in play it is necessary to arbitrate all the individual requests. The flocking model used to create Fig. 11.4.2 employs a variety of techniques to arbitrate independent behaviors. These techniques are based on a prioritization of all the component behaviors and their acceleration requests. Depending on the situation different requests get a

11.4.1 The character Johnny Storm, from the feature film *Fantastic Four*, was transformed into the *Human Torch* by using particle systems techniques and other types of procedural animation. The life-like movement of the animated character was based on the motion captured from a live actor. (Animation by Mr. Film, Venice, CA. Courtesy of Wavefront Technologies, Inc.)

11.4.2 Animating flocks of bats in the film *Batman Returns*. The behavior of the bats is based on a flock animation computer model created by Craig Reynolds in 1987, with additional software written by Andy Kopra to satisfy the special requirements of the motion picture. (*Batman Returns* ™ and © 1992 by DC Comics. Image courtesy of VIFX.)

higher priority. For example, maintaining all the birds in the flock together can receive a low priority if the flock is about to collide with a large obstacle.

Computer animations of flocks can also be created with a combination of particle animation and keyframe animation. This is especially useful in cases when the computer animation software does not provide a full-fledged rule-based system. An example of this simplified technique for creating flock animation is illustrated in Fig. 11.4.3. In this case, the flock animation is controlled mostly with simple parameters that are adjusted at the keyframes, but the relation between flock members cannot be specified in the form or rules. The basic technique here starts by creating a set number of particles that will represent the members of the flock as they move from a **source mesh** for particles to a **destination mesh**. The precise path of the motion can be controlled by the magnitude and direction of a simulated force of gravity, and also by the way in which the particles select the points (or vertices) on the source mesh to leave from and the points on the destination mesh to arrive to. The distribution of the particles on both meshes can be easily controlled by the shape of the meshes and by whether the source and destination meshes have the same shape and number of vertices. The distribution of particles can also be controlled with numerical values that randomize the mesh, or by concentrating most flock members on a small group of vertices. The behavior of the flock as it moves from one point to another can be controlled in this example by numerical values that specify the amount of back-and-forth change, or jittering, in each of the geometric transforma-

ADVANCED ANIMATION TECHNIQUES

tions, and the shape of the models being controlled by the particles. The shape of the three-dimensional model that is controlled by the moving particles can be specified in the form of one or several key shapes.

Goal-Oriented Animation

Some computer animation systems are capable of automatically choreographing the motion of an animated character based on a specific goal that has to be achieved. The animated characters in goal-oriented systems range from a simple robot arm or a fantastic creature to a more complex human-looking character. The goal for the character can be as simple as turning its head towards the light, or as complex as grabbing an object with the left hand, passing it to the right hand, and running out of the room while avoiding all the obstacles along the way. **Goal-oriented** computer animation is also often called **intention-based** or **automated** animation. Goal-oriented animation has its roots in the fields of robotics and expert systems where computer systems are designed so that they can be as autonomous as possible, including the ability to plan different strategies to achieve a goal, evaluate the results, and continue to develop the strategies that were succesful while avoiding the strategies that lead to failure.

Goal-oriented animation techniques still belong by and large in research laboratories. Nevertheless their usefulness is slowly, turning them into commercial products. The most important component of a goal-oriented animation system is the set of rules and procedures that allows characters to analyze and evaluate its environment and to determine the best way to achieve a goal, usually by reacting with motion, gestures, and manipulations of objects in the environment. Many goal-oriented animation systems also include an inverse kinematics module to deal with the position of jointed figures, and/or a motion dynamics module that deals with basic issues, including weights, forces, and collision detection.

Goal-based computer animation systems include the **codified procedures** that are necessary to analyze a goal, break it into tasks, evaluate the environment, predict and try to avoid potential obstacles, recover from mistakes, develop new strategies as a result of those experiences, and ultimately achieve the goal. Most existing goal-oriented computer animation systems specialize in a specific type of goal or a specific type of motion, other-

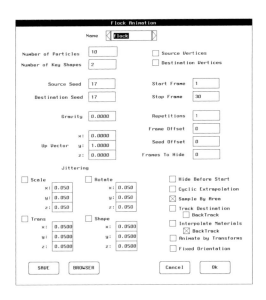

11.4.3 Parameters for a flock animation. (Dialog box from Softimage 3D. © Microsoft Corporation. All rights reserved.)

11.4.4 These still frames from a goal-oriented animation illustrate how the software can generate the motion paths necessary for a character to manipulate a pair of glasses with both hands. The motion of the arms is achieved with both inverse kinematics and a sensorimotor model based on neurophysiological studies. (Images from "Planning Motions with Intentions" by Yoshihito Koga, Koichi Kondo, James Kuffner, and Jean-Claude Latombe in the SIGGRAPH '94 Conference Proceedings. Courtesy of Yoshihito Koga, Stanford University.)

wise their tasks would be too complex to implement. (When the complexity of goal-oriented animation approaches the complexity of human motion it is often more practical to record human motion itself directly on video or film.) Some goal-oriented systems, for example, specialize in simulating human gaits and other forms of multilegged locomotion. Others can animate hands grasping and manipulating objects, or even body gestures and facial expressions.

One of the main tasks of goal-oriented animation system consists of determining what sequences and paths of motions are necessary to achieve a certain goal. Finding an optimal motion path that will allow the goal to be completed involves testing for collision detection, angles of motion, and grasp ability of limbs. Establishing a **sequence of motions** involves determining how many steps are necessary to complete a motion and what is the optimal order of execution. Simple goals that involve motion usually translate into simple motion paths and simple motion sequences. But as the goal increases in complexity so do the paths and sequences of motions necessary to complete the goal.

One of the biggest challenges of goal-oriented computer animation is to deal effectively with complex sequences of motions, both in terms of being able to complete the tasks and achieve the goal, and also in terms of producing natural motion when human figures are animated. For this reason, most are based on some sort of **motion planner**. The systems that animate characters that grasp and manipulate objects utilize a **manipulation planner**. In addition, goal-oriented systems include kinematics or dynamics techniques for calculating motion. The manipulation planner used to create the sequence of images in Fig. 11.4.4, for example, defines paths in terms of transit paths and transfer paths. In this case, the goal for the animated figure consisted of reaching for the glasses and wearing them. The task of the animator is limited to selecting the object that has to be moved and the location where the object has to be repositioned. The motion planner of this goal-based animation system determines that the character has to use both hands in order to complete the action. Not too many individuals can grab a pair of lenses and put them on with just one hand. The **transit paths** define the motions of the character without the objects being manipulated, for example, getting the arm to a

Do you have a blank check?

Will you help me get fifty dollars?

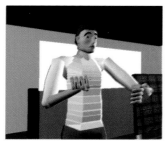

you can write the check.

I will wait for you to withdraw fifty dollars for me.

position from which it can reach the object. The **transfer paths** define arm motions that also move the object. Transfer tasks are generated by analyzing and planning the motion of the object from its initial position through the completion of the goal. During the calculation of the path the manipulation planner identifies all the possible ways of grasping the object and the configurations of the object requiring a grasp or regrasp.

The majority of motion planners have a simplified set of rules that specify how motion takes place in general, and which motions are allowed in particular. The animation system illustrated in Fig. 11.4.4, for example, allows only the arms of the animated character to touch the objects in the environment that are to be grasped. Objects in the environment that are obstacles can only be touched for the purpose of achieving static stability. In the interest of efficiency, most goal-oriented systems limit the number of possible motions and grasps, or types of static and dynamic obstacles that are considered, or the number of possible solutions to situations when collisions occur.

A few goal-oriented animation systems attempt to automate the animation of human figures based on instructions given in plain English—or other human natural languages—as opposed to special-purpose animation languages. One example of such an approach is illustrated in Fig. 11.4.5. This animation system is able to automatically generate and animate conversations between human-looking figures. The conversations include motions such as facial expressions and arm gestures. The facial expressions are associated with motions of the head, eyes, and

11.4.5 These four gestures were automatically generated by a goal-based animation system that creates a sequence of simple actions in response to a statement. In the first image, an iconic gesture representing a rectangular check is generated from the words "blank check." In the second image, a gesture requesting help accompanies the verbal request for money. In the third image, an iconic gesture representing writing on a piece of paper is generated from the mention of the concrete action of writing a check. In the fourth image, a motion of the hands up and down emphasizes the notion of waiting. (From "Animated Conversation: Rule-based Generation of Facial Expression, Gesture and Spoken Intonation for Multiple Conversational Agents," by J. Cassell et al., published in the SIGGRAPH '94 Conference Proceedings. Courtesy of Dr. Justine Cassell.)

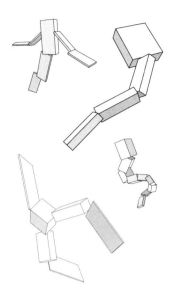

11.4.6 These creatures are the result of a simulation that seeks to optimize a locomotion system for swimming. Both their shape and motion behavior were determined by a computer program that simulates genetic evolution. Most of their motion is achieved by paddling, sculling, or wagging their tail and flippers, or by winding with sinusoidal motions. (Images from "Evolving Virtual Creatures," by Karl Sims. Courtesy of Karl Sims, Thinking Machines Corporation.)

lips. The arm gestures include coordinated motions of the arms, wrists, and hands. The rules underlying this system are based on the relation between verbal and nonverbal communication. The combined meaning of speech, body language, and facial expressions can result in animated characters that are consistent, believable, and somewhat autonomous.

One of the most unique features of this rule-based animation system is that it is capable of accepting the text of the dialog within the context of a database that contains facts, goals, and beliefs of the animated characters about the world and about one another. The text of the dialog is preprocessed so that the linguistic and semantic aspects of a conversation can be interpreted by computer programs in charge of the speech synthesis, semantic analysis, and generation of gestures and facial expressions.

The rules of the program used to create the images in Fig. 11.4.5 are based on a topology, or classification, of facial expressions and hand gestures that assign a meaning to a selection of gestures and expressions. It also establishes a semiotic relationship and a temporal synchronization between speech, gestures, and expressions. Much of the sequencing and coordination of actions is created with a computer model that activates transitions between actions based on conditions being met, or on rules of probability.

Within the computer animation program that was used to generate Fig. 11.4.5 the **gesture motion** is specified with information about the location, type, timing, and handshape of individual gestures. The hand, wrist, and arm positions can be controlled independently. An interesting feature of this system allows users to control the expressiveness of the gesturing of a character by modifying the size of its **gesture space**, which is usually dependent on the virtual age group and culture of the animated characters. The facial expressions are generated both automatically when based on the intonation and phoneme—or spoken sounds—and by hand when they add meaning to the spoken discourse. Gazing, one action involved in facial expression, is controlled automatically based on the purpose of looking, for example, whether to look away to gain concentration or look at the other character to reinforce a point in the conversation.

In addition to simulating human-looking characters it is also possible to simulate and animate artificial types of life with goal-oriented computer animation techniques. The three-dimensional creatures illustrated in Figs. 11.4.6 and 11.4.7 were created with a computer program that uses genetic algorithms to define the shape of the creatures and the processes by which their motion is controlled. These creatures are the result of a genetic evolution simulation that seeks to optimize a specific goal: their locomotion on water or land. This is achieved by running survival

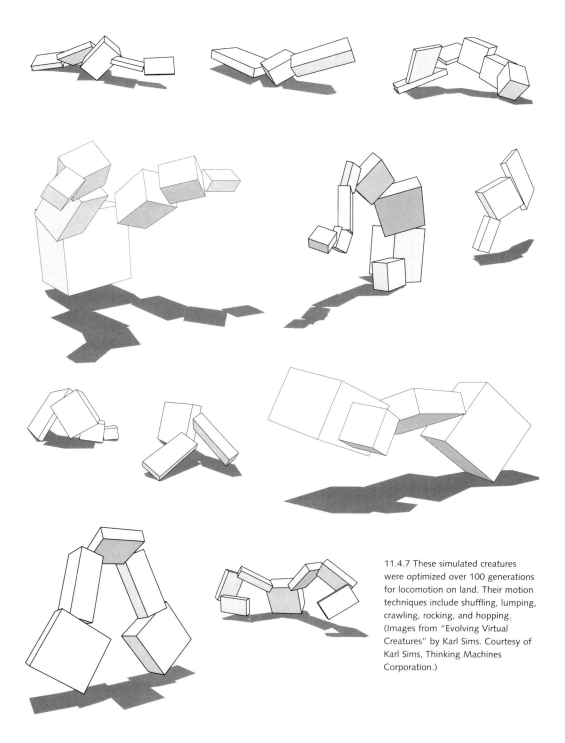

11.4.7 These simulated creatures were optimized over 100 generations for locomotion on land. Their motion techniques include shuffling, lumping, crawling, rocking, and hopping. (Images from "Evolving Virtual Creatures" by Karl Sims. Courtesy of Karl Sims, Thinking Machines Corporation.)

tests throughout 100 generations of approximately 300 members each. The survival tests consisted of a physical simulation where the creatures are tested for fitness based mostly on their speed and ability to control their speed and direction of motion. The fittest creatures within a generation are selected by the program for survival and reproduction.

The creatures in this example are able to sense contact with their own selves and with the environment, and can avoid obstacles. These creatures have a morphology that evolves from a simple control system that senses the environment, evaluates the situation, and reacts to it. The evolutionary process starts with a random generation of sets of nodes (body, limbs and head) and the connections between them. A clear set of rules and procedures governs all the stages of this simulated world including the initial assembly of the creatures, their behavior, their fitness evaluation, and their reproduction and optimization.

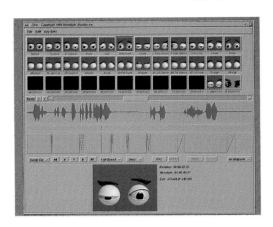

11.4.8 Lip-Sync and Soundwave software were used to choose lip configurations from a library of key positions, and then align them to a graph representing the voice soundtrack of the main character in Weldon Pond, a pilot television program. (Software developed by Alias Research and Windlight Studios. Courtesy of CBS, Inc., and Windlight Studios.)

Facial Animation

There are many techniques for animating **facial expressions**, including libraries of key poses, motion dynamics, and goal-oriented techniques. Facial animation is very often generated with a combination of some or all of these techniques and is usually applied to the character only after the primary motion has been established.

A **library of key expressions** is a simple and convenient way to store and retrieve many facial expressions. Libraries of key expressions are based on keyframing techniques and, therefore, require a fair amount of interactive work for placing the required expressions along the time line. Figure 11.4.8 illustrates a library of lip key positions and an interface that allows animators to place those keyframes in the animation while viewing a graphic representation of the soundtrack. The **motion transitions** between facial expressions have to be checked for details in the interpolation that may look unnatural and, therefore, be distracting.

Facial animation that uses motion dynamics techniques is often based on **simulated muscles** that control both the way in which the skin moves and the facial expression. Some of the techniques for simulating muscle forces are based on small muscles that contract or relax (Fig. 11.4.9). This change is transmitted to a flexible lattice that represents facial tissue. In order to simulate a realistic propagation of dynamic forces throughout the simulated skin, some animation systems employ a multilayer flexible lattice that permits an increased interaction of the spring forces.

The image shown in Fig. 11.4.10 was created with a multi-

 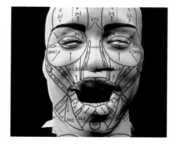

11.4.9 Two views of a head model showing the relationship between simulated facial muscles and expressions. (Courtesy of Acclaim Entertainment, Inc., Advanced Technologies Group.)

track facial animation system that combines simulated muscles and key expressions—called snapshots in this system—that correspond to phonemes and emotions. The snapshots for phonemes consist of the lip positions that correspond to the emission of a particular sound. Both the emotion and the phoneme snapshots can be specified with intensity parameters that control the motion of different virtual muscles. For example, a specific facial expression could be defined as:

```
raise_sup_lip  30%
lower_inf_lip  20%
open_jaw       15%
```

The emotions can also be specified in a parametric fashion by defining the change, intensity, and duration of facial expressions over time. Some parameters of emotion that can be used to control virtual muscles include the length of time that it takes for the expression to start and to decay, its overall duration, and its transition to a relaxed state. Facial animation based on goal-oriented techniques is illustrated in Fig. 11.4.5.

11.5 Channel Animation

Channel animation allows the collection or capture of all kinds of information in real time through a variety of input peripherals that are attached to a computer. The motion capture animation techniques covered earlier in this chapter are one of the most popular forms of channel animation. The data contained in the channels can also be used to control other aspects of the animation, such as the intensity of a light source, the density of a texture, the force of gravity, or the speed of a motion (Fig. 11.5.1). The sets of data brought into the system are assigned to one or several **channels** in the **animation score** and used to drive the aspects of the animation controlled by those channels. For ease of work, the captured data is displayed in the form of **function curves**. The result of the live motion

11.4.10 The facial animation of this surprised virtual Marilyn Monroe is generated using the SMILE system, which is a multilayer animation system with muscle deformation at the lower level and a high-level language to specify the emotions, the speech, and the eye motions. (© 1991 Nadia Magnenat Thalmann, MIRALab, University of Geneva, and Daniel Thalmann, Computer Graphics Lab, EPFL, Lausanne.)

capture process, for example, is presented by most computer animation software in the form of function curves that control different aspects of the animation.

In principle, all kinds of input peripherals can be used to input time-based information to the animation software. This includes **peripheral input devices** such as a joystick, a microphone, a music keyboard, a trackball, or a variety of motion capture gear. In all cases, a **device driver** is necessary for the animation software to be able to communicate with the peripherals.

The basic process of channel animation starts by identifying the active input devices and assigning each of them to one or several channels based on the number of degrees of freedom that they have. The degrees of freedom of input peripherals are

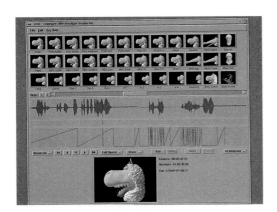

defined by the rotations and translation that the device is capable of. A joystick with one button, for example, has three degrees of freedom because it can move along two axes and the button can be clicked. Motion capture gear can generate dozens of channels depending on the number of position points—each with XYZ degrees of freedom—that the gear is built with, which usually ranges between a low value of ten and a high of seventy. Once each degree of freedom in the device is assigned to a channel, the second stage of the channel animation process consists of assigning each channel to the motion of an object. Figure 11.5.2 illustrates this process.

11.5.1 Eye-Sync and Soundwave software were used to align the eye animation of a character to the voice soundtrack in *Weldon Pond*, a pilot television program. These software programs allow animators to choose eye configurations from a library of key positions, assemble a motion sequence (red and blue lines), and then playback a motion test in real time in synchronization with the soundtrack (green lines). (Courtesy of CBS, Inc., and Windlight Studios.)

During the data capture process some computer animation systems allow animators to preview the effect of the captured data and the links between the channels and the elements on the animation. But if the number of live channels is too large then the display of the animation can overburden the computer and slow down the sampling rate of the capture process. For that reason, it is often more practical to capture the data in a blind mode, and to preview the resulting animation only after the live data capture is complete. Afterwards any changes can be made to the resulting motion by editing the function curves of each channel.

11.6 Location-Based and Interactive Entertainment

The entertainment industry has recently applied many computer animation techniques to areas that go beyond the confines of a traditional movie theater or a television set. Both motion rides and interactive games have unique creative, and technical requirements that differentiate them from other applications of animation. **Location-based entertainment** is another name given to both motion rides and large—usually multiplayer—videogames that are bound to a specific location due to their size and equipment requirements (Figs. 11.6.1 and 11.6.2). The name of **virtual reality** is sometimes given to entertainment applications that are based on computer animations that try to simulate reality.

Motion Rides

Motion rides are a kind of movie rollercoaster where computer animations are shown in a theater constructed on a motion simulator. **Motion simulators** are platforms or bases that move—usually with pneumatic mechanisms—in response to a script of programmed motion. The motion of the platform is choreographed in conjunction with the motion of the camera in the computer animation. The size of motion simulators varies, but on average they hold between ten and thirty seats. Motion rides can simulate the motion of the observer through space, or the motion of the environment around the observer, or both. Entertainment rides plunge viewers into fantasy worlds and they almost always take place in scenic theatrical environments. Rides usually explore realistic looking environments, but sometimes the environments are fantastic and have their own laws of physics. Typically the observer (the audience) rides a vehicle that can move at high speeds. This generates one of the most typical characteristics of motion rides—sudden changes of speed and direction.

The **entertainment value** of most motion rides is based on the story they tell, the synchronization of the motions of the simulated camera and environment, with those of the motion simulator, and the consistency of the motions and environments presented. Unlike computer animations that are meant to be *watched*, motion rides are meant to be *experienced*. Much of the effect of motion rides is based on the physical experience derived from fooling the sense of balance and orientation of the audience. This is done by simulating not only the moving images that the audience would see if they were moving, but also some of the physical sensations that they would feel if they were moving. For these reasons, the **synchronization of motions** between the motion simulator and the computer animation is essential for the success of a motion ride.

From the production point of view the synchronization of the motions is a process that requires a lot of trial and error, including the display or projection of wireframe motion tests of the computer animation while the motion of the base is fine tuned. The **field of view** and the **lines of sight** have to be carefully orchestrated so that the simulated and real motions are synchronized. An important issue to consider is the fact that the motion of the platform should be affected by both the motion of the simulated camera and some of the actions that take place

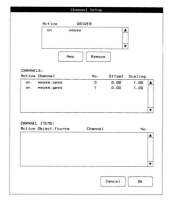

11.5.2 One-dimensional data captured by each of the input devices is assigned to a channel, and then channels are linked to one dimension of the motion of an animated element. (Dialog box from Softimage 3D. © Microsoft Corporation. All rights reserved.)

11.6.1 In the *Loch Ness Expedition* game eight vehicles—each carrying six participants—are connected to a high-performance computer that generates high-resolution three-dimensional computer graphics in real time. The real vehicles where the players sit contain a three-dimensional digital-audio system that delivers sound effects in real time in sync with the movements of each of the virtual vehicles. (Game developed by Iwerks Entertainment and Evans & Sutherland. Courtesy of Evans & Sutherland Computer Corporation.)

in the simulated three-dimensional environment. The motion of the platform is mostly determined by camera-related issues like orientation and speed, but also by other motions, for example, an explosion or a giant monster trying to blow us away. The action in the three-dimensional environment is sometimes articulated in a simple way to the actions of the participants through the actions in the story line. For example, if the simulated spaceship that carries the audience shoots at a monster in the scene, the motion platform would move based on the recoiling motion of the ship as well as the turbulent forces generated by the monster as it tried to escape.

Another factor that is essential to the success of a motion ride is the **consistency of the motion** in the environments simulated on the motion platform. Consistency of motion implies that the platform will always move in a consistent and similar way in anticipation or in reaction to the actions shown in the animation. In cases when the motion ride is based on the simulation of real motion, it is crucial that this realism of motion is always consistent. One inaccurate motion is enough to destroy the illusion of realism sought by so many motion rides. But consistent motion does not necessarily imply that the motion style will try to simulate real motion. A fantastic motion ride could have its own particular laws of physics, or just gravity forces for example, different from the natural laws of our reality. The audience can quickly adapt to any motion as long as the motion is consistent.

During the stage of preproduction it is important to design the animation based on the types of motions and effects that the motion simulator is capable of. It is useless to design a computer animation for a motion ride without taking into consideration the weaknesses and strengths of the motion base. The integration of computer animation and motion simulation technologies has to be seamless for motion rides to be effective. From this point of view the computer animations for motion rides are somewhat stylistically slave to the capabilities of motion simulation technology. Even platforms with six degrees of freedom (rotations and translations on XYZ) have motion limitations. A debate between creators of motion rides focuses on whether the images in a ride should be stylized versions of fantastic worlds or photorealistic simulations of our world. Most agree on one issue: regardless of what the imagery looks like the motion should be outstanding. This is especially important in cases when the renderings are simple.

Production schedules for motion rides are usually longer than those of a computer animation intended for a traditional delivery format due to the additional task of synchronizing the motion of the animation to the motion of the platform and vice versa. This usually requires an animation design that takes into

11.6.2 *Seafari* is a hyperrealistic computer-generated motion ride that takes the audience on an underwater rescue mission. (© 1994 MCA/Universal. Courtesy of Rhythm & Hues Studios.)

account what the motion base can do, and also the extended production times required to fine tune the motion of the platform to the animation motion tests back and forth until the desired effects are achieved.

The film formats usually employed to record computer animations for motion rides require larger sizes and higher resolutions than other delivery formats. These formats include 70 mm film with five, eight and fifteen perforations (also called 5, 8, and 15 perf). Both the size and resolution of the images have an impact on the computing and production times required to create animation for motion rides.

Even though motion rides typically involve a fair amount of action most of them are, in essence, passive forms of entertainment from the point of view of **audience participation**. Most forms of location-based entertainment that include interactivity are in the form of games where the audience interacts with computer animations. But this interaction does not usually take place on motion simulators.

Interactive Games

The functionality and image quality of today's interactive games continue to improve along with thechnological innovations. Popular technologies like the CD-ROM and the 24-bit color standard have redefined the meaning of state-of-the-art in the latest generation of interactive games, especially as it applies to three-dimensional computer animation. Interactive games are, in fact, so bound by technology that before dealing with creative issues it is imperative to understand the ways in which technology defines the creative boundaries in an interactive game. Early designs for an interactive game that do not consider the technical lilmitations of the delivery system result in wasted creative energy and costly production delays.

One of the critical aspects of many interactive games—especially action games—is the **response speed** of the game to the commands, actions, and requests of the user. This speed is determined by the processing speed of the hardware on which the game is played on, and it defines strategies for saving and displaying the three-dimensional computer animation that may be part of the game.

Most **action-based games** for arcade use are delivered in self-contained kiosks with specialized hardware that is typically capable of very fast response speeds. The versions of arcade action games for home use are delivered in electronic cartridges that plug into proprietary game systems that are typically faster than most computer systems for home use. **Dialog-based games** are commonly delivered on a CD-ROM that can be played on one or several brands of computer systems.

The interactive games that incorporate three-dimensional computer animation are generally based on one of two display strategies: playback of prerendered two-dimensional images, or real-time navigation and rendering of a three-dimensional scene. Playing back a sequence of prerendered two-dimensional images is common, for example, when the processing power of the system is limited, or when exceptional savings in storage are derived from saving compressed two-dimensional files instead of a full-fledged three-dimensional database. This is effective with games that are played off a CD-ROM or a fast hard disk. A three-dimensional scene database can be rendered in real time as the player moves through the environment only when a fast graphics processor is available, along with the assortment of electronics that accelerate the display of images. Needless to say, there is a wide range of rendering resolutions in today's interactive videogames ranging all the way from 32-bit full color to 8-bit dithered color (read Chapter 12 for more information on color resolution).

As said earlier, when designing computer animation for interactive games it is of paramount importance to consider the playback limitations of the computer or game system. Action sequences that can be effective in the movie theatre environment invariably require a major amount of creative and technical work to be adapted to the medium and format of interactive games. Two of the issues that always come up in these adaptations include the modeling complexity of the three-dimensional scene and the color and image resolution of the rendered images. It is often the task of creative game designers and artists to find the best compromise between playing fun, aesthetic qualities, technological capabilities, response time, modeling complexity, and image resolution. A challenging task.

Review and Practice

Matching

_____ Motion dynamics

_____ Inverse kinematics

_____ Environmental density

_____ Mass

_____ Collision detection

_____ Filtered motion

_____ Rigid objects

_____ Channel animation

_____ Conical force

_____ Torques

_____ Virtual reality

_____ Location-based entertainment

_____ Rotoscoping

a. Allows to capture all kinds of information in real time through a variety of input peripherals.

b. Name given to both motion rides and large—usually multi-player—videogames.

c. Animation techniques that generate realistic motion of objects by simulating their physical properties and the natural laws of physical motion.

d. Their surfaces do not move much after a collision.

e. When it impacts a surface it is strongest at the center of the impact area and weaker at the edges.

f. Entertainment applications that are based on computer animations that try to simulate reality.

g. Calculates the motion of entire skeletons by specifying the final angle positions of some of the key joints that define the motion.

h. Using it can add a lot of processing time and production expense to a scene because the position and dynamic properties of objects must be constantly checked to avoid overlapping objects.

i. A form of motion capture that is usually based on tracing joint positions from live action footage.

j. Occurs during the motion-capture process when the hierarchies of real actors and virtual actors are structured in different ways.

k. An example of a resisting force.

l. Determined by the product of the volume of an object and its density.

m. The motion they produce is in the form of rotations or torsions with varying amounts of rotational velocity and acceleration, and changing orientations.

True/False

_____ a. The data collected with a motion capture system should never be subjected to any post processing because that degrades its quality.

_____ b. The synchronization of motions between a motion simulator and the computer animation is essential for the success of a motion ride.

_____ c. In most computer animation productions of a scientific nature, it makes more sense to use animation shortcuts instead of computing expensive and time-consuming dynamics simulations of the events in question.

_____ d. The motion of live actors can be captured and applied to the animated characters in real time.

_____ e. A simple and economical method for collision detection can be implemented by visually identifying the obstacles that a moving object is likely to encounter along its collision path and repositioning the objects.

_____ f. A common solution to the occlusion problem in optical capture of motion is to increase the number of cameras used to look at the sample points.

_____ g. Potentiometers are devices capable of measuring force and motion based on the amount of acoustic energy that passes through the device as a result of the motion of a joint.

_____ h. Unfiltered captured human motion applied to a cartoon character makes them look real.

_____ i. The skin of three-dimensional models can only be defined as a continuous flexible surface.

_____ j. Inverse kinematics animation techniques require that the three-dimensional models to be animated are built as hierarchical structures.

Answers True/False: a. False, b. True, c. False, d. True, e. True, f. True, g. False, h. False, i. False, j. True.

Key Terms

Acceleration
Acoustic motion capture
Action-based games
Animation score
Attracting forces
Audience participation
Automated
Automatic collision detection
Basic tracks of motion
Bounding boxes
Broken hierarchy
Center of mass
Chain root
Channel
Codified procedures
Collision detection
Collision path
Conical force
Consistency of the motion
Density
Destination mesh
Device driver
Dialog-based games
Direction
Distribution of mass
Dynamic simulation
Effector
End effector
Elasticity
Entertainment value
Environmental density
Facial expressions
Field of view
Filtered
Flexible lattice
Flexible objects
Force
Friction
Function curves
Gelatin
Gesture motion
Gesture space
Global forces
Goal-oriented
Gravity
Hard rubber

Hybrid environment
Impacting forces
Intensity
Intention-based
Inverse kinematics
Joint
Library of key expressions
Linear force
Lines of sight
Live control
Local forces
Location-based entertainment
Magnetic motion capture
Manipulation planner
Mass
Motion capture
Motion constrains
Motion dynamics
Motion planner
Motion simulators
Motion transitions
Multiple layers of motion
Number of motion sensors
Obstacles
Optical motion capture
Particle systems
Peripheral input devices
Placement of the sensors
Point force
Positions
Potentiometers
Procedural-based motion
Prosthetic motion capture
Radial force
Raw motion
Real actors
Receivers
Resisting forces
Response speed
Rest position
Rigid objects
Rotational velocity
Rotoscoping
Rule-based motion
Sampling points
Secondary motion
Sequence of motions
Shortcuts in the simulation

Simulated muscles
Simulation domain
Source mesh
Springs
Stiffness
Strength
Stretched position
Synchronization of motions
Torques

Transfer paths
Transit paths
Transponders
Velocity
Virtual actors
Virtual reality
Viscosity
Volume

Post Production

CHAPTER 12

Post Processing

Summary

Once the three-dimensional scenes have been rendered, then the resulting two-dimensional images can be subject to further processing. Post processing techniques are typically used for enhancement purposes including color balance and correction, image retouching, compositing, and sequencing.

12.1 Basic Concepts of Image Manipulation

There is a myriad of techniques for enhancing and combining two-dimensional renderings of three-dimensional environments. Post processing has its roots in traditional retouching just like three-dimensional computer modeling can be compared to the work of a sculptor working with traditional materials, and the rendering process can be compared to the work of lighting designers, make-up artists, photographers, and painters. Post processing the resulting computer-generated images can be compared to the work that photographers do in the darkroom, once the images have been recorded on film but before the final prints are made. **Image manipulation** techniques are used to modify the color, contrast, and brightness of computer-generated images, as well as their content. These techniques can increase the overall brightness of an image, or lower the contrast between light and dark tones. Image manipulation techniques can also be used to remove mistakes or to combine areas of different sources into a single image. Some of the basic concepts behind image manipulation techniques include pixel and color resampling, editing with parameter curves and histograms, and compositing with alpha channels and transition effects.

Resampling the Pixel Resolution

One of the key techniques of image manipulation consists of

changing the spatial resolution of an image. This is called **resampling an image** and is often used when the dimensions or the spatial resolution of an image need to be increased or decreased. It is necessary to resample an image, for example, when a scene has been rendered at a resolution of 72 **pixels per inch** (ppi) but the final output requires 300 dots per inch (dpi), or when a scene was rendered at a size of 1,000 x 1,000 pixels but the client only needs it at 500 x 500 pixels.

The continuous values of a live scene or a photograph are sampled when the live scene is digitized with a digitizing camera, or when a continuous tone photograph is scanned with a scanner. In both of these cases, the frequency of the sampling determines the resolution of the digital image. Many samples, or point measurements, of color result in many pixels. A few samples yield few pixels and a low resolution.

When images are resampled the information contained in a digital file can change subtly or dramatically. When images are sampled down, the software averages the values of several pixels and discards some of the original information. When images are sampled up, the software averages the values of several pixels and creates new information. In either case, this averaging of pixel values is based on one of many **interpolation techniques** that create new pixel values by averaging the existing pixel values in different ways.

There are simple interpolations, such as **neighbor pixel interpolation**, that determine the value of a new pixel by averaging the values of only two pixels. When an image is resampled in order to double its original size, for example, the number of pixels that has to be created is twice the number of original pixels. With a simple interpolation technique each new pixel is created between two existing pixels, and its value is determined by averaging the value of just those two pixels. Resampling based on simple or linear interpolation techniques usually creates images with small defects like banding, aliased edges, or loss of detail.

There are more sophisticated resampling techniques on the other end of the interpolation spectrum. Some determine the value of a new pixel by averaging the values of many pixels and by assigning each of them a priority or weight based on their proximity to the new pixel being calculated. An example of a

weighted interpolation technique is illustrated in Fig. 12.1.1 where the values of several pixels are averaged in order to created a new single pixel. When an image is sampled down, some of its original information is lost, and the resampled image will look quite different from the original if it is resampled up again after having been resampled down.

Regardless of the pixel interpolation method used, when resampling an image it is important to determine whether maintaining the **file size** (the amount of space it takes to store it) is important. If maintaining the file size constant is an issue the the physical **image dimensions** (height and width) of the file will surely change. Inversely, if the file size may change as a result of the resampling, then the dimensions remain constant. For example, a 46 kb image that measures 2 x 1.5 in. at 72 ppi can be resampled at 300 ppi and keep its file size of 46 kb constant but the dimensions change to .48 x .36 in. (Fig. 12.1.2). If the file size must remain constant then the absolute number of pixels also remains constant, but the image dimensions change because at the higher resolution more pixels are required to create an inch. If the file size can grow the so does the resolution and the number of pixels while the dimensions remain unchanged. But if the 72 ppi image would be resampled to the dimension of 2 x 1.5 in. at the increased resolution of 300 ppi then its file size would increase to 792 kb.

Resampling the Color Resolution

Another useful technique for manipulating images of three-dimensional rendered scenes consists of changing, or resampling, their color resolution. Satisfactory results when **resampling the color resolution** of a rendered image are obtained only when it is necessary to lower the color resolution but not when it is necessary to increase it. Increasing the color resolution of an image can only be achieved with good results by re-rendering the three-dimensional scene at a higher color resolution. Color resampling is useful—and even necessary—when the image has been rendered at high color resolutions but needs to be displayed at a low resolution. This would be the case, for example, of renderings created at a resolution of 32-bit color for the purpose of feature film presentations that are adapted to the home videogame format and that had to be resampled down to 16-bit color in order to be displayed efficiently. Resampling the color resolution of entire projects is common now that many works and intellectual properties previously developed for high-resolution formats are now being released in home entertainment systems at lower color resolutions.

Most three-dimensional computer rendering systems create 24-bit or 32-bit color images. When color resampling is needed

a

b

c

12.1.2 An image with a resolution of 72 ppi and a total of 15,552 pixels (a), compared with two 300 ppi files each with a total of 15,552 pixels (b), and 269,400 pixels (c).

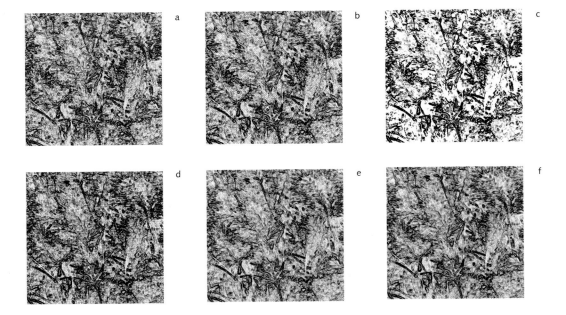

a   b   c

d   e   f

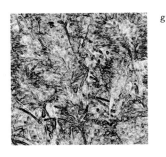

g

12.1.3 This sequence of images shows the same image rendered at different color resolutions, in each case the values of each of the bit-planes are added to determine the final value of the pixels. A 1-level bitmap can only display black and white images (a). A pixel in a 2-level bitmap displays one of four levels of gray (b). A 4-level bitmap can display 16 colors (c), and the color accuracy is often improved with dithering techniques (d). An 8-bit color image contains 256 colors (e) which can be compressed into a color look-up table (f). A 16-bit color contains 65,536 colors (g).

the process is very straightforward and is usually implemented in the form of choices listed in a dialog box or a pull-down menu. The most common resolutions for color images include 32, 24, 16, 8 and 4-bit color (Fig. 12.1.3). But the loss in color detail due to color resampling can be severe, for example, when going from the sixteen million colors of 24-bit color to the 256 colors available in 8-bit color. For this reason, the techniques of color dithering and color look-up tables are often used to minimize the artifacts and loss of detail created by color resampling. Both of these techniques are especially effective when 8-bit color is utilized.

Color dithering simulates shades of color with dot patterns of several colors. Dithering preserves some of the color detail that tends to be lost when 24-bit color images are sampled down to 4-bit or 8-bit color. But at the same time dithering lowers the apparent spatial resolution of an image because the dot patterns used to simulate shades of color often look like enlarged pixels (Fig. 12.1.3).

Color look-up tables, also called **indexed color**, are a popular technique in interactive projects where three-dimensional animated sequences are rendered in real-time in response to the users playing the game. A **color look-up table** is a limited palette of colors that represents quite faithfully a much larger selection of colors. Color look-up tables contain a tight selection of colors (256 in the 8-bit color mode) that gives the impression of a much larger palette. The main purpose of color look-up tables is to optimize color accuracy in a low color resolution environment. When a full color RGB image or sequence is converted to indexed color there are different methods for choosing the colors that go in the look-up table. These methods include using a generic color look-up table, or customizing the color manually or automatically.

It is convenient to use a generic color look-up table, often called a **system palette**, because it is a standard feature of most image manipulation software programs. A generic color look-up table produces acceptable results with images that have a balanced distribution of color. But generic palettes usually produce poor results in cases when the colors in the sequence are biased towards a single hue, for example, a scene at dusk with mostly dark colors. In such cases, generic palettes usually lack the variety of color that is required to represent the subtle variations of color within a narrow chromatic range. One of the advantages of using a generic color look-up table is that it reduces memory requirements and increases performance because the generic color look-up table can be used with a variety of different images. In an indexed color environment, a generic look-up table only has to be loaded once for all images, as opposed to customized palettes which have to be loaded every time the image is used.

Custom color look-up tables can be built for a specific image or sequence by *manually* selecting the colors that best convey the variety of colors contained in the original full color version. Color look-up tables that are built especially for a series of sequences in a project should contain the most commonly used colors throughout the project (Fig. 12.1.4). Custom color look-up tables can also be built *automatically* by letting the software decide which limited color palette would best represent the thousands of subtle colors contained in a scene.

Parameter Curves

The parameter or function curves are graphs that represent and control different attributes of an image, such as brightness or color. These attributes can be easily modified by manipulating the function curves without having to alter the image directly with a retouching tool. Making image manipulations that involve all of the image, or large portions of it, are best performed with function curves. The parameter curves used for image manipulation are similar to those used for controlling animation interpolations (read Chapter 10 for more information on animation interpolation).

Parameter curves for image manipulation are usually represented by a line that starts at the lower left corner of a square and ends at the upper right corner. The **straight diagonal line** (in a parameter curve) represents one or several untouched attributes of the original image. Any changes made to the line will

12.1.4 A full 8-bit color image (a) that is converted to indexed color (b) can retain a fair amount of color fidelity and crispness when a custom color look-up table is used. (Screen shot from Myst CD-ROM computer game. Game and screen shot are © 1993 by Cyan, Inc. All rights reserved.)

12.1.5 The unretouched image displays its brightness function curve as a straight diagonal line.

result in changes to the image. Generally, if the line is pulled above the straight diagonal path the attribute increases, and if the line is moved below the diagonal path the the attribute being controlled by the line decreases (Fig. 12.1.5).

The manner in which the parameter curve is redrawn also influences the way in which the attribute is controlled. If the parameter curve is redrawn with a series of **soft curves** then the attributes of the image change gradually as in a curved interpolation. If the parameter curve is redrawn with a series of **angular straight lines** then the attributes change abruptly as they sometimes do at the junction of two linear interpolations (Fig. 12.1.6).

The Histogram

One of the principles of traditional painting as well as classic photography recommends the creation of images with a rich

tonal range. In the case of a monochromatic image, that means a sample of gray values that is evenly and continuously distributed across the grayscale. In the case of a color image, a rich tonal range includes color values as well as brightness and contrast. An image, a black and white photograph for example, that contains small amounts of pure black and pure white plus a continuous and even distribution of gray values usually has a wider expressive range than a manierist image that dwells exclusively on the dark or light tones of the scale.

Looking at the histogram of an image is an effective way of analyzing the distribution of gray values in the image. A **histogram** consists of a graphical representation of the distribution throughout the grayscale of the pixels that constitute an image. In a monochromatic image, the horizontal line in a histogram represents the range of gray values between pure black, usually represented with a value of 0 on the left side, and pure white represented with a value of 255 in an 8-bit color scale. In a full color image, RGB for example, each component color has a histogram. The combined component colors can also be controlled with a single histogram. The number of pixels that have intensity values between black and white are represented with a vertical line or bar. The larger the number of pixels on a single value the taller the line. These lines are located throughout the horizontal line in

12.1.6 The brightness of the image increases in the midtones when the function curve is pulled up (a), the smooth curve results in a gradual change of the brightness values. Abrupt changes in the curve result in abrupt changes in the brightness values (b), in this case flattening the lightest and darkest values and compressing the midtones.

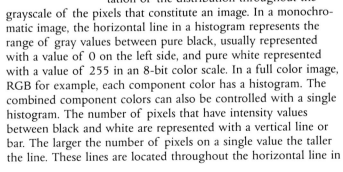

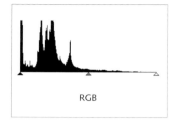

RGB

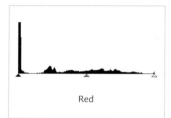

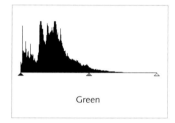

Red

Green

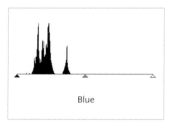

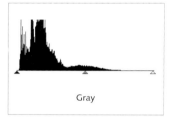

Blue

Gray

12.1.7 The histograms represent the distribution of pixels in the image throughout the tonal range. The continuity of the vertical lines in the graph reflects the continuity or discontinuity of levels in the image.

accordance with the pixel values contained in the image. An image with pixels that are evenly distributed throughout the grayscale has vertical lines all across the histogram, while an image with only dark and light values—but no midtones, for example—has vertical lines on the extremes of the histogram but not in its center. The histogram of an image with many dark values has lines mostly on its left side (Fig. 12.1.7).

Image Layers

The numerical values and some of the components that define a two-dimensional rendered image can be organized in layers. Working with multiple **image layers** or **channels** is similar to the process of painting on transparent acetate overlays that is still used in traditional cel animation. In this case, different components of the image are painted each on a cel, and the finished image can only be seen when all the layers are assembled in sequence. But when each layer or cel is viewed separately only a part of the image is visible. The principle of using image layers is also the basis of four-color separation and a staple process in the graphic arts (Fig. 12.1.8).

12.1.8 A CMYK full color image is created when the four image layers are viewed together. Four-color separation is employed in the four-color mechanical reproduction of color images on paper-based magazines and books.

Image layers are used for a variety of image manipulation purposes. As previously mentioned, image layers are used to display separately each of the component or primary colors of an image in several color modes including RGB, CMYK, and HSL. It is possible to work on a single layer separately from the other layers, for example, increase the brightness or apply a filter to just a single layer, and then merge the layers again and view the combined results.

The Alpha Channel and Masks

Image layers can also be used to composite and blend the contents of several layers and place the resulting image in a separate set of image layers. This process is called image compositing or blending depending on the specific techniques used to combine the contents of the image layers. An **alpha channel** is commonly used to aid in the compositing of multiple layers, because it may contain a black and white image that masks or protects select parts of one or several of the layers being composited. One or several alpha channels may be used in the compositing process. The **mask** contained in the alpha channel is like the **stencils** traditionally used to label wooden cargo containers or to aid in the creation of images with the delicate techniques of airbrushing or silkscreen. In either case, the stencil is perforated with a design or with letterforms and placed on a surface. The solid areas of the stencil protect the surface underneath and the perforated areas allow the paint to reach the wooden plank, in the case of the cargo container, or the paper surface being airbrushed or silkscreened (Fig. 12.3.1).

Transition Effects

Image layers, alpha channels, and masks are commonly used to combine still images, but they are also used to combine sequences of computer animation. The techniques used to blend and composite moving images are called **transition effects**. The range of transition effects is quite extensive even though the most commonly used transitions include a dozen or so effects, such as a fade-in, a fade-out, and a cross-dissolve (Fig. 12.1.9).

12.2 Image Retouching

Digital image manipulation techniques can provide the best that both the **darkroom** of a photographer and the **studio** of a painter have to offer. For example, with image manipulation software we can fine tune the tonal range of rendered images, adjust their contrast and brightness, and apply digital filters to create special effects.

Post processing programs facilitate the blending of computer-generated images with photographic or painted images. The final result can be output onto a variety of media only after the two types of images are combined with integrated tools and techniques. These capabilities are opening new creative avenues that were not possible with traditional tools.

Before computers came along it was impractical to combine painting with photography because each occurred in very different, almost incompatible, media. Bringing the photographic image onto the canvas was cumbersome, and painting on photographic paper was limiting. The narrow focus of the traditional tools did not help either. Brushes and paint did not work too well on photographic images, and many of photography's essential tools such as lenses and filters could not even be used to paint. The closest these two media ever got before computers was in the form of retouching photographs for commercial advertisements, or in the form of artistic collages. In the former case, the process of blending the painted image with the photograph was painstaking, limited, and extremely expensive. In the latter case, the painted image and the photographic image usually remained quite independent from each other.

Retouching Tools

There is a wide variety of tools for **retouching** rendered images. Some of these digital tools are inspired by the tools of painters and illustrators, and others are based on the tools used by photographers. Retouching tools are typically used to touch up small mistakes in the rendered file or to add details that are missing. As a general rule, when mistakes are made in the modeling or rendering process it is best to model and render the scene again. But in a few cases, the production schedule or budget does not permit to fix minor mistakes by remodeling or rendering again. This is especially true when the time it would take to render is beyond the production scope of the project, or when the computer-generated animation, for example, has already been composited with live action.

Some of the digital retouching tools that are inspired by **traditional painting tools** include brushes, pencils, and rubber stamps. These painting tools are used to paint over selected areas of the rendered image, and their simulated attributes, such as width or pressure, can be customized. In addition, the way in which these paint tools "deposit" the paint can also be customized in many different ways. The digital paint, for example, can have different degrees of transparency or can affect only a certain range of pixels with a certain color or brightness value. A variety of simulated paper textures can also be applied to the surface of the rendered image.

12.1.9 A cross dissolve is a popular transition effect between two animated sequences where the end of the first sequence gradually blends into the beginning of the second sequence, and vice versa.

The retouching tools based on **photographic procedures** include a tool for lightening or darkening selective parts of the image interactively, just like dodging and burning are performed on photographs as the image on the film negative is projected onto photosensitive paper. The histogram editor itself and all the parameter curves are also retouching tools that are rooted in the photographic tradition because they help define an image by adjusting the settings in which the imaging process occurs.

The **digital retouching tools** that are truly unique to computers are those that allow the selection of different parts of the image. These selection tools provide techniques for selecting the pixels or areas of the rendered image that need to be retouched. The most common selection tools provided by retouching software are those that let the user enclose the selected area with a tool like a marquee or a freeform lasso. The more sophisticated selection tools allow the selection of image areas based on their pixel values. This method of selection works on contiguous pixels as well as pixels scattered throughout the image. All the pixels in an image within a specific color range can be easily manipulated or replaced with this selection method.

Editing the Tonal Range

One of the most useful tools provided by many image manipulation programs is the histogram. The histogram is a graph that shows the distribution of light, middle, and dark values in an image. Using a **histogram editor** makes it possible to modify with extreme accuracy the tonal range of an image, which defines many of the characteristics that give images their distinctive character. **Tonal range** includes the distribution of values throughout the grayscale and the relation between the highlights, mid-tones, and the shadows, the brightness and contrast levels, and the color balance of images.

The histograms in Fig. 12.1.7 show an uneven distribution of pixel values across the tonal range represented by the width of the horizontal line. Each of the vertical lines represents the number of pixels in the image at each of the tonal values between black and white. The higher lines represent the most number of pixels at that tone of gray or particular color. The three triangles below the tonal range represent (from left to right) the shadow editor, the mid-tone editor, and the highlight editor. Their normal values are 0, 1, and 255 respectively. These markers are used to redistribute the pixel values across the tonal range. By sliding any or all of the editors to the right, for example, the darker values are given more prominence in the tonal range. Moving just the **shadow** editor to the right relocates the position of the pure black to a higher position in the tonal range (from 0 to 31), therefore increasing the proportion of

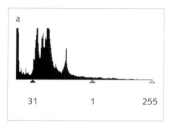

a

31　　　　1　　　　255

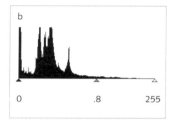

b

0　　　　.8　　　　255

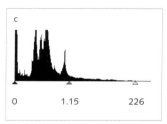

c

0　　　　1.15　　　　226

dark values in the image (Fig. 12.2.1a). Moving the **mid-tone** editor to the right expands the presence of the dark values within the tonal range (Fig. 12.2.1b). Moving both the **highlight** editor and the mid-tone editor to the left, for example, increases the range of the light values in the image (Fig. 12.2.1c).

Using a histogram to effectively edit the tonal range of an image requires practice. A more straightforward method for editing the tonal range of an image is based on using simpler controls for **brightness** and **contrast**. These controls are often in the form of sliders, parametric curves, or fields that accept numerical values typed directly on the keyboard.

12.2.1 A histogram editor can be used to redistribute the color values in an image.

Digital Filters

Digital filters are not used during the actual rendering process. Digital filters are applied to the two-dimensional images of three-dimensional scenes after the scenes have been rendered. Like their photographic relatives, digital filters modify the appearance of an image, but are able to change many more attributes and with much more precision than it is possible to change with photographic filters. Digital filters can be applied selectively to all of the image or only some areas. This capability turns digital filters into extraordinary retouching tools. Digital filters cover a wide range of special effects ranging from a simple blurring filter to a compound filter that adds lens flare and motion blur.

Digital filters work by submitting single pixels in the image or groups of them to a series of mathematical operations. Each type of filter is based on a unique combination of mathematical operations that process the numerical values of pixels, both independently and in relation to the neighboring pixels. The matrix

12.2.2 In this example of custom filters applied to the image in Fig. 5.6.1, the cel in the center of the 5 x 5 matrix contains the value that is to be used in the mathematical operation applied to the brightness of the pixel being evaluated. The cels adjacent to the center cel represent the pixels immediately surrounding the pixel being evaluated. The outer cels represent a second group of pixels that are a pixel away from the pixel being evaluated. The values used in each of the filtering variations are shown next to each image.

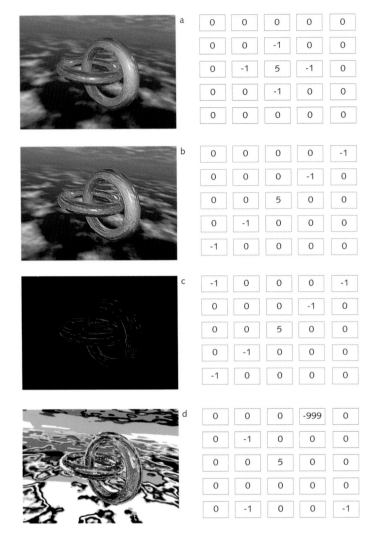

a

0	0	0	0	0
0	0	-1	0	0
0	-1	5	-1	0
0	0	-1	0	0
0	0	0	0	0

b

0	0	0	0	-1
0	0	0	-1	0
0	0	5	0	0
0	-1	0	0	0
-1	0	0	0	0

c

-1	0	0	0	-1
0	0	0	-1	0
0	0	5	0	0
0	-1	0	0	0
-1	0	0	0	0

d

0	0	0	-999	0
0	-1	0	0	0
0	0	5	0	0
0	0	0	0	0
0	-1	0	0	-1

and values of a **custom filter** that convolutes, or "twists," the brightness of the pixels in the image are illustrated in Fig. 12.2.2.

Sharpening filters are commonly used to increase the contrast of adjacent pixels in areas of an image that may be blurred, for example, due to the lack of lighting during the rendering process. Sharpening filters can also be used to bring out more detail in surfaces that have been texture mapped or in images that have been resampled to a higher resolution. These filters use a variety of sharpening techniques that increase contrast based, for example, on differences of color or brightness, or only where edges of shapes are found. Even though sharpening filters are applied to every pixel of the selected image area in some cases a **filter radius** is specified to determine the size of the filter as it looks for edges and determines how much sharpening should be applied (Fig. 12.2.3).

    Blurring filters can be used to soften the areas of rendered images where too much contrast between adjacent pixels create jagged edges or **texture noise**. Blurring usually works by bringing the intensity or color values of adjacent pixels closer to one another (Fig. 12.2.4). On occasions, blurring filters are used as an antialiasing retouching tool. Blurring filters can also soften the sharp edges of polygonal renderings, and the edges of masks. This technique is very effective for eliminating the jagged edges and color aliasing that happen during compositing when the mask is too sharp and displays jagged edges.

    A couple of additional filters that can be quite functional include the edge detection filters, and the NTSC (National Television Standards Commission) and field de-interlacing filters. **Edge detection filters** identify the edges of a shape, isolate them, and even trace a contour around them. When combined with selection tools both of these techniques are useful for creating the masks used in the compositing of images. Edge detection filters create tight masks quickly and avoid the repetitive manual work that is required to create masks otherwise (Fig. 12.2.5). An **NTSC color filter** clips the colors in an RGB image that are beyond the chromatic range of the NTSC video signal. NTSC color filters are extremely useful in maintaining the quality of color, and in making sure that colors are not too "hot" for the video standard (Fig. 12.2.6). **De-interlacing filters** can be used in conjunction with NTSC filters to improve the quality of video images displayed on RGB monitors (Fig. 12.2.7). (For more details on NTSC read Chapter 13.)

    In addition to the basic digital filters, there are dozens of striking visual effects that can be achieved by filtering an image. A select group of these filters helps to fine tune and refine renderings of three-dimensional scenes. But the majority of filters have such an overwhelming effect on the image that they are better suited to aid in the creation of special effects that visibly alter the original renderings or to prepare the two-dimensional images that are used as image maps. When used appropriately, even the filters that distort the image can create startling effects like bold changes in color, sensuous undulations and ripplings, delicate embossing and contouring, tingling textures, and faceted brushstrokes (Fig. 12.2.8).

12.3 Image Compositing and Blending

Image compositing consists of combining two or more different images into one in such a way that an illusion of time and space

12.2.3 A sharpening filter applied to an image.

12.2.4 A blurring filter applied to an image.

12.2.5 The edges of a rendered image were traced with an edge tracing filter to extract a two-dimensional contour.

a

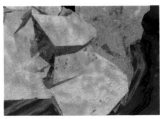

b

12.2.6 Before (a) and after (b) an NTSC filter was applied to the image in order to remove the RGB colors that are beyond the chromatic range of NTSC video. The histograms for the colors red and green show (in the brighter colors) the hues that were clipped by the filter.

is created: it seems that all the images happened at the same time and place and were recorded together. When created with traditional tools—such as scissors, glue and paper—image compositing results in a **collage**, which is an assembly or composition of image fragments or materials from different sources. In the film industry image compositing is also known as **matting** because of the masks, or mattes, used in the compositing process.

The purpose of image compositing is usually to save expensive production costs or to simulate something that is physically impossible to create in our reality—for example, a family having a picnic on the surface of Saturn while their chauffer drives their spaceship through the rings around the planet.

The process of compositing images from different sources into a single visually coherent image can be performed on both still and moving images. Still composites are often called collages, while moving composites result in dynamic composites or transition effects. Combining several shots from different sources into a single still or sequence is at the heart of all special visual effects, and also of many avant-garde artistic movements—such as Surrealism—that seek to subvert our notions of reality. Images are usually composited with masks (described earlier in this chapter), but when images are composited without masks the process is called image blending.

Compositing With Masks

A mask used in the compositing process consists of a monochromatic image that protects portions of another image being composited. As described earlier in this chapter, masks are like stencils: its solid areas protect the surface being masked, and its perforated areas expose the surface being masked. In many instances the mask or masks used in the compositing process are kept in the alpha channel, which is independent from each of the red, green, and blue channels that make up an RGB color image (Fig. 12.3.1).

Compositing with masks allows select portions of images to be composited as **foreground elements** in front of a **background**, which can also be composed of multiple images. Figure 12.3.2 illustrates the compositing of a foreground image with a background. The compositing is done using all the possible combinations of masks derived from the simple shapes in the foreground (inside and outside) and the background (top and bottom).

Image compositing with masks allows us to isolate and consolidate seamlessly multiple images (Figs. 12.3.3 and 12.3.4). Image compositing also facilitates the rendering of complex three-dimensional scenes in separate parts or layers. Environments that are too large can be rendered in parts, and the resulting images can be assembled back together in two-dimensions with image compositing.

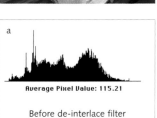

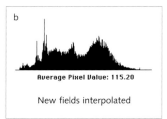

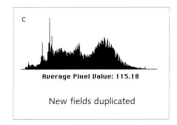

a	b	c
Average Pixel Value: 115.21	Average Pixel Value: 115.20	Average Pixel Value: 115.18
Before de-interlace filter	New fields interpolated	New fields duplicated

The idea of compositing foreground elements over a background is also a staple concept in traditional keyframe animation: motion is simulated with two-dimensional foreground shapes that move over a background. The foreground shapes can be, for example, drawings of cartoon characters, letterforms, or scanned photographs. The backgrounds may be painted or photographic images. The image compositing in this instance is sometimes done "in the camera," by placing the foreground elements on a cel over the background, or with masks and multiple exposures.

12.2.7 The histogram detail of the original image (a) can be compared with the histograms of images processed with a de-interlace filter. One histogram shows the result of new fields created—to replace those that were removed—by interpolation (b). The other histogram shows the result of new fields created by duplication (c).

Compositing Without Masks

It is also possible to digitally composite images from multiple sources without using masks; in such cases the image compositing process is usually referred to as **image blending**. With this process multiple images can simply be blended, and the result looks like a collection of transluscent, or ghosted, images. Blending can also be controlled with a many combinations of operators such as addition, difference, multiplication and difference (Fig. 12.3.5).

Two-Dimensional Morphing

Morphing is based on two-dimensional interpolation techniques that can be applied to renderings of three-dimensional scenes. Two-dimensional morphing is different from the three-dimensional interpolation techniques—sometimes also called morphing techniques—that blend the three-dimensional shape of objects in a simulated scene. **Two-dimensional morphing** is a special type of image blending that interpolates the values of pixels.

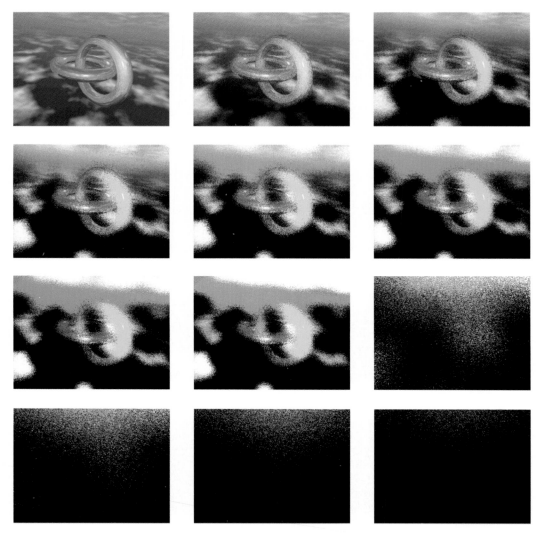

12.2.8 This sequence of images was created by applying the same filter to the initial image and to each of the subsequent images.

This interpolation is based not only on the color value of pixels but also controlled by a grid that helps to match and interpolate the shapes of the two images or sequences being morphed (Fig. 12.3.6). The control grid is placed on the two images to be morphed or on two keyframes of the sequence to be morphed. The grid is adjusted in each of the images so that the points on the grid correspond to the areas that have to be morphed. The grid points control the color interpolation of the pixels as well as the spatial interpolation that is necessary for a pixel in the first image to be moved to the XY location of the corresponding pixel in the second image.

Traditional Matting Techniques

Before computers, matting and compositing were primarily done with the **optical printer**, a camera that photographs film projected onto the camera by a projector mounted in front of it. The optical printer was developed in the early 1940s, and it transformed the way special effects in movies were created for decades. The optical printer can duplicate an entire film onto a new roll, and it can also be used for compositing, slowing or reversing the motion, reshooting through anamorphic lenses, balancing the contrast and the color values, zooming, panning, and creating transition effects. Today the optical printer is still used in conjunction with digital and high-resolution video technology, but it has been largely replaced by digital compositing, now the primary form of dynamic compositing.

The technique of **matte painting** was developed in the 1920s by making detailed paintings on glass but leaving some areas empty so that the live action can be matted, or inserted, there. This is the simplest kind of matting and it is called a **stationary matte.** Initially the partially painted glass was placed in front of the camera, far enough away that both the painting and the live action could be seen through the unpainted areas in the glass, and recorded together. As this technique developed, the clear areas through which the camera photographed the background action were painted black instead of being left transparent. This way it became possible to add the live action later by rewinding the film and making a double exposure. This innovation made possible the matting of figures in the foreground of the scene.

A **travelling matte** is a more complex type of matting. In this case, the blocked areas change every frame in exact synchronization with the foreground image action. There are several methods in use today for producing a travelling matte, including blue screen, rotoscoping, and computer-generation.

With the **blue screen** method the actor or model to be matted over a background is positioned in between the camera and a blue screen. Since the background is of a uniform blue color, it is easy to isolate it from the rest of the colors in the scene and eliminate it from the negative. The blue background can also be made black by using color filtering and color correction techniques. Blue screen results in a monochromatic matte composed of a flat background and the flat silhouettes of foreground objects or actors. This matte is used to composite, or combine, the color image of the background and the color image of the foreground. The blue screen matting method is still used extensively in the production of special effects, especially those that incorporate flying figures.

Rotoscoping is an animation technique that combines ani-

12.3.1 An alpha channel contains a black and white image that can be used as a stencil to mask some areas of the layers being composited with other images.

mated images with live action. The rotoscoping technique can be used to create masks by tracing portions of still frames of a live action scene. Those tracings can be used as masks with which three-dimensional objects can be laid over a live action sequence.

Rear and front projection are two compositing techniques extensively used in special effects that do not involve the creation of a mask or matte. The actors or foreground objects act themselves as masks. In both rear and front projection the matting is achieved by recording the actors or objects to be matted over live projections of the background. In **rear projection**, a translucent screen behind the actor or model is used to project previously shot material. While the actor acts or the model is moved the scene is photographed by a camera situated in front of the action. This simple trick was devised in the early 1930s and it is a common technique still used in the filming of dialogues between actors inside mock-up cars. Street scenes are rear-projected while the fake car is moved to simulate the vibration produced by motion. When color photography became the standard of the motion picture industry, rear projection posed many technical problems. This was because the large amounts of light that were needed to illuminate the scene bright enough for the slow color film of the time also washed out the images projected on the rear translucent screen behind the live action. So front projection was developed, and in 1968 it was used with excellent results in the milestone film *2001: A Space Odyssey* to composite the image of a human actor in an ape costume with images of real apes shot elsewhere.

Front projection is based on a projector that is aligned at a 90 degree angle with the camera and a half-silvered mirror aligned at a 45 degree angle in relation to the camera and the projector. A front projection screen made of a highly reflective material is placed in front of the camera, and the actor or model is positioned in between the screen and the camera. The image is projected on the half-silvered mirror positioned at a 45 degree angle, which sends it to the screen. Ninety-five percent of the image bounces back from the reflective screen, passes through the two-way mirror, and goes directly to the camera.

12.4 Image Sequencing

A great deal of a story narrated with images is actually told by the order and timing in which sequences of images are presented to the audience. The arrangement and composition of moving images is called **image sequencing** or **image editing**. The stage of image sequencing in any computer animation project is an important moment in the production process for two reasons. It is when ideas presented in the original storyboard can be finalized in a faithful and flawless way. Image sequencing is also

12.3.2 (opposite page) Two original images were composited using eight different masks. The background is a photograph of the tropical rain forest, and the foreground is a synthetic rock.

BACKGROUND   FOREGROUND   MASK   COMPOSITE

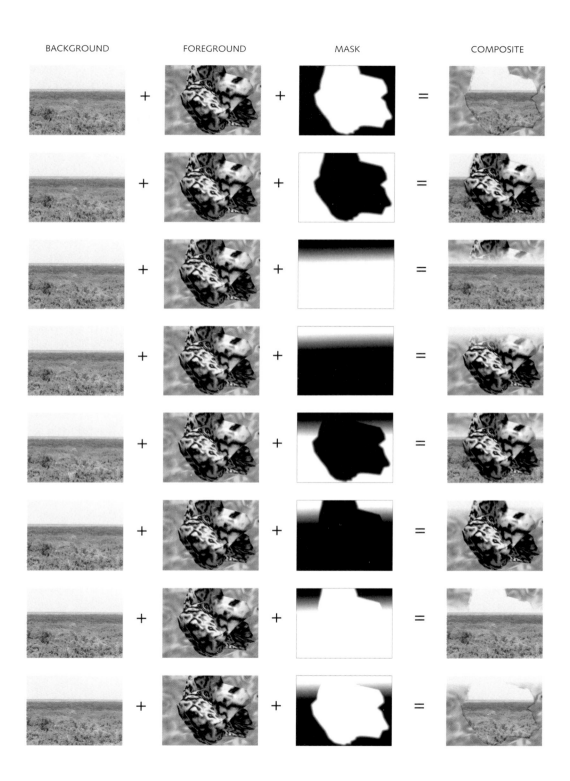

the moment in the creative process when ideas can be fine tuned to make the project more expressive or to conform to unexpected changes, such as a shorter or a longer running time.

In most computer animation productions, the image sequencing process is usually not done by the individual or production team that produced the computer animation in the first place. The final sequencing of images—and their subsequent output onto film, video, or photographic media—is a specialized process that involves specialized techniques and skills. This is especially true when the image sequencing is done with nondigital film or video production techniques. But increasingly, as more of the final image sequencing process migrates to the digital realm, it is common for those involved in producing the computer animation to also be involved in some or all of the image sequencing.

The most common reason for computer animators to get involved with image sequencing is to create an animatic or a rough cut of the project. An **animatic** is a preliminary version of a computer animation and is used to visualize how the final project may look. Animatics are based on preliminary visual material such as wireframe or low-resolution motion tests. None of the special effects in an animatic is meant to be final, and often they are implemented with techniques that are cruder and less expensive than the techniques that are actually planned for the finished project. Simple hand drawn sketches and still photographs are common replacements for complex dynamic effects

12.3.3 Another example of compositing live images (with masks) with renderings of virtual environments. (From the music video *Agolo* by Angelique Kidjo. Courtesy of Telecreateurs, Medialab Paris, Phonogram, Michel Meyer, and ZAP-DAN.)

when these are presented in the form of an animatic. In more than one way, animatics happen earlier in the production process than motion tests because most animatics are not concerned with the same level of motion detail that must be included in a motion test. For example, the motion of an animated character in an animatic may be jerky and only insinuated, while the same motion in a motion test must be as close as possible to the final motion. Animatics are like motion sketches while motion tests contain the actual action that has already been laid out and is in the process of being refined. Animatics are commonly shown to a client or an executive producer before the final production actually starts. In today's production environment, animatics are usually assembled from digital flipbooks and simple live-action sequences that are composited digitally. It is partly for that reason that animatics are increasingly produced in-house at the same place where computer animation is created; both happen in a digital format.

Unlike an animatic, a **rough cut** of a computer animation usually contains the finished renderings and final motion. However, the final arrangement of the sequences presented in a rough cut is yet to be locked, and the transitions between sequences are not implemented. Rough cuts are used to preview the rhythm and timing of the sequences already arranged in the order specified in the storyboard. Rough cuts often result in modifications to the original plan in terms of the duration or length

12.3.4 The four-minute music video of the Pet Shop Boys song, "Liberation," uses three-dimensional objects and photographs of the group members to create the feeling of a virtual reality excursion through an unusual landscape. (Image by Ian Bird and John Wake of 601FX, London. Courtesy of Wavefront Technologies, Inc.)

of a particular shot, scene, or sequence, or in terms of the order in which a series of shots, scenes, or sequences are presented.

Building a Sequence of Images

Most image sequencing software provides at least one pair of channels or **video tracks** for placing the different shots that are being edited as well as the transition effects that link them. The idea of using tracks to build a sequence of dynamic information comes from the pre-digital worlds of video and sound editing. Since its early days sound editing used multiple tracks of sound to composite simultaneous sounds—such as dialogue, background music, and sound effects—from a variety of sources. This layering of sound was possible because pre-digital sound editing systems had multiple tracks. The standard editing technique in pre-digital film and video, the **A/B roll editing** technique, is based on building a sequence by combining images arranged linearly in two different sources. Most image sequencing software today permits to sequence and combine images from two or more tracks, and in any order. This is commonly called **nonlinear editing**, and it makes reference to the fact that digital editing systems do not have to scan a linear medium (such as film or videotape) in order to find the source images.

Editing the different shots of a computer animation with digital sequencing software is usually done through a visual interface that allows the editor to arrange animated segments by manipulating icons. This is done by dragging the icons that represent the source images into the proper position on the track and dropping them into place. Their location and duration can be further adjusted by sliding them on the video track or time line. This common method of image sequencing is called **copy-and-paste editing** because images are copied from the source files and then pasted in the sequence being built. In addition to the tracks that hold the animation clips, there are tracks for the transition effects between shots placed on different video tracks, and tracks for sound information.

Visual Rhythm and Tempo

Two of the key principles of dynamic image composition include rhythm and tempo (a thorough examination of *all* the principles of dynamic image composition is beyond the scope of this book). In practical terms, the visual rhythm sets the pace of a computer animation, and tempo sets the speed. In the context of image sequencing, the **visual rhythm** of a sequence or an animated project is the visual pattern created by the frequency of transitions between shots. The rhythm of image sequences can be, for example, predictable or surprising, regular and soothing,

12.3.5 Three pairs of images are composited (without masks) with the Darker, Lighter, and Difference functions.

syncopated and lively, or irregular and chaotic. The tempo of image sequences ranges from slow to very fast. **Visual tempo**, or visual pace, is set primarily by the length of the individual shots in the sequence. The pace is fast when shots in a sequence stay only a couple of seconds on the screen, the pace is slow when shots are longer in length. When used in conjunction with the action contained in the animated images, rhythm and pace are effective ways of reinforcing the emotional content of a scene.

Transitions Between Shots

The techniques used to blend and composite moving images are called **transition effects**. Transitions between shots, as they are also called, can be simple or complex ranging, for example, from a straight cut to a cross-dissolve combined with a wipe.

Transition effects are useful from the visual point of view because they add visual interest and variation to a sequence. Transition effects can add funkiness and ornamentation. In addition the their immediate embellishment functions, transition effects are also an effective way to communicate the passage of time and to anticipate or play down the upcoming action. Transition effects, for example, break the continuity of one sequence or announce the beginning of a new one.

In addition to the information provided by the story line and the action shown by the camera, transition effects help to define the **temporal** and **spatial relation** between shots or scenes. A quick and simple transition effect, such as a straight cut, for example, reinforces the fact that the action shown in the

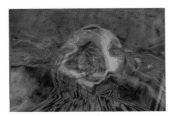

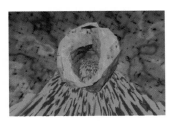

12.3.6 Morphing is a technique that blends two-dimensional still images into one another. The blending of the pixel color values is controlled by a grid that tags areas of the image to be blended with one another.

second shot of a sequence occurs right after the final shot and also in the same physical location. A long cross-dissolve, on the other hand, hints that two consecutive shots happen in different places and also that a fair amount of time takes place between them. Some of the most commonly used transition effects include the cut, fades, cross-dissolves, and wipes.

A **cut** is a plain and immediate change from one shot to another. A cut is the simplest transition and also the most common. Cuts are made by placing the last frame of a sequence, or tail, right next to the first frame, or head, of another sequence (Fig. 12.4.1). A cut gets its name from the fact that when editing film a transition of this type is achieved by actually cutting two strips of film and then splicing them together with transparent glue or tape. A **soft cut** is a combination of a cross-dissolve and a cut. This effect provides a cut that is slightly expanded in time, and softened, by the effect of the two shots quickly fading into each other.

In a **fade-out**, the end of a shot vanishes gradually and reveals a still frame of solid color. When a shot fades into a black still frame the effect is called **fade to black**. Fade-out transitions can also be made between shots so that the end of the first shot gradually vanishes into the early frames of the consecutive shot which suddenly pops into the sequence (Fig. 12.4.2). In a **fade-in** transition—which is the inverse of a fade-out—the first shot usually consists of a still black frame so that the second half of the transition seems to emerge from black. Sometimes a fade-in also starts with a first sequence of frames that is suddenly cut when the second sequence has fully appeared. Fades are defined by their length and by their intensity. Most fades are just a couple of seconds long, but a slow fade can last ten seconds or more and a quick fade lasts less than a dozen frames. The intensity of a fade is expressed in percentages. Fades usually go from zero percent to 100 percent or vice versa, so that when the images are fully faded they are either fully invisible or fully visible. But in some situations partial fades can create interesting effects—for example, a sequence of shots that start their fade-in with a 20 percent fade-in value and are cut when they reach 80 percent.

A **cross-dissolve** is a transition effect where two shots fade into each other, as the first shot fades out the second shot fades in (Fig. 12.1.9). Cross-dissolves are an effective way to give the audience a moment to pause and think about what they have just seen or what they are about to see. Cross-dissolves are effective links between two shots and can be used as adverbs in the visual grammar of computer animation. A cross-dissolve can say, for example, "and then," or "in the meantime," or "years later." Cross-dissolve transitions are effective ways to connect actions that happen in the distant past or in the future, or to present

12.4.1 A cut between two animated sequences.

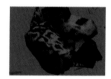

12.4.2 A fade-out transition.

12.4.3 A wipe transition.

actions that occur only in the imagination of a protagonist in parallel with the real action.

There are many variations of cross-dissolve transitions. The most common form of a cross-dissolve consists of a gradual and delicate simultaneous transition from one shot to another. The length and intensity of cross-dissolves is expressed—as it is in fades—in terms of frames and percentages respectively. A very short cross-dissolve is often called a soft cut and is barely perceptible, but it adds an accent of slowness or acceleration to the transition between two shots. Slow cross-dissolves create a ghostly effect where the objects and characters in the scene seem to be transparent. Blending and **layering moving images** is best achieved with cross-dissolves. A dream sequence, for example, where images overlap with one another and objects suddenly materialize or vanish is a classic example of using cross-dissolve transitions for layering images. A **dither cross-dissolve** uses a coarse pattern to fade the two shots into one another.

Wipes are transition effects where the basic idea is that the second shot displaces the first shot by sliding into the frame, dropping or spreading over it. There is a myriad variations of wipes and some are illustrated in Fig. 12.4.3. In the most common form of a wipe, called plainly a **wipe** or a side wipe, the second shot slides across the frame over the first shot. Wipes can also slide diagonally, along the vertical axis, radially, or using any geometric shape or edge as a template. Elaborate wipes include screen splits, spin wipes, interlaced wipes like venetian blinds, and page turns.

Review and Practice

Matching

_____ Soft cut

_____ Dither cross-dissolve

_____ Image layers

_____ NTSC color filters

_____ Cross-dissolve

_____ Histogram

_____ Color dithering

_____ Animatic

_____ Tempo

_____ Transition effects

_____ Resampling

_____ Masks

_____ Rough cut

_____ Parameter curves

_____ Sharpening filters

_____ Nonlinear editing

_____ Cut

_____ Rhythm

_____ Digital filters

_____ Transition effects

_____ Alpha channel

_____ Image sequencing

_____ Interpolation techniques

_____ Color look-up table

a. Contains a black and white image that masks or protects parts of one or several of the image layers.

b. Set primarily by the length of the shots in a sequence.

c. Protect portions of the image during the compositing process.

d. Apply mathematical operations to single pixels or groups of them in order to change their color value.

e. Made by placing the tail of a sequence right next to the head of another sequence.

f. Used to separately display each of the component or primary colors of an image in several color modes including RGB, CMYK, and HSL.

g. Uses a coarse pattern to fade a pair of shots into one another.

h. Graphs that represent and control different attributes of an image, such as brightness and color.

i. Commonly used to increase the contrast of adjacent pixels.

j. Contains the finished renderings and final motion in a computer animation, but the final arrangement of the sequences and the transitions are not implemented.

k. Term used to describe image sequencing systems that have instant access to the source images.

l. Used to create new pixel values by averaging the values of existing pixels in different ways.

m. Clip the RGB colors that are beyond the chromatic range of video.

n. Transition effect where two shots fade into each other.

o. Changing the spatial or color resolution of an image.

p. Techniques used to blend and composite moving images.

q. A preliminary version of a computer animation used to visualize how the final project may look.

r. The arrangement and composition of moving images.

s. Limited palette that represents a larger selection of colors.

t. Combination of a cut and a cross-dissolve.

u. Simulates shades of color with dot patterns.

v. Define the temporal and spatial relation between shots.

w. Graph of the distribution of the image pixels throughout the grayscale.

x. Sets the pace of a computer animation.

True/False

_____ a. Dream sequences are classic examples of using cross-dissolve transitions for layering images.

_____ b. Morphing is a technique that blends the color values of pixels, and also displaces their position based on a grid that tags areas of two images to be blended with one another.

_____ c. The compositing of images from different sources is made less efficient by the use of multiple layers.

_____ d. Pans are transition effects where the second shot displaces the first shot by sliding into the frame.

_____ e. An image with pixels that are evenly distributed throughout the grayscale has vertical lines all across the histogram.

_____ f. When images are sampled down the software averages the values of several pixels and discards some of the original information.

_____ g. In copy-and-paste editing, the images are copied from the sequence being built and then pasted in the source files.

_____ h. The attributes of an image change gradually if its parameter curve is redrawn with smooth curves.

_____ i. One digital retouching tool that is unique to computers selects different parts of the image based on their pixel values.

_____ j. Hand drawn sketches and still photographs are not common replacements for complex dynamic effects in an animatic.

_____ k. When mistakes are made in the modeling or rendering process it is never easier to retouch instead of modeling and rendering the scene again.

_____ l. Image manipulation techniques are used to modify the color, contrast, and brightness of computer-generated images.

_____ m. Radial wipes are effective to present actions that occurred in the distant past or the future.

_____ n. It is possible to increase the brightness of just a single image layer, and then merge all the layers again and view the composite results.

_____ o. Resampling based on linear interpolation techniques often creates defects like banding, aliased edges, or loss of detail.

_____ p. The rhythm of an animated sequence is the visual pattern created by the frequency of transitions between shots.

_____ q. An image with only dark and light values but no midtones has vertical lines on the extremes of the histogram but not in its center.

_____ r. A mask in the alpha channel is like a stencil with a perforated design that allows the paint to reach the surface underneath the perforated areas.

_____ s. Digital post processing filters are applied as images are rendered.

_____ t. Some of the digital retouching techniques are inspired by the tools of painters and photographers.

_____ u. When resampling a file if the size (the amount of space it takes to store it) is maintained constant then the physical image dimensions (height and width) of the file change.

_____ v. A cut is a plain and immediate change from one shot to another.

Answers Matching: a. Alpha channel, b. Tempo, c. Masks, d. Digital filters, e. Cut, f. Image layers, g. Dither cross-dissolve, h. Parameter curves, i. Sharpening filters, j. Rough cut, k. Nonlinear editing, l. Interpolation techniques, m. NTSC color filters, n. Cross-dissolve, o. Resampling, p. Transition effects, q. Animatic, r. Image sequencing, s. Color look-up table, t. Soft cut, u. Color dithering, v. Transition effects, w. Histogram, x. Rhythm.

Answers True/False: a. True, b. True, c. False, d. True, e. True, f. True, g. False, h. True, i. True, j. False, k. True, l. False, m. False, n. True, o. True, p. True, q. True, r. True, s. False, t. True, u. True, v. True.

Key Terms

A/B roll editing
Alpha channel
Angular straight lines
Animatic
Background
Blue screen
Blurring filters
Brightness
Channels
Collages
Color dithering
Color look-up table
Color resolution
Contrast
Copy-and-paste editing
Cross-dissolve
Custom filter
Cut
Darkroom
De-interlacing filters
Digital filters
Digital retouching tools
Dither cross-dissolve
Edge detection filters
Fade to black
Fade-in
Fade-out
File size
Filter radius
Foreground elements
Front projection
Highlight
Histogram
Histogram editor
Image blending
Image dimensions
Image editing
Image layers
Image manipulation
Image sequencing

Indexed color
Interpolation techniques
Layering moving images
Mask
Matting
Matte painting
Mid-tone
Neighbor pixel interpolation
Nonlinear editing
NTSC color filter
Optical printer
Parameter curves
Photographic procedures
Pixels per inch
Rear projection
Resampling an image
Resampling the color resolution
Retouching
Rotoscoping
Rough cut
Shadow
Sharpening filters
Soft curves
Soft cut
Spatial relation
Stationary matte
Stencils
Straight diagonal line
Studio
System palette
Temporal relation
Texture noise
Tonal range
Traditional painting tools
Transition effects
Travelling Matte
Two-dimensional morphing
Video tracks
Visual rhythm
Visual tempo
Weighted interpolation
Wipe

CHAPTER 13

Output

Summary

This chapter presents the basic concepts required to output computer-generated images in a variety of media. The three types of image resolution—color, spatial, and temporal—are examined in detail. File formats are reviewed, as well as the most popular delivery media, including paper, film, video, and CD-ROM.

13.1 Basic Concepts of Digital Output

Each of the professions and industries where three-dimensional computer imaging is used today has different output requirements. This is due to the differences in the final product, and the different forms of final delivery and distribution of products in each of these areas. The output of three-dimensional imagery in many of the art and design areas that deal with two-dimensional creation, for example, occurs primarily in the form of paper printouts and film slides, or transparencies. These areas include, for example, illustration, photography, and graphic arts. The new areas of interactive visual creation that include interactive videogames and on-line information services, for example, require that images are delivered in a variety of digital file formats, often on magnetic or optical media. In some of the three-dimensional areas, including product design, sculpture, and architecture, the digital output includes both printouts for presentation purposes and digital files for computer-aided design and computer-aided manufacturing (CAD/CAM). In the four-dimensional, or time-based activities, including computer animation and location-based entertainment, delivery usually takes place in the form of video or film.

The digital output process starts when rendered images are taken out of the computer system with the **output peripherals**. These include an array of devices such as printers, pen plotters, recorders, and three-dimensional milling machines. Output peripherals are used for fixing the images created on the monitor onto other media that may include paper, film, video, and CD-ROM. This capture process is not automatic, it is based instead on a **translation of data**. This translation is made by software and electronic components of output peripherals called **digital-to-analog** converters or **DTAs**. The DTAs convert the digital information created with software back into continuous information. This process is just the inverse of scanning an image on paper that is to be used as a texture map or a background in a three-dimensional scene. In this case, the sensors in the input peripherals—called analog-to-digital converters—convert the continuous information contained in the image into digital information that can be manipulated by the program. DTAs convert the binary numbers that describe an image back into analog voltages that are subsequently converted into light, heat, or pressure by the imaging components of the output peripherals. The quality and sophistication of the digital-to-analog converters—their precision, definition and speed—often defines the quality of the final output as well as the cost of the output peripheral. High quality DTAs provide digital output with low noise, high image resolution, and a wide chromatic range.

13.2 Image Resolution

Image resolution can be defined as the amount of detail contained in an image or sequence of images. The resolution of an image is also called **image definition**, and it is related to many factors such as the quality of the input and output peripherals, the color depth of the computer system, the capabilities of the software that was used to create the image, and the quality of the output media. Having a good understanding of the basic issues of image resolution is fundamental in order to use three-dimensional computer imaging techniques to their fullest. There are three types of image resolution that are relevant to visual creators: spatial resolution, chromatic resolution, and temporal resolution.

Spatial Resolution

Computer-generated images are made of **pixels,** or picture elements, which are the little dots that we see when we get very close to the computer screen. **Spatial resolution** has to do with the total number of pixels in an image, and is defined by the relation between the dimensions of an image and the number of pixels in the image. Spatial resolution can be expressed in terms of pixels, dots, or lines per inch.

The number of pixels that exist in an **image file** is measured in **pixels per inch** or **ppi**. When rendering a three-dimensional scene, for example, it is necessary to indicate the

13.2.1 Four different spatial resolutions at the same 150 lpi halftone screen resolution: 300 ppi (a), 200 ppi (b), 150 ppi (c), and 100 ppi (d).

pixel resolution at which the image is to be rendered. The most general way to specify the absolute spatial resolution of a file is by using pixels per inch, even though this resolution contained in the image file may be displayed in different ways when using a variety of techniques and output peripherals, regardless of the resolution of the output peripheral used to print or display the image. The spatial resolution of image files ranges from a low of 100 ppi to a high of 4,000 ppi.

The spatial resolution of a specific input or output **peripheral device** can be measured in **dots per inch** or **dpi**. This unit of resolution is often related to the number of sensors in an input peripheral, or the number of imaging heads in an output peripheral. A medium resolution ranges from 300 to 600 dpi, and high resolution ranges from 1,000 dpi and up.

Lines per inch or **lpi** is another unit for measuring spatial resolutions. lpi is used almost exclusively in digital prepress or in desktop publishing for measuring the number of lines—or rows of dots—in **halftone screens**. These screens are used for printing an image with traditional graphic arts mechanical reproduction techniques. Halftone screens of 65 lpi, for example, are commonly used for newspaper image quality while 150 lpi halftone screens yield great image definition on high-quality coated paper. A simple formula that can help determine the pixel (ppi) resolution needed when preparing files for **halftone output** specifies that the ppi resolution should not exceed 2.5 times the target lpi resolution. For example, a resolution of 300 ppi would be adequate when using halftone screens of 100 lpi but not sufficient if 150 lpi screens were used (Fig. 13.2.1).

When the **dot resolution** of the output peripheral matches exactly the **pixel resolution** of an image file then we can see the contents of the file displayed in optimal fashion, but these cases are rare. Most often we work with files whose ppi resolution does not match the dpi resolution of an output peripheral. In those cases, we can use specialized software to **resample** the pixel resolution of the file and match it to the dot resolution of the output peripheral. We can also let the internal (ROM) software of the peripheral do the resampling for us. However, the results are generally better and more predictable when we do it.

Using pixels per inch as the unit to convey spatial resolution is convenient because oftentimes the resolution of the rendered images is different from the resolution of the peripherals used to output them. Images may be rendered at one resolution and displayed at another. For example, when an image is rendered in high resolution and then displayed in high or in low resolution, the high resolution image loses detail when displayed on a low resolution display, but it shows its true resolution when shown on a display with a higher resolution (Fig. 13.2.2). The fact that an image may look low resolution on a specific printout or monitor does not necessarily mean that the image is low resolution.

For example, a three-dimensional scene rendered at a resolution of 300 dpi, and horizontal and vertical dimensions of 3 x 2 in. has an absolute pixel size of 900 x 600 pixels. On a monitor with a resolution of 300 dpi, for example, there would be a 1:1 match so that each pixel in the file corresponds to a dot on the monitor. On a monitor with a resolution of 100 dpi the results would be different due to the 1:3 ratio, one dot for every 3 pixels. In cases such as this one, the discrepancy can be solved without resampling the file by keeping either the resolution or the dimensions constant. If the resolution is kept constant, then each pixel in the image file is assigned to one dot in the output peripheral. In this case, the resolution is untouched but the physical dimensions change. In the example of the 300 dpi 3 x 2 in. file the new dimensions at 100 dpi would be 9 x 6 in. If the dimensions are kept constant then every three pixels in the image file are assigned to one dot in the output peripheral. This leads to a significant loss of spatial resolution, but the dimensions remained untouched. The 300 dpi 3 x 2 in. file remains at the same size but with a lower resolution.

Color Resolution

The **color resolution** of an image is related to the amount of colors that may be contained in an image. Color, or chromatic, resolution is determined by the number of bitplanes used to create and display that image. A **bitplane** can be described as a grid where each cell in the bitplane stores a one-digit number. Since each cell on the grid is assigned to a **pixel**, or picture ele-

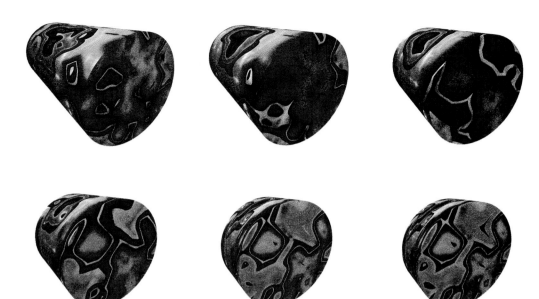

ment, on the computer screen, the numerical value is translated into the color that is displayed on the pixel controlled by that cell. Multiple bitplanes can be thought of as layers in the **graphics memory** or **bitmap**. It is the number of layers in a bitmap that determines the number of colors that each pixel on the screen may have.

A pixel in a bitmap with just one plane, for example, is capable of displaying only one of two colors: black or white. This is because each cell in a one-level bitmap grid can only store a one-digit number, in this case a zero or a one (Fig. 12.1.3). When a bitmap has more than one plane then the numbers in the corresponding cells of each plane are added—using the conventions of the binary numerical system—to make a longer value.

A bitmap with two planes is capable of displaying one of four possible colors—or values of gray—in each pixel (Fig. 12.1.3). This is because when we add the ones or zeros in the corresponding cells of each plane we end up with four possibilities: 00, 01, 10, and 11. In the binary numerical system, 00 equals our decimal 0. Binary 01 equals decimal 1, 10 equals 2, and 11 equals 3.

A bitmap with three planes is capable of displaying one of eight colors per pixel (Fig. 13.2.3). When we add the binary values (1 or 0) in the corresponding cells of each bitplane we end up with eight possible values expressed here, first in binary and then in decimal form.

13.2.2 This sequence shows the 300 dpi images from Fig. 8.6.8 output at the lower resolution of 72 dpi.

$$000 = 0$$
$$001 = 1$$
$$010 = 2$$
$$011 = 3$$
$$100 = 4$$
$$101 = 5$$
$$110 = 6$$
$$111 = 7$$

In the **binary system**, numerical values are read from right to left. The digits in the first (rightmost) column represent the units, and their decimal value can be found by multiplying them times the number one, which is the result of two to the power of zero (2^0). The digits in the second column are multiplied times two, which is the result of 2^1. The digits in the third column are multiplied times 2^2.

BINARY	$2^2 = 4$	$2^1 = 2$	$2^0 = 1$	
DECIMAL	x 1	x 1	x 0	
	4	+ 2	+ 0	= **6**

The rule is very simple: the more bitplanes in a bitmap, the more color may be displayed in an image. This simple rule can be summarized in the following formula:

$$2^{\text{(bitplanes)}} = \text{possible colors}$$

The maximum number of colors that may exist in a computer-generated image can be calculated by elevating the number two—the base number in the binary system—to the power of the number of bitplanes. Standard configurations of color resolution include 8-bit color with 256 colors, 16-bit color with 65,000 plus colors, and 24-bit color with 16 million plus colors. Here is a list of several possible configurations:

$$2^1 = 2 \text{ colors}$$
$$2^2 = 4 \text{ colors}$$
$$2^3 = 8 \text{ colors}$$
$$2^4 = 16 \text{ colors}$$
$$2^5 = 32 \text{ colors}$$
$$2^6 = 64 \text{ colors}$$
$$2^7 = 128 \text{ colors}$$
$$2^8 = 256 \text{ colors}$$
$$2^{10} = 1,024 \text{ colors}$$
$$2^{16} = 65,536 \text{ colors}$$
$$2^{20} = 1,048,576 \text{ colors}$$
$$2^{24} = 16,777,216 \text{ colors}$$
$$2^{32} = 4,214,967,296 \text{ colors}$$

In addition to the color resolution of an output peripheral, it is also important to consider its chromatic range, as well as the color conversion techniques used to convert color values from one color space to another. The **chromatic range** of any device defines the range of colors in the visible spectrum that the device is capable of reproducing. Not all media and techniques for creating color are capable of creating exactly the same colors. The CIE chromaticity diagram (Fig. 5.2.1) is a useful tool for visualizing the chromatic ranges of different media. This diagram can be used to bridge the different ranges or gamuts of color that are obtained when different color systems are used. It can also be used to narrow the amount of color that gets lost when an image file is output. Knowing which colors overlap across different media helps to work around the physical limitations of color reproduction.

The fact that many of the colors created with RGB computer monitors are too bright and saturated for display on standard television sets is an example that illustrates a limitation created by the different chromatic ranges of different media. Many of these RGB colors have to be clipped before the image is transferred to videotape, otherwise these saturated colors would fall outside the chromatic range of video. Clipping the colors that fall outside a chromatic range does not mean that the colors are removed altogether, instead they are replaced with a color that is within the chromatic range and that resembles it the most. This **color clipping** is useful for avoiding distortions such as color bleeding in the final video recording. **Color bleeding** is the streaking and overflowing of colors that occurs on a television set when the colors in the video signal are too saturated. (To create color bleeding turn the saturation controls on your television set all the way up.)

It is often necessary to **convert colors** from one color space to another, for example from the RGB color space to CMYK, as we convert an image rendered and retouched in the RGB color space into a **CMYK four-color separation** suitable for reproduction in a magazine. Each of the colors in an image is separated into its CMYK components because the printing presses used in mechanical reproduction reproduce color images by printing each of the CMYK layers with a different plate and ink (Fig. 12.1.8). In most cases, this color conversion and separation is done automatically by the computer software, and the quality of this conversion varies from program to program. In general, this conversion takes into account many production details—such as type of paper, ink, and printing press characteristics—related to the final printing of an image with a CMYK medium. The color conversion software will use default values if those details are unknown at the time of conversion.

It is important to make sure that the RGB monitor connect-

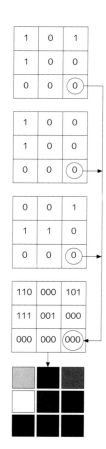

13.2.3 A three-level bitmap can display eight colors. The values of each of the bitplanes are added to determine the final value of the pixels.

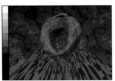

13.2.4 The gamma factor of an RGB monitor is used to calibrate the image on the display according to what the final output will be. The values of 1.0, 1.4, 1.8, and 2.2 are illustrated here.

ed to the computer system being used is properly calibrated so that the colors displayed on the screen are as close as possible to the color values contained in the image file. For optimum color resolution it is always best to get involved in the color balancing and correction, or at least enlist the help of a color experienced user. But in any event the gamma factor of an RGB monitor should be checked. The **gamma factor** is one of many useful aids in making sure that the image displayed on an RGB monitor looks its best. The gamma factor is a number used to scale the brightness of the image according to the characteristics of the final output media. When the gamma factor has a value of one, for example, the numerical values of RGB color sent by the computer are used as they are to determine the voltages used by the RGB color guns located inside the monitor to create color. When the gamma factor has a value higher than one, the RGB numerical values are scaled by that number before they are applied to the voltages that control the colors emitted by the monitor (Fig. 13.2.4). A typical value used for video output, for example, is 2.2.

Temporal Resolution

Temporal resolution is related to the number of still images contained in a sequence of images displayed over time. Temporal resolution is almost always measured in terms of the number of images displayed within a specific amount of time, usually a second. Images in a sequence are often called **frames** because of the still frames contained in a strip of photographic film. A common unit for measuring temporal resolution is called **frames per second** or **fps**.

Each output media has a typical temporal resolution. Sequences displayed on NTSC video for example—the standard used in the U.S.A., Japan, and most of Latin America—have a rate of 30 fps. (NTSC is the acronym for the National Television Standards Commission.) On 35 mm film that rate is 24 fps. Temporal resolution in multimedia projects can range from 8 fps to 60 fps depending on the nature of the sequence, and on the playback power of the computer system.

13.3 File Formats for Image Output

Files that contain images are called **picture files** or image files. Computer imaging programs can save and retrieve images in a variety of **file formats**. Some of these formats are native to a specific program. This means that the files can only be retrieved

ADVANCED ANIMATION TECHNIQUES

by the program that was used to create them, and not by any other program. One solution to the lack of compatibility between **native file formats** consists of saving the visual information in **universal** or **portable image file formats**. Some of these portable file formats include PICT, TIFF and QuickTime, and are described below.

In those few cases when the images cannot be saved in a portable format, it is possible to convert one native file format into the native file format of another program. This alternative solution to the file incompatibility problem is called **file format conversion**, and it is a standard feature in many computer imaging programs in the form of **import** and **export tools**. These tools translate image data files from and into other native or universal file formats. The results obtained with different file conversion utilities vary widely. Some file conversions are almost flawless while others rarely produce desirable results. There is no easy way to know if a file conversion program will work or not; each has to be tried and evaluated. All file format conversions are directed by so-called **import** and **export filters**, which are tables that instruct the conversion utility how to translate each and all of the elements encountered in the original file.

There are several file formats for both still and moving images. Each of these file formats has been designed with a specific goal in mind and, therefore, is better suited for a particular task. There are always trade-offs between the characteristics of a file, for example, a file format that preserves the fine detail in the image may also take up a lot of storage space (Fig. 13.3.1).

It is common in everyday productions to integrate images in different file formats into one single document. It is also quite common to save an image in a variety of file formats as the image is created with different programs, or transferred between different computer platforms through a network. The image in Fig. 5.6.1, for example, was created on a Silicon Graphics computer and saved in the SGI file format, sent through an Ethernet network, retouched on an Apple Macintosh computer, and saved as a TGA file, then sent back through the network, and finally imaged with a film recorder driven by a PC-compatible computer.

Format	Size
EPS	2,460 kb (ASCII format, without preview)
EPS	1,240 kb (binary format, with an 8-bit color preview)
EPS	1,220 kb (binary format, without preview)
TGA	1,220 kb (32-bit color)
TGA	920 kb (24-bit color)
TIFF	920 kb (without LZW compression)
PICT	560 kb (32-bit color)
JPEG	560 kb (without compression)
Photoshop	560 kb (native, v. 2.5)
TIFF	440 kb (with LZW compression)
PICT	380 kb (16-bit color)
JPEG	150 kb (maximum quality)
GIF	115 kb (8-bit color)
JPEG	110 kb (high quality)
JPEG	60 kb (medium quality)
JPEG	40 kb (low quality)

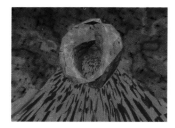

13.3.1 This chart compares the amount of storage required by the same image in a variety of file formats.

Still Images

Some of the most popular portable file formats for saving two-dimensional visual information include: PICT, TIFF, EPS, TGA,

```
%!PS-Adobe-3.0 EPSF-3.0
%%Title: Sims-1.eps
%%BoundingBox: 0 0 200 200
%%EndComments

200 200 scale
.001 setlinewidth
1.5 setmiterlimit
/quad { setgray newpath moveto lineto lineto lineto closepath
  gsave fill grestore .0 setgray stroke } def

0.4531 0.1716 0.4111 0.0544 0.6423 0.1391 0.6648 0.2546 1 quad
0.6648 0.2546 0.6423 0.1391 0.6456 0.1343 0.6677 0.2502 0.865 quad
0.6997 0.5376 0.7810 0.5643 0.8535 0.9500 0.7641 0.8703 1 quad
0.7073 0.5358 0.7898 0.5622 0.7810 0.5643 0.6997 0.5376 1 quad
0.6456 0.1343 0.6423 0.1391 0.4111 0.0544 0.4145 0.0500 1 quad
0.7392 0.3909 0.6664 0.4162 0.6398 0.2082 0.7161 0.1902 0.975 quad
0.5966 0.2084 0.6724 0.1909 0.7161 0.1902 0.6398 0.2082 1 quad
0.5966 0.2084 0.6398 0.2082 0.6664 0.4162 0.6240 0.4105 1 quad
0.6061 0.4571 0.6747 0.3831 0.6606 0.4622 0.5828 0.5444 1 quad
0.6747 0.3831 0.7774 0.4697 0.7777 0.5593 0.6606 0.4622 0.887 quad
0.7810 0.5643 0.7898 0.5622 0.8620 0.9474 0.8535 0.9500 1 quad
0.6985 0.6377 0.5828 0.5444 0.6606 0.4622 0.7777 0.5593 1 quad
0.6347 0.5379 0.5792 0.5772 0.3892 0.6422 0.4382 0.6031 0.956 quad
0.4382 0.6031 0.4076 0.5317 0.6053 0.4730 0.6347 0.5379 1 quad
0.4382 0.6031 0.3892 0.6422 0.3608 0.5746 0.4076 0.5317 1 quad
0.1447 0.3282 0.2239 0.2544 0.4006 0.5145 0.3501 0.6173 0.831 quad
0.1447 0.3282 0.1380 0.3320 0.2179 0.2579 0.2239 0.2544 1 quad
0.3501 0.6173 0.3436 0.6204 0.1380 0.3320 0.1447 0.3282 1 quad
showpage

%%EndDocument
```

13.3.2 Listing of the EPS program that generated the lower left image in Fig. 11.4.6.

JPEG, and GIF. There are many other portable file formats for saving still images, but an exhaustive listing is beyond the scope of this book. In addition to the dozens of universal file formats, there are also many native file formats that can only be read by the software that created them.

It is important to realize that these universal file formats are used to save single still images and also **series of still images**. The majority of computer animations that are eventually recorded on film or videotape are rendered as series of still frames because each frame has to be recorded, one at a time, on film or videotape.

The **PICT** file format, from the word picture, is a very versatile format used by many drawing and photo-retouching programs. PICT is a popular file format because it offers good image quality with a relatively small file size. The PICT file format is very popular in multimedia applications because of its compact size and compatibility across computer platforms. Series of numbered PICT files are commonly used to save the still frames in a computer animation sequence. The numbering of sequential files is usually done automatically by the animation program that creates them. One convention for numbering files in a sequence consists of adding an extension to the filename, for example, Dance.0001 for the first frame, Dance.0010 for the tenth frame, and so on.

The **TIFF** file format, from Tagged Image File Format, is popular with prepress and publishing software, and very useful when the rendered image has to be reproduced in a publication. The TIFF format preserves detailed grayscale information that is fundamental for generating the high-quality halftones (grids of dots of varying size) used in the graphic arts. TIFF files tend to be large in size so many applications usually provide options or

ADVANCED ANIMATION TECHNIQUES

utilities for automatically compressing and expanding them.

The **EPS** file format, or Encapsulated PostScript, is also popular in prepress applications, and can be quite useful and effective when high-quality line wireframe drawings are needed. Information saved in the EPS file format is always imaged at the best resolution possible in EPS-compatible output peripherals because EPS is a **device-independent file format**. EPS files usually require significant amounts of memory for storage and transfer. EPS files are almost identical to PostScript files except for the **header information** that is found at the beginning of EPS files. This header information is inserted automatically by the application that generates the EPS file, and it includes data that is needed in order to import the file into another application program and output it properly (Fig. 13.3.2).

The **TGA** file format is popular with video-oriented software because it saves the files in a format that is quite convenient for transferring the digital data into the video environment. TGA is short for TARGA, the name of the family of graphics boards products developed in the early 1980s that pioneered video input and output with microcomputers. The TGA file format is not as dominant as it used to be, but it is still widely used.

The **JPEG** file format, from Joint Photographic Experts Group, is one of the most popular formats that offers image compression. This is useful when large amounts of data have to be archived or transmitted over computer networks. JPEG works by removing data that is redundant or data whose removal is almost imperceptible to the human eye. One of the main strengths of the JPEG format lies in the fact that it provides great compression and decompression speed as well as huge savings in file size (Fig. 13.3.3). The JPEG file format uses a **lossy compression** technique because it discards image information as it compresses the file. For this reason, the settings of the JPEG compression should be chosen with care, keeping in mind that increasing the compression decreases the image quality and vice versa. A copy of the original uncompressed file should always be archived in case the compression settings applied to the file were too extreme and the image becomes illegible.

In addition to JPEG, there are other compression techniques that do not discard the original information. These methods are called **lossless compressions** because they retain the original information as they compress a file. In spite of their preservation of information some lossless techniques yield expanded files that are slightly different from the original file.

The **GIF** file format, from Graphics Interchange Format, is popular for compressing and storing images that are distributed through on-line services—in fact, GIF was developed by the Compuserve on-line service. This file format is also compact enough to facilitate the uploading and downloading of still

13.3.3 JPEG compression options (JPEG none is 556 kb, maximum is 149 kb, high is 105 kb, medium is 61 kb, and low is 39 kb). The image degradation can be clearly appreciated in the enlarged details.

images over e-mail and Internet-based bulletin boards and on-line services. GIF is based on an 8-bit color standard that allows for a maximum of 256 colors, usually chosen from a customized color look-up table. GIF also employs a lossless compression technique that requires a decompression utility before the file can be displayed on the receiving end.

Sequences of Moving Images

Some of the most popular file formats for saving sequences of two-dimensional images in a **self-contained format** include: PICS, QuickTime, and MPEG. These file formats are commonly used when the animated sequence is played back directly from a fast peripheral storage of the computer—as is the case with many interactive projects—or through computer networks. But sequences of images that are not played directly on the computer monitor, especially those destined to be recorded on film or videotape, are commonly saved in some of the same file formats used to save still images—mostly PICT and JPEG. In these cases, each individual sequential frame is assigned a number that reflects its place in the sequence.

The **PICS** file format derives its name from the word pictures and is very convenient when a series of low resolution images is required. The PICS file format saves information in a compact way. One drawback of using the PICS file format is that it lacks built-in compression controls, and that it is somewhat cumbersome to edit long sequences of images saved in this format. A very common alternative, or complement, to the PICS file format is a series of numbered PICT files that can be read by many programs and displayed in sequence as if they were a single PICS file.

The **QuickTime** file format stores both visual data and audio in one or several tracks. In most cases, a QuickTime file is displayed within a window that has a **playback controller,** such as those available in videotape players (Fig. 13.3.4). QuickTime is a versatile format that facilitates saving computer animation files at different spatial resolutions, and at different window sizes, for example, ranging from a small 160 x 120 pixels to a full-screen 640 x 480 pixels. QuickTime also plays the files back at different temporal resolutions, for example 10 frames per second (fps) or 30 fps.

The QuickTime file format provides a variety of compression options for video or animated images. As with other compressed file formats, the quality and effectiveness of a QuickTime file is based on the relation between the compression ratio, the playback speed, and the image fidelity. The QuickTime file format provides five compression options. One of them is especially designed to compress computer animation, another

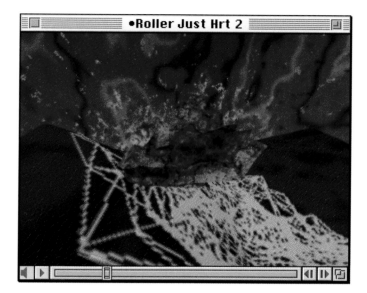

13.3.4 Computer animations saved in the QuickTime format usually display a playback controller at the bottom of the window. In this example, a sequence of wireframe images was applied as an animated texture to the surface of a moving three-dimensional object. The animated wireframe images are one of the many surface layers animated in this environment.

one is designed to compress photographic images and is based on the JPEG compression method. The differences between each of these five compression techniques are related to the time that it takes to compress and decompress an image. With some options the compression speed is high so that users do not have to wait long as the file is compressed but the compression ratio is low. With other options the compression ratio is good and that results in great space savings, but the compression time is slow.

The **MPEG** file format is another popular format for compressed moving images including video and animation. This file format was developed by the Motion Pictures Experts Group, which is related to the International Standards Organization (**ISO**). The data compression in MPEG is based on the removal of data that is identical or similar from one frame to another. This lossy compression technique can realize impressive savings in file size while keeping a reasonable quality for most applications. MPEG files can only be displayed with utility programs called **MPEG viewers**, that usually provide a variety of dithering techniques for improving the final image quality.

13.4 Output on Paper

There is a great variety of printing technologies used for creating digital prints on paper. Some of these include, for example, electrostatic, dye sublimation, ink jet, and pen plotters. Each of these printing technologies has strengths and weaknesses in the areas of resolution, paper size (Fig. 13.4.1), chromatic range, dye stability, and cost.

Metric ISO A Sizes		
AO	841 x 1,189 mm	(33.11 x 46.81 in.)
A1	594 x 841 mm	(23.39 x 33.11 in.)
A2	420 x 594 mm	(16.54 x 23.39 in.)
A3	297 x 420 mm	(11.69 x 16.54 in.)
A4	210 x 297 mm	(8.27 x 11.69 in.)
A5	148 x 210 mm	(5.83 x 8.27 in.)
A6	105 x 148 mm	(4.13 x 5.83 in.)
A7	74 x 105 mm	(2.91 x 4.13 in.)
A8	52 x 74 mm	(2.05 x 2.91 in.)
A9	37 x 52 mm	(1.46 x 2.05 in.)
A10	26 x 37 mm	(1.02 x 1.46 in.)

American ANSI Sizes		
A	8.5 x 11 in.	(215.9 x 279.4 mm)
B	11 x 17 in.	(279.4 x 431.8 mm)
C	17 x 22 in.	(431.8 x 558.8 mm)
D	24 x 36 in.	(609.6 x 914.4 mm)
E	36 x 48 in.	(914.4 x 1219.2 mm)

Architectural Sizes		
A	9 x 12 in.	(228.6 x 304.8 mm)
B	12 x 18 in.	(304.8 x 457.2 mm)
C	18 x 24 in.	(457.2 x 609.6 mm)
D	24 x 36 in.	(609.6 x 914.4 mm)
E	36 x 48 in.	(914.4 x 1219.2 mm)

13.4.1 International standard paper sizes used to specify the size of computer output on paper.

Electrostatic Printing

Electrostatic output technology is the most popular method for creating medium resolution black and white prints, but is also used to create color prints. **Electrostatic** technology is commonly known as **laser printing**, and it is capable of resolutions that range from 300 to 1,000 dpi. The output process with this technology typically consists of a laser beam that draws the image with electrical charges on a rotating metal drum, which in turn transfers charges onto the sheet of paper. Then the electrostatic energy on the paper attracts fine powder, or **toner**, to create an image directly on the surface of the paper. Finally, the toner is melted with heat on the paper. Many laser printers are able to print PostScript files and this further enhances the quality of their output, especially of line drawings. Electrostatic printing offers an affordable way of creating proofs on paper and heat-resistant acetate with sizes that range from letter size (8.5 x 11 in.) to tabloid size (11 x 17 in.).

Dye Sublimation Printing

Dye sublimation is a color printing technology that uses extreme heat to sublimate the dyes contained on a roll of acetate onto a sheet of paper. Sublimation happens to materials with such physical properties that when heated they are transformed from a solid state directly into a gaseous state, without passing through the liquid state. The sublimated dyes reach the paper in a gaseous state, and the pattern that they create on the paper is irregular but delicate. This pattern resembles the shape and pattern of the grains in photographic emulsions. For this reason, and also because of the pearl finish of the paper used in dye sublimation, prints created with this technology resemble traditional photographic prints on paper. The irregular pattern created by the sublimated dyes that reach the paper in a gaseous state also softens the regularity of the grid of pins (dpi) that apply heat to form the image. This softening helps to increase the apparent resolution of dye sublimation printers, which is usually around 300 dpi, but looks more detailed. Dye sublimation prints also offer great dye stability and excellent color range, but their cost is still higher than other techniques, and the maximum paper size rarely exceeds 11 x 14 in. This printing technology usually requires that RGB files are converted into the CMYK color format before they can be printed.

Ink Jet Printing

Ink jet printers work like miniature airbrushes that spray micro-scopic drops of color ink on a sheet or a roll of paper. The noz-zles through which the ink is sprayed are so thin that most of the ink dyes used in ink jet printers are based on vegetable dyes that have very small molecules. The small molecular size of the dyes allows the ink to pass through the narrow nozzles of the ink jet printers. However, another characteristic of vegetable dyes—as oppossed to mineral dyes—is that they are **fugitive dyes**, which means that they fade rapidly when exposed to the ultraviolet radi-ation present in sunlight. This makes the ink jet printouts unstable unless they are coated with a transparent substance that acts as a filter of ultraviolet radiation. The strengths of ink jet printing include the excellent color and image fidelity, and the great avail-ability of paper sizes and types. Ink jet printing also requires that RGB files are converted into the CMYK color format before they can be printed. In fact, most ink jet printers spray CMYK or CMY ink simultaneously on the paper, each color through a different nozzle. Of all the technologies for printing on paper that do not involve photographic processes, ink jet and dye sublimation are unique because of their good image and color fidelity.

Pen Plotters

Pen plotters have long been the preferred output technology for creating line drawings that do not require shading. **Pen plotters** create line drawings on paper with one or several pens. Unlike other peripherals that also output onto paper, pen plotters do not create images with dots. Instead, pen plotters create drawings with continuous lines. As a result the image definition of line drawings created with pen plotters is excellent. The image defin-ition of continuous tone images created with pen plotters, how-ever, is quite limited because shading can only be simulated with cross-hatching patterns. Pen plotters are still quite popular in applications such as industrial design or architecture where drawings in very large formats, 36 x 48 in. for example, are nec-essary. High resolution electrostatic printers are an alternative to pen plotters when smaller size output is required.

13.5 Output on Photographic Media

In spite of the technological advances and innovations in the area of image output, photographic media are still the medium of choice when superb image quality and flexible size are required. The imaging devices that output on photographic media have a wide range of applications. Some are used to cre-ate and assemble images on high-contrast film for use in graphic arts mechanical reproduction. Others are used to record stills on transparency film or photographic paper, or to record high-quality animation for projection in public theatres.

Imagesetters

Imagesetters are high resolution output peripherals that create black and white images. They are the preferred peripheral for outputting the films that contain the CMYK or spot color separations required for mechanical reproduction. (All the reproduction of three-dimensional imagery contained in this book, for example, were color separated, and output with digital imagesetters.) **Imagesetters** get their name from the photographic typesetters that were used to set type before digital technology transformed the typesetting industry. Imagesetters are capable of spatial resolutions in excess of 2,500 dpi both for line art and for shaded images with halftone screens. Typically a laser beam is used to draw the image directly on photosensitive film or paper, which is then developed and fixed with chemical solutions. The paper used in most imagesetters comes in rolls. Typical sizes range from 8.5 x 11 in. to 14 in. wide and several feet long.

Film Recorders

Film recorders are used to record computer images on both photographic film and paper. In essence, **film recorders** consist of a box containing a photographic camera focused on a monitor that displays the computer image to be recorded. Film recorders typically use a laser beam or a black and white monitor with filters for imaging on the film. The high-end film recorders provide excellent resolution, chromatic range, and image permanence. Output on photographic film almost always requires that the images are sent to the film recorder in the RGB color format. Film recorders for still images provide a convenient way to generate still images on transparency or negative film, and most accept the major film formats including 35 mm, 4 x 5 in., and 8 x 10 in. The film recorders used for motion picture film accept a variety of film formats including 16 mm, 35 mm, and 70 mm. It is interesting to point out that there are differences between software programs in the aspect ratios specified for the standard output formats (Figs. 13.5.1 and 6.2.3–4).

13.6 Output on Video

Videotape is the medium of choice for recording sequences of moving images intended for display on television sets, but video is sometimes also used to record still images. Output on video is possible on all the major video formats including Hi-8 mm, VHS

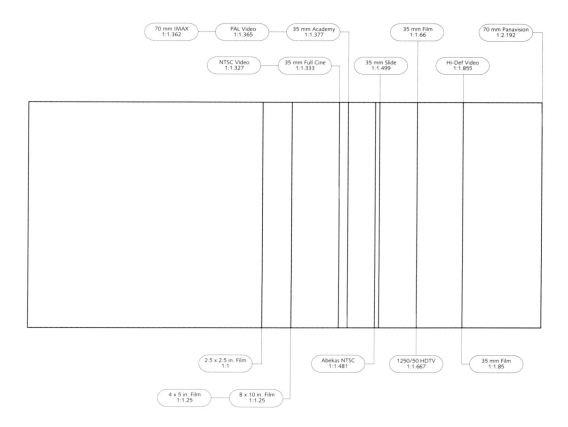

70 mm IMAX
1:1.362

PAL Video
1:1.365

35 mm Academy
1:1.377

35 mm Film
1:1.66

70 mm Panavision
1:2.192

NTSC Video
1:1.327

35 mm Full Cine
1:1.333

35 mm Slide
1:1.499

Hi-Def Video
1:1.855

2.5 x 2.5 in. Film
1:1

Abekas NTSC
1:1.481

1250/50 HDTV
1:1.667

35 mm Film
1:1.85

4 x 5 in. Film
1:1.25

8 x 10 in. Film
1:1.25

1/2 in., U-matic 3/4 in., Betacam, and D-1.

Two of the most popular standards for encoding video signals include NTSC and PAL. The NTSC signal (National Television Standards Commission) is used in the U.S.A., Japan, and most of Latin America. The PAL signal (Phase Alternating Line) is used in most of the world, including most countries in Europe. The NTSC video standards were developed in the early 1950s while PAL was developed almost ten years later. NTSC is a composite video signal that carries different types of information including: picture luminance, color saturation, color hue, horizontal line synchronizing pulses, color reference burst, reference black level, and both horizontal and vertical blanking intervals. The NTSC video standard displays 525 lines of information at the rate of 30 frames per second. The PAL video standard displays 625 lines of information at the rate of 30 frames per second. PAL also has a unique automatic color correction system. Both NTSC and PAL use interlaced display of fields, but PAL does it at 50 hz while NTSC does it at almost 60 hz.

The quality of the video output is largely determined by

13.5.1 Aspect ratios of a variety of formats common in photographic media (exact measurements vary slightly between software programs).

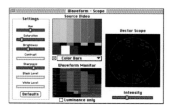
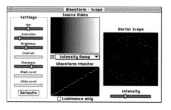
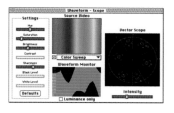
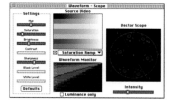

13.6.1 Computer-simulated wave-form monitors and vectorscope displays of properly adjusted split field vertical color bars (a), continuous color bars (b), a continuous grayscale (c), and split field horizontal color bars (d). (Adobe Premiere™ dialog boxes are reprinted with express permission by Adobe Systems Incorporated. Adobe and Adobe Premiere are trademarks of Adobe Systems Incorporated or its subsidiaries and are registered in certain jurisdictions.)

the video format, the quality of the videotape, and the video recording equipment. The quality of video output is also influenced by the proper balance and correction of RGB colors before they are recorded onto video, and by the calibration of the gamma factor. As mentioned earlier, the chromatic range of the RGB color model exceeds the range of video media, and often images in the RGB format contain colors that are outside the chromatic range of video and that create severe color distortions when displayed on video. For that reason, it is necessary to prepare images that were created in the RGB format before they are output to video. This is achieved through a **color correction** process that clips—or removes—the RGB colors that exceed the chromatic range of video, and replaces them with the closest equivalent color within the chromatic range of video.

Another technical detail that has major consequences when outputting computer images onto video is the calibration of the **gamma factor**. The gamma factor—also known as gamma—makes the video image look as close as possible to the original RGB information by compensating for the loss of information between the voltages sent by the computer to the monitor, and the amount of light output by the monitor (Fig. 13.2.4). Other tools that are also useful in monitoring the quality of the video signal include the **vectorscope** and the **waveform monitor**. Both of these devices—whether real or simulated with software—display a graphical representation of the video signal. These graphs help to make sure, for example, that the colors fall within "legal" limits, or that they are distributed evenly throughout the color spectrum, or that the transitions between color gradations are smooth and constant (Fig. 13.6.1).

Flickering is another common problem that occurs when computer-generated images are recorded onto NTSC video. **Flickering** happens for a variety of reasons but mostly due to that fact that each frame of NTSC video is displayed as two **interlaced fields**. One field contains all the even scan lines in the frame, and the other field contains the odd scan lines. RGB monitors are usually **noninterlaced**, so flickering occurs when a computer-generated image contains visual data such as horizontal lines or textures that are only one pixel high. This happens because that information appears only on one of the video fields and not on the other one (using antialiasing techniques can greatly reduce this problem). Flickering also happens when regular video cameras are used to record off an RGB monitor. This happens because the **refresh rate**, also called scanning rate, of most NTSC video equipment is 60 Hz while most RGB monitors usually have a faster rate. This type of flickering results in a diagonal line that rolls continuously from the top to the bottom of the video screen.

The aspect ration of video has to be taken into consideration when recording computer-generated images onto videotape. Not only is the aspect ratio of video different from the aspect ratio of several RGB monitors, but also up to 20 percent of the image is cut off when computer-animation is displayed on television video monitors. (This has to do with the fact that the video signal uses some of the scan lines at the bottom of the screen to carry sync information.) An easy way to avoid having computer animations cut off is to leave a generous amount of unused space on the edges of the image. Using the field guides that specify the **action safe areas** of video can also help to solve this limitation (Fig. 6.2.4).

13.7 Output on Digital Media

A considerable amount of three-dimensional computer renderings are delivered today in formats that can be readily used in digital media such as videogames or multimedia presentations. Professionals from a wide variety of visual disciplines are increasingly working with three-dimensional computer graphics in a **digital creative environment.** The traditional fields of graphic arts, broadcasting, and film each uses three-dimensional creations in a specialized way. But they are all able to share their imagery in the form of **digital information**.

Three-dimensional images are output on digital media when they need to be played directly on the RGB monitor directly from the computer. This is the case, for example, when an animator wants to preview a motion test in the form of a sequence of low resolution files, or flipbook, stored in the hard disk. Other examples include the distribution of three-dimensional imagery and animation on CD-ROMs or through networks of computers.

One of the main concerns with images delivered in digital media is that they are compact enough to load fast. But image detail is also important. So finding the right balance between speed and detail is a challenge typical of delivering images on digital media. In order to find this balance, it is necessary to perform tests that compare the amount of image detail against the loading speed and storage efficiency. Very few mainstream videogames, for example, utilize sequences of 24-bit color images for this reason. The image quality would be superb—better than the standard 8-bit or 16-bit color—but the price of hardware required to display these images would make the videogames too expensive for the mainstream. On the other hand, we can expect this challenge to fade away as graphics hardware becomes more sophisticated and less expensive.

CD-ROM

One of the most successful output media of recent times is the **compact disk-read only memory**, commonly known as **CD-ROM**. Technically speaking, CD-ROMs are a type of peripheral memory, but they can also be defined as output media because of their popularity for distributing visual projects. This medium is extremely convenient because it uses optical technology to store large amounts of information per disk, about 660 mb, in a format that is as permanent and stable as can be. Furthermore, the **read-time**—or time that it takes for the computer to find and read information from the CD-ROM—is minimal due to the laser beam technology utilized for this purpose.

CD-ROMs can contain all types of information. One CD-ROM, for example, may be filled up with over 60 minutes of very high-quality audio sampled at 44 kHz and in 16-bit stereo format, or with 450 images in 24-bit color RGB format at 640 x 480 pixel resolution. The same CD-ROM could also be filled up with over 20 hours of low resolution audio sampled at 11 kHz and in 8-bit stereo format, or with 26,500 monochromatic images at 512 x 342 pixel resolution. (Fig. 13.7.1).

Network Distribution and Real Time Digital Playback

During the decade of the 1980s it would have been adventurous trying to play computer animations in real time through a network. But advances in network technology today are contributing to make the distribution of computer-generated images and animations commonplace.

The distribution of computer-generated images through a network serves different needs, and the system requirements in each case can have significant differences. A simple application of network distribution consists of playing back a sequence of images—sometimes called a **digital flipbook**—from one computer on the network directly on the monitor of another computer connected to the network and typically in the same room. In this case, a single digital file travels through the **local area network**, or **LAN**, at the request of a **single user**. Another example would consist of the same animation file being accessed through the network simultaneously by **multiple users**. This would be the case if several individuals in different locations, a client in the meeting room, and the production team in their studios, for example, needed to play back the same digital file as they spoke over the phone. A situation such as this one would require either a network with a wide bandwidth and/or the digital files having some form of data compression. There already are several networks in use that allow multiple simultaneous users to access a file without a loss in speed or resolution. Some of these solutions, however, still require deep pockets. Many networks that allow simultaneous playing of animation files still display different degrees of loss of speed or resolution.

The speed at which images are transmitted though networks of computers is an issue that influences the performance of playing back files remotely. The speeds at which files can travel through networks is related primarily to the bandwidth of the communication paths that files travel through between computers as well as inside a single computer. These paths can be divided in three types: paths in a digital network, phone lines and modems, and paths inside the computer itself. The **bandwidth**, or transmission capacity, of these different media is measured with different units that express the amount of information that travels through the path per second. The bandwidth of digital networks is generally measured in **megabits per second**. The bandwidth or speeds of modems operating on phone lines is measured in bits or **kilobits per second**. The bandwidth of computer internal data channels is measured in **megabytes per second**. This seemingly arbitrary variety of bandwidth units is rooted in very different magnitudes of transmission capacity and in different traditions that date back to the early days of telephone transmission and computer engineering.

Planning the live playback of digital files through a network requires a wide variety of strategies depending on the purpose of the playback. Using networks that are controlled environments is different from using open-ended networks that go into the outside world. In a controlled network environment, for example, it is possible to use specialized hardware for compression and decompression that increase the playback speed of an animation file through any network. In controlled network environments, each node can also be setup with specialized hardware

How many images fill one tenth of a CD-ROM?	
45 images	640 x 480 (24-bit color)
147 images	512 x 384 (8-bit color)
2650 images	512 x 342 (monochrome)

How much audio fits on a CD-ROM?	
30 minutes (50%)	16-bit resolution stereo, 44.1 kHz
30 minutes (15%)	8-bit resolution stereo, 22 kHz
30 minutes (3%)	8-bit resolution mono, 11 kHz

13.7.1 Different ways of storing visuals in a CD-ROM.

and high bandwidth lines. In cases such as this, it makes sense to design the playback of the file by making extensive use of real time file compression and decompression and high bandwidths. But in situations when the file is played in a wide variety of environments and throughout different bandwidths it is usually wiser to choose the lowest common denominator so that the file can be played by the largest number of viewers.

The speed of digital networks is based on many factors, including the type of material that the network lines are made of (optic fiber or copper for example), and the type of communications protocol (Ethernet or ATM for example). The speed of modems and computer spreads a broad range. It is difficult to say that there is a standard network communications speed or bandwidth because this type of technology is still changing dramatically every couple of years. The ranges go, for example, from 56 kilobits per second (kps) for a Digital Signal Level Zero (DS-0) data channel to 135 megabits per second (or 135,000 kps) for a Broadband Integrated Services Digital Network (ISDN). However, the internal data channels of specialized computers for visual creation is in the range of 10 to 40 megabytes per second. The range of modem bandwidth goes from a low of 2,400 bits per second (bps) to 64,000 bps (64 kps) and higher. The total bandwidth and performance of file transmission over networks takes into account a multitude of factors, and cannot be determined by just one of the three data paths. In many instances, the performance of network distribution and playback of digital files is fast inside the computer, slow as the files are sent through the modem, and then fast again or very fast as the files travel through a network. For example, a file would travel fast inside a computer with an internal bus bandwidth of 40 megabytes (320 megabits) per second, it would then slow down as it goes through a 14,400 bits per second modem, zip through a high-speed optical fiber network at 135 megabits per second, slow down again through an Ethernet connection at 10 megabits per second, and playback even slower at a computer with a bus bandwidth of 2 megabytes (16 megabits) per second.

Interactive Media

Interactive multimedia systems are usually built around a computer that responds to the requests of users with a multitude of media, including still and moving images, sound, and text. Many interactive systems inform, educate, or entertain by responding to the user's queries. The **interactivity** of a computer system is based on the **dialogue** established between the system itself and the individuals using it. Interactive systems are often built around one or several computer systems that are able to control the flow of information stored in a variety of media, formats and systems. Hence the name of **interactive multimedia**. Individuals using interactive systems can make their choices through standard input peripherals such as mice, joysticks, and keyboards, or unique ones such as ultrasonic and light sensors, and gloves and bodysuits, that can determine the position, orientation, and physical gestures of a person.

In most media, visual communication and story telling happens in a linear way because images, sounds and text follow each other in just one single predetermined order. But in an interactive project there may be many possible sequences because users can make different requests and also establish different types of dialogue with it. Each time interactive projects are played they may follow different paths, and may have multiple endings and even multiple beginnings. Because of the **nonlinearity** of the medium, planning and creating for interactive multimedia requires unique techniques. Creators of an interactive project have in flowcharts a powerful tool for planning the project, and for determining the many paths the project may follow.

Flowcharts are diagrams that clearly lay out all the **branching** options that may occur in the **flow of events** in an interactive dialogue. The branching structure in an interactive system may be simple if few options are offered or complex if the options are multiple. Each branching node in a flowchart is controlled by a choice made by the individual or individuals interacting with the system. When a choice is made at a branching node the flow of events advances to another hierarchy level in the flowchart. On occasions the sequencing of events in an interactive project may also be sketched in the form of a traditional storyboard.

Flowcharts describe in an abstract manner the overall structure and dynamics of an interactive project. But **scripts** actually control the flow of events in an interactive project; they are the practical implementation of a the ideas contained in a flowchart. Scripts are computer programs that collect and evaluate information about the choices made by the users of the system, and then direct the program in the appropriate direction. Scripts trigger events that may include displaying an image, playing a sequence of images or sounds, or moving the arm of a robot or a section of an interactive sculpture.

Interactive media is not made to be watched. Instead it is made to be used by people. For this reason the functionality of an interactive system should always be checked with extensive **user-testing**. The feedback and suggestions of users usually uncover the moments in the flow of events that may be confusing, or important functionalities that may be missing, or requests from the users that crash the program and freeze the system. Only after a thorough user-testing process can interactive projects be released to the public.

One of the aspects that is paid special attention during the user-testing process is the **computer-human interface,** or interface for short. An interface is the collection of techniques that facilitate the dialogue between an individual and an interactive computer system. The **interface design** of a project has to do with the graphical conventions such as the shape of icons, typography, and color, but also with the sequencing of events, selection techniques, and interplay of sound, text, and images.

13.8 Output on Three-Dimensional Media

The data used to describe three-dimensional models in virtual environments can also be used in a variety of ways to actually

13.8.1 *Foray* is a bronze sculpture created by Bruce Beasley, who uses computers to both compose and fabricate his sculptures. (Photograph by Lee Fatherree. Courtesy of Bruce Beasley.)

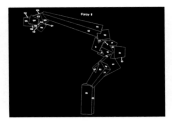

build the object with real material. The details of the techniques used to translate digital three-dimensional data into real three-dimensional objects are beyond the scope of this book. But some of the basic techniques are implemented with cutting machines, milling machines, and stereo lithography machines.

Computer-controlled **cutting machines** are able to cut two-dimensional shapes usually with a laser beam. These shapes are parts in structure that can be assembled by hand or under robot control. The shape of these parts is described as a series of XY coordinates or complex curves that are followed by the cutting tool. The work illustrated in Fig. 13.8.1 was assembled from two-dimensional shapes created by unfolding a three-dimensional model with software designed for that purpose. This example was composed directly on the computer (a), by previewing a large combination of shapes (b). All the planes in the sculpture were numbered (c) and dimensioned (d) on the computer screen. Once the composition was fully resolved the patterns were previewed on the screen (e), plotted directly on foamcore, and a model was constructed. This model was sent to the foundry, and was burned out for a traditional lost wax casting. (If a sculpture is going to be fabricated rather than cast, the patterns are plotted on pattern paper for transfer to bronze plate.)

Milling machines are able to shape blocks of material such as plastic, wood, or stone by placing a rotating cutter on

13.8.2 The stereo lithography process hardens liquid polymer with two computer-controlled laser beams.

their surface, and moving across from top to bottom. The continuous motion of the cutting head along the three axes results in the modeling of a three-dimensional object. A wide variety of shapes can be created by using different cutting paths and by attaching different cutting tools to the milling machine.

Stereo lithography is a process by which a liquid plastic is shaped and solidified by two computer-controlled laser beams. The beams are perpendicular to each other and they move according to the XYZ positions on the surface of an object that has been modeled with software but is yet to be built in the physical world. One laser beam is focused at the transparent container from the front, and the other beam is focused from the side. The liquid plastic solidifies where the two laser beams intersect in the liquid inside the container. With stereo lithography, shell surfaces or solid objects can be built by using the data contained in the digital model file to direct the motion of the two laser beams (Fig. 13.8.2).

Review and Practice

Matching

_____ Kilobits per second

_____ JPEG

_____ Lpi

_____ Field guides

_____ Film recorder

_____ Playback controller

_____ DTAs

_____ Spatial resolution

_____ Dpi

_____ Pixel

_____ Megabits per second

_____ Resolution

_____ Gamma

_____ MPEG

_____ 10-40 mb per second

a. Used to measure the image resolution of a specific input or output peripheral device.

b. Indicate the action safe areas of NTSC video that keep the edges of computer animations from being off the video frame.

c. Used to measure the bandwidth of digital networks.

d. The amount of detailed information contained in an image or a sequence of images.

e. Factor that helps to compensate for the loss of information that happens between the voltages sent by the computer to the monitor and the light output by the monitor.

f. The smallest unit used to measure image resolution.

g. Used to measure the bandwidth or speeds of modems operating on phone lines.

h. Based on a "lossy" compression scheme that removes data that is redundant or imperceptible to the human eye.

i. Usually contains a photographic camera that records the image displayed on a black and white monitor through a wheel of color filters.

j. Common bandwidth of the internal data channels of computers used for visual creation.

k. Defined by the relation between the dimensions of an image and the number of pixels in the image.

l. The compression technique of this popular file format is based on the removal of data that is identical or similar from one frame to another.

m. Displayed right below the window of a QuickTime file.

n. Used to measure the number of rows of dots in the halftone screens of mechanical reproduction techniques.

o. Components of all output.

Answers Matching: a. dpi, b. Field guides, c. Megabits per second, d. Resolution, e. Gamma, f. Pixel, g. Kilobits per second, h. JPEG, i. Film recorder, j. 10-40 mb per second, k. Spatial resolution, l. MPEG, m. Playback controller, n. Lpi, o. DTAs.

True/False

_____ a. The chromatic range of video media exceeds the range of the RGB color model.

_____ b. The QuickTime file format stores both visual and audio data.

_____ c. The JPEG file format is useful when large amounts of data have to be transmitted over slow networks because it discards image information as is compresses the file.

_____ d. A standard bandwith of Ethernet local area networks is 10 megabits per second.

_____ e. The resampling technique can be used to match the ppi resolution of an image file to the dpi resolution of an output peripheral.

_____ f. Dye sublimation and ink jet are two technologies for printing on nonsilver paper with superior spatial resolution and color fidelity.

_____ g. QuickTime files may easily play back at different temporal resolutions.

_____ h. A binary value of 10 equals a decimal value of five.

_____ i. One of the five compression options by the QuickTime file format is based on the JPEG format.

_____ j. Specialized hardware for compression and decompression may increase the playback speed of a computer animation file through a computer network.

_____ k. Bitmaps can have a maximum of eight bitplanes.

_____ l. The three types of image resolution most commonly used by visual professionals include: chromatic, spatial, and temporal resolution.

_____ m. The QuickTime file format provides five compression options, including one that is especially designed to compress computer animation.

_____ n. The bandwidth of computer internal data channels is measured in megabytes per second.

_____ o. It is possible to know exactly how many colors can be displayed by a computer graphics system by elevating the number two to a power that equals the number of bitplanes in the system.

_____ p. Output peripherals include printers, pen plotters, recorders, and three-dimensional milling machines.

_____ q. Computer animation files can be accessed simultaneously by multiple users through a network.

_____ r. One CD-ROM may be filled up with approximately 450 images in 24-bit color RGB format at 640 x 480 pixel resolution.

_____ s. One second of NTSC video has a rate of 30 fps.

_____ t. Video flickering is common when computer-generated images with horizontal lines or textures that are only one pixel high are recorded onto videotape.

_____ u. The number of pixels that exist in an image file is measured in dots per image.

_____ v. The majority of prints created with vegetal dyes used by ink jet printers fade when exposed to ultraviolet radiations.

_____ w. Video flickering happens because NTSC video still frames are displayed as two interlaced fields and RGB monitors are usually non-interlaced.

_____ x. Dye sublimation printing techniques use extreme heat to transform solid dyes into vapors that are deposited onto film or paper.

Answers True/False: a. False, b. True, c. True, d. True, e. True, f. True, g. True, h. False, i. True, j. True, k. False, l. True, m. True, n. True, o. True, p. True, q. True, r. True, s. True, t. True, u. False, v. True, w. True, x. True.

Key Terms

Action safe areas
Bandwidth
Binary system
Bitmap
Bitplane
Branching
CD-ROM
Chromatic range
CMYK four-color separation
Color bleeding
Color clipping
Color correction
Color resolution
Compact disk-read only memory
Computer-human interface
Convert colors
Cutting machines
Device-independent file format
Dialogue
Digital creative environment
Digital flipbook
Digital information
Digital-to-analog
Dot resolution
Dots per inch
Dpi
DTAs
Dye sublimation
Electrostatic
EPS
Export filters
Export tools
File format conversion
File formats
Film recorders
Flickering
Flow of events
Flowcharts
Fps
Frames
Frames per second
Fugitive dyes
Gamma factor
Graphics memory
Halftone output
Halftone screens

Header information
Image definition
Image file
Image resolution
Imagesetters
Import filters
Import tools
Ink jet printers
Interactive multimedia
Interactivity
Interface design
Interlaced fields
ISO
JPEG
Kilobits per second
LAN
Laser printing
Lines per inch
Local area network
Lossless compression
Lossy compression
Lpi
Megabits per second
Megabytes per second
Milling machines
MPEG
MPEG viewers
Multiple users
Native file formats
Non interlaced fields
Nonlinearity
Output peripherals
Pen plotters
Peripheral device
PICS
PICT
Picture files
Pixel
Pixel resolution
Pixels
Pixels per inch
Playback controller
Portable image file formats
Ppi
QuickTime
Read-time
Refresh rate
Resample

Scripts
Self-contained format
Series of still images
Simultaneous access
Single user
Spatial resolution
Stereo lithography
Temporal resolution

TGA
TIFF
Toner
Translation of data
Universal image file formats
User-testing
Vectorscope
Waveform monitor

APPENDIX I

Computer Graphics Visual Effects for Terminator 2: Judgment Day

by Lincoln Hu

Director of Advanced Technologies
Industrial Light & Magic,
a division of Lucas Digital Ltd.
San Rafael, CA

Summary

This paper describes some of the basic tools, techniques, and production processes used in the creation of the computer graphics visual effects for the film *Terminator 2: Judgment Day*. It describes a myriad of T1000 Terminator transformation processes and how they were accomplished. It also outlines some methods for accurate human facial and body modeling, and ways to precisely and seamlessly integrate these computer generated images into live action photography.

Introduction

Many people have said that *Terminator 2* marked an important milestone in computer graphics history. It was the first feature film ever made that could not have been done without computer generated effects. There have been many previous examples of computer generated images in films, *Tron*, the "Genesis Effect" in *Star Trek II*, the stained glass knight in *Young Sherlock Holmes*, the space ships in *The Last Starfighter*, the Raziel transformation sequence in *Willow*, the pseudopod sequence in *The Abyss* and several others, but this was the first time computer animation was used as an essential integral element of the story. The success or failure of T2 largely depended on the completion of a number of difficult computer graphics shots, and it all had to be done in a very short amount of time.

While a detailed algorithmic description of our tools is beyond the scope of this paper, we will outline some of the most important basic tools and techniques developed for this project. Modeling and animation references can be found in numerous computer graphics textbooks as well as past SIGGRAPH proceedings and SIGGRAPH course notes.

Some History

Writer and Director James Cameron's previous experience with ILM involved the "pseudopod" sequence from *The Abyss* (1989). The pseudopod was a snake-like creature made entirely of seawater and brought to life by aliens. Approximately 73 seconds of computer animation was created and inserted into a five minute sequence in which the pseudopod entered and explored an underwater habitat and interacted with the actors and the physical environment (Ref. 1).

The basic pseudopod had the appearance of a tube of water which formed its tip into replicas of the actors' faces, mimicking their expressions. It was constructed by defining a spline that controlled the basic placement and movement of the pod, and numerous cross sections that defined the overall shape of the pod. To make the facial data and expression animation accurate, we digitized the actors' faces, manipulated the data to achieve the correct expressions, then fit it onto our pseudopod model. Due to the large number of surface deviations and rippling required for the surface detail of the pseudopod model and the related facial animation, we employed data amplification methods in the cross section interpolation, skinning and rippling processes. The finished pseudopod model contained anywhere from 7,500 to 50,000 patches; the patch count varied with the requirements of each particular shot. Two good references that described how the effects were done are (Ref. 2 and 3)

A great deal of knowledge was gained from working on the pod. We learned about the limits of our tools and the efficiency and soundness of our techniques. It also helped us define a new production process for computer graphics visual effects. It gave us an opportunity to experiment with what looked good on the screen, how to make the computer generated element come to life and blend in with live action footage. It also taught us how to communicate effectively with directors and producers in order to understand and create their vision.

A New Terminator

For *Terminator 2*, James Cameron designed a new generation of terminators. Unlike its predecessor, the T800 metal endoskeleton-based Arnold Schwarzenegger version, the new prototype, the T1000, was made from an intelligent polyalloy liquid metal. It can mimic any object or person of similar mass by sampling the object and obtaining the necessary shape and surface characteristics. It is then able to transform itself at will into that entity.

Computer generated effects were necessary to help portray the T1000 character, played by actor Robert Patrick. The intricate effects allowed this character to take on chameleon-like abilities and transform itself effortlessly and seamlessly from one character or state into another. It could also melt perfectly into the surrounding environment. Even so, complex visual transformations only represented half of the

story. The computer animation and effects must also help to define and establish the T1000's character as intelligent, purposeful, confident, efficient, completely invincible, and indestructible (well, almost). This helped to convey the T1000's menacing presence and establish its unrelenting, single-minded quest to terminate its target.

To be convincing, these effects must be completely and seamlessly integrated with the live action photography. It is only with this integration that the audience will suspend reality and begin to believe in the character and the story. For example, the motion must possess a certain fluid quality as it pours itself through an opening, yet it must maintain the feeling of mass and momentum. The computer generated character must retain an accurate human-like quality to augment the actor's performance. The lighting and surface characteristics must not only reflect and blend in with the surroundings, it must also, in some cases, interact with the environment (Ref. 4 and 5).

Computer-Generated Effects Design and Planning

As with most every job, we began with concept art and storyboards. The concept sketches, developed by Cameron and a team of artists, helped us focus on an accurate visual representation as well as solidify the technical research and development efforts needed to achieve these results. An example of this was the T1000 transformation process. It was divided into five stages:

(1) amorphous liquid metal blob
(2) generic, smooth, featureless human form
(3) human form with soft outline of clothing and some distinct features
(4) crisp, accurate and detailed human form with all the clothing and accessories (badge, gun belt, walkie-talkie, buttons, folds in the uniform, etc.) that closely replicated actor Robert Patrick's features, and

(5) the live-action "real" Robert Patrick

Each and every shot was storyboarded and thoroughly analyzed before principle photography began. This set the proper ground work for an efficient production process throughout the show. Each shot was categorized by difficulty into four levels: simple, medium, difficult, and miraculous. We could then better gauge the volume of work. The effects were also divided into five classes:

(1) polyalloy, for all the flowing chrome, pseudopod-like effects
(2) human, for the human modeling, motion and transformation sequences
(3) morph, to deal with all the two-dimensional metamorphosis transformations
(4) "3D on Live Action," for a number of special live-action-mapped-on-three-dimensional-element effects
(5) and finally, "death," which deal with the big finale/T1000 death sequence

The research and development phase focused on a large collection of software tools. Older programs, such as the ones used to create the pseudopod, were revived and greatly improved. New tools in human body modeling, object deformation, surface resampling, interactive lighting, texture map projection, matching the moves of a motion-control camera with a target-tracking technique, and many others were designed and implemented by a team of innovative programmers.

Plate Photography

Many of the effects shots were filmed early in the principle photography schedule to permit the longest post production time possible and to avoid bad weather at outdoor locations. ILM's T2 Visual Effects Supervisor, Dennis Muren, and one of the computer graphics sequence supervisors were always present during a plate shoot. This proved to be extremely valuable because things never go as planned, and being able to anticipate and respond quickly to changes was essential in the creative process. Being on location also allowed us to analyze and understand the physical spatial characteristics as well as take accurate measurements and reference photos. This information was necessary for the construction of the simulated computer graphics environment.

An extensive target tracking system was also developed for accurate camera movement alignment and simulation. When the live-action plates were shot, a reference target was substituted for the primary computer graphics element and shot with the live background. This reference footage was then digitized and its two-dimensional target coordinates in image space were used to inversely derive a set of appropriate three-dimensional world coordinates. This process can be automated and was originally published by (Ref. 6). For motion-controlled shots with the camera run by computer-controlled mechanical motors, we obtained the data from the camera computer system and (theoretically) converted it to accurate rotation, translation, zoom, and focus information. Unfortunately, these mechanically derived data were never 100 percent accurate. But with the help of our target evaluation system, we were able to advance that idea one step further and use the same inverse computation to incrementally refine the motion control move until it was perfect.

Almost all the plates dealing with computer generated effects were shot in VistaVision (35 mm 8 perf) format on either Eastman Kodak 5296 or 5245 film stock.

Building the Models

For a medium or complex shot, one of the first modeling tasks was the recreation of the physical set. This allowed the animator to become familiar with the environment and also served as a guide for any interaction that may be required between the computer generated element and the physical objects.

One of the greatest challenges was to build an accurate human model that resembled the real actor. To do this, we stripped Robert Patrick down to his skivvies, painted a grid on his body and took reference photos. Our animators closely studied the actor's physical form and applied their knowledge of human anatomy to construct an accurate three-dimensional human skeleton and body model from the reference photographs. This set the basis for our stage two T1000 (generic, smooth, and featureless human form). A similar approach was used to construct a stage three (soft, with some details) and four (highly detailed, accurate) T1000. These models were built early in the production phase and used for most of the computer animated human action and three-dimensional transformation sequences. The final death sequence called for a series of dramatic deformations and transformations requiring a more complex, custom-constructed human body topology. Other human forms, such as Janelle (John Connor's foster mother) and Louis (the hospital security guard), were also constructed from the same basic stage 2 model.

For facial features, Patrick's head was scanned by a Cyberware scanner and the data was used by our animators to sculpt a highly detailed model. The generic Cyberware data was too noisy and dense to be usable. This, coupled with the fact that our facial construction and animation required a specific geometric topology, meant we must custom model each head.

Depending on the complexity of the shot, a flowing chrome pseudopod-like object may require anywhere from a few dozen to several hundred patches to model. For the generic human body model, approximately two dozen meshes of varying sizes were used to defined the torso and limbs, while another several dozen meshes formed the head, neck, face, hands, and feet/shoes. All of the complementary police officer's accessories (gun belt, gun, walkie-talkie, ammo holster, etc.) were also accurately reproduced.

Additional Modeling Tools

Since different versions of the body models were made to showcase the various stages of transformation, we developed a set of tools to manipulate, cut, replace, and interpolate between the different models. This allowed the animator to sculpt entire bodies and surfaces and not be bogged down with the details of managing and organizing the hierarchical models or its animation data. When the body animates, the patch meshes that form the static model will move apart. To ensure proper continuity across adjoining meshes and corners, a major piece of software tool was developed to "sew" the model together. This tool permitted a tremendous amount of freedom because the models can now be animated, displaced, or stretched and there will not be seams across any surfaces. Deformation tools such as bendy boxes were also implemented to help simulate some of the clothing wrinkle movements for the stage 4 T1000. For the head-rising-from-the-floor shot, a ray-casting modeling tool was written to fire rays from a predefined launch surface at a set of target objects. The resulting points from the ray-surface intersections were then used to form the desired b-spline or cardinal surface.

Even with such good tools, there was never a substitute for great modeling skills by talented animators.

Animation

Several shots in T2 required a moving camera to track the action. In order to accurately simulate the physical environment, our first task was to duplicate this physical camera move using techniques such as the one described in the Plate Photography section above. Once we had a good computer graphics camera move and a properly recreated set, we began to accurately insert our computer generated element.

Much of our animation is character-oriented. In addition to defining the appropriate motion needed in the scene, our computer generated character must also convey certain emotion. To help accomplish this, we examined and applied many of the principles used in traditional two-dimensional animation such as timing, anticipation, staging, follow through, overlap, exaggeration, and secondary action. Timing or the speed of the action defines how well the idea behind the action will read to the audience. It reflects the weight and size of an object and can project emotional meaning. Proper timing is critical to making the action readable. It is important to spend just the right amount of time preparing the audience for the anticipation of an action, the action itself and the reaction to the action. A secondary action is an action that results directly from another (mostly primary) action. These secondary actions are imperative because they add a realistic complexity to the motion which is critical for simulating reality.

To study Robert Patrick's motion and mannerism, we filmed him using multiple synchronized cameras. The footage was then carefully studied and rotoscoped by animators. This technique of capturing motion proved to be very effective and is the same underlying basis for automated motion capture systems. An example to help illustrate this is when we first see the T1000 walking out of the blazing truck wreck in the canal chase sequence. This shot was critical in establishing the T1000 character because it was the first time the audience saw the transforming terminator. It must be believable, in every sense, for the audience to accept it. Technically, this was difficult to achieve because we, as normal human beings, are very accustomed, visually, to human movements. We know instinctively what walking, running, and talking humans are supposed to look like. Our visual perception, either consciously or subconsciously, can detect the slightest abnormality or imperfection in the animation so our human motion must be near perfect. In addition to getting the T1000's movement to be technically accurate, we also must project the proper persona through its body language. The walking out of the fire must project confidence, determination and invincibility.

The only line of dialog the computer animated T1000 had in the film was when he ordered the helicopter pilot to "Get out!" To correctly model and animate the speaking facial expressions, we digitized Robert Patrick's face in different poses using the Cyberware system, cleaned up the data and interpolated between the different models. Much of the animation

required critical accuracy in matching to the live action photography. In the above example, the computer generated T1000 should match the real Robert Patrick perfectly for a smooth transition from the chrome character to the live action actor. Other examples of critical matchmoves include the healing and closing bullet wounds. They must track perfectly to Robert Patrick's body or the illusion is destroyed.

A great deal of the animation was accomplished by animating individual control vertices on b-spline patchmeshes. This was a labor intensive approach but when executed correctly, it often provided the most dramatic results, as demonstrated in the shot where Arnold punched through the T1000's head or when the T1000 poured itself into the helicopter.

Rendering

Rendering an element so it can be integrated with live action requires accurate simulation of the lighting condition and other environmental influences such as haze, fog, reflections, refractions, and shadows. To accurately duplicate the surface reflection or refraction on a computer generated object, we photograph the surrounding environment and exactly reconstruct the live action set. A six-sided environment cube is normally sufficient for reflection maps. In theatric visual effects, it is also imperative that we properly simulate an object's motion blur and the changes in depth of field as they are created by a real camera's shutter and lens.

Another very useful tool in high quality image synthesis is the flexibility and ease-of-use of a programmable shader. A shading function calculates the appearance of the visible surfaces. The ability to alter this shading computation allows us to easily control and adjust subtleties in lighting and surface appearance, which in turn produces better looking imagery.

The T1000 needed to accurately reflect as well as interact with the physical environment. Reflection maps, either static photos or running footage, must be properly color corrected and placed into the synthetic environment. Sometimes optically and theoretically correct reflection maps just didn't look good because what people expect isn't always what would really happen, so distorting and cheating the reflecting image was necessary. The character's chrome surface also needs to be reflected in other objects, such as puddles of water, and shadows must be cast on the surrounding surfaces. In our programmable shader, we also provided the ability to place additional arbitrary reflection planes to accommodate special reflection elements such as blazes of fire. Small amounts of surface imperfections were also incorporated for added realism.

To simulate the proper lighting, a lighting editor was developed to allow the animators to interactively position the light sources and obtain quick visual feedback. The lighting editor also permitted the user to specify exactly where to place a highlight on a surface and the software will automatically calculate where the computer light source should be positioned in three-dimensional space.

An example of subtle yet effective lighting was the shot where the T1000's severed crowbar hand joined with his feet as he walked up. The lighting of the computer generated crowbar/blob changed significantly during the shot. At the beginning, it was lit as normal street lighting, but towards the end of the shot the object was surrounded on both sides by the actor's feet so its highlights and reflections had to be blocked out.

Several shots, such as the one where the T1000 walks through the bars or where it reforms its head after being split open by a shot gun blast, were difficult challenges. To achieve these effects, the computer model was accurately match-animated to the live action performance of the actor, then each frame was projected onto the three-dimensional geometry, which could then be deformed or altered.

Morph

The two-dimensional image warping technique, also known as morph, was used in several instances to assist in the proper alignment of three-dimensional computer generated elements to real objects. Morph was also used for sequences that did not involve any three-dimensional geometry. A stunning example of the effectiveness of this simple, direct two-dimensional metamorphosis was when the T1000 got thrown, front first, into a wall. Instead of turning around, which would take more time, it chose a more efficient fighting technique of bouncing off the wall, reforming itself to face backwards to continue to fight.

Three plates were shot for this effect: Robert Patrick running forward into the wall, Robert peeling himself off the wall, and a clean plate without the actor. The first two plates were used for the metamorphosis while the third plate provided clean background areas to comp over.

Compositing

Compositing is the process of combining multiple images into a single image, as when a space battle scene is built up from a number of separately filmed scale models. Traditionally, compositing is done by projecting each image onto unexposed film using an optical printer.

Digital compositing is similar in many ways to traditional optical composites but it offers several advantages not available in the photochemical process. Digitally composited images do not suffer from generation loss. We can do many multiple layer composites at the same time. The computer allows us localized controls and provides quick interactive feedback. Compositing computer generated imagery with live-action photography must deal with correct color matching and balancing. Other issues such as matching the appropriate film grain of the background scene also have to be considered.

Combining the Different Tools and Techniques

One of the most exciting parts of T2 was the opportunity to combine and truly integrate many of these concepts described above. Some of the transformations were not just a simple three-dimensional model interpolation or a two-dimensional morph but a combination of all the techniques. A good example of combining two-dimensional and three-dimensional techniques is the bullet healing wounds where two-dimensional morphs of the clothing movement are added to the animated three-dimensional chrome closing bullet holes to enhance the effect.

A more intricate and sophisticated combination of these techniques is demonstrated in the shot where Janelle/T1000 (John Connor's foster mother) after killing John's foster father in the kitchen, transforms from Janelle into the chrome computer generated T1000, shape-shifts into the chrome cop and right before walking out, changes to the real Robert Patrick. The metamorphosis from Janelle to the match-animated chrome computer-generated character was done with a two-dimensional morph. The transformation from a smooth Janelle-like chrome character to a stage 4 T1000 was accomplished with three-dimensional model interpolation and the real Robert Patrick was revealed by a specially designed wipe-off of the animated chrome terminator. Several plates were used to achieve this effect: plate shot with Janelle, plate with Robert Patrick and a clean plate with no actors, (except the dead one on the floor.) Many cleverly concealed splits were used to match the different pieces of film together. Special image processing had to be done to all the footage to make them match perfectly because the fluorescent lighting on the set caused bad flickering in the different plates.

Film Input Scanning and Output Recording

To manipulate film images digitally, we must first scan (or digitize) the image. After manipulation, we also need to record the images back out to film. Input scanning need to address several requirements such as fast image acquisition, high spatial resolution, good radiometric resolution, and frame to frame stability and registration. Output film recording must offer accurate color reproduction, good resolution and frame registration. Efficient and inexpensive data I/O is also an important aspect of digital visual effects production.

What Did It Take?

Forty-three computer graphics effects shots were generated in a seven month period for T2. The computer graphics production and software development crew, some of whom had never done production work before coming to ILM, was assembled in a very short time.

The modeling and animation were done using a combination of Alias 2.4.2 software and several dozen custom-developed tools. Approximately 100,000 lines of code were written by ILM for this film including software for three-dimensional model and animation channel manipulation, skinning, two-dimensional morph, image processing and compositing, and some of the tools mentioned above. The rendering was done using RenderMan, ILM-custom shaders and the in-house developed interactive lighting tool. The shots were digitally composited using ILM proprietary image processing software. All of the computations were performed on two dozen Silicon Graphics workstations. Approximately 800 8 mm Exabyte cassettes were used during the T2 production to store and backup the data.

References

1. *The Abyss* (Motion Picture), Twentieth Century Fox, 1989.
2. Anderson, Scott E. "Making a Pseudopod". *SIGGRAPH '90 Course Notes*, "Computer Graphics in Visual Effects."
3. *Cinefex 39*: Dancing on the Edge of the Abyss. August 1989.
4. *Terminator 2*: Judgment Day (Motion Picture), Carolco Pictures, 1991.
5. *Cinefex 47*: A Once and Future War. August 1991.
6. Yuncai Liu, Thomas Huang and O.D. Faugeras. "Determination of Camera Location From 2D to 3D Line and Point Correspondences." IEEE 1988.

Biography

Lincoln Hu joined Industrial Light & Magic in 1986 as one of the original five founding members of the Computer Graphics Department. He has worked on several Academy Award-winning feature films, performing a wide array of roles including modeler, animator, rendering and compositing technical director, project supervisor, hardware designer and software programmer. Lincoln has developed three input film scanners while at ILM: the first R & D prototype in 1987, the second in conjunction with Eastman Kodak in 1989, and the third which was completed in 1994. He received a Scientific and Engineering Academy Award for his work in this field.

Lincoln's current role as the Director of Advanced Technologies for ILM include long term digital technology research and development as well as technical supervision for ILM productions. He is actively involved in new technology developments in interactive modeling, animation, rendering and compositing, and a number of other related areas. He received a Bachelor of Science and a Master of Science degrees in Computer Science from Columbia University.

(Text first appeared in the SIGGRAPH 1993 Course "Computer Graphics in Visual Effects." © 1993 by Lincoln Hu.)

Recommended Reading

Adamson, Joe. *Tex Avery: King of Cartoons*. New York: Da Capo Press, 1975.

Ames, Patrick. *Beyond Paper*. New York: Adobe Press/Hayden Books, 1993.

Apple Computer Inc. *Apple CD-ROM Handbook: A Guide to Planning, Creating and Producing a CD-ROM*. Reading, MA: Addison-Wesley, 1992.

Arijon, Daniel. *Grammar of the Film Language*. Los Angeles: Silman-James Press, 1991.

Aukstakalnis, Steve, and David Blatner. *Silicon Mirage: The Art and Science of Virtual Reality*. Berkley, CA: Peachpit Press, 1992.

Blair, Preston. *Animation*. Tustin, CA: Walter T. Foster, 1949.

Campbell, Joseph. *The Hero with a Thousand Faces*, Second Edition. Princeton University Press, 1968.

Collins, Maynard. *Norman McLaren*. Ottawa: Canadian Film Institute, 1976.

Cotton, Bob, and Richard Oliver. *Understanding Hypermedia: From Multimedia to Virtual Reality*. London: Phaidon, 1993.

Crafton, Donald. *Before Mickey: The Animated Film 1898-1928*. Cambridge, MA: MIT Press, 1982.

Derfler, Frank J., ed. *How Networks Work*. Emeryville, CA: Ziff-Davis Press, 1993.

Dreyfus, Hubert L. *What Computers Still Can't Do, A Critique of Artificial Reason*. Cambridge, MA: The MIT Press, 1992.

Edera, Bruno. *Full Length Animated Feature Films*. New York: Hastings House, 1977.

Field, Syd. *The Screenwriter's Workbook*. New York: Dell, 1984.

Finch, Christopher. *Special Effects: Creating Movie Magic*. New York: Abbeville, 1984.

Foley, James, A.Van Dam, et al. *Fundamentals of Interactive Computer Graphics*, Second Edition. Reading: Addison-Wesley, 1990.

Glassner, Andrew S. *3D Computer Graphics: A User's Guide for Artists and Designers*, Second Edition. New York: Design Press, 1989.

Glassner, Andrew, ed. *An Introduction to Ray Tracing*. New York: Academic Press, 1989.

Goodman, Cynthia. *Digital Visions, Computers and Art*. New York: Abrams, 1987.

Halas, John, and Roger Manvell. *The Technique of Film Animation*. London/New York: Hastings House, 1959.

Halas, John. *Graphics in Motion*. New York: Van Nostrand Reinhold, 1981.

Hall, Roy. *Illumination and Color in Computer Generated Imagery*. New York: Springer-Verlag, 1989.

Holsinger, Erik. *MacWeek Guide to Desktop Video*. Emeryville, CA: Ziff-Davis Press, 1993.

Kawaguchi, Yoichiro. *Growth Morphogenesis*. Tokyo: JICC Publishing, 1985.

Kerlow, Isaac Victor, and Judson Rosebush. *Computer Graphics for Designers and Artists*, Second Edition. New York: Van Nostrand Reinhold, 1994.

Kitson, Claire. *Fifty Years of American Animation*. Los Angeles: American Film Institute, 1972.

MacNicol, Gregory. *Desktop Computer Animation:*

A Guide to Low-Cost Computer Animation. Boston: Focal Press, 1992.

Magnenat-Thalmann, Nadia, and Daniel Thalmann. *Synthetic Actors in Computer-Generated 3D Films.* New York: Springer-Verlag, 1990.

Maltin, Leonard. *Of Mice and Magic.* New York: McGraw-Hill, 1980.

Mandelbrot, Benoit. *The Fractal Geometry of Nature.* San Francisco: Freeman, 1982.

Manvell, Roger. *The Art of Animation.* New York: Hastings House, 1980.

Mealing, Stuart. *The Art and Science of Computer Animation.* Oxford, England: Intellect Books, 1992.

Mitchell, William, R. Liggett, and T. Kvan. *The Art of Computer Graphics Programming.* New York: Van Nostrand Reinhold, 1987.

Pascarelli, Emil, and Deborah Quilter. *Repetitive Strain Injury, A Computer User's Guide.* New York: John Wiley and Sons, 1994.

Peters, David, ed. *Terminal Health, Reports from Five Specialists on the Risks of the New Technology.* New York: AIGA/NY, 1992.

Pilbrow, Richard. *Stage Lighting,* Revised Edition. New York: Drama Book Publishers, 1991.

Popper, Frank. *Art of the Electronic Age.* New York: Harry N. Abrams Publishers, 1993.

Prusinkiewicz, Przemyslaw, and Aristid Lindenmayer. *The Algorithmic Beauty of Plants.* New York: Springer-Verlag, 1990.

Rogers, David, and J. Alan Adams. *Mathematical Elements for Computer Graphics.* New York: McGraw-Hill, 1976.

Roncarelli, Robi. *The Computer Animation Dictionary.* New York: Springer-Verlag, 1989.

Smith, Thomas, G. *Industrial Light and Magic: The Art of Special Effects.* New York: Ballantine Books, 1986.

Thomas, Frank, and Ollie Johnston. *Disney Animation, The Illusion of Life.* New York: Abbeville Press, 1981.

Upstill, Steve. *The RenderMan Companion: A Programmer's Guide to Realistic Computer Graphics.* Reading, MA: Addison-Wesley Publishing Company, 1990.

Vince, John. *3-D Computer Animation.* Wokingham, England: Addison-Wesley Publishing Company, 1992.

Whitaker, Harold, and John Halas. *Timing for Animation.* London/New York: Focal Press, 1981.

White, Tony. *The Animator's Workbook.* New York: Watson-Guptill, 1986.

Whitney, John. *Digital Harmony: On the Complimentarity of Music and Visual Art.* Petersborough, NH: McGraw-Hill, 1980.

Cinefex Journal

1. *Alien, Star Trek–The Motion Picture.* March 1980.
2. *The Empire Strikes Back, Star Trek–The Motion Picture,* Greg Jein. August 1980.
3. *The Empire Strikes Back,* Phase IV, Walter Murch. December 1980.
4. *Altered States, Outland.* April 1981.
5. Ray Harryhausen, *Clash of the Titans,* Roy Arbogast, *Caveman.* July 1981.
6. *Raiders of the Lost Ark, Dragonslayer,* Computer Generated Imagery. October 1981.
7. Willis O'Brien. January 1982.
8. *Tron, Silent Running.* April 1982.
9. *Blade Runner.* July 1982.
10. *Poltergeist, Firefox.* October 1982.
11. *E.T.,* Robert Swarthe. January 1983.
12. *Something Wicked This Way Comes,* Stop-Motion Update, *Dream Quest.* April 1983.
13. *Return of the Jedi.* July 1983.
14. *The Right Stuff, Brainstorm, Twilight Zone–The Movie.* October 1983.
15. *Never Say Never Again, The Day After,* Ralph Hammeras. January 1984.
16. Rick Baker. April 1984.
17. *Ghostbusters, The Last Starfighter.* June 1984.
18. *Indiana Jones and the Temple of Doom, Star Trek III.* August 1984.
19. *Gremlins, Buckaroo Banzai, Dreamscape.* November 1984.
20. *2010.* January 1985.
21. *The Terminator, Dune.* April 1985.
22. *Return to Oz, Baby.* June 1985.
23. *Explorers, Lifeforce, My Science Project.* August 1985.
24. *Cocoon, Back to the Future, The Goonies.* November 1985.
25. *Enemy Mine,* German Special Effects, *Fright Night.* February 1986.
26. *Poltergeist II, Young Sherlock Holmes.* May 1986.
27. *Aliens.* August 1986.
28. *The Fly, Big Trouble in Little China, Short Circuit.* November 1986.
29. *Star Trek IV, King Kong Lives, Top Gun.* February 1987.
30. *Little Shop of Horrors, The Gate, The Golden Child.* May 1987.
31. *Spaceballs, The Witches of Eastwick, Masters of the Universe.* August 1987.
32. *Robocop, Innerspace.* November 1987.
33. Dick Smith, *James Bond, Predator.* February 1988.
34. *Beetlejuice, Batteries Not Included.* May 1988.
35. *Who Framed Roger Rabbit, Willow.* August 1988.
36. *Dead Ringers, Alien Nation, The Blob, Die Hard.* November 1988.
37. *Star Trek–The Next Generation, The Fly II,* Oxford Scientific Films. February 1989.
38. *Time Bandits, Brazil, Baron Munchausen.* May 1989.
39. *The Abyss.* August 1989.
40. *Indiana Jones and the Last Crusade, Ghostbusters II.* November 1989.
41. *Batman, Honey I Shrunk the Kids.* February 1990.
42. *The Hunt for Red October, Tremors, Star Trek*

V. May 1990.

43. *Total Recall, Back to the Future II & III.* August 1990.
44. *Dick Tracy, Ghost, Always.* November 1990.
45. *RoboCop 2, Die Hard 2, Flight of the Intruder.* February 1991.
46. Rick Baker Update, Simulator Rides, *Godfather* Trilogy. May 1991.
47. *Terminator 2.* August 1991.
48. *The Rocketeer, Backdraft, Cast A Deadly Spell.* November 1991.
49. *Hook, Naked Lunch, Star Trek VI.* February 1992.
50. *Alien 3, The Lawnmower Man,* Cinefex Index (1-50). May 1992.
51. *Batman Returns,* August 1992.
52. *Honey, I Blew Up the Kid, Death Becomes Her.* November 1992.
53. *Bram Stoker's Dracula, Close Encounters of the Third Kind.* February 1993.
54. *Cliffhanger,* Toys. May 1993.
55. *Jurassic Park.* August 1993.
56. *The Nightmare Before Christmas, Last Action Hero, RoboCop 3.* November 1993.
57. *Attack of the 50 Foot Woman, Demolition Man.* February 1994.
58. *The Flintstones, The Hudsucker Proxy.* May 1994.
59. *True Lies.* August 1994.
60. *The Mask, Forrest Gump, Mary Shelley's Frankenstein.* December 1994.
61. *Interview With the Vampire, Star Trek Generations, Stargate.* March 1995.

SIGGRAPH Video Review

Summary

The following is a selection of the videotapes about three-dimensional computer animation published by the SIGGRAPH Video Review. This list includes the issues that contain mostly artistic and commercial animations created between 1979 and 1994. (Ordering information can be found at the end of the appendix.)

1. SIGGRAPH 79 Film and Video Show
1. TOPES/Bell Laboratories
2. Newshole/University of Toronto
3. Videocel/Computer Creations
4. Sunstone/Emschwiller
5. Voyager 2/Blinn et al.
6. Information International Demo Reel
7. DNA with Ethidium/Max et al.

2. SIGGRAPH 80 Film and Video Show
1. The Compleat Angler/Whitted
2. Vol Libre/Carpenter
3. JPL/Saturn/Blinn et al.
4. Peak/Snitly
5. Doxorubicin/DNA/Max et al.
6. Digital Effects Demo Reel
7. MAGI Synthavision Demo Reel
8. Spatial Data Mgt. System/Herot et al.
9. Pantomation/DeWitt et al.
10. Artifacts/The Vasulkas

3. SIGGRAPH 80 Film and Video Show
1. CT5 Flight Simulator/Evans & Sutherland
2. Time Rider/JVC
3. Imagination/Acme Cartoon Company
4. Dubner Demo Tape
5. Vidsizer/Franzblau
6. ZGRASS Paint Demo/Giloth et al.

4. SIGGRAPH 81 Film and Video Show
1. Abel Demo Reel/Kovacs et al.
2. Image West Demo Reel
3. OSU Computer Graphics Research Group Terrain Model/Csuri et al.
4. Computer-Assisted Dance Notation/Calvert et al.
5. The Grip-75 Man-machine Interface/UNC
6. Graphics Interactions at NRC/Wein et al., National Film Board of Canada

5. SIGGRAPH 82 Film and Video Show
1. Evans & Sutherland Demo '82
2. The Tactical Edge/Evans & Sutherland
3. Carla's Island/Max et al.
4. Aurora Demo
5. Digital Effects Sampler '82
6. Real Time Design ZGRASS Demo
7. Marks & Marks Demo

6. SIGGRAPH 82 Film and Video Show
1. Abel '82 Demo Reel
2. Galileo/Blinn et al., JPL
3. Mimas/Voyager II/Blinn et al., JPL
4. Non-Edge Computer Image Gen./Grumman
5. DISSPLA Animation/ISSCO

6. Tomato Bushy Stunt Virus/Olson
7. Interactive Raster Graphics Sampler/UNC
8. Ron Hays Music-Image Sampler

7. SIGGRAPH 82 Film and Video Show
1. Triple-I Digital Scene Simulation Reel
2. TRON reference/Disney
3. MAGI/Synthavision '82 Demo
4. Videocel '82/Computer Creations
5. Cranston/Csuri Demo Reel
6. Four Seasons of Japan/Expo '85/NHK
7. Acme Cartoon Company Samples '82
8. ADAM/Olson and O'Donnell
9. 1982 Experimental Works/Texnai CGL
10. Sorting Out Sorting Excerpt/University of Toronto

9. SIGGRAPH 83 Film and Video Show
1. Economars Earth Tours/Upson
2. Toyo Links Demo
3. Antics/Abe
4. Japan Computer Graphics Lab
5. Bo Gehring Demo
6. Omnibus Video
7. Translation Part 3/Moran
8. Julia I Excerpts/Peitgen and Saupe
9. Space Simulator/Galicki
10. Marks & Marks/Novocon
11. Solid Modeling/Zaritsky and Herr

10. SIGGRAPH 83 Film and Video Show
1. When Mandrills Ruled.../Watterberg
2. Cranston-Csuri Productions
3. OSU/Zeltzer and Van Baerle
4. Pan Optica Preview '83/Gordon
5. Ray Tracing/Barr and Lorig
6. Pacific Data Images
7. NHK Special Programs Division
8. Humanon/Francois
9. Light & Shadow/Nakamae
10. UNC Sampler
11. Benesh Notation/Singh
12. Blooming Stars Excerpt/Genda

11. SIGGRAPH 83 Film and Video Show
1. Star Trek II: Genesis/Paramount and Lucasfilm
2. Non-Edge CIG/Grumman

3. Digital Effects Demo
4. The Cube CUBE/Gerhard
5. SPN/SEIBU Productions Network
6. Symmetry Test 11A/Newell
7. Composite News/Burson
8. A/V Tour at SIGGRAPH 83/Veeder and Morton
9. Shirogumi Sampler
10. Movie Maker/IPS
11. Pixel Play/Nakajima
12. Growth/Mysterious Galaxy/Kawaguchi
13. Digital Harmony/Whitney, Sr. et al.

14. SIGGRAPH 84 Electronic Theater
1. Martian Magnolia/Mareda
2. Tantra '84/Nakajima
3. Puzzle/RPI CICG
4. Ray Tracing, A Silent Movie/Sweeney and Forsey
5. The Cube's Transformation/Resch
6. 9600 Bauds/Huitric, Nahas, and Bret
7. Wag the Flag/Kesler and Balch
8. Whispers in a Plane of Light/Gillerman and Piche
9. Sharkey's Day/Anderson and Winkler
10. Floater Final Sequence/Veeder
11. Before the Law/Seiden

15. SIGGRAPH 84 Electronic Theater
1. Bio-Sensor/Osaka University and Toyo Links
2. Robert Abel and Associates 1984 Demo Reel
3. OSU Computer Graphics Research Group
4. JCGL Demo/Japan Computer Graphics Lab
5. The Bicycle Company/Landor Associates
6. First Flight/Bisogno and Ferraro
7. Warnings from the 21st Century/Shonosuke and Kitayama
8. Dream House/Pryor
9. SIGGRAPH 84 Time Lapse/Naimark
10. Omnimax Documentary/Liedtke
11. A Brief Visual History of Computer Graphics/Ellingson

16. SIGGRAPH 84 Electronic Theater
1. Demo Reel 1984/MAGI Synthavision

2. Cranston/Csuri Productions Demo Reel
3. Renault Electronic Now!/M.C.A.V. Renault
4. Sogitec Showreel
5. Omnibus Computer Graphics
6. Visual Image Presentation/Acme Graphics
7. Vertigo Computer Imagery
8. Wonderworks/Durinsky, Omnibus
9. Joblove/Kay Inc. Sample Reel
10. Show Reel/EIDOS
11. Graphics at GLOBO/TV GLOBO
12. Digital Productions Demo Reel
13. Our Favorites/Digital Effects

17. SIGGRAPH 84 Electronic Theater
1. The Mechanical Universe/JPL Computer Graphics Lab
2. Clinical Aspects of Alcoholism/VA Medical Center
3. The Last Supper at the Computer/Computervision
4. Still-Life Etude-1/Hiroshima University
5. Star Rider Laser Disk Video Game/Computer Creations VideoCel
6. The Sudanese Mobius Band/Lerner and Asimov
7. Fly Lorenz/Juergens and Peitgen
8. Link Flight Simulation Demo/The Singer Company Link Division
9. Beethoven's Sixth in CIG/Gardner

20. SIGGRAPH 85 Film and Video Show
1. The Mechanical Universe/JPL
2. The Making of BRILLIANCE/Abel
3. GM Saturn Robot Assembly/Z-Axis
4. Feast of Lights/Nakamae
5. GED Science/Chute
6. Computer Cowboy/Artronics
7. UNC '85 Interactive Graphics Sampler
8. Mr. Yorick Skull .../Liebman
9. Grasp Lab/Voxel Demo/University of Pennsylvania
10. Terms of Entrapment/Olson
11. Fractal Generation/Lathrop
12. Have a Koch/Kirk
13. Tori in the Hypersphere/Margolis
14. Videoplace Sampler/Krueger

21. SIGGRAPH 85 Film and Video Show
1. Tuber's Two Step/Wedge
2. Eurythmy/Amkraut, Girard, and Karl
3. Cranston/Csuri 1985 Demo Reel
4. Quest/Sciulli, Arvo, and White
5. Digital Effects Demo Reel
6. Omnibus Demo Reel '85
7. Intelligent Light 1985 Demo Reel
8. JCGL Demo Reel '85
9. Sogitec Demo Reel 1985
10. Advanced Computer Animation Course Notes, SIGGRAPH 85/Rosebush and Bergeron

22. SIGGRAPH 85 Film and Video Show
1. PDI Animation Assortment
2. Calculated Movements/Cuba
3. Luminare/Sanborn and Winkler
4. Growth III: Origin/Kawaguchi
5. Mt. Fuji/Nakajima
6. The Last Starfighter Excerpts/Digital Productions
7. Nursery Song/Technofront
8. Ralph the Punk/Athanas and Horn
9. Precision Bathroom/Weil and Helman
10. Flow Fantasia '85/Sasaki
11. CFD Workstation/NASA Ames
12. Telepresence Technology/Rappaport

23. SIGGRAPH 85 Film and Video Show
1. Pixels at an Exhibition/Bacon
2. Trees/California Institute of Technology
3. Molecular Dynamics/Lerner
4. MAGI Demo Reel 1985
5. Bosch FGS4000 Demo Tape
6. Silicon Graphics Demo
7. Interpolating Splines/Kochanek
8. Robert Abel & Associates
9. Digital Productions
10. Limbo Land/Reitzer

24. SIGGRAPH 86 Electronic Theater
1. Serenity/Omnibus
2. Abel Image Research '86
3. Pacific Data Images-Opera Industrial
4. Digital Productions '86
5. Toyo Links '86
6. Sogitec '86

7. Omnibus Demo Reel '86
8. Interiors/San Francisco Production Group
9. Knot Reel/Schlumberger
10. New Threads/AT&T Bell Labs
11. Wood Turning/Imagenisis
12. Lenses over Rolling Chrome/Clark
13. Life on Titan
14. Dogumaster
15. Caron's World/NHK
16. Motion Studies/Girard and Karl
17. Vision Obious/Leeman
18. Blue Chair & Ghoti/Seideman
19. Metafable
20. Soft II
21. Z./Weinberger
22. Human Vectors Excerpt/Jacobson

25. SIGGRAPH 86 Electronic Theater
1. SIGGRAPH Opening/Cranston/Csuri Productions
2. Obelisk/JVC
3. Fantastic Animation Machine '86
4. Details Count/GE
5. CalTech Demo & Flyby
6. Hot Air/Sandia National Labs
7. Simulation Excellence/Evans & Sutherland
8. Visitor on a Foggy Night/Hiroshima University
9. Light Beams/Max, LLNL
10. JCGL '86
11. Bosch FGS4000
12. Computer Animation Laboratory '86
13. Vertigo Demo Reel
14. R/Greenberg Demo Reel
15. Speeder
16. Mechanical Universe/JPL
17. Dynamics/Norton, IBM
18. Super Resolution/MIT
19. Two Bit/Pixel Full Color Encoding/DeFanti, UIC
20. 4K Tape/Veeder
21. Artist as a Performer

26. CHI + GI '87 Electronic Theatre
1. Commercial productions. From the U.S., Japan, and Europe: Omnibus/Abel, Sogitec, TDI, NYIT, Toyo Links; From Canada: Greenlight, Vertigo, Mobile Image, CBC, Alias Research, Andre Perry Video, and the University of Calgary
2. Best commercials submitted. Benson & Hedges Carousel, Benson & Hedges Power, Prudential, TRW, Hawaiian Punch/Omnibus/Abel
3. Research computer graphics and visual synthesis. LeGame/CBC Engineering; Waves/Pixar; Dynamics/IBM; Knot Reel/Schlumberger; New Threads/AT&T Bell Labs; Work in Progress/MIT Media Lab; Motion Studies/OSU; BSP Trees/AT&T Bell Labs; Simulation Excellence/Evans & Sutherland; Demo & Flyby/CalTech
4. Research human interaction. Lego Logo/MIT Media Lab; Hook-up/MIT Media Lab; Animating Programs/Tektronix; DataGlove/VPL Research; Virtual Environment/NASA Ames; Interactive Font Design/MIT Visible Language Workshop; Color Selection Tools/Xerox PARC; Intelligent Graphic Layout/MIT Visible Language Workshop; Conversational Desktop/MIT Media Lab; SemNet/MCC; Alternate Reality Kit/Xerox PARC
5. Animation projects as either research or demonstration pieces. Digitoons and User Abuser/NYIT; Opera Industriel/Pacific Data Images; Digital Productions '86/Digital Productions; Interiors/San Francisco Production Group; Luxo Jr./Pixar; Hot Air/Sandia National Labs

28. Visualization in Scientific Computing: Domain
1. L.A.-The Movie/JPL
2. Instabilities in Supersonic Flows/Norman et al., NCSA
3. CalTech Studies in Modeling and Motion/Barr et al., CalTech
4. Evolution of Structure in the Universe/Centrella, Drexel
5. Dynamic Crack Propagation with Step Function Stress Loading/Haber et al., NCSA

6. Numerical Simulation of a Thunderstorm Outflow/Wilhelmson et al., NCSA
7. Scientific Visualization/Science Data Systems Group, JPL
8. Poliovirus/Olson et al., Research Institute of Scripps Clinic
9. Inertial Confinement Fusion/Max, LLNL
10. RPI Scientific Visualization/RPI CICG
11. Rigid Body Dynamics/Hahn, OSU
12. NASA CFD Highlights
13. Computational Fluid Dynamics/Winkler et al., LANL
14. Aerospace Applications of ADAM and Postprocessor/Mechanical Dynamics

30. Visualization/State of the Art Special Issue
1. Interactivity
2. Workstation Trends
3. Expansion Boards
4. Input/Output Peripherals
5. Lighting: Theory and Practice
6. Update: Graphic Art Systems
7. Dynamics: The New Realism
8. Visualization in Scientific Computing
9. Medical Imaging & Volumetrics
10. Parallel Processors: Accelerators & Image Computers
11. Looking Ahead/Herr and Zaritsky, Pacific Interface

31. Educational Systems
1. Interactive Image/DeFanti, UIC
2. Fractal Exploration/Sandin, UIC
3. Animation Pipeline/Csuri, OSU
4. Image Processing on PIPE/Kent, Philips Lab

32. Educational Systems
1. A Close Encounter in the Fourth Dimension/Norton, IBM
2. Quantum Mechanical Universe/Blinn, JPL
3. BALSA/Van Dam, Brown University
4. Designing with PLAID/Badler, University of Pennsylvania

36. SIGGRAPH 87 Film and Video Show
1. Stanley and Stella: Breaking the Ice/Symbolics Graphics and Whitney Demos Productions
2. Balloon Guy/OSU ACCAD
3. Red's Dream (excerpt)/Pixar
4. Fabricated Rhythm/AT&T Bell Labs
5. Mental Images/mental images GmbH & Co. KG
6. Cooking with Kurt/Schlumberger Palo Alto Research
7. Dynamic Simulations of Flexible Objects/OSU ACCAD
8. Sun and Shade/Max, LLNL
9. Moon/Max, LLNL
10. C.G. Town/Hiroshima University
11. Agusta A-129 Real-Time Simulation/GE
12. Molecular Dynamics of Solutions/IBM
13. Boom Boom Boom/AT&T Bell Labs
14. Curtain/Haumann, OSU ACCAD
15. Sign of the Times/Mix Efex/Pacific Video
16. One Minute Past Forever/NHK Osaka
17. Computer Graphics and Animation Group/MIT Media Lab
18. Jo, Beauberg, and CIO/TDI
19. TDI Science & Industry/TDI
20. Syntex Opener/Lazerus
21. JCGL Demo for SIGGRAPH 87/JCGL
22. Sogitec Show Reel/Sogitec
23. Deja Vu/4D Art & Design

37. SIGGRAPH 88 Animation Screening Room Highlights
1. Cootie Gets Scared/Zeltzer, MIT
2. Post Perfect Demo Reel/Winkler, Post Perfect
3. Interaction of Cosmic Strings/Fangmeier, NCSA
4. Robochicken-Poultry in Motion/Amour, Camerawork
5. The Sky/Nakamae, Hiroshima University
6. Anchoring Unit of Protamine with DNA/Max, LLNL
7. KHD Commercial/Steiner
8. Refraction Effects in Radiosity/Sillion, LIENS
9. Mars Rover Sample Return Mission/Sabionski, NASA
10. Hair/Weil, Whitney Demos Productions

11. ReZ-N8 Demo Reel/Stolow, ReZ-N8
12. Metalmorphosis/Burrows, OSU ACCAD
13. F-16 Flight Dynamics/Bancroft, NASA Ames
14. Animals (excerpt)/Bravais, Mac Guff Ligne
15. Technoquest Demo Reel/Hirokane, Technoquest
16. Sonic Map Study/Evans, NCSA
17. Visualization of 4D Meteorological Data/Hibbard, University of Wisconsin
18. Channel 26 ID/Hirokane, Technoquest
19. Return to the Titanic -Sinking Scenario/Whitney, Mix Efex
20. Helicopter!/Briggs, Evans & Sutherland
21. Chalk Talk/Lamb
22. Project Sci-Vi/Fangmeier, NCSA

38. SIGGRAPH 88 Film and Video Show
 0. Opening Animation/Dixon, Pacific Data Images
 1. Technological Threat (excerpt)/Kroyer Films, Inc.
 2. Key Change/Bogart, University of Utah
 3. Mickey Mouth/Harris, Topix
 4. VH1 Demo/Scott Miller and Associates
 5. Mathematica: The Theorem of Pythagoras/Blinn, CalTech
 6. Flying Logos, Inc./Conn, Homer & Associates
 7. NCSA Scientific Visualization 1988/Fangmeier, NCSA
 8. Jumpin' Jacques Splash/Nicolas, Sogitec
 9. CT6 Automobile/Briggs, Evans & Sutherland
10. Broken Heart/Staveley, OSU ACCAD
11. Digital Pictures Ads/Woodfield, Digital Pictures
12. The Art Dream/Haxton, William Paterson College
13. Great Train Rubbery/Wyvill, University of Calgary
14. Krypto and the Supremes/Seydoux, BSCA
15. Burning Love/St. John, Pacific Data Images
16. Organic Architecture/Greene, NYIT
17. Sextone for President/Kleiser-Walczak Construction Company
18. Stuff We Did/St. John, Pacific Data Images
19. Links Corporation Demo Reel for SIG-GRAPH 88/Odaka, Links Corporation
20. Embryo (excerpt)/Kawaguchi, Nippon Electronics College
21. Going Bananas/Barr, CalTech
22. Tin Toy (excerpt)/Guggenheim, Pixar

39. SIGGRAPH 88 Film and Video Show
 0. Live Performance/de Graf/Wahrman
23. Soaron and Blastarr Character Animation/Price, ARCCA Animation
24. Dinosaur Stuff/Donkin, OSU ACCAD
25. Space Station/Casey, Production Masters
26. Smarties "Blue Print"/Edwards, Robinson Lambie-Nairn Ltd.
27. Scrubbing Bubbles/Leeman, Cranston/Csuri Productions
28. Footsteps/Zerouni, Computer FX Ltd.
29. Beat Dedication/Sabiston, MIT Media Lab
30. A Close Encounter in the Fourth Dimension/Norton and Melton, IBM
31. Polly Gone/Lake
32. Pencil Test/Susman, Apple
33. Function of the Brain Cells/Atelier Bister Animation Art GmbH
34. Rhythm & Hues SIGGRAPH Show Reel/Riccio and Ross, Rhythm & Hues
35. Stylo/Eurocitel
36. Space-time Constraints/Witkin, Schlumberger Palo Alto Research
37. Formation of Venus Plasma Clouds and Streamers/Wolff, Apple and Norman, NCSA
38. Pencil Polka/McMahon, Electric Picture Works
39. Oh Atsimenu Nameli/Wilson
40. Natural Phenomena/Miller, Alias Research
41. Sio-Benbor/Lacroix, Fantome
42. Particle Dreams/Sims, Whitney Demos Productions

40. SIGGRAPH 88 Art Show: Interactive and Video Artists
 1. Very Nervous System/Rokeby

2. Self Search/Axelrad
3. Plasm: A Nano Sample/Myers et, al.,
   Silicon Graphics
4. Videoplace '88/Krueger
5. Interactive Video Kaleidoscope/Sims
6. Lego/Logo/Conn, MIT Media Lab.
7. Bird Cage and Word Processor/Rath
8. Interactive Image/DeFanti et al., UIC

41. SIGGRAPH 88 Art Show: Interactive and Video Artists
9. The Countdown/Foltz
10. JabJabLand/Debuchi
11. Polly Gone/Lake
12. Eclipse/Hirata
13. Looking In/Caldwell
14. Deltoid ... A Drinking Man/Banchero
15. Bau/Ono
16. Fractal Fantasy/Brinsmead
17. The Open School/Conn
18. Oh Atsimenu Nameli/Wilson
19. Urban Memories/Hahn
20. The Thundering Scream of the
    Seraphim's Delight/Weidenaar

42. Visualization in Scientific Computing '89: Research
1. Thinking Machines: Best of
   Visualization/Salem, TMI
2. Random Dot Motion/Sandin, UIC
3. Spectral Density Functions/Rogan, Alcoa
4. Volume Rendering for Scientific
   Visualization/McMillan, Sun
5. MATLAB on Ardent Titan/Moler, Ardent
6. Fractal Transitions/Norton, IBM
7. Dynamics in the Quaternions/Hart, UIC
8. Cubic Polynomial Volume
   Rendering/Gunn, Minn. Supercomputer
   Inst.
9. Fluoropolymer Simulations/Dixon, du
   Pont
10. Molecular Genesis/Rogers, du Pont
11. Imine Ion Interactions in the Gramicidin
    Channel/Chen, Brown University
12. Tempest in a Teapot/Desmarais, Battelle
13. Rendering of PLIF Flowfield Images/van
    Cruyningen, Stanford

43. Visualization in Scientific Computing '89: Research
1. BRL Scientific Visualization
   Highlights/Muuss, BRL
2. Stress Wave Propagation in
   Graphite/Epoxy Material/Cardwell, PVI
3. SEA Accident Reconstruction/Leeman,
   SEA
4. Earthquake and Structural
   Response/Suzuki, Shimizu Corp.
5. Interactive Earth Science
   Visualization/Hibbard, Univ. of Wisc.
6. A Little About Bones and Points of
   Insertion/Doria, Swiss Inst. of
   Biomechanics
7. Visualization of Brain/Toga, UCLA
   Medical School
8. Volume Microscopy of Biological
   Structures/Argiro, Vital Images
9. AML Total Hip System and
   Porocoat/Reed Productions
10. Ray Tracing of Computed
    Tomograms/Meinzer, Cancer Research
    Heidelberg
11. UNC Computer Graphics Sampler
    '89/Fuchs, UNC

44. Volume Visualization/State of the Art-Special Issue
1. What is Volume Visualization?
2. How is Volume Visualization being used
   right now?
3. Why has Volume Visualization suddenly
   come to the forefront?
4. How does it work?
5. What are the basic concepts?
6. What are the advantages and disadvantages?
7. Where will it lead? Herr, Pacific Interface

49 Visualization in Scientific Computing
1. Mars: The Movie/Hall, JPL
2. Earth: The Movie/Hall, JPL
3. 1988 CFD Highlights/Watson, NASA
   Ames
4. Visualizing Shuttle Flow Physics and
   Fluid Dynamics/Bancroft, NASA Ames
5. Self-Portrait/Goldsmith, JPL

6. The Etruscan Venus/Francis, UIUC
7. Numerical Relativity: Black Hole
    Spacetimes/Hobill, NCSA
8. The Lorenz Attractor/Hobill, NCSA
9. Kodak's Supercomputational Science
    '88/Ray, Kodak
10. Hydrogen Diffusion on a Platinum
    Surface/Ray, Kodak
11. Double Diffusive Convection:
    Saltfingering/Rosenblum, NRL
12. Simulated Treatment of an Ocular
    Tumor/Lytle, CNSF

50. Visualization in Scientific Computing
1. Pittsburgh Supercomputing Center
    '89/Welling, PSC
2. Interaction of Cosmic Jets with an
    Intergalactic Medium/Elvins, SDSC
3. SDSC Scientific Visualization
    '88/Sheddon, SDSC
4. Monte Carlo Simulation of Excited
    Electrons in GaAs/Brady, NCSA
5. Molecular Diffusion on Crystal Gold
    Surface/Brady, NCSA
6. Two-Armed Instability of a Rotating
    Polytropic Star/Brady, NCSA
7. Large-Scale Structure in the
    Universe/Brady, NCSA
8. Enzyme Reaction in Triophosphate
    Isomerase/Brady, NCSA
9. Quantum Molecular Dynamics/Brady,
    NCSA
10. Cajon Paass Scientific Drilling
    Project/Brady, NCSA
11. Topology of Coma Supercluster
    Region/Brady, NCSA
12. VIEW: Ames Virtual Environment
    Workstation/Fisher, NASA Ames

**51. SIGGRAPH 89 Computer Graphics
    Theater**
1. The Little Death/Elson, Symbolics
2. A Moonlit Spring Night at Ma-ma
    Temple/Motoyoshi, HighTech Lab.
3. Inforum/Design/Effects
4. Her Majesty's Secret Serpent/Apple
5. Treadmill/Campbell
6. Locomotion/Goldberg, Pacific Data

Images
7. The Conquest of Form/IBM UKSC
8. NBC 1988 Olympic Open/Kanner,
    Filigree Films
9. Gibbon Event/Ridenour, UCLA Design
    Dept.
10. Visualization of Simulated Treatment of
    an Ocular Tumor/Lytle, CNSF
11. Continuum 1. Initiation/Post Perfect
12. Mars-The Movie/JPL
13. In Search of New Axis/Polygon Pictures
14. Megacycles/Mitchell, AT&T Bell Labs
15. Sio-Benbor Junior/Fantome
16. Mathematics!/Blinn, CalTech
17. Study of a Numerically Modeled Severe
    Storm/NCSA
18. Margaux Cartoon/Warshafsky, Electric
    Picture Works
19. L'Anniversaire/Anniversary (An
    Excerpt)/Centre d'Animatique, National
    Film Board of Canada
20. Paris: 1789/Nicolas, ExMachina
21. A Public Service
    Announcement/WATARP
22. Breeze/Xaos
23. Send in the Clouds/Gardner, Grumman
24. The Making of "Without
    Borders"/Berson, Design/Effects
25. The Virtual Lobby/Rohlf, UNC

**52. SIGGRAPH 89 Computer Graphics
    Theater and Animation Screening
    Room Highlights**
1. Complexly Simple/Kajima Corp.
2. Night Cafe/Calahan, Cubicomp Canada
    Ltd.
3. Excerpts from "Leonardo's Deluge"/Sims,
    Optomystic
4. Voyager: Journey to the Outer
    Planets/Rueff, JPL
5. Don't Touch Me/Kleiser-Walczak
    Construction Company
6. Parfums de Vie/Ortega, Sogitec
7. Tipsy Turvy/Norton, IBM Research
8. Eurhythmy/Amkraut and Girard, OSU
    ACCAD
9. Numerical Experiments on the Interaction
    of Disk Galaxies/Bancroft, NASA Ames

10. Gas Turbine Flowfield Simulation/NASA Ames
11. Tempest in a Teapot/Desmarais, Battelle
12. knickknack (excerpt)/Guggenheim, Pixar
13. Displacement Animation of Intelligent Objects/Elson, Symbolics
14. Dirty Power/Lurye, OSU ACCAD
15. ALEA/Anderson, MIT Media Lab
16. Plastic Landing/Dech, UIC
17. Leela/Shriram
18. PeeDee Meets the Dragon/Weil, Optomystic

53. SIGGRAPH 89 Animation Screening Room Highlights
1. Random House/Johnson, SVA
2. Trouble in the Basement/Johnson, SVA
3. Galaxy Sweetheart/Thalmann, Swiss Federal Inst. of Technology
4. Columbus On the Edge/Haxton, William Paterson College
5. Ziggraf/Banchero, Jr.
6. Vegetables/Lehn, Lamb & Company
7. Tempest/Litwinowicz,Williams, et al., Apple
8. Soft Landing/RGB Computer Graphics Service
9. First Contact/Wolff, Apple
10. Crack Fish/Ray, Byte by Byte Corp.
11. Autodesk Animator/Bennett, Autodesk
12. Kawasaki Safety Intelligent Plaza/Howe and Kasahara, Kajima Corp.
13. Scenes at a Street Corner/Nakamae, Hiroshima Univ.
14. Pool/Volny
15. A Journey Into Sound/CMP GmbH & Co. KG
16. Multivisual's 1989 Demo Reel/Lowe and Mellenhorst
17. Demon Reel/Berenguer, ANIMATICA
18. In Time ... It Happens/Banchero, Jr.
19. Lamb & Company Character Demo Reel/Lehn, Lamb & Co.
20. Music for the Eyes/Conahan & Amour, Camerawork
21. 1989 PPS Selected Animations/Polk, Post Production Services
22. New Explorers Opening/Cully, Post

Effects
23. Metrolight Studios Show Reel/DiNoble, MetroLight Studios
24. McEwan's L.A. "Walk In A Straight Line"/Forrest, Snapper Films
25. Pepsi Presents: Wired/Forrest, et al., Snapper Films
26. Digital Pictures Animation/Woodfield, Digital Pictures
27. Stuff We Did/Seydoux, BSCA
28. The Sound of One Hand Clapping/Stroukoff

54. SIGGRAPH 89 Animation Screening Room Highlights
1. Viomechawars/Debuchi, HighTech Lab
2. Lorelei/Casey et al., Production Masters
3. Once a Pawn a Foggy Knight.../Ebert et al., OSU
4. Esmerelda/Kantor, SVA
5. Let It Rain/Wilson
6. Birdbrainstorm/Voci, NYIT Media & Arts
7. PDI "Selected Cuts"/Gaeta, Pacific Data Images
8. Honey, I Shrunk the Kids (Opening Titles)/Kroyer Films
9. Philomene/Fantome
10. Fish/Bock
11. Karkador/Callas
12. Revolve Evolve/Hirata
13. A View of a Room/Gerth
14. Gallia/Stenger
15. Rednose Rabbit/Hulsbergen, Digital Art Production
16. Coredump/Fujii, OSU ACCAD
17. The Universe Within/NHK
18. Pygmalion/Nahas, Université Paris
19. Faux Pas/Davies, Softimage

60 HDTV & The Quest For Virtual Reality-Special
HDTV
1. HDTV Around the World
2. Classical Television
3. High Definition Television
4. What You Can Buy Now on the TV Continuum
5. TV & Film Production & Distribution

6. The Economics of HDTV
7. New HDTV Applications
8. HDTV & Telecommunications
9. The Digital Video Telecomputer HDTV and Industrial Leadership

The Quest For Virtual Reality
1. Introduction to the Desktop of the Future
2. Virtual Reality
3. The Evolution of Today's Workstation
4. Display Hardware
5. Data Highways
6. The Journey to Virtual Reality Herr and Rosebush, Pacific Interface

61. Supercomputing '90 Featuring Pieces from SIGGRAPH 90
1. The Politics of Pleasure/Meyers, EVL-UIC
2. Splash Dance/Kass, Apple Computer, Inc.
3. 1990 CFD Highlights/Gong, NASA Ames Research Center
4. Visualizing Fermat's Last Theorem/Hanson, Indiana University
5. Numerical Simulations of Cosmic Jets/Elvins, SDSC
6. The Formation of the Solar System/Nadeau, SDSC
7. Sierpinski Blows His Gasket/Hart, EVL-UIC
8. PSC 1990 Sampler/Welling, PSC
9. Lively IFS/Lescinsky, EVL-UIC
10. Cold Front Moving Across the North Atlantic/Hibbard, University of Wisconsin
11. ANL's Scientific Visualization Promo Tape/Dech, ANL
12. Ductile Flow/Reynolds, Symbolics, Inc.
13. Electron Densities of the AZT Molecule/Dech & O'Donnell, UIC
14. Forest Fire Simulation/Gardner, Grumman Data Systems
15. Landscape Dynamics of Yellowstone Park/Walker, NCSA
16. Computational Quantum Chemistry in Catalysis Research/Walker, NCSA

62. Supercomputing '90 Featuring Pieces from SIGGRAPH 90
17. Smog: Visualizing the Components/Walker, NCSA
18. More Bells and Whistles/Lytle, Cornell National Supercomputer Facility
19. Artificial Reality at UNC-Chapel Hill/Robinett, UNC-Chapel Hill
20. A Sequence from the Evolution of Form/Latham, IBM UK Scientific Centre
21. Mathematics! Similarity and The Story of pie/Corrigan, CalTech
22. A Volume of 2-D Julia Sets/Sandin, EVL-UIC
23. Panspermia/Sims, Thinking Machines Corp.
24. The Process of Wound Healing/Bister, Atelier Bister-Animation Art GmbH
25. Flight Over Mandelbrot Set/Jurgens, University of Bremen
26. Neptune Encounter/Hall, Jet Propulsion Lab.
27. Invertebrate Models/Clark, Florida Institute of Technology
29. Graftals/Rawlings, EVL-UIC

66. SIGGRAPH 90 Film and Video Theater
0. Opening Animation/Grower, Santa Barbara Studios
1. This is not Frank's Planet/Swain, Cal. State University
2. McDonald's "Save the Universe"/DiNoble, MetroLight Studios
3. ABC's World of Discovery/DiNoble, MetroLight Studios
4. AMC "Feature Presentation"/DiNoble, MetroLight Studios
5. Total Recall/Schiff, MetroLight Studios
6. 1990 SIGGRAPH Demo/Lamb & Company, Inc.
7. Gas Pipe/Hurrell, SVC Television
8. Dirty Power/Lurye, OSU-ACCAD
9. Nissan "Time Machine"/Gibson, Rhythm & Hues, Inc.
10. 7-UP "Saxophone"/Gibson, Rhythm & Hues, Inc.
11. A Passing Shower/Nakamae, Hiroshima University
12. Lava Jr./Bauer, Luxo-Klone Productions
13. Trillo's Adventures/Di Biagio, Intermedia

Audiovisivi S.N.C
14. The Audition/Miller, Apple Computer, Inc.
15. Pigment Promenade/Litwinowicz, Apple Computer, Inc.
16. Styro/Sinnott
17. The Hole/Sakakibara
18. I Have Never Seen, But I Know.../De Leon, Texas A&M University
19. Under the Puddle/Corson, OSU-ACCAD
20. The Nature/Taira, Dentsu

67. SIGGRAPH 90 Film and Video Theater and SIGGRAPH 90 Animation Screening Room
1. Prebirth/Hashem
2. Blue Sky Productions Demo Reel/Brown, Blue Sky Productions, Inc.
3. The Great "Blue Ouah Ouah"/Baudart, Fantome
4. Grinning Evil Death/McKenna & Sabiston, MIT Media Lab
★ Closing Animation/Grower, Santa Barbara Studios
5. Screen Play/Martinez, Pygmee Communication
6. The Robe of an Angel/Motoyoshi
7. Sity Savvy/Stredney & Chadwick, Ohio State University
8. Le Pantin/Nagorny & Perrin, Relief
9. IAD/Thalmann, Swiss Federal Institute of Technology
10. Flashback/Thalmann, Swiss Federal Institute of Technology
11. The Adventures of Chromie "On the Rocks"/Casey, Prod. Masters, Inc.
12. Reveil (Alarm Clock)/Fourneaux, Eurocitel
13. Occam's Razor/Bridgeford, EVL-UIC
14. Interstitial Dreamin'/Mara, Intelligent Light
15. Thought Grid/King
16. Camera Work/Haxton, William Paterson College
17. Acolytes/White, Simmons College
18. Vision d'une Schizophrene/High Tech. Lab. Japan
19. Top tHat/Grotke, Anim. Lab, Capital Children's Museum

20. Luke Le Block's Daring Escape/Foster

68. SIGGRAPH 90 Animation Screening Room
1. Hadrosaurus/Rosenfeld
2. Stegosaurus: The Roof Lizard/Donkin, Ohio State University
3. Magma Tours/Ajisawa, Tanseisah Co., Ltd.
4. In Search of the Fingerprints of God/Bushell
5. Edo/Sugimoto, IBM Tokyo Research Laboratory
6. The Dream of Mr. M/Sakamoto, Fuji TV Network
7. Hubble Space Telescope/Rossman
8. S.S. Freedom- The Ultimate Challenge/Legensky, Intelligent Light
9. An Afternoon with John Whitney/Em & Em

69. SIGGRAPH 90 Animation Screening Room
1. Pacific Data Images/Gaeta, PDI
2. Special Effects/Stone, Apple Computer, Inc.
3. Rush Hour/Hastings
4. Paris Dakar 90/Guiot, Videosystem
5. Earthtecture Sub-I/Sawai, Plus One, Inc.
6. The Effects of Forces, Masses & Springs on Airborne Typography/Dempsey, Design/Effects
7. Tribune Broadcasting Group Christmas ID/Smith, Design/Effects
8. Scenes from CPUAX, GaAs INFO/Henry, TRW
9. One Night/Ono, High Tec. Lab. Japan Inc.
10. Open Road/Hoeg, Post Effects
11. Kiddipick Television Commercial/McIntosh, Pixel Perfect
12. Pepsi Power Hour/Price, Topix Computer Graphics & Anim. Inc.
13. CGI Demo #4/Winkler, Post Perfect, Inc.
14. Face/King
15. Calibre Digital Design Compilation Reel/Cosenzo, Calibre Digital Design, Inc.
16. 1990 Namco/Watanabe, NAMCO CG Project
17. sfpg-Selected Graphics/Wills

Animation Art GmbH

4. Welcome to My Living Room/Rawlings, EVL-UIC
5. Lost in Thought/Weinberg and Fischer, Forced Media
6. Crunchy Peach Pie (Apple Pie)/Sharpe
7. Memory of Moholy-Nagy/Halas and Waliczky, Educ. Film Centre, London
8. Discours du 1er avril/Aii/ENSAD
9. Immersion/Koulias, ARTSystems
10. Moon/de Kerangal
11. Endless Wave/Coggeshall, EVL-UIC
12. Curtain Call/Rossman
13. The Making of "Don Quichotte"/Videosystem
14. Les Xons-Baston/Ex Nihilo-Mac Guff Ligne

74. SIGGRAPH 91 Computer Graphics Screening Room

15. Computer Home/B.S.C.A.
16. Rose from the Dead/Design EFX and Biomechanics
17. Venus & Milo/Cox, NCSA
18. Garbage/Cox, NCSA
19. Cronicas Urbanas/TVE
20. Numerical Simulation of the Flow through the Penn State Artificial Heart/NASA
21. A Molecular Dynamics Simulation of Atomic Force Microscope/Landel, Advanced Scientific Visualization Lab.
22. Subsurface Geology of a Soviet Nuclear Test Site/USGS
23. El Nino Satellite Observations and Downburst Simulation/Hibbard, Paul, University of Wisconsin, Madison
24. Robotics in Space/Carnahan and Bacon, Advanced Technology and Research Corporation
25. EVA Development Flight Experiment/STS 37/NASA
26. R. Aquarii/Berry, Space Telescope Science Institute
27. Using Sound to Extract Meaning from Complex Data/NCSA
28. Visibility Analysis Through the Animation of a Backhoe Work Cycle/NCSA

29. The House That Radiosity Built: An Introduction to the Radiosity Method/Baum and Smith, SGI
30. Unfortunate Kid/Hayashida, LINKS Corp.
31. Still Walking/Thalmann and Thalmann
32. Realistic Rendering of Lace-Victoria's Dress Shop/Becket, Vigliotti and Badler, University of Pennsylvania

80. Historical Computer Animation-Special, The First Decade: 1960-1970

* Videotape
* Filmography
* Chronology

81. SIGGRAPH 92 Electronic Theater Part 1 of 2

1. Windy City/R/Greenberg Associates, Inc. New York
2. Coca-Cola/AMC/MetroLight Studios
3. "Let's Get Rocked"/Limelight
4. S.C.A.M. Starving Computer Artist's Market/NYIT
5. Ex memoriam/AGAVE SA
6. Caustic Sky: A portrait of regional acid deposition/NCSC
7. The Living Room/Texas A&M University
8. Rien Qu'un Souffle (A slight breeze)/Videosystem
9. The Seven Wonders of the World/Electric Images/UK, Ltd.
10. The Ancient World Revisited, Part II/Taisei Corporation
11. Sketches of Rome/William Paterson College
12. Banri no Chojo (Odyssey of the Great Wall)/TBS
13. Fire and Air/OSTRA DELTA
14. Fractal Ellipsoid Fire/Geoffrey Y. Gardner
15. Sound Rendering/George Washington University
16. In Search of Performing Axis/Polygon Picture
17. Eccentric Dance/META Corporation, Japan
18. Tagada & Fugue/Little Big One/Guionne Leroy/La Cambre
19. Returning Waves (Namigaeshi)/Dai

Nippon Printing Co.

20. Bande-Annonce de la Quinzaine/Fani Films/DHD PostImage
21. Le Concombre Masque/The Lone Cuke/Neurones Cartoon
22. PDI Scenes from "The Last Halloween"/PDI
23. Siemens "Aliens"/Spans & Partner
24. SpaceBoy in "SKY HIGH SCRAM-BLE"/Blue Sky Product.
24. The Incredible Crash Dummies/Lamb & Company
26. MandelSplat/Booker C. Bense
27. FIGURE to FIELD/Barbara Mones-Hattal and Ken O'Connell
28. Shield Soap/MetroLight Studios
29. Reebok "Cowardly Baskets"/Rhythm & Hues

82. SIGGRAPH 92 Electronic Theater Part 2 of 2

30. Does this Pulsar Have Orbiting Planets?/Cornell Theory Center
31. "Batman Returns" Visual Effects/Video Image Associates
32. Penguin Blues/Ex Machina and HD/CG New York
33. Best of Geometric Fables (2 eb 3)/Fantome Animation
34. Energy Generation by Controlled Thunderstorm/Hibbard
35. Dance in the Pants/Animal Logic
36. Lawnmower Man (particulation sequence)/Xaos Computer Animation & Design
37. The Lawnmower Man/Angel Studios for Allied Vision Lane Pringle Productions
38. Coming Attractions/Susan Alexis Collins
39. Liquid Selves/Karl Sims
40. PDI Music Video Effects/Pacific Data Images
    Science Reel
41. Patellar Reflex/META Corporation
42. Hubble Space Telescope: Image Deblurring with a Parallel Computer/NASA/Goddard Space Flight Center
43. Visualization of Tectonic Features:

Colorado River Extension Corridor JPL/CALTECH
44. Scientific Visualization 1992/PSC
45. Three Dimensional Fractal Growth (DLA)/BM
46. LANL Video Sampler/Los Alamos National Laboratory
47. Visualization of Human Biomechanics/Engineering Animation, Inc. and Iowa State University
48. Computer Graphics for CT and MRI/Cemax, Inc.

83. SIGGRAPH 92 Computer Graphics Screening Room Part 1, Art Reel

1. Have You Been Waiting Long?/Patricia A. Abt
2. "Laberint," from the series, "Postals de Barcelona"/Animatica/TVC
3. idiolect.JAM/SCSU Art Department
4. Zen3 Tao2/ACCAD/Ohio State University
5. CHANCEFormation/Yau Chen
6. Frozen Gods/Ryoichiro Debuchi/HighTech Lab. Japan, Inc.
7. Venus and Mars/Ray Eales
8. acacia mosaics/Brian Evans
9. Infinity/The Media Studio
10. Falling Apart/Marcos Martins
11. Off the Map/Sylvain Moreau
12. Lost Ground/Deanna Morse
13. LIPS/John Paul
14. A Certain Uncertainty/Lynn Pocock-Williams
15. Angels/Nicole Stenger
16. Jaguar Moon/Apple Computer, Inc.
17. S.C.A.M. Starving Computer Artist's Market/New York Institute of Technology
18. Coming Attractions/Susan Alexis Collins

84. SIGGRAPH 92 Computer Graphics Screening Room Part 2, Entertainment/Commercial Reel

1. After Birth/N.C.C.A., U.K.
2. DEC: Windows of Opportunity/TOPIX
3. Styro II/Sinnott & Associates
4. Meggamorphosis/Sean Schur

5. Ryder Transportation Solutions/ReZ.n8 Productions
6. Bob the Frog in "BURP"/Darren D. Kiner
7. How to Make a Decision/Visualization Laboratory, Texas A&M
8. AMC Features Presentation II/MetroLight Studios
9. Moe's World/MetroLight Studios
10. Bosch "Map"/MetroLight Studios
11. Fat Lulu is Going Back to Venice/Videoscop
12. R/Greenberg Associates Morph Reel/R/Greenberg Associates, Inc.
13. Around Again/University of British Columbia, GraFiC Lab
14. SI/MIT Media Lab
15. The Insider "L'Homme Oblique"/Terminal Image
16. Unburied Bones/CFA
17. BFT 2/The Moving Picture Company
18. The Best of SRC '92/Societé Radio-Canada
19. Xanadu City/Jerome Estienne/Xavier Duval
20. Quarxs Pilote: The ELASTO-FRAGMEN-TOPLAST is Back/Z.A Production
21. Day Break/The Bureau
22. Innatube Smarties/The Bureau
23. PEPIN GEANT de ARP/PANDORE
24. The Cyberiad/Cyberiad Project

85. SIGGRAPH 92 Computer Graphics Screening Room Part 3, Technical Reel
1. Sam's Water/CAL
2. Water Colors/Hiroshima University
3. Windy Moment/Hitachi
4. Nano-Vision/NHK
5. Sculpt/MIT Media Lab
6. Kodak "Let the Memories Begin"/R/Greenberg Associates
7. Humming Along/IBM T.J. Watson Research Center
8. Fun With Octrees: Graph Topologies on the Recurrent Cube/John C. Hart
9. Graphic Violence/The George Washington University
10. Four-Sight/Andrew J. Hanson & Pheng

A. Heng
11. Iwate '92/Iwate University
12. Flux Jon McCormack
13. Party Hardy/Homer & Associates
14. Bugsy for Prez/Realta
    Architecture Reel
15. Quatre Ans Café/Genevieve Yee
16. Pavilon de la Once/EDE Infografics
17. "El Idioma Español" Pabellon de España Expo '92/COM4
    Education Reel
18. Highlights from Knotty (1)/Hewlett Packard
19. Engineering Animation, Inc./Demonstration Tape
20. Regular Convex Polytopes/Texas A&M University
21. Spending = Q x P/Federal Reserve Bank of San Francisco

86. SIGGRAPH 92 Video Supplement to the Conference Proceedings
1. Scheduled Fourier Volume Morphing/Brown University
2. Shape Transformation for Polyhedral Objects ACCAD/OSU
3. Surface Reconstruction from Unorganized Points/Hugues Hoppe
4. Smoothing Polyhedra with Implicit Algebraic Splines/Purdue University
5. Pump It Up: Computer Animation of a Biomechanically Based Model of Muscle Using the Finite Element Method/MIT Media Lab
6. A Simple Method for Extracting the Natural Beauty of Hair/Hitachi, Ltd.
7. Variational Surface Modeling/William Welch, Andrew Witkin
8. Direct Manipulation of Free-Form Deformations/DEC
9. Surface Modeling with Oriented Particle Systems/DEC
10. High Resolution Virtual Reality/Sun Microsystems
11. Sound Rendering/The George Washington University
12. An Algorithm with Linear Complexity for Interactive, Physically-Based Modeling of

Large Proteins/Surles

13. Interactive Spacetime Control for Animation/Cohen
14. Through-the-Lens Camera Control/CMU Video Papers
15. Using Deformations to Explore 3D Widget Design/Brown University Computer Graphics Group
16. Interactive Inspection of Solids: Cross-Sections and Interferences/IBM T.J. Watson Research Center

91. SIGGRAPH 93 Electronic Theater
1. Project MATHEMATICS! Polynomials & Sines & Cosines/Blinn, et al.
2. Last Word/Blue Sky Productions, Inc.
3. Go Fish!/University of Toronto
4. MEGALOPOLICE Tokyo City Battle/Sega Enterprises, Ltd.
5. Heart Beat/Hokkaido University
6. Mercury/Brozsek
7. Doom and the Dog/Dagget
8. Stripe Box/Taiyo Kikaku Co., Ltd.
9. Fruit Tracing/Caltech
10. Studies for the Garden/Wallada Bioscop, Ltd.
11. Rhapsody in Light & Blue/Hiroshima University
12. Michelob Golden Draft 'Evolution'/Rhythm & Hues Studios
13. Sister of Pain/Vince Neil/Homer & Associates
14. Visualizing DNA Crystal Packing Interactions/The Scripps Research Institute
15. Pacific Data Images Montage/Pacific Data Images
16. Deus ex Machina/Georgia Institute of Technology
17. Walking Figure in Sight/Taiyo Kikaku Corporation
18. ODORO ODORO (The Mysterious Dance)/LINKS Corporation
19. joram/Rosen, Broersma
20. Video Supplement to the Conference Proceedings/Hart, Blinn
21. Data Driven: The Story of Franz K./NCSC
22. Flow/Apple Computer, Inc.

23. The Dangers of Glitziness and Other Visualization Faux Pas/Cornell Theory Center
24. Legacy/Butts
25. Dr. Scratch/Mr. Film
26. JuJu Shampoo/MetroLight Studios
27. PDI 'Toys' Visual Effects/Pacific Data Images
28. CAA-Coca-Cola Polar Bears/Rhythm & Hues Studios
29. Gas Planet/Pacific Data Images
30. GOKU/Magic Box Productions, Inc.

92. SIGGRAPH 93 Small Animation Theater Art Reel
1. Triangle Eat Triangle/Hallam
2. Night Moves/Klimley
3. Gasping for Air/Bishko
4. When I Was Six/Robinson
5. Brilliant Days/Hsieh
6. air, water part 2/Tonkin
7. The First Political Speech/Mah
8. The Allegory of the Cave/Kelley
9. Minute Georgienne/Mongeau
10. Power of Dreams/Kaul
11. Coup de Théâtre/Pasdeloup, Cazenave
12. Sintu/Popa
13. Cybercrazed/von Ruggins
14. Fantastic Dreams/Inakage

93. SIGGRAPH 93 Small Animation Theater Science Reel
1. knot4/Indiana University
2. JASON IV Real-Time Visualization/NASA/GSFC
3. Timbre Trees/George Washington University
4. Reconstruction and Visualization of a Human Embryo Heart/DEC
5. New Life Forms Sighted in Toronto!/University of Toronto
6. Animated Electronic Wiring Buck/Creative Industries
7. Climatology of Global Stratospheric Ozone (1979-1991)/IBM T. J. Watson Research Center
8. Air on the Dirac Strings/Sandin, EVL
9. Visualizing Seafloor Structures with

Satellite Altimetry/SDSC
10. Biomechanics: Dynamics and Playback/CEIT
11. Advanced Visualization for Transportation Engineering/Parsons, Brinckerhoff/4D Imaging

94. SIGGRAPH 93 Small Animation Theater Entertainment/Commercial Reel

1. Merck Corporate ID/DHD PostImage
2. StarQuest Adventure/MetroLight Studios
3. Barry's Trip/TELEZIGN
4. Mr. Hops/MetroLight Studios
5. NBC Sports '92/MetroLight Studios
6. Oreo: Word Play/TOPIX Computer Graphics and Animation, Inc.
7. Stabbur Makrell/CAL Ltd.
8. Nestle-Milky Bar/Animal Logic Pty Ltd.
9. Robo Jr./Microtech Graphics & Animation, Inc.
10. Warts and All/Ronin Animation
11. The Adventures of Korky, the Corkscrew/Saldanha
12. Ruby's Dream/SAS Institute Inc.
13. Colorado Interstate Gas Campaign/Windstar Studios
14. Smart Drive/Power and Vision Ltd.
15. Arcelik/Gribouille
16. Dimension 'Intro'/Canal Uno Producciones
17. Sony 'Bajo'/Canal Uno Producciones
18. TISEA Opening Animation/McCormack
19. La Goutte/DHD PostImage
20. Moonwalk/Imagic, Inc.
21. Countdown Contraption/Henninger Video, Inc.
22. Transformers/Lamb and Company
23. The Incredible Crash Dummies/Lamb and Company
24. Carpet Stains/Art Center College of Design
24. Computer Puppetry Demo Reel/Medialab
26. The Donor Party/Apple Computer, Inc.
27. Journey to Technopia/Boss Film Studios
28. The World of Materials: The Tiger, an excerpt/Ex Machina

95. SIGGRAPH 93 Small Animation Theater Architecture Reel

1. From Ruins to Reality/IBM UK Scientific Centre
2. Sendai Castle/CAD Center Corporation
3. Center for Ecology Research and Training Flyby/U.S. EPA Scientific Visualization Center
4. Tokyo International Forum/Rafael Viñoly Architects
5. Cluny/IBM France
6. De Karnak à Louqsor: La Machine à Remonter le Temps/Ex Machina
7. Ginza Walk Through/Shiseido Co., Ltd.

96. SIGGRAPH 93 Video Supplement to the Conference Proceedings

1. Interactive Texture Mapping
2. Implementing Rotation Matrix Constraints in Analog VLSI
3. Pad: An Alternative Approach to the Computer Interface
4. A Toolkit for Interactive Construction of 3D Interfaces
5. VIEW/An Exploratory Molecular Visualization System with User-definable Interaction Sequences
6. The Nanomanipulator: A Virtual Reality Interface for a Scanning Tunneling Microscope
7. Surround-screen Projection-based Virtual Reality: The Design and Implementation of the CAVE
8. Display of the Earth Taking into Account Atmospheric Scattering
9. Smooth Transitions between Bump-rendering Algorithms
10. Adaptive Display Algorithm for Interactive Frame Rates During Visualization of Complex Virtual Environments
11. View Interpolation for Image Synthesis
12. Spatial Anti-aliasing for Animation Sequences with Spatio- temporal Filtering
13. Space Diffusion: An Improved Parallel Half-toning Technique Using Space-filling Curves
14. An Implicit Formulation for Precise

Contact Modeling Between Flexible
Solids
15. Sensor-actuator Networks
16. Spacetime Constraints Revisited
17. Animation of Plant Development
18. Modeling Soil: Real-time Dynamic
Models for Soil Slippage and
Manipulation
19. Turbulent Wind Fields for Gaseous
Phenomena

98. New Directions in Virtual Reality
1. Virtual Reality: Immersed in High
Performance Computing and
Communications
2. NASA Telepresence Video
3. Advanced Computing Group Visualization
Laboratory
4. Discovering Virtual Reality: An
Experiment in Learning
5. Observing a Volume Rendered Fetus
Within a Pregnant Patient
6. The Smart Endoscopic Environment
7. Scientists in Wonderland: A Report on
Visualization, Applications in the
CAVE, Virtual Reality Environment.

**99. Entertainment Simulations and
Theme Park Visualizations**
1. The Devil's Mine
2. Seafari
3. Scuba Dog
4. Deep Earth Exploration
5. Space Shuttle America
6. Journey to Technopia
7. Alien Invasion
8. The Loch Ness Expedition
9. Atlantis Submarine Race
10. StarQuest Adventure
11. Galactic Flight
12. The Adventure of Peter Pan 2

100. Fifteen Years of Computer Graphics
Selected Excerpts from the SIGGRAPH
Video Review 1979-1994

101. SIGGRAPH 94 Electronic Theatre
1. shadow puppets/Gamble

2. A Nice Easy Turquoise/Sharpe
3. Listerine 'Arrows'/Pixar
4. Cells/Fleisher
5. D'Apres Le Naufrage/Marchal
6. ENDGAME/Stanford Computer Science
Robotics Laboratory
7. The Holy Bird/Debuchi
8. Danse Interactif/NYU Media Research
Lab
9. Coke 'Comic Hero' Japan/Pacific Data
Images
10. The True Story of the Roman
Arena/Digital Pictures Ltd.
11. Dead Air (Mind Over Matter)/Tylevich
12. Smirnoff 'Message in a Bottle'/The Mill
13. Outside In/The Geometry Center
14. Moxy/(Colossal) Pictures and Cartoon
Network
15. Motion Capture Samples from the Alien
Trilogy/Acclaim Entertainment, Inc.
16. THE QUARXS (They're Here!)
Extract/Z.A. Production
17. 20,000 Leagues Under the Sea/Gribouille
18. 500 NATIONS visual effects/Santa
Barbara Studios

**102. SIGGRAPH 94 Screening Room,
Entertainment and Commercial
Program**
1. ETB 2 Station identity/Ostra Delta, S.A.
2. Nick Boy/Blue Sky Productions, Inc.
3. Sugar Crisp: Tour/Topix Computer
Graphics & Animation
4. Mr. Sticky Bubble Gum/Tysowsky
5. Carefree Gum 'Bursting Bubbles'/Pacific
Data Images
6. Dream Dweller/McLaughlin
7. Oat Revolt/Editel
8. Mandarina Duck/Menfond Electronic Art
& Computer Design Co. Ltd.
9. The Fall/Ronai
10. Wild Flavors/Blue Sky Productions, Inc.
11. The Hit/Moragues
12. Smarties 'Smart-I-LLusions'/The Mill
13. RACOON/Renault Design
14. Nestle: Old Woman/Topix Computer
Graphics & Animation
15. Card Trick/Russ

16. La Victoria 'A Mind of Their Own'/Pacific Data Images
17. Moving/Ex Machina
18. AJAX 'BEYOND'/The Frame Store
19. 'M. Butterfly' Title Sequence/Syzygy Digital Cinema

103. SIGGRAPH 94 Screening Room, Architecture and Industrial Design Program

1. Chen Lung Tien/CG Computer Graphics Co.
2. The Roman Baths of Paris/Artway and IBM France
3. The Ancient World Revisited Part 3 (Rome)/Taisei Corporation
4. La bonificazione di Venezia/Taisei Corporation
5. My Sweet Home/CG Computer Graphics Co.
6. Edo City/Dai Nippon Printing Co., Ltd.
7. US EPA Center for Ecology Research and Training/US EPA
8. AKASHI KAIKYO Bridge/OBAYASHI Corporation
9. Renault Design Team/Renault Design

104. SIGGRAPH 94 Screening Room Art and Design Program

1. Color Control: flags
2. Reaching the Light
3. Metamorfosi
4. Tableau D'Amour
5. 'SOUL. [placed] beyond glass'
6. Sextuor
7. Crystal Paradise
8. Oscillation
9. Displaced Dice
10. FURBLE
11. Memory
12. Mirage Illimité
13. Bolero

105. SIGGRAPH 94 Screening Room Science and Technology Program

1. Impact of Comet Shoemaker-Levy 9 on Jupiter: The First 40 Minutes
2. Real-time Volume Rendering of Downbursts
3. Visualization of Stratospheric Ozone and Atmospheric Dynamics
4. Hurricane Gilbert
5. Mount Redoubt Volcano Eruption
6. Rain
7. Plastic Operation
8. MRI Face Mask
9. Pump Up the Volume
10. Cell Quakes
11. ECO-R1
12. Virtual Reality in Computational Neuroscience
13. Electro-magnetic Distributions in an Induction Motor
14. NASA/JSC Excerpts

More information by e-mail: info.videoreviews@siggraph.org
Ordering by e-mail: svrorders@siggraph.org
Ordering by phone within USA: 1-800-523-5503
Ordering by phone outside USA: 1-708-250-0807

Index

Cubical environment mapping, 177-178
Cubical projection, 168
Cubic splines, 70
Curvature, 51
Curve-based modeling, 39
Curved interpolation, 237, 238-239
Curved lines, 49-50
  tension of, 51
Curved patches, 70
Curved surfaces, freeform, 69-76
Curves, soft, 316
Custom file formats, 34-35. *See also* File formats
Custom filters, 322
Cut-copy-paste technique, 24
Cuts, 334
Cutting machines, 364
Cyan, magenta, yellow, black (CMYK) color model, 99-100
Cylinders, 53
Cylindrical projection, 168-169, 180

Darkroom, 318
Database amplification, 85
Data files, 24
Data translation, 342
Decay value of light, 142
Default camera, 121-122
Default light, 137
  checking, 155
Deformation
  freeform, 56-57
  with lattices, 58
  with splines and patches, 81
Deformation parameters, 73-74
Deformed surfaces, 79-81
Degree of curve, 51
Degrees of freedom, 262-264
De-interlacing filters, 323
Delayed motion capture, 280
Density, of objects, 282
Depth-fading, 189
Depth of field, 124-125, 254-255
Depth sort method, 105
Derivative modeling techniques, 88
DES format, 35
Destination mesh, 292
Device drivers, 300
Device-independent file formats, 351
Dialog-based games, 304
Dialogue, system-individual, 362
Diameter, 52
Die, defined, 54
Difference operator, 76
Diffuse interreflections, 108, 144

Diffuse reflection, 174
Digital backups, 231
Digital camera, 167
Digital creative environment, 3-4, 359
Digital filters, 321-323
Digital flipbook, 264-265, 360-361
Digital format, for computer animation, 209
Digital imaging techniques, 3
Digital information, 3, 359
Digital media, output on, 359-360
Digital output, 341-365. *See also* Output
  basic concepts of, 341-342
Digital painting, 167
Digital playback, real time, 360-362
Digital postproduction group, 226
Digital retouching tools, 319-320
Digital scanner, 167
Digital Signal Level Zero (DS-0), 362
Digital studios, 220-223
Digital-to-analog converters (DTAs), 342
Dimensions, 21
Dioramas, 168
Directional light, 139
Direct numerical description, 24
Direct point manipulation, 57-58
Discrete numerical values, 167
Displacement maps, 180, 183
Distributed rendering, 191. *See also* Rendering
Distribution of mass, 288
Dither cross-dissolve, 336
Dithering, 314
Dodecahedron, 54
Dolly, 34, 131, 251
Dot resolution, 343-344
Dots per inch (dpi), 343
Downward compatibility, 221
Drawing Interchange Format (DXF), 35, 36
Drawings, storyboard, 213
Duplicating, 60
Dye sublimation printing, 354
Dynamics, 207
Dynamic simulations, 282-283

Ease functions, 240
Ease in/out, 239
Edge detection filters, 323
Edges, 25
Edison, Thomas Alva, 13
Editing
  A/B roll, 332
  captured-motion, 281

copy-and-paste, 332
  image, 328-332
  nonlinear, 332
  tonal-range, 320-321
Effector (end effector), 273
Elapsed time, 213
Elasticity, of objects, 283
Electronic game industry, 8. *See also* Games
Electrostatic printing, 354
Em, David, 9
Emotion, expression of, 218-220
Entertainment
  differing viewpoints on, 13-14
  location-based and interactive, 300-304
Environmental density, 287
Environmentally-sensitive L-systems, 85
Environment-dependent shading, 187-191
Environment maps, 175-178
EPS (Encapsulated PostScript) file format, 55, 116, 351
Evans, David, 6
Event flow, 211, 363
Events, in storytelling, 210
Exclusive links, 144
Export filters, 349
Export tools, 349
External control structures, 247-248
Extreme close-up shots, 127
Extreme long shots, 128
Extrusion, 43
  cross section, 71
  freeform, 55
  simple, 54-55

Faceted shading, 162
Facetracker system, 11
Facets, 26
Facial animation, 298-299. *See also* Animation
Facial expressions, 217
  library of, 298
Facing-away surfaces, 87
Fade-ins, 334
Fade-outs, 334
Fade to black, 334
Fake hold, 203
Fall-off, 142
Fantastic transformation, 250
Far clipping plane, 123
Feature films, teams involved in, 224-225
Fetter, William, 5
Fiber Distributed Data Interface